ACTA UNIVERSITATIS UPSALIENSIS
Studia Doctrinae Christianae Upsaliensia
18

Fredrik Brosché

LUTHER ON PREDESTINATION

The Antinomy and the Unity Between Love and Wrath
in Luther's Concept of God

UPPSALA 1978

Distributed by Almqvist & Wiksell International, Stockholm, Sweden

Doctoral dissertation at Uppsala University 1978

© Fredrik Brosché

ISBN 91-554-0705-6
ISSN 0585-508 x

230.41
L977Ybr
7908027

To Anna-Stina

Printed in Sweden by LiberTryck Stockholm 1977 716258

Contents

1. Introduction

1.1. The Question in General

There have been allegations that Luther preached *the love of God* in a new, sonorous mode. A famous work by Anders Nygren describes Luther's contribution to the history of the Christian concept of love as a "Copernican revolution". The reformer radically breaks off the *eros* theology of the Middle Ages, and presents God tenaciously and consistently as *agape*. God is love: this is Luther's great discovery.[1]

It has also been asserted that Luther takes up anew the heavy emphasis on *divine wrath*. God's judgement and punishment—not least in the human conscience—comes to the fore in descriptions which bear witness to shaking, personal experiences thereof. The revelation from heaven of God's wrath against all iniquity: this is also forcefully underlined by Luther.[2]

What is the relationship between wrath and love in Luther's concept of God? Is wrath a *means* in the service of love, so that wrath and love are a unit? Or does God's avenging displeasure involve an *end in itself*, so that it does not serve the purposes of love; this leads to a tension between wrath and love in the concept of God. Or is the wrath sometimes a means, and sometimes an end, so that we must here assume both a unity and a contradiction in the reformer's concept of God?

1.2. The Two Trains of Thought in the Research

If we read two fairly recent Luther dissertations which deal, up to a point, with the relationship between love and wrath in the concept of God, we encounter two diametrically opposed theories:

Gerhard Rost, the German scholar, analyses Luther's concept of the wrath of God as it is manifested in the doctrine of predestination. After a penetrating and interesting review he concludes that the reformer's intention can be comprehended by means of the complemental theory in modern physics. Both love and wrath in the concept of God are objective

---

[1] A. Nygren, *Agape and Eros* II (1939)463ff.
[2] See the account of Th. Harnack (1.2 n. 12–14) and K. Holl (1.2 n. 5) below. L. Pinomaa, *Faith Victorious* (1963)51 stresses the same fact.

and total realities. Both represent one and the same truth: one and the same God. The aspect encountered depends on the situation of the individual in relation to God. The focus of this thesis is, in many respects, the *contradictory* element in the conception of God.[1]

But another German interpreter of Luther, *Ulrich Asendorf*, is not content with this conclusion. The contradiction between the divine love and the divine wrath is not the whole truth. The analogy with the law of complements is only valid when we assume that the paradox is not the most profound secret of the essence of God. Here the emphasis is laid on the *unity* of the concept of God as it emerges most distinctly in the reformer's doctrine of justification.[2]

(1) If we penetrate deeply into Luther research we discover that Asendorf is by no means the first to advocate this line of thought. In fact, a whole series of interpretations of Luther, while differing in many respects one from another, agree on the accentuation of the *unity* of Luther's concept of God.

Albrecht Ritschl, with his concentration on knowledge through the revelation of Christ, and on the consolation of faith, emphasizes the nature of evil as education, which is used by the love of God. He rejects Theodosius Harnack's interpretation that love and wrath are co-ordinates in the concept of the divine.[3]

Reinhold Seeberg stands to some extent for the same tradition as Ritschl. When he makes faith the organizing principle in Luther's theology he also prefers to describe the aspect of the divine being which corresponds to this faith, namely the divine love. Wrath is not a reality of the Godhead in the same way as is the love. Consequently, he concentrates on the positive election by means of God's love in the doctrine of predestination.[4]

[1] G. Rost, *Der Prädestinationsgedanke in der Theologie Martin Luthers* (1966)172. A summary and a positive assessment is presented by A. Peters in ThLZ 93 (1968)364f. The objections to the interpretation of the role played by natural reason and natural theology by K. Schwarzwäller, *sibboleth* (1969)96ff. will be discussed in 3.2 n. 4 and 4.2.1 n. 2 below.

[2] U. Asendorf, *Eschatologie bei Luther* (1967)51 n. 139: "Rost übersieht dabei, dass nicht die Paradoxie das Letzte ist. Von dort aus ist auch die Komplementarität nur bedingt analogiefähig ."

[3] A. Ritschl, *Die christliche Lehre von der Rechtfertigung und Versöhnung* I[3] (1889)218ff. A detailed analysis is to be found in D. W. Lotz, *Ritschl and Luther* (1974) as regards the Luther interpretation of Ritschl. Concerning Th. Harnack see 1.2 n. 12–15 below. Cf. also F. Kattenbusch, *Luthers Lehre vom unfreien Willen und von der Prädestination nach ihren Entstehungsgründen untersucht* (1875).

[4] R. Seeberg, *Lehrbuch der Dogmengeschichte* II[1] (1898)283ff., IV:1[2–3] (1917)153ff., *ib.* 175f. An exposition which closely resembles R. Seeberg's view of predestination is put forward by C. Stange, *Studien zur Theologie Luthers* I (1928)75ff.

The so-called Luther renaissance in the 1920's derived great inspiration from the theories of *Karl Holl*, although he too was dependent on Ritschl's ethicizing outlook. But in consequence of his theocentric perspective he emphasizes that Luther revived the Pauline doctrine of the divine wrath. Nevertheless, he does not follow up this point, but shifts to the distinction between that which is "alien" to God and that which is God's "own" work. Thus wrath is subordinated to love, and the concept of God is homogeneous. In the interpretation of the theory of predestination the idea of *resignatio ad infernum*, which in the last resort concerns election to salvation, attracted most attention and became generally accepted.[5]

Gustaf Aulén, the Swedish theologian, tends to accept Holl's premises. But the basic Christian motif—God's *agape*—which emerges most clearly in the revelation of Christ becomes even more dominant. Love is "the whole" in the concept of God. Aulén indeed seeks to do justice to the divine wrath. But his endeavour to achieve "an organic outlook" leads him to conceive of both the "mild" and the "severe" wrath as means in the service of God's love. Therefore it should not be regarded as a contradiction in the concept of God but as a "dynamic synthesis". Predestination is thereby composite in such a way that election is a genuine religious motif insofar as it stands for *sola gratia* in all its starkness. The wrath of God, which is expressed in an abiding rejection, is pushed aside in the specific context of faith.[6]

Erich Vogelsang was also influenced by Holl. He tried first and foremost to outline the central role of Christology in Luther. Notwithstanding that he explicitly states that the wrath of God is not a fiction, and that Christ on the cross tasted actual condemnation by God, he follows Holl in neglecting the eternal damnation which is incompatible with the Christocentric outlook. The unity of wrath and love in the concept of God is not dissolved even by the Luther doctrine of predestination.[7]

[5] K. Holl, *Gesammelte Aufsätze zur Kirchengeschichte* I[2-3] (1923)2, *ib.* 35 ff., *ib.* 41f., *ib.*, 48f., *ib.* 148ff. A minor work which, more or less faithfully, follows Holl's conception, and is occasionally cited in the debate is E. Hirsch, *Luthers Gottesanschauung* (1918). Concerning Holl as a Luther scholar see R. Stupperich, *Karl Holl als Lutherforscher*, L 37 (1966)112ff. and W. Bodenstein, *Die Theologie Karl Holls im Spiegel des antiken und reformatorischen Christentums* (1968) *passim*.
[6] G. Aulén, *Den kristna gudsbilden* (1927)7, *ib.* 166, *ib.* 186, *ib.* 199, *ib.* 211, *ib.* 220ff. T. Bohlin, *Gudstro och Kristustro hos Luther* (1927) agrees in many ways closely with Aulén.
[7] E. Vogelsang, *Die Anfänge von Luthers Christologie* (1929)23f., *ib.* 36, *ib.* 98. See also *id.*, *Der angefochtene Christus bei Luther* (1932)20f., *ib.* 27, *ib.* 30, *ib.* 37, *ib.* 98.

1.2.

The most penetrating analysis of the divine wrath since the days of Theodosius Harnack comes from *Lennart Pinomaa,* the Finnish Luther scholar. The fundamental conception of his theory is the homogeneous feature of the concept of God, and the corresponding existential attitude which is inherent in faith. Judgement is "unreservedly in the service of the divine love". Predetermination is interpreted primarily as a personal matter for the believer. The theoretical problem of predestination to damnation tends to be overlooked.[8]

When discussing Luther's view of affliction ("Anfechtung"), scholars have also accentuated the unity of wrath and love in the concept of God. On the basis of a dualistic cast of thought *Paul Th. Bühler* regards the devil as the cause of tribulation. But when the temptation has been overcome and faith has conquered, the Christian can understand that the devil is nevertheless subject to God's will. There is no scope in this interpretation for a permanent assault which is never overcome by faith. God's love makes use of temporary tribulation in order to purify and to instruct. In this way, the whole theory results in the concept of God contained in faith, according to which God is pure love.[9]

This dualism is refuted by the German scholar, *Horst Beintker,* in a paper on affliction ("Anfechtung") in Luther. He holds that the starting point should be monistic: God is the cause of the tribulation. God assaults in order to justify. Consequently, the framework of this interpretation is the doctrine of justification and the faith corresponding thereto. An abiding wrath and affliction by God remains outside this framework. The damnation as an end in itself, is not discussed in detail. The emphasis is laid on the concept of God made consistent by the idea of love.[10]

---

[8] L. Pinomaa, *Der Zorn Gottes in der Theologie Luthers* (1938)11f., *ib.* 54, *ib.* 79, *ib.* 115ff., *ib.* 143ff., *ib.* 205. Cf. further *id., Der existentielle Charakter der Theologie Luthers* (1940) and *id., Unfreier Wille und Prädestination bei Luther,* ThZ 13 (1957)339ff.

A more popular account which accepts the interpretation of Holl, Aulén and Pinomaa is to be found in Ph. S. Watson, *Let God be God!* (1947). It has had some significance as a theological textbook in, *inter alia,* Sweden.

[9] P. Th. Bühler, *Die Anfechtung bei Martin Luther* (1942)1ff., *ib.* 74ff., *ib.* 213ff.

[10] H. Beintker, *Die Überwindung der Anfechtung bei Luther* (1954)12ff., *ib.* 38ff., *ib.* 98ff., *ib.* 106, *ib.* 134ff., *ib.* 164.

K. Schwarzwäller, *Theologia crucis* (1970) *passim* also focuses on the doctrine of justi-fication, and the task of achieving unity, whereby the antinomy in the concept of God recedes into the background. A synthesis of Schwarzwäller's view of Luther's doctrine of predestination in *De servo arbitrio* is presented in *id., Das Gotteslob der angefochtenen Gemeinde* (1970)10ff.

Here it is also important to observe that the theology which resembles that of Karl Barth with its proposal to derive the entire doctrine of faith from the second article of the creed, and its rejection of the natural knowledge of God, might represent an interpretation of Luther in which the unity of the conception of God is accentuated. Since Christology is the channel through which all theological ideas must pass, the result, so far as the concept of God is concerned, is that the love of God is fostered by the revelation of Christ. The devil is God's instrument, which performs *opus alienum dei* in order that the *opus proprium* can be realised. It is indeed possible to imply that, according to Luther, *deus absconditus* predetermines not only for salvation but also for damnation. Yet, since this whole complex of problems falls outside normative Christology it receives summary treatment.[11]

(2) Likewise it is easily established that the aforementioned Rost also has his forerunners, who reckoned with both *contradiction* and *unity* in the Luther concept of God. They pay attention to material which contained the idea of everlasting damnation. They accept the consequences thereof without blenching at the paradoxes which arise. In general we could probably say that these scholars represent a more conservative line of reasoning, and are less dependent on the frames of reference of liberal theology than the writers quoted above.

Theodosius Harnack is a prominent figure whose account, with copious quotations, of Luther's theology provided the initiative for many lines of modern Luther research.[12] He too makes faith in Christ the axis round which the greater part of the reformer's reflection revolves. Here his outlook resembles that of Ritschl. But Harnack's exposition is different. He is not content with examining the positive aspect: "Gott und Welt in Christo". He also speaks his mind about the negative side: "Gott und Welt ausser Christo" in Luther.[13] Where the Hofmann-Ritschl interpretation modified or omitted Luther's statements on the divine wrath as an end in itself, a permanent condition, Harnack emphatically singles them out. Since wrath and love in the conception of God are equally true, equally serious and equally eternal, it must be admitted that

---

[11] H.-M. Barth, *Der Teufel und Jesus Christus in der Theologie Martin Luthers* (1967)15ff., *ib.* 157ff., *ib.* 165f., *ib.* 183, *ib.* 188, *ib.* 200f., *ib.* 204ff.

By reason of the question of revelation theology H. Bandt, *Luthers Lehre vom verborgenen Gott* (1958) adopts a critical attitude to the doctrine of the almighty, predetermining God, cf. *Vorwort.*

[12] Th. Harnack, *Luthers Theologie mit besonderer Beziehung auf seine Versöhnungs- und Erlösungslehre* I (1862), II (1885). I refer to the new edition I–II (1927).

[13] *Id.,* I (1927)41ff., *ib.* 70, *ib.* 84.

there is a startling dualism inherent in the concept of God. But this "Nebenordnung" is only half the truth. According to Harnack, Luther also assumes an "Unterordnung" of the divine wrath to the love so that the image of God becomes a unity through this love.[14] Luther's ideas on predestination are set into this context. In a fashion highly reminiscent of Lutheran orthodoxy, damnation is made dependent on human guilt, while selection to salvation is derived solely from God's mercy. Predestination protects the nature of mercy as pure mercy, in contrast to any form of Pelagian theology.[15]

This account of the wrath of God and the need for propitiation made a deep impression on many later Luther scholars, not least *via* the new edition of Harnack's work in 1927. We find the same ideas in *Johannes v. Walter*. He emphasizes that wrath is just as real as love in the essence of God. For this reason Luther's concept of God must be described as paradoxical. In particular the idea of the Law's judgement and punishment of sin brings this antinomy to life for von Walter. Notwithstanding that he has a more positive assessment of the doctrine of predestination than that found in the Ritschl school, he does not bring out the contradiction which is implicit in the theory of double election. In addition to the paradox of the concept of God implied by the idea of retribution, the unity of the concept of God, with regard to the practice of faith, emerges in this interpretation.[16]

Another German scholar, *Erich Seeberg,* advocates a more original and independent theory. He would stress more forcefully than before the innate knowledge of God, and the radical theory of omnipotence in the Luther material. The doubleness inherent in the twofold outcome of the

---

[14] *Id.,* I (1927)10, *ib.* 221f., *ib.* 229, *ib.* 233, *ib.* 238f., *ib.* 242ff., *ib.* 335ff., *ib.* 348ff. *Id.* II (1927)49f., *ib.* 67.

[15] *Id.,* I (1927)117, *ib.* 127, *ib.* 133, *ib.* 142, *ib.* 174f., *ib.* 179ff. Referring to Harnack's interpretation of the doctrine of predestination F. Brunstäd, *Theologie der lutherischen Bekenntnisschriften* (1951)227ff. does not give due attention to the criticism of Harnack's view of the predestination, which is presented *e.g.* by E. Hirsch in his review of the new edition of Harnack's investigation, ThLZ 52 (1927)39ff.

E. Brunner, *Der Zorn Gottes und die Versöhnung durch Christus,* ZZ 5 (1927)93ff. asserts that Harnack is the Luther scholar who has best understood the importance of God's wrath and Christ's propitiation in the theology of Luther. O. Wolff, *Die Haupttypen der neueren Lutherdeutung* (1938)107ff. is in my opinion too critical of Harnack's sharp antithesis. Objections against Harnack's conception of the Law in Luther's theology are brought forward by R. C. Schultz, *Gesetz und Evangelium* (1958)136ff. and H. Olsson, *Schöpfung, Vernunft und Gesetz in Luthers Theologie* (1971)124ff.

[16] J. von Walter, *Die Theologie Luthers* (1940)103ff., *ib.* 122ff. The lectures in this book were given as early as 1927-28.

Last Judgement is returned *via* the concept of omnipotence into God's own being. Wrath in damnation and love in salvation are thus expressions of two diametrically opposed, immutable sides of God's eternal nature. Therefore, predetermination is not a meaningless and insignificant *locus* in Luther but indeed "das Erste und Letzte in Luthers Religion". But at the same time as Seeberg emphasizes this antinomy he is aware that a unity also exists: God Himself is the highest good and perfect love. All this is without doubt important for the understanding of the reformer's theology.[17]

Gustaf Ljunggren, a Swedish interpreter of Luther, makes a surprisingly complete synthesis of the above viewpoints, using some new material for his examples. He attributes to Luther a twofold theory of the innate knowledge of God. The idea of an everlasting punishment for sin leads to a doctrine of the divine wrath which is incompatible with love. We can only register the gulf between the wrath and the love in the divine concept. Ljunggren states: The predetermination to damnation is a reality, as is election for salvation. There is a "double" will in the immutable God. But at the same time as he is aware of the contradictions which the human reason discovers he also sees the material with the other aspect. When faith grasps at the divine revelation in Christ the believer encounters a God who is perfect love.[18]

The emphasis on the dualism of God and the devil, and the thesis of a special context of religious significance within which not *ratio* but *fides* is valid, gives the Luther dissertation of *Ragnar Bring* its special flavour.[19] Indeed, as the Lund theologians are wont to do, he depicts the Christian idea of love in the divine conception. But he also seeks to do justice to the reality of the divine wrath. Luther's interpretation of the hardening of Pharaoh's heart points to an avenging displeasure, involving a genuine end in itself.[20] In the analysis of the doctrine of predestination he focuses on the apposition of absolute love and absolute wrath in Luther's concept of God. There is a "tension", where we cannot evade "the paradox" according to the conclusion reached by reason. Yet, the "theocentric"

---

[17] E. Seeberg, *Luthers Theologie* I (1929)150ff., *ib.* 160ff., *ib.* 204f. Cf. also *id., Grundzüge der Theologie Luthers* (1940)64ff., *ib.* 76.

[18] G. Ljunggren, *Synd och skuld i Luthers teologi* (1928)378, *ib.* 389, *ib.* 429, *ib.* 440f., *ib.* 471ff., *ib.* 490.

[19] R. Bring, *Dualismen hos Luther* (1929)14ff. *ib.* 215ff., *ib.* 257f. A detailed analysis of Bring's theory of knowledge is to be found in J. Hemberg, *Religion och metafysik* (1966)236ff.

[20] R. Bring (1929)215ff., *ib.* 319, cf. *ib.* 334f.

attitude of faith leads to a certainty that, despite the rational contradiction, God is nothing but love.[21]

To return to Lutheran scholarship in Germany, we meet two famous names. *Werner Elert* would follow Theodosius Harnack in refuting the theory that the wrath of God can always be interpreted in terms of *opus alienum*, which aims at *opus proprium*. Occasionally the punishment is an end in itself, *e.g.* a hardening of heart. The divine image is here divided through a "Diastase zwischen Zorn und Barmherzigkeit".[22] Nevertheless, Elert is zealous to point out love as the predominant concept. From the Luther material which demonstrates how faith overcomes the fear of eternal damnation he draws decisive conclusions for the doctrine of predestination. The reformer pursues the idea of predetermination principally in order to show the prerequisite of the right "Dennoch-Glaube", which believes despite wrath and hell.[23]

Paul Althaus, his fellow professor in Erlangen, also refers to Harnack's work concerning the wrath of God in Luther. He clearly observes the eternal damnation and the double divine will thereby implied. But his attitude to the interpretation of the concept of predestination is critical. He considers it to be based on an over-interpretation of Pharaoh's hardening of heart. Moveover, it also invalidates Luther's basic doctrine of justification, with its universal application. Like Elert he too finds some positive value in the doctrine of predetermination. For this makes faith a pure "Dennoch-Glaube", which believes in God's perfect love, although many things contradict it, particularly the predetermination to damnation and everlasting torment.[24]

[21] *Ib.* 337ff., *ib.* 344ff.

[22] W. Elert, *Morphologie des Luthertums* I (1931)38, *ib.* 54, *ib.* 104ff., *ib.* 187f.

[23] *Ib.* 108ff. This train of thought has had a certain importance. In *Viljefrihet og forut-bestemmelse i den lutherske reformasjon inntil 1525* (1933) S. Normann, the Norwegian scholar, takes up Elert's thesis that the doctrine of predestination in Luther's theology is only of "subsidiary significance" (*ib.* 529f.). After an extensive, detailed exegesis Normann adopts a far too critical attitude to the doctrine of predestination.

Another Norwegian theologian, E. Erikstein, in *Luthers Praedestinationslehre geschicht-lich dargestellt bis einschliesslich 'De servo arbitrio'* (1957) IVff. takes over a lot of Normann's material but refutes his negative assessment.

[24] P. Althaus, *Die Theologie Martin Luthers*[2] (1963)151, *ib.* 238ff., *ib.* 243ff. He explicitly accepts the critical dismissal of the predestination theory in M. Doerne, *Gottes Ehre am gebundenen Willen*, LuJ 20 (1938)45ff.

Obviously this interpretation has its supporters also among modern Luther scholars. K. Schwarzwäller (1969)56 and *id.*, *Das Gotteslob* (1970)11ff., *ib.* 17 seems to share the basic thought of Doerne that the doctrine of justification is the central issue from which the statements of *The Bondage of the Will* are to be considered as "Spitzensätze".

From a more positive standpoint E. Grislis, *Luther's Understanding of the Wrath of God*, JR 41 (1961)277ff. gives an interesting outline.

Extensive study lies behind the interpretation of Luther presented by the Swedish scholar, *Herbert Olsson*. He gives a detailed account of the way in which the wrath and the love of God are demonstrated in the Creation. He notes that faith and blessedness are not conferred upon all men. We must expect both "Einheit" and "ein gewisser Gegensatz zwischen Gottes Zorn und Liebe" in Luther. Nevertheless it is astonishing that Olsson devotes so little attention to the predestination theory in this context.[25]

(3) To sum up, we may say that, concerning Luther's conception of God, two lines of thought seem to be stressed. The one emphasizes the unity of God's wrath and God's love, while the other brings out both the unity and the contradiction.[26] This short review will now help us to express the problem in exact terms.

1.3. The Question in Particular

First, we have the *temporal* evil in all its different forms. This suffering should not *per se* supersede the idea of the divine love. It should be possible to attribute the cause and the responsibility to man's free will, in the case of torments resulting from human actions. Natural disasters could be derived from the devil's handiwork. But Luther obviously accentuates the idea of God's omnipotence to the degree that these attempts to create a theodicy at least in part are vain. My task is thus to analyse why and how the reformer depicts the concept of omnipotence, and to give at least a hint of the context in which monism—the evil emanates from God—or dualism—evil comes from Satan—is the relevant category of explanation.

---

[25] H. Olsson (1971)376ff., cf. *id.*, *Calvin och reformationens teologi* (1943)5ff.

To mention a few other important expositions of Luther's theology I would briefly note that G. Ebeling makes surprisingly few comments on the material describing Luther's view of God's wrath and predestination, see *id.*, art. *Luther*, esp. IIf., in RGG and *id.*, *Luther* (1964)31, *ib.* 106, *ib.* 133, *ib.* 246, *ib.* 252. F. Gogarten, *Luthers Theologie* (1967)171ff. explicitly discusses the doctrine of predestination but this is done in a far too paraphrasing manner. R. Hermann, *Luthers Theologie*, ed. H. Beintker (1967)164ff. is not especially useful since he only gives a short presentation of the well known passage in WA 43.458.9ff. (Gen. 26:9). Finally, some valuable suggestions about Luther's doctrine of predestination are to be found in H.J. Iwand, *Luthers Theologie*, ed. J. Haar (1974)90ff.

[26] The author has a much more detailed survey of the research which, it is hoped, will be published in another context.

1.3.

Obviously it is right and important that temporal suffering can by faith become meaningful and good, when it is interpreted with the help of the dialectic between *opus dei alienum* and *opus dei proprium,* or between law and gospel. There is here an agreement so great that I need not enlarge upon this "practical" unity of the divine wrath and the divine love. But the thought of a permanent hardening of heart cannot be fitted into this scheme. Therefore, it is essential to discuss the intention underlying and the significance of this form of punishment, which seems to be an end in itself.

Then, we have *eternal* evil, as it is expressed in the concept of hell. We found several interpretations of Luther which did not explicitly state an irreconcilable contradiction in the Luther concept of God in this context, despite the fact that everlasting torment seems to nullify the doctrine of God's absolute love. But we also established that theologians have often, in so many words, pointed out the paradox which here seems to be inescapable.

There were *two* different ways to the contradictory feature in the divine image. One underlined the Law and the Law's extreme punishment of sin in the form of definitive rejection. The second derived this everlasting rejection from predestination.

Without doubt the problem of eternal evil and the consequent antinomy in the concept of God is most strongly expressed in the second line of reasoning. The concept of retribution—hell as God's punishment of sin—expresses an intelligible relationship between human guilt and God's rejection. God's retaliatory displeasure is not arbitrary but is related to something reprehensible in man. Yet, there appears to be no human merit in the idea of election. God's will alone decides which individuals will be rescued from the "doomed mass", and which will be abandoned for all time.[1]

---

[1] E. W. Gritsch & R. W. Jenson, *Lutheranism* (1976)161 state the doctrinal difficulty in this way: "The God who is the absoluteness of the gospel is pure love. But the will behind all events is by no means easily apprehensible as pure love or even pure justice—if we judge merely by what happens around us, we must deny either God's existence or his goodness. How are we to deal with this split in our image of God? That is the theological problem of predestination ."

Obviously the critical remarks against Calvin in J. Hick, *Evil and the God of Love*[3] (1974)129 on this point should also hit Luther's doctrine of predestination: "Calvin so emphasizes the sovereign divine freedom, in abstraction from the total Christian conception of the divine nature, as to call God's goodness and love seriously into question. For the arbitrary saving of some and damning of the others would be an act that is free not only from external constraint but also from inner moral selfdirection. There would be nothing admirable, still less worthy of worship, in a free activity that consisted in creating beings whom the Creator has predetermined shall deserve and receive unending punishment ."

The difficulty of depicting a unity between the love and the wrath of God reaches its peak in *the doctrine of predestination*. And when the leading role played by predetermination in Luther's theology has been forgotten, or modified in the shadow of Calvin, the most important task proves to be the illumination of our problem with Luther material on predestination. I by no means deny that the retribution idea is extremely important in the reformer's theology. Nevertheless, I hold that I must assign priority to predetermination. Thus my task is to demonstrate both the contradiction in the concept of God and the unity which still exists.

1.4. The Background in terms of the History of Ideas

The historical context of Luther has been left out of account far too often. The danger of such a procedure is self-evident. Both the continuity and the breach with earlier theology become obscure. In order to avoid this, it seems necessary to devote some consideration to the *Sitz im Leben*. But the more the Luther scholar immerses himself in the historical background, the clearer it becomes that we are here faced with a serious dilemma between, on the one hand, the historical demand for background illumination and, on the other, the difficulty of presenting adequate information. For, notwithstanding that an unprecedented amount of work has been done by diligent scholars, we are not yet wholly sure of the roots of Lutheran theology.[1] In this situation it is reasonable to impose certain limitations, so that at least the most important background is included.

(1) It seems fairly clear that the young Luther was brought up in the tradition of William of Ockham, as represented by, in particular, Gabriel Biel. The University of Erfurt obviously bore the stamp of the many-sided phenomenon designated *via moderna*. There is evidence that some of the most prominent teachers at the university represented this trend. Thus, when Luther was studying for his master's degree he was presumably trained in the fundamental principles of Biel's Ockhamism.[2] It seems probable that the school of the Hermits of St. Augustine also based its teaching on this tradition, since Luther's Ockhamistic

[1] Cf. *e.g.* H. Bornkamm, *Probleme der Lutherbiographie,* Luh p. 16 and H. A. Oberman, *Headwaters of the Reformation: Initia Lutheri—Initia Reformationis,* LuD p. 88.
[2] O. Scheel, *Martin Luther* I[3] (1921)174ff. presents a very thorough investigation.

tendencies are documented from 1509–1510, and one of his chief tutors is thought to have studied under Biel himself.[3] It is also feasible to point out that in statements written much later Luther accepted the status of a disciple *vis-à-vis* these Ockhamistic views, although the tendency to demote grace and the Holy Spirit to a non-essential condition for meritorious acts is sharply criticised.[4]

It is also essential to bear in mind Biel's eclectic use of Augustine, Thomas Aquinas, Duns Scotus and other theologians. Even by his study of Biel Luther had read numerous quotations from other contexts. Nor can we exclude the possibility that Biel's theology gave Luther some insight into the mysticism known as *devotio moderna*.[5]

If there was any contemporary theological trend in particular against which Luther reacted, and which he sought to reform, it was this late Medieval nominalism as interpreted by Biel. Its doctrine of penance, whereby redeeming grace is more or less dependent on man's preparatory intentions and achievements, was in high degree the great unbiblical heresy which could not give peace to Luther's troubled conscience. This theory Luther was trying to correct when he developed his new conception of justification *sola gratia* and *sola fide*.[6] Research has also shown that the theology of Biel was the main target when Luther, in his *Disputatio contra scholasticam theologiam* in 1517[7], expressed his first

[3] See further L. Grane, *Contra Gabrielem* (1962)10ff., *ib.* 17f., *id., Protest og Konsekvens* (1968)18ff., and *id., Modus loquendi Theologicus* (1975)110ff.
[4] In detail in L. Grane (1962)15. O. Scheel, *Dokumente zu Luthers Entwicklung*[2] (1929)199 quotes Melanchthon's famous assertion about Luther's acquaintance with Biel (nr. 532): "Gabrielem et Cammeracensem pene ad verbum memoriter recitare poterat. Diu multumque legit scripta Occam. Huius acumen anteferebat Thomae et Scoto."
H. Bornkamm in Luh p. 18 describes Biel's *Collectorium* as "das Grundbuch von Luthers scholastischer Erziehung".
H. Volz, *Luthers Randbemerkungen zu zwei Schriften Gabriel Biels: Kritische Anmerkungen zu Hermann Degerings Publikation*, ZKG 81 (1970) 207–219 demonstrates that even some years later than 1517 Luther wrote notes in the margin of his copies of the *Collectorium* and the *Canonis misse expositio*. Consequently, he studied Biel much later than was previously assumed.
[5] H. A. Oberman, *The Harvest of Medieval Theology* (1963)327 n. 10.
[6] See further O. Scheel, *Martin Luther* II[3-4] (1930)231ff.; A. Gyllenkrok, *Rechtfertigung und Heiligung in der frühen evangelischen Theologie Luthers* (1952)2ff.; I. Öberg, *Himmelrikets nycklar och kyrklig bot i Luthers teologi 1517–1537* (1970)129ff.
[7] L. Grane (1962)42f., *ib.* 310ff. enlarges upon this point. The disputation is to be found in WA 1.224ff. The theses to the disputation of Bartholomäus Bernhardi (probably Sept. 1516) in WA 1.145.1ff. are to be regarded as a prelude to Luther's own general attack a year later. Luther's satisfaction over this early disputation is shown in a letter to Johann Lang in WAB 1.65. 18ff. (Oct. 1516).

general objections to the theological thought of the time within the later scholastic tradition.

Consequently it seems reasonable to assume that in many respects the Luther view of predestination implied a reaction against Biel's theory of predetermination. This assumption was also made.[8] Thus, there is comparatively good reason to attain a certain understanding of the major features of Biel's doctrine of predestination, and the view of the tension and unity in the image of God, concerning the relationship between wrath and love. So we can discover the ideas to which Luther objected, and the way in which he too was a reformer of the predestination conception.[9] When all this has been said, I wish to point out that I do not repudiate the possibility of some influence from earlier theologians within the *via moderna*, such as Gregory of Rimini, Pierre D'Ailly and Johannes Gerson.[10] I would merely argue that there is a direct study of and a direct rejection of Biel in Luther which justifies the preferential treatment of these background data.

(2) I cannot avoid commenting on the relationship between Luther and the theologian who was the Medieval authority *par excellence*, namely *Augustine*. I have already said that Luther encountered Augustinian tenets and theories in his textbooks. The monastery school was also an environment in which Augustine's world was alive in a particular way. We must certainly assume an Augustinism which was in all its complexity a widespread phenomenon at that time.[11] But we also know that Brother

---

[8] W. Pannenberg, *Die Prädestinationslehre des Duns Scotus* (1954)148: "Luthers deterministischer Prädestinationsbegriff in De servo arbitrio ist wohl noch als Reaktion gegen Biel im Rahmen der nominalistischen Fragestellung zu verstehen." Cf. also G. Rost (1966)92f., *ib.* 102.

[9] Major works on the theology of Ockham and Biel are C. Feckes, *Die Rechtfertigungslehre des Gabriel Biels und ihre Stellung innerhalb der nominalistischen Schule* (1925), P. Vignaux, *Justification et prédestination au XIVe siècle* (1934), H. A. Oberman (1963), H. Junghans, *Ockham im Lichte der neueren Forschung* (1968), F. J. Burkard, *Philosophische Lehrgehalte in Gabriel Biels Sentenzenkommentar unter besonderer Berücksichtigung seiner Erkenntnislehre* (1974).

G. Rost (1966)89ff. has defined Biel's predestination doctrine so laconically that similarities and differences are not clearly discernible with regard to Luther.

[10] Cf. further *e.g.* P. Vignaux (1934)165ff., W. Pannenberg (1954)143ff., L. Grane, *Gregor von Rimini und Luthers Leipziger Disputation*, StTh 22 (1968)29ff., H. A. Oberman in LuD p. 54ff.

[11] D. C. Steinmetz, *Luther and late Medieval Augustinians: Another Look*, in: Concordia Theol. Monthly 44 (1973)245ff., H. A. Oberman in LuD p. 69ff., and L. Spitz, *Headwaters of the Reformation: Studia Humanitatis, Luther Senior, et Initia Reformationis*, in: LuD p. 93ff.

Martin was engaged in a direct study of several of Augustine's writings.[12] Bearing in mind the significance to Augustine of the doctrine of predestination in his teaching of grace we have good reason to assume that there are lines of reasoning about this particular theme which Luther took over.

An investigation already made reveals that in his *Commentary on Romans*—the most important source of data on the reformer's ideas about predestination in his youth—Luther tends to accept Augustinian reasoning on this point. It goes without saying that Luther contributed other ideas, *i.e.* the distinction between *deus absconditus* and *deus revelatus*. On the whole, however, he seems, as on other issues, to have intended to follow Augustine and to regard himself as a disciple of the *doctor gratiae*.[13]

A further reason for me to refrain from special study of the theme Augustine/Luther with reference to predestination, apart from a few comments, is more pragmatic. It would seem to be well nigh impossible, in the framework of this investigation, to present a survey of the material and secondary literature in Augustine which would be both accurate and suitable for comparison when this research would be concerned with accents and shades of meaning.[14]

(3) Another major trend of piety which influenced Luther was *Medieval mysticism*. He was familiar with Dionysius the Areopagite, Bernhard of Clairvaux, Bonaventura, Hugo St Victor, and Gerson, to name but a few. The vicar general of his order, von Staupitz, to some extent advocated attitudes from mysticism which may have been handed down to Luther. The reformer did indeed forcefully reject certain forms of mysticism, especially that represented by Dionysius.[15] At the same

[12] The basic investigation is A. Hamel, *Der junge Luther und Augustin* I–II (1934–5). Cf. further W. Link, *Das Ringen Luthers um die Freiheit der Theologie von der Philosophie* (1940)210ff., A. Nygren, *Augustin und Luther,* Aufsätze und Vorträge zur Theologie und Religionswissenschaft, H. 3 (1958), W. von Loewenich, *Zur Gnadenlehre bei Augustin und bei Luther,* in: *Von Augustin zu Luther* (1959)75ff., R. Schwarz, *Fides, Spes und Charitas beim jungen Luther* (1962) *passim,* B. Lohse, *Die Bedeutung Augustins für den jungen Luther,* KuD 11 (1965)116ff., L. Grane (1975)23ff., *ib.* 63ff., *ib.* 87ff. For discussion of literature, see *ib.* 27ff.

[13] A. Hamel II (1935)107ff. Cf. L. Grane (1975)131.

[14] *E.g.* G. Nygren, *Das Prädestinationsproblem in der Theologie Augustins* (1956) gives an idea of the wide extent of the sources and the literature.

[15] The basic extensive investigation is E. Wolf, *Staupitz und Luther* (1927). To this issue cf. further E. Vogelsang, *Luther und die Mystik,* LuJ 19 (1937)32ff.; H. A. Oberman, *Simul gemitus et raptus: Luther und die Mystik,* in: *Kirche, Mystik, Heiligung und das Natürliche bei Luther,* hrsg. I. Asheim (1967)20ff.; L. Grane (1975)125f.

time, however, he emphatically expressed his acceptance of theories and experiences to be found, *e.g.* in Tauler. The anonymous manuscript entitled *Theologia deutsch* was, as is well known, the first work which Luther recommended for printing. In the preface he explicitly states that this booklet taught him most after the Bible and Augustine.[16] Evidently more mystical experiences than are generally realised can be glimpsed in the theology of the mature Luther.[17]

So far as we are concerned, two aspects in particular reveal experiences of mysticism underlying Luther's theology. First of all, there is the fascinating theory that Luther's vivid concept of omnipotence and theological determinism originates in a personal experience of the majesty of God.[18] Secondly, attention has been drawn to the profound significance of experience in the form not only of judgement and punishment under the Law but also of the fruit and witness of the Holy Spirit in the heart of the believer. This would prompt the hypothesis that experience plays an important part in Luther's postulation of the unity of God's image through faith and revelation.[19]

I must draw a sharp line also concerning this background of the history of ideas. Any attempt to report a representative material from the mystics here cited, except in some short references, goes beyond the realms of practical possibility. I must be content with these more general hints, in order to define the essential role of personal experience later on in the Luther material.

---

[16] WA 1.153 (*Vorrede.* 1516). The following version is especially explicit, WA 1.378.21ff. (*Vorrede.* 1518): "Und das ich nach meynem alten narren rüme, ist myr nehst der Biblien und S. Augustino nit vorkummen eyn buch, dar auss *ich mehr erlernet hab und will,* was got, Christus, mensch und alle ding seyn."
  Concerning a discussion of the ideas derived by Luther from Tauler, see W. Link (1940)315ff., L. Grane (1968)82ff., G. Wrede, *Unio mystica* (1974)30ff., H. Bornkamm, *Luther: Gestalt und Wirkung* (1975)136ff., L. Grane (1975)121ff.
[17] B. Hoffman, *Luther and the Mystics* (1976)25ff. shows how accounts of Luther's relationship to mysticism are far too often unduly general, and at times downright misleading.
[18] *Ib.* 108f., *ib.* 125f. I elaborate this issue in 3.3–4 below.
[19] Important interpretations of this theme are to be found in H.-M. Müller, *Erfahrung und Glaube bei Luther* (1929) *passim,* S. von Engeström, *Luthers trosbegrepp* (1933)170ff., W. von Loewenich, *Luthers Theologia crucis*[3] (1939)118ff. An extensive study of Luther's pneumatology is R. Prenter, *Spiritus creator*[2], (1946). Fundamental objections to Prenter's exposition are made by H. Gerdes, *Zu Luthers Lehre vom Wirken des Geistes,* LuJ 25 (1958)42ff. See further the suggestions in K. G. Steck, *Lehre und Kirche bei Luther* (1963)106ff., G. Heintze, *Luthers Pfingstpredigten,* LuJ 34 (1967)117ff., K. Schwarzwäller, *Zur Struktur von Luthers Pneumatologie,* LuJ 38 (1971)26ff., B. Hoffman (1976)148ff.
  In 4.5.5.2 below I deal further with this topic.

(4) Scholars seem to be more or less agreed that Luther had a comparatively superficial knowledge of Thomas' theology. His judgements of the tradition are evidently based not on his own studies of the primary material but principally on generalisations derived from fragmentary quotations from other sources.[20] Nevertheless in the ecumenical dialogue between Catholic and Protestant it is extremely important to elucidate similarities and differences between the foremost theologian of the *via antiqua* and Luther. The erudite investigations so far carried out concerning Thomas Aquinas/Martin Luther, not least by Catholic scholars, have demonstrated a number of interesting similarities.[21] With regard to the idea of liberty and the doctrine of predestination, I can refer to competent analysis by both Evangelical and Catholic scholars, who have relevant views of the features which unite and divide.[22]

(5) Naturally many more factors contributed to the development of Luther's frame of mind. We know that he read the writings of Duns Scotus.[23] A more detailed study of the background would inevitably call for a penetrating examination of, *e.g.*, humanism and late Medieval apocalyptics.[24] But the lack of space excludes any possibility of a further description of these phenomena.

---

[20] Review of research in H. McSorley, *Luther: Right or Wrong?* (1969)139ff.

[21] See further *e.g.* St. Pfürtner, *Luther und Thomas im Gespräch: Unser Heil zwischen Gewissheit und Gefährdung* (1961), A. Brandenburg, *Thomas und Luther im Gespräch*, C 16 (1962)77ff., O. H. Pesch, *Zum Gespräch zwischen Luther und Thomas*, C 18 (1964)27ff., *id.*, *Die Theologie der Rechtfertigung bei Martin Luther und Thomas von Aquin* (1967) which is a very extensive investigation. A popular summary is given by O. H. Pesch in: *Existential and Sapiential Theology—The Theological Confrontation between Luther and Thomas Aquinas*, in: *Catholic Scholars' Dialogue with Luther*, ed. J. Wicks (1970)61ff. E. Iserloh, *Luther und die Reformation* (1974) presents an ecumenical interpretation of Luther.

In H. Bornkamm (1975)74ff. we find a survey of the Catholic opinion of Luther during the history from the 16th century to our time.

[22] H. McSorley, *Luther und Thomas von Aquin über die Prädestination*, in: *Oekumenica: Prof. E. Schlink zum 60. Geburtstag* (1963)17ff., O. H. Pesch, *Freiheitsbegriff und Freiheitslehre bei Thomas von Aquin und Luther*, C 17 (1963)197ff., H. Vorster, *Das Freiheitsverständnis bei Thomas von Aquin und Martin Luther* (1965), H. McSorley (1969)138ff., *ib.* 217ff., *ib.* 297ff., O. H. Pesch, *Die Frage nach Gott bei Thomas von Aquin und Martin Luther*, L 41 (1970)16ff.

[23] Cf. *e.g.* WATR 3.564.3ff. (1538), WATR 4.611.7f. (1540).

[24] See further in LuD the papers by H. A. Oberman (*ib.* 40ff.), L. Spitz (*ib.* 89ff.), W. J. Bouwsma (*ib.* 127ff.), and B. Hägglund (*ib.* 150 ff.). On Luther's humanism see also literature and discussion in L. Grane (1975)104ff.

1.5. The Material

The material as presented in the scholarly edition of Luther's works—the so-called Weimar Edition—will be discussed along the lines which are generally accepted in research.[1]

a) The most reliable material, of course, consists of Luther's own manuscripts, and printed works approved by him. In my analysis of *Dictata super Psalterium* (1513–1515) I shall compare this material with the new edition now in preparation, in which the notes, rather than the text, have been amended.[2]

b) A major part of the material is composed of notes by others from Luther's lectures and sermons. Scholars have long been aware that the most reliable of these consist of material derived from Georg Rörer, Luther's loyal colleague.

c) Finally we have some material of somewhat controversial value. It seems clear that the large *Commentary on Genesis* cannot be regarded without reserve as a source for the theology of Luther's declining years, since it shows signs of editing and secondary additions. Any tenet which Luther had not previously taught which crops up in this lecture series should be regarded with scepticism. But when the reformer's own "diction", not least in the form of forceful comments in German or Latin, appears, and when there are clear agreements between the arguments in the Genesis commentary and the theology of the young Luther, this material deserves credence.[3] We also have a number of volumes of *Tischreden*. I shall only cite evidence from these to shed additional light on trains of thought which are guaranteed by more reliable material.[4]

[1] Cf. E. Vogelsang (1932)81f., L. Pinomaa (1938)15f., *id.,* (1963)XVII, I. Öberg (1970)XIIIf. An instructive survey of the various editions is to be found in R. Hermann (1967)26f. For the benefit of the reader I quote both the headline and the year from the Weimar edition after each reference to WA.

[2] Psalms 1–15 (Vulgate) are to be found in WA 55.I.1.1 and WA 55.II.1.1 (1963), Psalms 16–30 (Vulgate) in WA 55.I.1.2 and WA 55.II.1.2 (1973). H. Rückert describes methods of work and views of source material in *Die Weimarer Lutherausgabe,* Luh p. 113 ff. See also R. Schwarz (1962)76f. n 1.

[3] P. Meinhold, *Die Genesisvorlesung Luthers und ihre Herausgeber* (1936) 118ff., *ib.* 150ff., *ib.* 427f.

[4] Cf. further B. Stolt, *Die Sprachmischung in Luthers Tischreden* (1964).

1.6. The Method

The material described above will be quoted and analysed historically and systematically. The quotations will be given almost invariably in chronological order. In this way one can keep track of both the continuity and the shifts in focus.[1] My framework does not permit of a complete account of the material. I shall instead follow the principle of citing relevant texts from different periods.

(1) We meet the young Luther in the early marginal notes, the first lecture on the Psalms and the lecture on Romans, to mention but a part of the extensive material. It is not necessary for me to try to fix a date for the highly controversial "reformation breakthrough". I state only that this discovery was the fruit of a theological conversion on a wide front, rooted far back in time, which did not come into full flower until later.[2] Intensive research has revealed how very complicated a phenomenon we must here consider.[3]

(2) There is indeed disagreement on the exact point at which the mature, consistent, reformed outlook appears. Many scholars hold, however, that on the whole there is a high degree of homogeneity in Luther's theology from the first years of the 1520's onwards.[4] The book *The Bondage of the Will*—so important for my theme—from 1525 surely belongs to this period; unlike a great deal of other material it was explicitly approved by the reformer much later.[5]

(3) Finally, during the 1530's, comes the material which may be described as representing the aging Luther. Obviously it is not possible, or indeed necessary, to set a definite limit when this phase begins. From the point of view of method it must be regarded as an advantage when we can find documentation not only in the Genesis commentary but also in letters, sermons, disputations, etc.

---

[1] A well-balanced discussion is to be found in I. Öberg (1970)XIVff. See also L. Pinomaa, *Methodische Gesichtspunkte zur Lutherforschung*, LuJ 43 (1976)109ff. With this historical method some repetitions are unavoidable since the same material often sheds light on different subjects. But I consider this a minor disadvantage compared with the well-founded broad perspective gained by analysing relevant passages from different phases of Luther's life. Further, I wish to point out that *the italics* in the quotations are my own.

[2] O. H. Pesch, *Zur Frage nach Luthers reformatorischer Wende*, C 20 (1966)216ff., *ib.* 264ff. is perhaps the most complete survey of the current discussion of this question.

[3] Cf. 1.4 n. 1. An attempt to clarify the problem is made by H. A. Oberman in LuD p.41ff. For a complete biography of Luther and his work J. Köstlin & G. Kawerau, *Martin Luther.* I–II[5] (1903) is still valuable.

[4] Important works on this issue are listed by I. Öberg (1970)XIVf.

[5] See the well known passage in WAB 8.99.5ff. (1537).

1.7. The Definitions

My terminology will be special with regard to two concepts. Indeed, I have chosen them in association with Luther's own mode of expression. Nonetheless, these are not descriptions of two already existing terms. They are merely two stipulatory definitions[1], which are introduced to make the presentation more succinct and comprehensive.

a) By *notitia* level I mean the understanding which implies a general theoretical knowledge or an unspecified conception.

b) By *usus* level I mean the understanding which implies a knowledge which is applied and specified *pro me*. This is a matter of a personal knowledge, a theoretical and existential application of the doctrine in life. The term *usus* is furthest realised and best known in the context of the application of the Law.[2]

As is well known, Luther assumes a starkly dualistic anthropology. Man can live, work, meditate and evaluate, either on the basis of an anthropocentric outlook which is expressed by such concepts as flesh, reason, unbelief, or from a theocentric attitude, when the mainspring is the Spirit, revelation, faith.[3] Thus we may expect two different forms of concrete expression on the *usus* level: a false one which is accomplished by carnal unbelief, and a true one which is achieved by faith conferred through the Spirit and the Word.

1.8. The Disposition

First of all I shall illustrate Luther's theory of the *natural knowledge of God*. This proves to be more differentiated than is usually imagined. He accepts a knowledge of certain divine attributes on the *notitia* level in pagan man. But he rejects totally the possibility of a valid realisation through reason of this understanding on the *usus* level. The chief authority for this twofold theory is Rom 1:19ff. I have thus outlined some of the premises for what follows.

---

[1] Cf. further A. Naess, *Empirisk semantik* (1966)30ff.

[2] Documentation and further references are to be found in M. Schloemann, *Natürliches und gepredigtes Gesetz bei Luther* (1961)22ff.

[3] We find extensive investigations of this dualism *e.g.* in B. Lohse, *Ratio und Fides* (1958)55ff., B. Hägglund, *De homine* (1959)293ff., W. Joest, *Ontologie der Person bei Luther* (1967)196ff.

1.8.

Secondly I intend to illustrate Luther's view of *God's omnipotence*. I shall show that he assumes a certain rational knowledge of the divine omnipotence, which is in line with his view of the natural knowledge of God. Nevertheless I shall also demonstrate how the central issue is the concept of omnipotence which is inherent in the Biblical revelation, and which Luther wishes to emphasize anew. This affords me an opportunity to analyse the bond between the temporal evil and God, and the way in which hardening of heart is provoked by God's omnipotence. An attempt will also be made to shed light on the dialectic between monism and dualism.

Thirdly, I shall discuss Luther's highly complicated *doctrine of predestination*. This will reveal how a rigid double conception of predestination forms an integral part of the reformer's concept of God. He accepts a knowledge thereof on the *notitia* level, while rejecting a transposition of this knowledge to the *usus* level by means of the inquisitive speculations of reason. I intend to show that predetermination is the cause of justification and sanctification. In his practical teaching, however, Luther underlines the necessity of first believing oneself to be justified without deeds for the sake of Christ. Consequently, the idea of election can be realised on the *usus* level only through faith. I shall show that in this context Luther teaches certainty of election. Finally, I can counter the paradoxical concept of God, in which eternal wrath and eternal love stand side by side, with the homogeneous concept of God through love, which faith encounters and perceives through the Word and the Spirit: God in Jesus is love.

2. The Natural Theology

2.1. Background

The Pauline account in Rom 1:19–21 seems to imply that human reason has a certain capacity for envisaging the existence and nature of God on the basis of His acts in the world.

This very passage from Romans provides the Scriptural basis for the examination of natural theology in *Peter Lombard's* famous textbook, *Sententiarum Libri Quattuor*, which is known to have been a significant starting point for theological instruction and reflection over a long period. He states somewhat laconically that in various ways *ratio* derives knowledge of the Creator from the Creation. The visible and the mutable presume a cause which is invisible and immutable. The constant continuation of created things reveals the eternity of their founder, their magnitude His omnipotence, their order and disposition His wisdom, and their steering His goodness.[1]

The roots of the late Medieval development of Ockhamism are to be found in high scholasticism, which effects an extensive expansion of these ideas, with an abundance of distinctions and shades of meaning. Indeed, *Thomas Aquinas* emphasizes in his system that man lacks direct, "intuitive", knowledge of the divine being. This is a consequence of his doctrine of knowledge. But he also states strongly that reason has the capacity to arrive at a certain abstract and fragmentary understanding of the supernatural by way of rational arguments based on the evidence of the senses. Philosophy can, by means of the famous proofs, demonstrate the existence of God, that He is one, and that He manifests His perfect nature in the Creation. Accordingly, philosophy can present truths which belong to the same "materia" which theology treats.[2]

The new principle of reasoning in *Duns Scotus*, and the heavier emphasis on God as free, creative will, and on the individual objects as contingent phenomena, herald the later development. Duns Scotus asserts, however, that the existence of God can be proved *a posteriori* from the visible world. By means of innate common sense, man can

[1] MPL 192, 529f. (Dist. 3). Luther refers directly to this passage in his exposition of Rom 1:19–21 in the Lecture on Romans, WA 56.174.11ff.
[2] For an illuminating introduction and references see *e.g.* F. Copleston, *A History of Philosophy II* (1959)312ff., *ib.* 336ff., *ib.* 347ff.

2.1.

conclude that God is one, and that He is the highest good. Metaphysics can comprehend many of His essential attributes.[3]

The complex phenomenon known as *via moderna* in the 14th and 15th centuries provoked a more forceful criticism of the grounds of the great metaphysical systems. Many conventional theories about *William of Ockham, e.g.* that he was *the* radical revolutionary, do not hold water in the face of the material which recent research has brought to light.[4] On the one hand, he criticizes the logic of the traditional proofs of the existence of God. On the other, it is obvious that he considers it possible to give rational reasons for the existence of God as conservator of this Creation.[5] *Venerabilis inceptor* also takes the middle course with regard to the possibility of demonstrating the divine attributes. Some qualities, *e.g.* creativity, cannot be strictly proved. Duns Scotus is attacked on this point. Yet, other attributes, *e.g.* God's goodness, can be justified by reasoning. His view of the possibility that philosophy can attain valid knowledge of God is more positive than is often thought. It falls to a great extent within the traditional framework.[6]

As a faithful and independent interpreter of William of Ockham's ideas *Biel* also represents the *via media* in many respects. In the discussion of the proofs of the existence of God he appears to be influenced by Pierre D'Ailly. The existence of God cannot be proved by "demonstration". Nevertheless it can be made feasible by "good probable argument". Like Ockham he considers it more valid to hold fast to the conception of *causa conservationis* rather than of the *causa productionis*.[7] Thus there is "sufficient" but not conclusive evidence that there is a *primum conservans*.[8]

We cannot adduce any absolutely binding evidence for the belief that God is one. But it is possible to present arguments indicating a certain probability. Nevertheless these seem to fall short of the proofs of the existence of God. On the whole, it is an article of belief that God is one.[9]

[3] See *e.g.* A. Adam, *Lehrbuch der Dogmengeschichte II* (1968)116ff., F. Copleston (1959)518ff.

[4] H. Junghans (1968)326ff.

[5] *Ib.* 221ff., cf. F. Copleston, *A History of Philosophy III* (1960)83ff.

[6] H. Junghans (1968)228ff., F. Copleston III (1960)84ff. Cf. H. Olsson, *Den naturliga gudskunskapens problem enligt den senmedeltida nominalismen*, SvTK 26 (1950)381f.

[7] Coll I, Dist. 2, q. 10, C—H. Cf. also F. J. Burkard (1974)157ff.

[8] Coll I, Dist. 2, q. 10, H: "Sed non est possibile esse processum in infinitum in conservantibus, quia tunc actu essent infinita, quod est impossibile, saltem naturaliter, sicut posset probari per rationes *Philosophi* et *aliorum*, quae sunt satis rationabiles. Et per consequens per istam rationem patet sufficienter (licet non evidenter), quod oportet dare primum conservans et ita primum efficiens." Cf. Coll I, Dist. 3, q. 4.

[9] Coll I, Dist. 2, q. 10, B, F, G. Cf.F. J. Burkard (1974)163.

In his theory of knowledge Biel asserts that man acquires understanding of the world from the senses. Since God is not a part of this Creation, we cannot "intuitively" attain knowledge of Him as long as we are but "on the way". But the man who is "at home" and can see God is given direct knowledge. Consequently, the first conclusion is that reason "along the way" cannot know God, in the sense of God Himself, His nature or His reality *per se*.[10] Yet Biel adduces further conclusions which demonstrate that we are not abandoned to total agnosticism. We can form valid concepts of God, simple concepts which are the due of God and the world (*conceptus communes simplices*), and complex concepts which are attributes of God alone but whose constituent elements derive from the experience of the senses (*conceptus proprii complexi*). Reason can also attain certain simple connotative concepts, which are associated with empirical knowledge but belong to God alone, *e.g. prima causa, immutabilis*.[11] These concepts have the same meaning with regard to both the Creator and the Creation, although this univocity is not entirely rigid.[12]

But Biel not only discusses in detail how it is possible to form concepts which make an adequate statement about God. It goes without saying that he also assumes a real knowledge of God. This is given not only by *revelatio* but also by *ratio*. Some truths, which are part of theology, are also known by instinct. The divine epithets, *bonus, vivens, sapiens, intelligens*, are adduced as examples. Other truths, such as God's incarnation, can only be understood by man by means of supernatural revelation and acceptance on trust.[13]

[10] Coll I, Dist. 3, q. 2, C: "Nec Deus 'nec aliquid, quod est realiter Deus', sive dicatur et sit essentia sive quidditas sive quocumque modo intrinsecum Deo, naturaliter potest hic pro statu viae cognosci in se a nobis sive distincte, 'ita quod nihil aliud a Deo concurrat in ratione obiecti'." Cf. Coll I, Dist. 8, q. 5, A, con 1: "Deus non potest diffinitione proprie dicta et primo modo accepta diffiniri. Patet, quia res incompositae simplices non possunt diffiniri; qualis est Deus." See further L. Grane, *Gabriel Biels Lehre von der Allmacht Gottes*, ZThK 53 (1956)54f, *id.* (1962)69ff.

[11] Coll I, Dist. 3, q. 2, D, F. Cf. Coll. Prol. q. 2, G; *ib.* q. 7, D. Cf. also F. J. Burkard (1974)149f.

[12] F. J. Burkard (1974)152ff.

[13] Coll, Prol. q. 1, D: "Ex illo sequitur quod aliquae veritates naturaliter notae sunt theologicae, ut 'Deus est bonus, vivens, sapiens, intelligens', quas etiam *Philosophus* demonstrat XII Metaphysicae. Et per hoc veritates illae pertinent tam ad metaphysicam quam ad theologiam. In metaphysica demonstrantur demonstratione quia, in theologia propter quid. Secundo sequitur quod veritatum theologicarum aliquae sunt naturaliter notae, aliquae sunt supernaturaliter cognitae et tantum fide creditae, ut 'Deus est trinus et unus', 'Deus est incarnatus' etc." Cf. F. J. Burkard (1974)192f.

2.2. The Propositio Maior According to Rom 1:19–21

The philosophical terms used by Luther in his exposition of the positive and negative content of Rom 1:19ff are derived from the battery of concepts of scholastic logic, which he learned to understand and practice during his university studies. The major premise of a "practical" syllogism was known as "synteresis". Jodokus Trutfetter, his teacher, defined this as "a natural inclination", "an inextinguishable spark of reason", and "an inborn habit". This helps us to arrive at a clear understanding of the form and content of natural theology according to Luther.[1]

1. The natural starting point is the exegesis of Rom 1:19ff in the *Commentary on Romans* (1515–1516).[2] Luther here begins by saying that man, from Creation, possesses "the natural knowledge of God". This is a knowledge of the divinity in the human heart. This explains why idols and other created things can be the object of religious veneration and cult. Man holds fast with all his soul to this worship, and demonstrates it in his actions. Thus it follows that

> "Cognoverunt ergo, Quod divinitatis sive eius, qui est Deus, sit esse potentem, Invisibilem, Iustum, immortalem, bonum; ergo cognoverunt Invisibilia Dei sempiternamque virtutem eius et divinitatem."

Even idolaters possess a knowledge of God which can be identified with *propositio maior*, which contains the predicate of the conclusion, in practical reasoning. Of this basic knowledge we can namely say with truth:

> "Hec *Maior syllogismi* practici, hec Syntheresis theologica est inobscurabilis in omnibus."

Taken merely as an awareness of certain divine attributes, this knowledge is naturally abstract and general. It is an understanding which is only valid on the *notitia* level. Yet, I emphasize that this awareness is

---

[1] Martin Luther, *Vorlesung über den Römerbrief,* ed. H. H. Borcherdt & G. Merz, *Ausgewählte Werke II²* (1957)484 n. 25. Cf. also H. A. Oberman (1963)65f. about Biel's view of syntheresis. H. Olsson (1971)156f. has noticed Luther's use of the "practical" syllogism concept.

[2] WA 56. 176.15ff., LW 25.156ff.

in no way dependent on, or genetically secondary to, the knowledge born of faith. The innate knowledge of God is an understanding *sui generis*.

The *propositio minor*, which contains the subject of the conclusion, *i.e.* the contention that Jupiter or the like is God, on the other hand, is false. When, in the minor premise, an attempt is made to "subsume" the divine predicates subjectively, heresy and idolatry are a fact. This results in a definition and transfer to the *usus* level which is misleading.

Thus Luther regards the natural archetype of God as positive until it is actually applied. This is confirmed not least by what follows. If we were content with the major premise, there would even be an hypothetical possibility of redemption! For the exposition goes on to say: "If they had stayed with this feeling and had said: 'Look, we know this: Whoever this God, or this Divinity, may be whose nature is to be immortal and powerful and able to hear those who call upon Him, let us worship and adore Him, let us not call Him Jupiter and say that He is like this or that image, but let us simply worship Him, no matter who He is (for He must have being)', then without a doubt they would have been saved, even though they had not recognized Him as the Creator of heaven and earth, or taken note of any other specific work of His hands".

Then, there is no erroneous definition of the logical subject. As one man helps another, and as the higher helps the lower, God appears as the power in the universe which is almighty, the helper of all. When this natural knowledge of God is simple it is also adequate. But when it is made complex, without regarding the revelation in Christ, it becomes insufficient.[3]

2. In connection with his discussion of the first commandment of the Decalogue in *Sermons on Deuteronomy*, 1529, Luther takes up the question of the universal worship of God. Augustine's *Civitas Dei* prompted him to reflect on the religion of the ancient Romans. He is referring to the Roman cult when he says: "Da spurt man, quod ratio tantum scit ut Paulus: 'Notum dei est eis manifestum, quod deus sit', das

---

[3] R. Josefson, *Den naturliga teologins problem hos Luther* (1943)26, *ib.* 36f. includes a discussion of this Luther material, which I consider unsatisfactory for two reasons: (1) When J. begins with "the practical-concrete religion of man", and asserts that "in his speeches on the natural knowledge of God Luther assumes the concrete religion", it is not clear that the reformer's fundamental starting point is also St. Paul's words in Rom 1:19ff. (2) Luther's dialectical reasoning is not given its due, when J. writes: "It is obvious that with this basic viewpoint Luther cannot allow heathen religion to be an entity composed of a knowledge of God which is partly true and partly false." But is not this—in a way—the very point expressed by Luther in the true major premise and the false minor premise? Cf. further B. Lohse (1958)45ff., G. Rost (1966)59f.

got nutz sey und helff in noten".[4] The latter comment is true. Indeed, the Bible makes the same assertion: "Ergo Deus in scriptura dicitur ein nothelffer et dator omnis boni". Thus on this point the knowledge from *ratio* and from *revelatio* coincide. We observe that there is no concrete, personal application of this rational understanding. Using my definitions I may say that it is a knowledge on the *notitia* level.

The fact that the *propositio maior* is containing these general divine predicates emerges from the further exposition:

"Sed subsumere in *minore*, da teilt sichs.
Ratio dicit: Der, der, dieser sols thun.
Ibi fiunt tam variae sectae ut iam sunt."

Reason *per se* has an accurate conception of God's attributes as the main premise is wholly correct. We note that faith in Christ is not stipulated as essential for the truth of knowledge in this sense. Thus it is an independent form of knowledge of God.

Only the *propositio minor* is erroneous. Heresy derives from the concrete application. Reason cannot attain to the true God. It is possible to speak of Him and yet be ignorant of His identity.[5] Only if man—Luther is also referring to such a religious and Christian man as a monk—shares in the knowledge mediated by the Bible can he attribute the divine predicate to the right object and the right person.[6]

3. On at least one occasion in the large *Lecture on Galatians*, 1531/1535, the terminology of scholastic logic reappears. When Luther gives his exegesis of Gal 3:10, he emphasizes that the verb *facere* has one meaning in philosophy and another in theology.[7] In theology good will and sound sense take priority over deeds. The tree must be good if the fruit is to be sound. This state of affairs is "inverted" in philosophy. Therefore, in this respect, Luther must adjudge reason to be

---

[4] WA 28.610.3ff. (R). Cf. WA 7.205.16ff. (*Eyn kurcz form der zcehn gepott.* 1520): : "Dan das leret die natur, das eyn gott sey, der do alles gutis gebe und yn allen ubel helffe, wie das antzeygen die Abgotter bey den Heyden."

[5] WA 28.611.6f (R). Cf. *ib.* 9f (R): "Sic ratio non habens verbum dei weis von im zusagen, sed non scit treffen." Cf. also WA 10 I.1.239.20ff. and 240.22ff. (*Kirchenpostille.* 1522).

[6] WA 31.II.235.15ff. (*Vorlesung über Jesaias.* 1527-30) takes up the same argument in connection with Isa. 37:16. The expression "Deus Israel" is expounded as follows: "Hoc magnum est certum scire deum. Nam omnes idolatriae habent aliquem deum, dicunt: Deus est colendus. Sed in *minori* falluntur, faciunt multos deos. Augustinianus, Franciscanus facit suum cultum deum. Hic cultus venditur nomine veri dei, ita racio deluditur in cultu divino, sicut omnes gentiles sapientissimi illusi sunt."

[7] WA 40.I.410.1ff. (Hs)

unreservedly negative. "Et dicimus philosophiam moralem nihil scire de deo".[8]

Yet, philosophy contains some divine knowledge. For rational knowledge and ethics only assume the visible and the utilitarian. The moral philosopher does not integrate eternal life into his reasoning, and therefore does not seek to deserve salvation by his own efforts. In this sense philosophy remains pure and unadulterated.

Certain individuals, however, seek to use the insight of reason in order to attain eternal life. Thus, they create a synthesis of philosophy and theology:

> "Sic etiam faciunt hypocritae, Sophistae; habent quidem *illam maiorem*: divinitas est, sed transformant etc.: quae sic sit affecta, quae spectat meam monialem vitam, bonam voluntatem. Ibi miscent divinitatem et polluunt etc."[9]

Luther does not repudiate the major premise as long as it remains non-specific. The *propositio maior* containing the predicate of the conclusion is true at the *notitia* level. The Word, or faith, are not essential conditions. This is an autonomous form of divine knowledge.

The error lies in the minor premise, containing the subject of the conclusion when this innate, objective understanding of God is "transformed" and related to our practical needs and desires. There is an erroneous realisation on the *usus* level. Thus a confusion arises, and a soiling of the divine concept.

Nevertheless, this abuse does not *per se* cancel out the truth of the major premise. This is manifest from the end of this section. For here we encounter the unusual feature that Luther sees something exemplary in Aristotle's theory of God: God remains the pure form. "Philosophus Aristoteles est melior, qui habet rationem honestatis, non miscet."[10] Accordingly the positive feature is that he stops short at the theoretical understanding of God and does not, by reason of his own egocentric wishes, introduce the concrete category which I described as the *usus* level.

Finally, we turn to *the lecture series on Genesis* from 1535–1545, and adduce a last example of exegesis in the vocabulary of syllogism. This is

---

[8] *Ib.* 410.11 (Hs)
[9] *Ib.* 411.3ff. (Hs). Cf. *ib.* 608.25ff. (Dr).
[10] *Ib.* 411.6f. (Hs). Cf. WA 48.385.9 (*Veit Dietrichs Nachschriften der Tischreden*): "Philosophia est quasi theologia gentium et rationis."

the exposition of Gen 43:23–5.[11] It is alleged in this context that all men possess an archetype of God and of God's power and protection. The heathens, Luther says, invoke Mars and other gods. By this cult they show that they regard God as a helper in danger and difficulty. But they bestow the name and honour which are God's due on created things. This is shown by Rom 1:19ff. Consequently there is an universal knowledge of God before, and independent of, the Biblical revelation. This *notitia* is inscribed in the hearts of all men, that they must turn to God in affliction. In order to define his reasoning more accurately Luther quotes the Aristotelian logic which was well known to his student audience:

"Ea est *maior in Syllogismo*, nec vocari potest in dubium, nisi a Saducaeis et Epicureis."

Accordingly, Luther attributes to all mankind, apart from atheists such as sadducees and epicureans, a sufficient knowledge of the divine predicates, that God exists, and that God is the refuge who offers support and help in time of need. This knowledge is indeed purely abstract, valid on the *notitia* level alone. Nonetheless it implies a true and independent form of divine awareness.

The misleading premise is put forward as a *propositio minor:*

"Sed *minor* est falsa: Hoc idolum est Deus.
Ibi corruptio naturae nostrae apparet,
qua fit, ut a vero Deo aberremus."

Reason perceives certain divine predicates, but not, without Christ, the specific form of the divine subject. Thus sin has not destroyed our capacity to comprehend that God exists, is powerful, helps, protects etc.

So the distinctions discussed here have shown:

a) that the innate knowledge of God is an independent form of knowledge, and that it involves awareness of certain divine predicates, that God is mighty, invisible, righteous, immortal, good etc.

b) that this universal knowledge of God is polluted and distorted when it is applied to inadequate subjects because of human needs and desires.

c) that the terms *propositio maior* and *propositio minor* are used in a way corresponding to our definitions of the *notitia* and *usus* levels respectively.

[11] WA 44.549.14ff. Cf. WA 16.42.8ff (*Predigten über das 2. Buch Mose.* 1524–27): "Sic gentes fecerunt deos ex naturali inclinatione, quod deus omnes iuvet. Paulus: Pro lumine non fuit, quod cognitionem habuerunt de divinitate, qua iuvet. Sed haec idololatria est, quod hoc auxilium dei non adscribitur vero deo. Scit deum esse, sed non verum." Cf. also R. Josefson (1943)39f.

2.3. Other Expositions of Rom. 1:19–21

The terminology analysed above is missing from other expositions of Rom. 1:19–21. The same positive and negative views of natural theology still stand, however.

1. I begin with an example which dates from 1517–1518, namely *the exposition of Heb* 11:6. In his commentary Luther focuses on the expression "credere Deum", which is referred to the natural knowledge of God. For both poets and philosophers accept the existence of God:

> " 'Credere Deum' adeo esse facile multis videtur, ut id et poetis et philosophis tribuerint, ut et Rom. 1. Apostolus asserit. Denique sunt, qui hoc per se notum arbitrentur."[1]

By way of the universal knowledge of God, man comes to comprehension of the divine predicate which we call *esse*. We also see that this predicate is not attributed to any specific subject, that the belief in Christ is not an essential condition, and that this is by no means an object for negative assessment. Thus, this tenet corresponds to the aforesaid *propositio maior*. Since *esse* is not here expressed in concrete terms, it is true knowledge according to the *notitia* category.

But when Luther takes up the absence of personal trust he becomes negative and critical. This innate objective knowledge of God is only "fides humana", which does not endure but surrenders to tribulation.[2] Man has not the courage to trust in this knowledge alone. The personal pronouns are not used aright, for the text suggests *esse pro me* or *esse pro nobis*. "Ideo, ut dicitur, est fides de Deo et non in Deum."[3] Only if this existential faith is present does an individual venture to believe that he personally belongs to the host for whom God exists and whom God will reward.

2. *The exposition of Jonah* from 1526 contains a famous passage about the natural knowledge of God, in connection with Chap. 1:5. The sailors' desperate cries to their gods amid the raging storm lead Luther's thoughts to Rom. 1:19: "all mankind can speak of God, and human reason knows

---

[1] WA 57.232.27ff. Cf. also WA 18.617.23ff. (*De servo arbitrio.* 1525).

[2] WA 57.233.1. Cf. WA 16.433.9f. (*Predigten über das 2. Buch Mose.* 1524–27): "Ro 1. naturaliter insita cordi cognitio dei et tamen in tentatione non videtur." Cf. also WA 39.I.180.19ff. (*Disputatio de homine.* 1536). See further H. Olsson (1950)384.

[3] WA 57.233.9f. Cf. WA 7.215.16ff. (*Eyn kurcz form der zcehn gepott.* 1520), WA 10.I.2.24.12 (*Adventspostille.* 1522). See also P. Lombard, *Sententiarum libri quattuor III*, Dist. 23.4 according to MPL 192, 805, which distinguishes between "credere Deo", "credere Deum" and "credere in Deum".

that God is greater than all created things."[4] This is modified still further. Although the crew of the ship does not believe in God, they possess the knowledge that God is such a being as can help in all emergencies. This spark of insight is innate in man. It can be neither suppressed nor extinguished. There are indeed atheists such as Epicurus, but these men speak against their better judgement. Their atheism is only empty words. Luther summarises the innate awareness of God as follows: "So let us here also learn from nature and reason what is to be thought about God. For these people believe that God is such as can rescue them from all evil. It follows too that human reason must confess that all good comes from God. For He who can save us from all evil and misfortune can also give all good and happiness. Sofar the natural light of reason reaches regarding God as good, gracious, merciful, tender, this is a deep understanding."[5] *Ratio per se* possesses knowledge of certain general, divine attributes. This awareness could be regarded as *propositio maior* in the sense discussed above. As long as it is confined to the *notitia* category it is not subject to criticism.

Since this natural knowledge is not included in existential trust, however, it is insufficient. Its shortcomings stand revealed. First of all, this knowledge of God provides no incentive to belief in God's personal help. Thus the universal awareness of God dare not trust in the assistance of the divine will in personal life. Secondly, knowledge through reason is too abstract. Reason does not perceive God's will in relation to physical reality. The inmost heart of God remains concealed.[6] There is "a great difference" between this general knowledge and personal definition.[7]

3. The same pattern is to be found in the large *Commentary on Galatians* from 1531/1535. According to Gal 4:8, the Galatians did not know God, although they were slaves to gods who were not gods in essence. This tenet seems to contain a contradiction.[8] This is only apparent, however. For, according to Luther, St Paul was referring to two different aspects.

---

[4] WA 19.205.28ff. Cf. B. Lohse (1958)59ff., H. Olsson (1971)150f., *ib.* 177. Cf. also WA 13.228.32ff. (*Praelectiones in prophetas minores.* 1524ff.)
[5] WA 19.206.7ff. Cf. WA 16.431.3f. (*Predigten über das 2. Buch Mose.* 1524–27): "Ratio docet nos, ut deum colamus Ro.1. omnes gentes habent cognitionem de deo."
[6] WA 19.206.13ff.
[7] *Ib.* 207.11. Cf. WA 13.229.7ff. (*Praelectiones in prophetas minores.* 1524ff.): "Omnes praetexunt nomen dei etc. Rom. 1. Divinitatem sciunt sed voluntatem et beneplacitum non sciunt."
[8] WA 40.I.607.5ff. (Hs). Cf. B. Lohse (1958)59f., H. Olsson (1971)151, *ib.* 176.

Firstly, the fact that they had any idea whatever about the divine nature depends on the natural knowledge of God:

> "Divinitas est naturaliter cognita. Deum esse per se notum Sophistae (sc. dicunt). Cultus satis testantur omnes homines habere *noticiam* dei per manus traditam."

Here the reformer evidently bases his reasoning on Rom 1:19ff. This knowledge is not qualified.

But, then, when this knowledge is to be defined, idolatry appears. The perversity of nature here plays its part. We do indeed possess a superficial knowledge of God. Yet, we are ignorant of God's inmost intention for us, that He will act in such a way as to redeem us. The heathens err in making use of the theoretical knowledge of God in specific situations. They know of God's *esse* but, without Christ, they are ignorant of His *velle*. It is one thing to be cognizant of the general attributes, another to understand God's particular intentions for mankind.[9]

As long as man's knowledge of God *via* reason alone remains on the *notitia* level it is true, although incomplete. But when the *usus* aspect enters the picture reason goes astray, It is, and remains, blind to the inmost nature of the divine being.[10] Thus we see again how Luther vacillates between a positive and a negative assessment of the natural knowledge of God.

---

[9] *Ib.* 608.7ff. (Hs). The printed text of the Lecture on Galatians develops these two aspects explicitly from Rom 1:19ff., which provides support for a "generalis *notitia* Dei", that God created heaven and earth, that He is righteous and punishes the ungodly (*ib.* 607.19ff.). But only a believer in "propria notitia Dei" (*ib.* 607.30ff.) knows what the All highest thinks of individual man, what He is willing to give and to do in order to redeem. This closely corresponds with the twofold aspect expressed in the manuscript. Luther also makes the distinction between universal and particular knowledge of God in WA 16.43.31ff. (*Predigten über das 2. Buch Mose.* 1524–27). R. Josefson (1943)41ff. tends to overlook the true, cognitive element of the natural knowledge of God when he one-sidedly emphasizes man's abuse of this knowledge.

[10] WA 40.I.607.9 (Hs). Cf. WA 30.I.192.10ff. (*Der grosse Katechismus.* 1529): "Denn was ausser der Christenheit ist, es seyen Heyden, Türcken, Jüden odder falsche Christen und heuchler, *ob sie gleich nur einen warhafftigen Gott gleuben und anbeten,* so wissen sie doch nicht, was er gegen yhn gesynnet ist, können sich auch keiner liebe noch guts zu yhm versehen, darümb sie ynn ewigen zorn und verdamnis bleiben"; WA 40.III.78.13ff. (*In XV Psalmos graduum.* 1532/33): "Ubi ablatum (sc. verbum Dei), Sihe in scholasticis, Monachis, Mahometis. Speculantur de attributis, distinctionibus et speculantur extra deum, sine verbo, suis rationibus naturalibus, et non cognoscunt, quid deus velit erga eos."

2.3.

I pass on to *the survey of Genesis* (1535–1545) by the aging Luther. In his exegesis of Gen 17:7 Luther emphasizes that we should comprehend the name of God in "relative" terms, namely by worship and veneration, and not "absolutely" according to the divine essence and majesty.[11] Man must turn to God, invoke Him, thank Him, and proclaim His beneficence. But we do not need the Bible for this advice. We already know it of our own knowledge:

> "Sicut hunc sensum naturali instinctu etiam gentes habent, quod sit aliquod supremum numen, quod colendum, invocandum, laudandum, ad quod in omnibus periculis confugiendum sit, sicut Paulus dicit, Romanorum 1:'Gentes agnovisse Deum natura.'
>
> Haec enim *notitia* divinitus plantata est in omnium hominum animis, quod vocant Deum auxiliatorem, beneficum, placabilem, etiamsi in eo postea errent, quis nam ille Deus sit, et quomodo velit coli."

We observe, as before, that the text assigns the innate knowledge of God to the *notitia* level. It is universal, and involves the understanding of certain divine predicates. This knowledge is possessed of independent truth. The belief in Christ need not enter in to correct it, but possibly to complement it, as long as only the *notitia* level is involved.

Yet, this true *propositio maior* becomes false "postea", when man ponders the particular will and specific worship of God. Or in other words: When the theoretical knowledge is applied and becomes concrete, apart from the revelation in Christ, mistakes and lies occur. I content myself with a single example, although other passages in the same Genesis lecture could be adduced.[12]

---

[11] WA 42.631.27ff. Cf. WA 44.84.15ff.: "Deus quidem promisit se velle esse Deum omnibus hominibus, quae *notitia* indita est animis hominum, sicut testatur Paulus Romanorum 1. Et testantur omnium gentium opera et cultus, quod Deum esse nihil aliud sit, quam benefacere hominibus. Ideo enim invocant alius Iovem, alius Martem etc. non alia opinione, nisi quod velint iuvari. Ita naturaliter omnes homines intelligunt et statuunt Deum esse numen aliquod beneficum, ...

Etsi igitur errant in Persona Dei propter idolatriam: tamen studia ibi sunt, quae debentur vero Deo, id est, invocatio et expectatio bonorum et auxilii."

[12] Two other passages from the Genesis lecture may be quoted here; WA 43.240.22ff.: "Non enim aliam *notitiam* de Deo (sc. Pontifex, Turci, Iudaei) habent, quam Philosophicam aut metaphysicam. Quod Deus est ens separatum a creaturis, ut ait Aristoteles, verax, intra se contemplans creaturas. Sed quid haec ad nos? Diabolus etiam sic Deum cognoscit, et scit esse veracem, sed in Theologia quando de agnitione Dei docetur, agnoscendus et appraehendendus est Deus, non intra se manens, sed ab extra veniens ad nos, ut videlicet statuamus eum nobis esse Deum.

In conclusion, we scrutinize a passage in Luther's *last academic disputation* in 1545. The thesis under discussion, which is relevant to our theme, reads: "Peccatum enim excaecavit naturam humanam, ut creatorem amplius non cognosceret, etsi opus eius praesertim gubernationis a longe olfaceret" (no. 24).[13] The respondent, Petrus Hegemon, develops the hypothesis of a twofold knowledge of God, one *via* the Creation and human nature, the other through Christ and the revelation.[14] Luther himself comments on this point in the dissertation and accepts the respondent's basic distinction.

He defines it still further:

"Non enim credebant (sc. gentes), Deum ex nihilo condidisse omnia, sed tamen illa cognitione, quae est philosophica, ex gubernatione aliquid cognoverunt, esse primum movens et summum ens, ut Plato, sed naturalis ratio non potest intelligere rationem creatoris, id est, opus illud, illam totam mundi machinam ex nihilo conditam esse."

Notwithstanding that reason is darkened by sin, so that it does not comprehend the special creation *ex nihilo*, yet it accepts that God is "the prime mover" and "the highest being".[15]

The opponent objects on the grounds: If now the heathens are nevertheless insufficiently aware of God, how can they be responsible,

Ille prior Aristotelicus vel Philosophicus Deus Iudaeorum, Turcarum, Papistarum Deus est, nihil vero is ad nos."

WA 44.591.34ff.: "Philosophi disputant et quaerunt speculative de Deo et perveniunt ad qualemcunque *notitiam*, sicut Plato intuetur et agnoscit gubernationem divinam. Sed omnia sunt obiectiva tantum, nondum est cognitio illa quam habet Ioseph, quod curet, quod exaudiat et opituletur adflictis, hoc non potest statuere Plato. Manet in cogitatione Metaphysica, wie ein kue ein newes thor ansihet." Cf. WA 45.90.2ff. (*Pred.* Rom. 11:33ff. 1537, R); WA 40.III.656.23ff. (*Enarratio capitis noni Esaiae.* 1543–44). B. Lohse (1958)63ff. asserts that the aging Luther sharpens his criticism of the natural knowledge of God: Ratio knows nothing of God. Nevertheless, as shown by our examples from the Genesis lecture, this refers only to the abuse of the rational perception of God. And this also has been his attitude throughout. He said earlier in this sense that reason knows nothing of God. But when speaking of divine knowledge *per se* the preceding evidence from the Genesis lecture clearly indicates that reason possesses a true *notitia*, which is "objective" and "metaphysical".

[13] WA 39.II.340.27f. = Drews 835 (*Die Promotionsdisputation von Petrus Hegemon.* 1545).
[14] WA 39.II.345.4ff. = Drews 840f.
[15] WA 39.II.345.27ff. = Drews 840f. Luther, like Biel, asserts on several occasions that philosophy and reason comprehend that God will not abandon His Creation, cf. WA 40.II.421.16ff. (*Enarratio Psalmi LI.* 1532), WA 40.III.231.35f. and 232.1ff. (*In XV Psalmos graduum.* 1532/33).

and how can Paul say that they have no excuse, according to Rom. 1:20? The respondent retorts that man can indeed know God in general terms. But he does not know of his own knowledge what is God's will, or that God is trinity in unity.[16]

Luther focuses on the opponent's quotation from St Paul. He draws attention to what follows it: "Etsi cognoverunt Deum, tamen non glorificaverunt verum Deum".[17] The heathens' archetype of God is indeed incomplete and insufficient. But it is not false *per se*. It does incorporate diverse correct abstract ideas. Otherwise, they could not be called to account. Being a natural knowledge of God as the first cause and God the ruler of the world, this insight possesses truth *per se* before, and independent of, belief and revelation. This *propositio maior*, this universal knowledge on the *notitia* level, means that all mankind can be held accountable and without excuse.

The guilt arises when men attach the divine predicates to the wrong subjects, to idols, and hold fast to these false gods, against their better judgement so to speak. When they apply the innate knowledge of God, and create their own divine images, they are rightly adjudged guilty and worthy of punishment. The universal knowledge of God is good *per se*. Sin grows from the perverted human heart.[18]

Consequently, we see here that Luther is speaking of the natural knowledge of God in two senses, and that this dialectic is intended to explain Paul's reasoning in Rom. 1:19ff.[19]

---

[16] WA 39.II.347.3ff. = Drews 842f.: "Non perfecte cognoverunt Deum, sicut debebant ex suo verbo, quo se patefecerat, etsi ad eam cognitionem venerant, quod sit mens aeterna, causa boni in natura, sed per istam philosophiam non cognoverunt voluntatem Dei et quod sint tres personae divinitatis et quod Deus Pater miserit Filium ad genus humanum redimendum."

[17] WA 39.II.347.11ff. = Drews 842f.

[18] WA 39.II.347.13ff. = Drews 842f.: "Illa quantulacunque cognitione, quamquam imperfecta, contempto agnito illo Deo ex gubernatione versi sunt ad cultum animalium, quadrupedum, volucrum, et non tribuerunt Deo gloriam. Gentes sciebant, unum esse Deum, sed tamen suas idolatrias non volebant omittere. Haec est causa, cur sint inexcusabiles, quia sciebant, sua idola esse lignea et lapidea, tamen adorabant et divinum honorem illis tribuebant." Cf. the mode of expression of the second manuscript (*ib*. 30f.): "Paulus ipse solvit in textu et explicat hanc quaestionem, quod gentes qualicunque hac cognitione non *usi* sint nec voluerunt *uti* ." Cf. also the same thought earlier, WA 14.588.26ff. (*Vorlesung über das Deuteronomium*. 1523–24, Dr).

[19] A number of anonymous manuscript pages are appended to the material on the disputation on John 1:14 (1539). Someone has presumably prepared for the dissertation on these sheets (cf. WA 39.II.3). Since we find none of these arguments in the actual text we may assume that the person concerned was not given an opportunity to speak. But his detailed arguments are of interest to us. For they are based on the wording of Rom 1:19ff.

Summarizing the Luther material in this section we can state finally:

a) that the universal, innate knowledge of God is true before, and independent of, the revelation in Christ, and that it incorporates the perception of certain divine attributes: God's might, power to help, that his due is worship and that He is the prime mover and the highest being.[20]

b) that this innate knowledge possessed by the self-centred individual is false when it is applied to inadequate subjects which are manifestations of selfish desires[21], and

c) that this oscillation between positive and negative assessments of the natural knowledge of God corresponds to a dialectic between the *notitia* and the *usus* levels, if we use our own definitions. Many of Luther's exegeses of Rom. 1:19ff. lack the technical terms, *propositio maior* and *propositio minor*. Nevertheless, they contain the points which these terms are intended to express.

---

and express the positive and negative aspects of the natural knowledge of God in terms which appear to be in accord with Luther's own dialectical viewpoint. WA 39.II.31.17ff. and Drews 528f.: "Hic videtur Paulus innuere, placuisse Deo istam ethnicorum de Deo inquisitionem et cognitionem, nec damnare eos ideo, quod Deum cognoverint in creaturis et operibus etc. Sed quia non glorificarunt nec grati fuerunt Deo, ideo tradidisse eos in reprobam mentem. Non igitur damnat Deus istam cognitionem naturae de Deo nec damnat dictamen illud rectae rationis, sed potius negligentiam, contemptum gloriae Dei et ingratitudinem. Hinc concluditur, non esse philosophiam et rationis dialecticam reiiciendam in christianismo. E regione vero vos male docetis excludendam rationem ab articulis fidei." Cf. WA 39.II.14.6ff. = Drews 500ff.

[20] I would agree with the assessment in F. X. Arnold, *Zur Frage des Naturrechts bei Martin Luther* (1937)11: "Man wird dem Reformator nicht gerecht, wenn man diese Frage (sc. nach dem Naturrecht) kurzerhand negativ beantwortet mit dem Hinweis auf die lutherische Lehre von der völligen Verderbnis der menschlichen Natur durch die Erbsünde, auf den damit zusammenhängenden Gedanken von der Allwirksamkeit Gottes und auf den reformatorischen Biblizismus. Es ist methodisch verfehlt, mit einem fest umrissenen Begriff von der 'natürlichen Theologie' an Luthers Schriften heranzugehen und aus der Tatsache, dass der Reformator gerade diese Art natürlicher Theologie ablehnt, den Schluss zu ziehen, dass es für ihn überhaupt keine allgemeine Gottesoffenbarung aus der Natur gibt." H. Gerdes, *Luthers Streit mit den Schwärmern um das rechte Verständnis des Gesetzes Mose* (1955)49 has a good summary. In H. Olsson (1971)149ff. we find an extensive exposition of this issue. Cf. also G. Ebeling (1964)263, G. Rost (1966)57, *ib.* 59, *ib.* 67 and *ib.* 87.

[21] This aspect is clearly demonstrated already by H. Vossberg, *Luthers Kritik aller Religion* (1922)60ff. This false use of the natural theology by natural man and the right use through reason illuminated by faith are emphasized by R. Josefson (1943) 24, when he tries to refute Arnold's theories (cf. n. 20 above). A similar emphasis is to be found in B. Hägglund, *Theologie und Philosophie bei Luther und in der occamistischen Tradition* (1955)67 and in B. Lohse (1958)135. Cf. also H. Bandt (1958)88. Concerning the natural knowledge of God according to the Lutheran confessions see E. Schlink, *Theologie der lutherischen Bekenntnisschriften³* (1948)85f. and H. Fagerberg, *A New Look at the Lutheran Confessions 1529–1537* (1972)114f.

2.4. Theologia gloriae According to Rom. 1:19–21

Prior to his participation in a chapter of the German Augustinians in Heidelberg in 1518, Luther wrote 40 theses, the first 28 of which were accompanied by diverse arguments. This *Heidelberg disputation* has played an important role in Luther research. Special attention has been devoted to the distinction between *theologia gloriae* and *theologia crucis*, which was prompted by the indulgences controversy. Already Walter v. Loewenich's standard monograph *Luthers Theologia Crucis* proposed that the theology of the cross is basic to the whole of Luther's theology. And it cannot be confined to a specific period in the development of his reforming zeal.[1] This interpretation has become more or less normative.

Whereas the *theologia gloriae* is based on an innate knowledge of God, which derives its authority from Rom. 1:19ff,[2] I here intend to investigate whether the previously analysed dialectic in the view of the rational discernment of God is also relevant in this context. Does this interpretation fit in naturally with Luther's other exegeses of Rom. 1:19ff? Or does something new crop up in the Heidelberg dissertation?

A number of Luther scholars have indeed noted that there is at least some truth in the *theologia gloriae*. It incorporates a certain measure of knowledge of God.[3] But this has, for the most part, remained "a marginal note". I have not found any scholar who has made a direct

---

[1] W. von Loewenich (1939)7. Cf. further P. Althaus (1963)37f., L. Pinomaa (1963)1ff., G. Ebeling (1964)259f., H. Bornkamm (1975)130f., L. Grane (1975)146ff.

[2] WA 1.361.31ff.

[3] W. von Loewenich (1939)13: "Luther lehnt diesen Weg nicht völlig ab (Th 24, W.I, 354,27). Es sollte eigentlich eine Erkenntnis Gottes 'ex operibus' geben (W.I, 354,23). Es sollte so sein, aber faktisch ist es nicht so." H. Bandt (1958)90f.: "Eigenartig erscheint in dem soeben angeführten Abschnitt aus der Heidelberger Disputation, dass Luther zunächst die cognitio Dei ex operibus als wirkliche Erkenntnis der invisibilia Dei (der göttlichen virtus, divinitas, sapientia, iustitia, bonitas etc!) ausspricht (1.361.35), dann aber sogleich fortfährt: haec omnia cognita non faciunt dignum nec sapientem (361.36). Das kann doch offensichtlich nur so gemeint sein, dass der *spekulative Weg* der Erkenntnis jener göttlichen Wesenseigenschaften (keineswegs die Erkenntnis jener Eigenschaften überhaupt) nicht weise macht. Wir hätten es demnach in den beiden Thesen nicht etwa mit zwei verschiedenen Erkenntnisgegenständen (invisibilia Dei—visibilia Dei), sondern vielmehr mit zwei verschiedenen Erkenntnisarten, nämlich der an der menschlichen Vernunft orientierten spekulativen Erkenntnis und der an der göttlicher Offenbarung orientierten Glaubenserkenntnis, zu tun." *Ib.* 91: "diesen in sich selbst möglichen und guten Erkenntnisweg". P. Althaus (1963)35: "Röm 1:20 ist eine urständliche Möglichkeit gewesen." L. Pinomaa (1963)1f.: "Luther does not reject in principle this way to knowledge of God. Obviously one ought to reach knowledge of God by means of God's works." Cf. also G. Ebeling (1964)260f.

comparison with other major Lutheran expositions of Rom. 1:19ff. Instead, scholars tend to overlook the meaning of the *theologia gloriae* in favour of the *theologia crucis*. Even Loewenich gives his interpretation the somewhat one-sided bent.[4]

The critical comments on the *theologia gloriae* have in consequence been interpreted as a refutation of *all kinds* of rational theology, whatever. It would be feasible to regard the front against "intellectualism" as a clear parallel to the line of battle against "moralism", *e.g.* the Pelagian tendencies in the conventional doctrine of justification.[5] Thus, the Heidelberg disputation has become the norm for an interpretation which permits Luther's theology to vacillate, more or less unreservedly, round two poles, namely faith, in contrast to the role of reason in the *theologia gloriae*, and the revelation through Christ, as contrasted with the knowledge of God in the *theologia gloriae* mediated by the Creation. Yet, I question whether this does Luther justice. Moreover I shall demonstrate that we must, more scrupulously than before, distinguish between different aspects of the *theologia gloriae*.

A reader who examines the entire material from this famous disputation is struck by the twofold nature of Luther's interpretation of a number of basic, theological concepts. A presentation may be wholly positive from one point of view and wholly negative from another. Already in *conclusio 1* we encounter an example of this twofold, contradictory mode of reasoning. "Lex Dei, saluberrima vitae doctrina, non potest hominem ad iusticiam promovere, sed magis obest."[6] If Luther is thinking of the knowledge of the law *per se*, the comprehension of the law as general doctrine, he describes it as both sensible and sound.

---

[4] W. von Loewenich (1939)16f. There is evidently a shift of emphasis in Loewenich concerning this question. For that which was "*eine* Erkenntnis Gottes" becomes "*keine* Erkenntnis Gottes". Nevertheless, WA 1.362.11ff., which is adduced, is no support of the latter opinion, since it by no means denies that the cognitive moment of *theologia gloriae* is *per se* true knowledge. The reference to Luther instead speaks of the false personal *application* and the *abuse* of this knowledge. Cf. further the same tendency in B. Lohse (1958)73f.: "*Alles*, was der Mensch weiss, will oder tut, ist Torheit und muss zunichte werden" (The note refers to the Heidelberg disputation in 1518); P. Althaus (1963)37: "das Kreuz ist Verhüllung Gottes und insofern das Ende für *alles* Er-denken Gottes durch die selbstbewusste Vernunft;" L. Pinomaa (1963)2: "He rejects completely *all* speculation. One must not meditate upon the majesty of God, for it is beyond reach. Luther has no interest in abstractions."

[5] P. Althaus, *Die Bedeutung des Kreuzes im Denken Luthers*, L 8 (1926)97ff.; W. von Loewenich (1939)14f. Cf. also P. Althaus (1963)36f., L. Pinomaa (1963)3.

[6] WA 1.355.30f.

In this respect the law is truly "sancta et immaculata, vera, iusta &c" (*conclusio 2*).[7]

Yet this knowledge is transferred from doctrine to life, from the *notitia* to the *usus* level. Luther thereby regards it in a completely different perspective. The knowledge of the law does not lead to righteousness in the life of the individual human being. On the contrary, it is a serious obstacle thereto. Nevertheless the cause does not lie in the knowledge of the law as such but in our perverted will (*conclusio 3*).[8] Men wrongly apply the abstract understanding inherent in the law, in order to deprive God of his meed of honour and retain it for themselves.[9] As shown in the continuation of the Heidelberg disputation, the concept "creatura" faces the same distinction between the positive "res" and the negative "usus" (*conclusio 11*).[10]

Consequently, if Luther distinguished earlier in the dissertation between knowledge *per se* and its application by human beings, it is by no means surprising that the same dialectic is to be found in the section on *theologia gloriae* (*conclusiones 19–24*).

If we consider, *first of all*, the positive side of this concept, we can establish that Luther in no way denies that man "per ea, quae facta sunt" is endowed with a knowledge of "invisibilia Dei", *i.e.* an understanding of the "virtus, divinitas, sapientia, iusticia, bonitas &c" of the divine being.[11] This comment is none other than a paraphrase of his exposition of Rom. 1:19ff. The Creation, which we observe and experience, mediates an evident knowledge of the divine predicates. This understanding is universal in the sense that it is not applied to the situation of individual human beings. It is a knowledge related to the *notitia* category. And Luther says explicitly that the natural knowledge of God, including comprehension of the law, is not evil: "Non tamen sapientia illa mala nec Lex fugienda, sed homo sine Theologia crucis *optimis* pessime abutitur" (*conclusio 24*).[12]

If we take into account the preceding context, we discover that this assertion joins two ideas which were incorporated in the two previous

---

[7] *Ib.* 356.8, cf. *ib.* 363.25ff.

[8] *Ib.* 356.16ff., cf. *ib.* 356.32ff.

[9] *Ib.* 358.4ff., cf. *ib.* 363.21ff. and 28ff.

[10] *Ib.* 359.18ff., cf. *ib.* 363.25ff. Cf. further WA 56.80.3ff. (*Rom.* 1515–16), WA 30.II.572.9ff. (*Kinder zur Schule halten.* 1530), WA 37.370.11ff. (*Pred.* 1534, R), WA 40.II.203.11ff. (*Enarratio Psalmi II.* 1532).

[11] WA 1.361.32ff.

[12] *Ib.* 363.25f.

theses. The expression "sapientia illa" refers to *conclusio 22*, and therefore means knowledge acquired because "invisibilia Dei operibus intellecta conspicit". Or in other words: this is a matter of the content of the *theologia gloriae*.[13] The term *Lex* refers to *conclusio 23*, which describes the accusatory and punitive functions of the law.[14] Thus, with the aforesaid *conclusio 24*, Luther protects himself against the misunderstanding which crops up after the assertion of the abuse of the knowledge of God and the law because of human sin (*conclusiones 22* and *23* respectively), namely that the natural knowledge of God or the law *per se* could be inadequate, false and reprehensible. This positive acceptance of the innate, objective knowledge of God, and cognizance of the law, is not only supported in Rom. 1:19ff. but also by the belief in the Creation in general. Thus the first stage of the reasoning concerning thesis 24 contains the point: "Quia Lex sancta et omne donum Dei bonum, omnis creatura bona valde Gene. 1." Consequently, if we only consider the cognitive aspect of *theologia gloriae*, we have lucid statements asserting that this *notitia*, this understanding of God's predicates, this *propositio maior*, is a good and independent truth, which we possess before and irrespective of "the theology of the cross"!

But if, *secondly*, we turn to the critical judgements concerning *theologia gloriae*, a far different light is shed on the issue. Here Luther is following the Vulgate text of Rom. 1:19ff. Already in the presentation of evidence on *conclusio 19* a *theologus gloriae* is called "foolish". And the reason is this: "haec omnia (sc. invisibilia Dei) cognita non faciunt dignum nec sapientem". On the basis of 1 Cor 1:21ff. this is developed in *conclusio 20*: "Quia enim homines cognitione Dei ex operibus *abusi* sunt, voluit rursus Deus ex passionibus cognosci et reprobare illam sapientiam invisibilium per sapientiam visibilium, ut sic, qui Deum non coluerunt manifestum ex operibus, colerent absconditum in passionibus, Sicut ait 1. Corinth. 1."[15]

Not knowledge *per se* but the wrongful application thereof to a specific situation has the result that *theologia gloriae* does not attain its goal! Luther's rejection of *theologia gloriae* is accordingly a rejection of a specific, personal abuse, prompted by the pursuit of one's own prestige.

---

[13] *Ib.* 362.35ff.

[14] *Ib.* 363.16ff.

[15] *Ib.* 362.5ff. Cf. WA 1.614.17ff. (*Resolutiones disputationum de indulgentiarum virtute.* 1518). Cf. also the expositions of Psalm 14:1 in WA 5.392.26ff. (*Operationes in Psalmos.* 1519–21) and in WA 31.I.307.28ff. (*Die ersten 25 Psalmen.* 1530).

2.4.

This is also emphasized in what follows.[16] The repudiation by Loewenich and other scholars of the direct knowledge of God mediated by the Creation is too general to do full justice to the reformer's double perspective in this question.

My survey of the Heidelberg dissertation with special reference to the interpretation of Rom. 1:19ff. thus leads me to the conclusion: in fact Luther explains this *locus* in Romans in the same way as in other commentaries on the same passage. The emotional controversy on indulgences did not impel him to abandon his fundamental exegesis of Rom. 1:19ff., which I analysed in the *Commentary on Romans* (2.2.). Consequently, the Heidelberg dissertation shows:

a) that the natural but abstract knowledge of God in the *theologia gloriae* is a true and independent form of divine awareness with reference to God's power, divinity, wisdom, righteousness etc.

b) that this knowledge of God is only rejected because it is misused by anthropocentric individuals who, without Christ, seek their own glory and not God's, and

c) that this dialectic between affirmative and negative statements may be regarded as an oscillation between the *notitia* and the *usus* levels.

---

[16] WA 1.363.28ff.: "Sed sicut supra dictum est, qui nondum est destructus, ad nihilum redactus per crucem et passionem, sibi tribuit opera et sapientiam, non autem Deo, et sic *abutitur* donis Dei eaque polluit." If Luther is here asserting the wrongful use, the question arises of the extent to which, in the Heidelberg disputation, he presumes a *rightful use* of the natural knowledge of God. This is indicated by the first two theses (29–30) *ex philosophia*, which scholars have not taken into account at all. Already in his arguments in favour of Thesis 22 Luther maintained that the longing is not slaked by the objects which are coveted (*ib.* 362.39ff.). Nor is the "curiositas sciendi" satisfied by the acquisition of learning, but being kindled still further for more knowledge. Therefore, the only way to satisfaction is not to seek it but to extinguish the longing. This is done in such a way that a man who wishes to be "wise" does not seek wisdom "procendo" but accepts the foolishness "retrocedendo". This is the wisdom from God. Thesis 29 links up with the reasoning: "Qui sine periculo volet in Aristotele Philosophari, necesse est ut ante bene stultificetur in Christo" (*ib.* 355.2f.). If one condition is present, namely the belief in God's foolishness in Christ, the possibility exists of using philosophical knowledge aright, even the Aristotelian philosophy! Indeed, Thesis 30 expounds this point: "Sicut libidinis malo non utitur bene nisi coniugatus, ita nemo Philosophatur bene nisi stultus, id est Christianus" (*ib.* 355.4f.).

2.5. Conclusions

a) Luther stands in the Medieval tradition, whereby the knowledge of God is to some extent derived from nature. His works, like those of Biel, contain positive comments on natural theology. This appears sometimes as a *propositio maior* in a practical syllogism, but is not always found. The issue is clearcut, however. Indeed *theologia gloriae* may be said to stand for a certain measure of natural knowledge of God. Man is generally aware by instinct, and by reason, that God exists, that He is active, that He is powerful and good etc. On occasions this has been brought out in Luther research. Yet, often too little attention has been paid to the positive aspect in favour of the negative judgement, which is also supported by Rom. 1:19ff.

b) This natural knowledge of God is misleading and false when it is adapted and subordinated to sinful man's own needs and desires. In a fashion similar to the scholastic theory, including that of Biel, Luther emphasizes the necessity for a special revelation to allow us to learn to know the divine Trinity, the Incarnation, and the Father's will to redeem mankind through His Son. Scholars have long been well aware of these critical views of natural theology.

c) The two new concepts, which I introduced, proved useful for the simple presentation of the dialectic with regard to the universal knowledge of God. In the chapters which follow, it will also become clear that the *notitia* and *usus* levels are relevant to the explanation of other material as well. After this review of the natural theology I can examine the extent to which the belief in God's omnipotence is based on reason and on revelation (Chap. 3). So, I can pursue this line of argument to justify the doctrine of predestination which is inherent in the universal knowledge of God, and in the special revelation of the Scriptures (Chap.4).

3. The Omnipotence

3.1. Background

1. As we have already seen, *Peter Lombard* asserts that man possesses a natural capacity to understand the omnipotence of God from the "magnitudo" of created things.[1] The *Sententiae* discuss the fundamental significance of this divine omnipotence. One important tenet is that God can do all He wishes, and that His will comes to pass in a manner beyond compare.[2]

This *locus* expands considerably in the works of the major theologians of high scholasticism, such as *Thomas Aquinas* and *Duns Scotus*.[3] The idea of divine omnipotence comes to the fore as a result of the continued reflection in the *via moderna*. It is not so much that God's omnipotence is understood in a new light but that it is more strongly focused than ever before. This is of far-reaching significance for the whole approach to God's relationship with the world. God's contingent will *vis-à-vis* the Creation becomes a dominant concept, and can therefore no longer be integrated in a stable, metaphysical system.[4] This may be interpreted as a means of articulating the Creation theology of the Bible.[5] According to *William of Ockham*, God, being all-powerful, can do everything which is possible. He shares Scotus' theory that a distinction must be made between two different kinds of omnipotence. Philosophy can demonstrate that, directly or indirectly, God is the cause of all things. Theology, however, which derives knowledge from revelation, regards God's omnipotence as the immediate cause of all things, in the sense that no result could follow without the divine cause, even if all other conditions were satisfied. To the eye of faith, the world appears to be a series of contingent phenomena dependent on God's almighty will.[6]

Biel accepts Scotus' distinction, when, following Ockham, he denies the possibility of proving the assertion that God can do everything

---

[1] 2.1 n. 1.
[2] MPL 192, 635ff. (Dist. 42).
[3] F. Copleston (1959)368f., 527f.
[4] L. Grane (1956)67f., *ib.* 63. Cf. further F. W. Schmidt, *Theozentrische Theologie im Nominalismus und bei Luther*, ZThK 12 (1931)359ff.
[5] L. Grane (1956) 74, cf. *ib.* 54.
[6] F. Copleston (1960)84f., *ib.* 94f., cf. H. Junghans (1968)228f.

possible without the co-operation of Creation. Reason can indeed arrive at the conclusion that the omnipotence of God effects everything possible "directly or indirectly".[7] For theology, however, the divine omnipotence implies the capacity to "immediately" produce every possible effect which is not essential *per se*, nor includes a contradiction.[8] Philosophy can obviously envisage the first way of comprehending God's omnipotence, provided that God is the only prime active cause. Human reason cannot evidently prove the second mode of understanding, which is peculiar to theology.[9] The omnipotence of God in theological terms can be demonstrated only by the authority of the Bible, the Creed and the saints. Nevertheless, we can give reasons for the belief that God is almighty in the sense presumed by faith.[10] There is, accordingly, scope for rational arguments. It is not possible, however, to prove beyond doubt, but this is a theory of God's omnipotence which is in line with, and not contradicted by, reason.

God's will in an exalted sense is *voluntas beneplaciti consequens*. Nothing in Creation can impede this will.[11] Provided that God wishes "alia a se" it can be proved that His will cannot be thwarted.[12] Consequently, on this point, theology can find help in philosophy, and support its view of God's almighty will by adducing the theory held by reason. *Voluntas dei signi*, however, is not always fulfilled. For many

---

[7] Coll I, Dist. 42, q. 1, A, a. 1, n. 1: "Notandum pro articulo primo, quod 'omnipotens' dupliciter accipitur:

Uno modo, quia est 'agens, quod potest in omne possibile, mediate vel immedite'." *Ib.* C, a. 2, con 1: "Supposito quod Deus solus sit primum efficiens, probatur evidenter quod est primo modo omnipotens."

[8] *Ib.* A, a. 1, n. 1: "Alio modo accipitur 'proprie theologice' pro illo 'qui potest in omnem effectum' immediate et in 'quodcumque possibile', 'quod non est ex se necessarium nec includit contradictionem; ita inquam immediate, quod sine omni cooperatione cuiuscumque alterius causae agentis' potest in quemlibet effectum."

[9] *Ib.* C, a. 2, con. 1–2. Cf. L. Grane (1956)60f.

[10] Coll I, Dist. 42, q. 1, D, a. 2, con. 3: "Deum esse omnipotentem est sola fide creditum. Probatur auctoritate sanctorum et Scripturae ac Symboli ... Potest nihilominus *rationabiliter persuaderi:* Nam Deus est causa omnium; ergo omnipotens.—Assumptum probatur: Quia omnia essentialiter dependent a Deo, et per consequens est causa omnium.—Antecedens probatur: Quia omne aliud a Deo non minus dependet a Deo quam una creatura ab alia; sed una creatura dependet ab alia; ergo etc." Cf. *ib.* Dist. 45, q. 1, B, a. 2, con. 1: "Voluntas divina sive essentia, quod omnino idem est, est causa immediata omnium quae fiunt, quamvis hoc ratione naturali probari non possit."

[11] *Ib.* Dist. 46, q. 1, A, a. 1, n. 1: "Secundo sequitur quod 'voluntas', proprie accipiendo vocabulum, dicit solum voluntatem beneplaciti consequentem." *Ib.* C, a. 2, con. 3: "Voluntas beneplaciti consequens non potest impediri."

[12] *Ib.* Dist. 46, q. 2, B, con. 2.

---

things happen in despite of God's commandments, covenant and counsel. Creation can act in a way divergent from the will of God.[13] Thus, in one sense, God's almighty will implies a monistic outlook: God's will alone is realised supremely *vis-à-vis* Creation. In another sense, we may assume a dualism: Creation sets itself above and contravenes the will of God.

2. Although Medieval theology, not least Ockhamism, firmly accepted omnipotence as a fundamental feature of the concept of God, it also introduced major reservations with reference to evil. In expounding his theory, *Peter Lombard* emphasizes that the omnipotence of God cannot be modified to the point that God wills or commits sin.[14] When man rejects the goodness of God he is himself the cause of sin and the evil consequent thereon. If the evil inherent in guilt is attributed to man's perverted will, it is asserted that God's will causes the evil consisting of the punishment of sin.[15] By his guilt man deserves the hardness of heart with which God chastises him. We can find the cause of human hardness of heart (*meritum obdurationis*) but not *meritum reprobationis* or even less *meritum praedestinationis*. For eternal damnation and eternal salvation are conferred without reference to temporal merits. The scriptural evidence for this is seen in the OT prophecies concerning Jacob and Esau, whose destiny was decided before their birth.[16]

A similar outlook is to be found in *Thomas Aquinas*. Man alone is regarded as the cause of *malum culpae*. This is punished by God, to whom accordingly is attributed *malum poenae*. This evil does not occur for its own sake, but in order that the good and just world order shall prevail. Behind moral evil we can only assume a divine concession. God wills a greater good, that man shall possess free will, and choose to love God. Physical evil emanates to some extent from Almighty God. But God's goodness cannot allow this evil to afflict mankind as an end in itself. It is instead a means for the highest good. When God, as the supreme artist, wishes to perfect the universe, He must use both immortal and mortal beings who, in the latter case, cannot evade suffering and death.[17]

The heavier emphasis on God's omnipotence in Ockhamism results in a weakening of the idea of universal order inherent in created things. Thus,

---

[13] *Ib.* Dist. 46, q. 1, C, a. 2, con. 1, and *ib.* D, con. 5.
[14] MPL 192, 636 (I, Dist. 42, q. 3).
[15] *Ib.* 733ff. (II, Dist. 34, q. 3; II, Dist. 35, q. 14).
[16] *Ib.* 633 (I, Dist. 41, q. 1).
[17] F. Copleston (1959)371ff., J. Hick (1974)99ff.
[18] H. Olsson (1950)376ff., L. Grane (1956)69f.

it is no longer feasible to refer to an ontological goodness inherent in Creation itself. The good can be determined, not from nature, or the law, but from revelation alone.[18] For *Biel*, however, it is self-evident to cling to the traditional belief that God does not effect evil for its own sake. Man himself is responsible for the purely negative evil inherent in sin and guilt. Yet God adds the evil which consists in the punishment of sin. This has a good purpose: penance and sanctification.[19] This results in a traditional repudiation of the Manichean heresy that nothing evil does emanate from "God, the Father, Almighty" but only from another, evil deity.[20] Therefore, we can interpret hardness of heart as the divine punishment for the impenitent sinner. Why does God allow such evil as damnation, which has no apparent benefit for the individual concerned, since a good prince avoids all evil as far as possible? The answer is that God does not permit any evil in Creation which does not result in good. For the sin of the ungodly increases the merit of the good, as St Augustine says, so long as evil men attack the faithful.[21] When the idea of God's omnipotence is comprehended by faith, all contingent relations and phenomena in Creation are seen as effects of God's omnipotence. Consequently, evil—including the evil which seems to be an end in itself—has a good purpose, since it is inflicted by the good God.

3.2. The Rational Perception of God's Omnipotence

1. Man's innate archetype of God that He is "potent" was mentioned already in the primary source for Luther's early view of natural theology (Rom. 1:19ff.) in the *Lecture on Romans*. Nevertheless it is also asserted that we must have revelation and faith in order to assign this attribute to the right object.[1] Moreover, the text goes on to emphasize that the very concept of omnipotence is inadequate. We can try to reach a

---

[19] Coll I, Dist. 47, q. 1, C, a. 2, con; *ib.* II, Dist. 34, q. 1, B. a. 1, n. 2: "Secundo notandum, quod cum sit malum culpae et malum poenae nunc solum loquimur de malo culpae; non enim dubium est malum poenae esse *quid positivum*, et habere causam positivam etiam ipsum deum secundum illud Amos. III: 'Si erit malum in civitate, quod dominus non fecerit', loquitur ibi propheta de malo poenae." Cf. *ib.* Dist. 10, q. 1, D, a. 3, con.

[20] *Ib.* Dist. 34, q. 1, A, a. 1, n. 1.

[21] *Ib.* I, Dist. 41, q. 1, L.

[1] 2.2 n. 2 above.

"metaphysical" understanding of God's power from the visible Creation, but He conceals His might in weakness. Only thus can we grasp the true sense of the divine power.[2]

2. Yet, there are signs that the mature Luther, like Biel, considered that reason is not opposed to the belief in God's omnipotence, but admits it to some extent. In *The Bondage of the Will* Luther writes in general terms: "To begin with, even Reason and Diatribe admit that God works all in all (1 Cor. 12:6) and that without him nothing is effected or effective; for he is omnipotent, and this belongs to his omnipotence, as Paul says to the Ephesians" (Eph. 1:11, 19).[3] Apart from this confession by *ratio* there are more categorical statements. God's omnipotence implies man's absolute dependence. Luther proposes this as a tentative argument: "Yet natural reason itself is forced to admit that the living and true God must be (oportere esse) one who by his freedom imposes necessity on us, since obviously he would be a ridiculous God, or idol rather, if he foresaw the future uncertainly, or could be proved mistaken by events, when even the heathen have given their gods an 'ineluctable fate'."[4] He goes on to state the issue in terms bordering on direct proof: "Even natural Reason herself, who is offended by this necessity and makes such efforts to get rid of it, is compelled to admit it by the force of her own judgement, even if there were no Scripture at all."[5] This could perhaps be an exaggeration, from which we should not deduce too much. Nevertheless, we can establish that in *The Bondage of the Will* Luther finds no obstacles presented by reason to the concept of God's omnipotence.

3. In an interesting passage in the large *Lecture on Galatians* Luther exhorts his hearers to pursue apologetic debate with all possible rational arguments.[6] Concerning man's justification, he repudiates the use of reason of the natural knowledge of God. But apart from this doctrine,

---

[2] WA 56.380.31ff. (*Rom.* 1515–16), LW 25.370. Similar thoughts have been brought forward from the Heidelberg disputation (1518) in 2.4 n. 15–16 above. Cf. also WA 7.145.15ff. (*Assertio omnium articulorum.* 1520).

[3] WA 18.709.10ff. (*De servo arbitrio.* 1525), LW 33.175. It is noteworthy that Luther can call God "caussa principalis omnium, quae fiunt", WA 18.716.22. Obviously Luther adopts an expression from Erasmus. In *De libero arbitrio* the latter says: "Hic non excutiam, an deus, qui est sine controversia primaria et summa causa omnium, quae fiunt, quaedam sic agat per causas secundarias, ut ipse interea nihil agat, an sic agat omnia, ut secundariae causae tantum cooperentur causae principali, tametsi non sunt alioqui necessariae". And further Erasmus writes: "Huic voluntati nemo potest resistere, sed ordinatae voluntati sive, ut scholae vocant, voluntati signi nimirum saepe resistur" (III. a. 8.).

[4] WA 18.718.15ff., LW 33.189. It is impossible to avoid the conclusion that Luther in this issue proves his statement not only by the authority of *the Scripture* but also by the judgement of *the reason*, in spite of his being critical of the attempts from reason to be in

agreement with the revealed truths, cf. *e.g.* WA 18.631.16ff. Sympathizing with the latter critical assessment of reason K. Schwarzwäller (1969)96ff. takes a far too negative attitude against the Luther interpretation in G. Rost (1966)56ff. where Rost expounds the former evaluation of the judgement of reason. In his own interpretation of the relevant passage Schwarzwäller, *Theologia crucis* (1970)192 seems to underestimate the importance of the argument derived from natural reason. Yet, he admits that Luther can produce arguments—valid arguments—which lie on "die Vernunftebene" (*ib.* 104). The probable reason why Schwarzwäller dislikes the natural theology is his dependence on Barth's theological viewpoint, cf. *ib.* 11: "Das Ernstnehmen dieses interpretatorischen Grunderfordernisses, ... mag den Ausführungen gelegentlich einen Klang gegeben haben, der als "barthianisch" empfunden werden könnte. In der Tat: Karl Barths energischer Ruf zum einen und einzigen Thema der Theologie, seine Bewährung dieser Haltung in Situationen, wo man die kyriotes des Christus nicht abstrichlos zu bekennen wagte, und die Freiheit, die er mit seiner christologischen Konzentration für Theologie und Kirche erstritt, das alles ist schwer zu überschätzende Hilfe und gibt Mut, sich auf Luthers christologische Konzentration einzulassen, obschon einem dabei die Konsequenzen den Atem verschlagen". Of course, even Schwarzwäller is sometimes critical against Barth, see *ib.* llf. and *Gotteslob* (1970)19ff. These objections, however, do not hit Barth's rejection of natural theology.

Maybe G. Rost (1966)56f. overlooks the tentative character of this statement which is implied by "oportere esse". It is no real proof. But the following assertion (n. 5) is, of course, stronger.

5 WA 18.719.20ff., LW 33.190. Even later Luther stresses the capacity of pagan man to know God's power, see *e.g.* WA 19.206.17 (*Propheten Jona ausgelegt.* 1526), WA 45.91.30f. (*Pred.* 1537, R).

6

WA 40 I.78.6ff. (Hs)	WA 40 I.78.27 ff. (Dr)	WATR 6.86.24ff.
"Sed si disputandum fuerit	"Alias extra hunc locum Iustificationis si quando disputandum est cum	"Wo sichs zuträget, dass du ausserhalb dieser Sache von der Rechtfertigung mit
cum *Iudeis, Turcis, Schwermeris de alia re,*	*Iudaeis, Turcis, Sectariis* de *sapienta, potentia* etc. *Dei,* Utere omni arte tua et, quantum potes, sis subtilis	*Jüden, Türken, Rotten* oder *Ketzern von Gottes Weisheit, Gewalt u.*
so disputir so bose du kanst,	et argutus disputator, tum enim es *in alio argumento.*	disputiren sollt, so gebrauch deiner Kunst aufs Beste, sei so scharf, subtil und spitzig, so du immer kannst. Da hat es keine Fahr, denn da hast
quia tum es *ynn eim anderm feld.*	In *causa* autem conscientiae, *iustitiae,* vitae (quod significanter dico), contra legem, peccatum,	du *mit einem andern Argument* zu schaffen. Aber *in dieser Sache* von *der*
Sed in *re iustitiae*	mortem et diabolum, ..."	*Rechtfertigung,* da wir unser Gewissen wider das Gesetze, unser Gerechtigkeit wider die
contra peccatum, mortem, diabolum..."		Sünde und unser Leben gegen dem Tode und Teufel fur Gott vertheidingen sollen..."

this knowledge plays a positive role. Jews and Turks, who do not accept arguments from the New Testament, recognise the proofs of universal reason.

When the printed text supplements "de alia re" in the manuscript with "de sapientia, potentia etc. Dei" these may well be Luther's own words, since there are major agreements between the manuscript and the printed version. The table conversation from Aurifaber's collection, which displays close resemblances to the printed text, is also of some interest in this context. Consequently, if we here have an authentic Luther text, we could say that he not only adduces the rational concept of God's omnipotence in, e.g., The Bondage of the Will, he also exhorts his students to argue in the same way.

The fundamental theses 1. and 2. of the Disputation on John 1:14 from 1539 presume that the same truth is not valid in different spheres, and that the incarnation is true in terms of theology but "impossible and absurd" in philosophy.[7] The opponent points to the philosophical knowledge of God's power.[8] If at least a few thinkers accept God as the absolute power, this is in the eyes of the respondent, probably Luther himself, a truth valid within both theology and philosophy. Although reason concedes (concedat) that God exists, and that He is omnipotent, it cannot accept the incarnation. For it seems impossible that something infinite could become as finite as a human being.[9] Thus, on the one hand, there is a knowledge common to both philosophy and theology, and, on the other, Luther draws a sharp distinction between these two spheres.

Consequently, there is in Luther a positive assessment of the view held by reason concerning the divine omnipotence, especially in The Bondage of the Will, so that it is relevant in theology. God's omnipotence in theological terms is in harmony with, and derives support from, the concepts of philosophy.[10] But since this theory has its limitations, we must also assume a critical view on Luther's part as regards the relevance of the philosophical concept of omnipotence within theology. This scholars have long observed.[11]

[7] WA 39 II.3.1ff. = Drews 487.
[8] WA 39 II.8.10ff. = Drews 492ff.
[9] WA 39 II.9.1ff. = Drews 492ff., cf. the B-manuscript.
[10] Cf. E. Seeberg (1929)205, G. Ljunggren (1928)378, W. Elert (1931)197f., G. Rost (1966)55ff.
[11] E.g. Th. Harnack I (1927)53f., R. Seeberg (1898)227f., id. (1917)146f., M. Doerne (1938)80f., ib. 86f., P. Althaus (1963)17, cf. ib. 27f., K. Schwarzwäller (1969)98.

3.3. The Biblical View of God's Omnipotence

Scholars have realised that Luther lays special emphasis on the dynamic feature of God's action with His Creation.[1] This interpretation is derived from his intensive struggle with the Bible, not least the Old Testament. A stimulus thereto gave the *via moderna*, as we have seen (3.1.1.).

1. A number of pregnant statements which illuminate Luther's vision of the divine omnipotence are to be found in the exposition of the *Magnificat* from 1521. Luke 1:49 is expounded as follows:

"Truly, in these words she takes away all might and power from every creature and bestows them on God alone. What great boldness and robbery on the part of so young and tender a maiden! She dares, by this one word, to make all the strong feeble, all the mighty weak, all the wise foolish, all the famous despised, and *God alone the Possessor of all strength, wisdom, and glory.* For this is the meaning of the phrase: 'He who is mighty'. There is none that does anything, but as St Paul says in Ephesians 1: 'God accomplishes all in all', and all creatures' works are God's work. Even as we confess in *the Creed*: 'I believe in God the Father, the Almighty'. He is almighty because it is His power alone that works in all and through all and over all.'"[2]

Everything in Creation is emptied of its own power and might. In the most profound sense, God's omnipotence brings out every phenomenon of existence. This is the essential and sufficient cause of all things.

---

[1] Th. Harnack I (1927)89ff., *ib.* 91: "Die Transzendenz und Immanenz Gottes erweist sich der Welt gegenüber in dem ewigen, unveränderlichen A l l w i s s e n   u n d   V o r h e r w i s s e n, und in dem stetigen und aktuosen A l l w i r k e n Gottes in der Welt." It is also clearly underlined by K. Holl (1923)45: "Die Welt erschien ihm (sc. Luther) jetzt nicht mehr wie den Griechen und der Scholastik als eine ruhende Ordnung. Er schaute sie als begriffen in nie rastender Bewegung, und auch ihre Ordnung sah er in jedem Augenblick neu erzeugt. Dadurch wird ihm die Lebendigkeit Gottes erst im eigentlichen Sinn anschaulich. Denn Gott war es, der als 'unruhige Treiber' die Dinge unaufhörlich zum Wirken drängte und ihr Ineinandergreifen schuf; die ganze Welt war ein ununterbrochenes Zeugnis seiner nie versiegenden Schöpferkraft." Cf. also *ib.* 89ff. H. Olsson, *Grundproblemet i Luthers socialetik I* (1934)51ff., *ib.* 84ff. was one of the first scholars in Scandinavia to interpret Luther's thoughts on the theology of creation. We find an extensive summary in H. Olsson (1971)7ff., *ib.* 369ff. Concerning this theme see, especially, D. Löfgren, *Die Theologie der Schöpfung bei Luther* (1960)21ff. For the important Old Testament background cf. H. Bornkamm, *Luther und das Alte Testament* (1948)38ff.

[2] WA 7.574.3ff. (*Das Magnificat verdeutschet und ausgeleget.* 1521), LW 21.328. See further H. W. Beyer, *Gott und die Geschichte nach Luthers Auslegung des Magnificat*, LuJ 21 (1939)110ff.

3.3.

2. *The Bondage of the Will* not only depicts the rational aspect of the concept of omnipotence, when God is seen as the prime mover, who directly or indirectly causes all things. Here too, the human experience of the divine omnipotence is present. The theologians' error consists in that they envisage God's omnipotence as a static phenomenon: "they do not sufficiently consider how unrestingly active God is in all His creatures, allowing none of them to take a holiday."[3] Luther explicitly states his intention of bringing out the Biblical aspect of omnipotence:

> "By the omnipotence of God, however, I do not mean the potentiality by which He could do many things which He does not, but the active power by which He potently works all in all, which is the sense in which *Scripture* calls Him omnipotent."[4]

When Christ's real presence in the Eucharist is stressed in the controversies with, *inter alios*, Zwingli, Luther once more illuminates the believer's experience of God's dynamic omnipotence:

> "*The Scriptures* teach us, however, that the right hand of God is not a specific place in which a body must or may be, such as on a golden throne, but is the almighty power of God, which at one and the same time can be nowhere and yet must be everywhere."
>
> "On the other hand, it must be essentially present at all places, even in the tiniest tree leaf. The reason is this: It is God who creates, effects, and preserves all things through his almighty power and right hand, as *our Creed* confesses. For he despatches no officials or angel when he creates or preserves something, but all this is the work of his divine power itself."[5]

[3] WA 18.710.38f. (*De servo arbitrio*. 1525), LW 33.178. Cf. R. Seeberg (1917)144.
[4] WA 18.718.28ff., LW 33.189. Cf. the thought in WA 18.631:21f.: "Cum contra *scriptura* dicat, arbitrio Dei et authoritate stare, cadere omnia,..." An important feature in Luther's perception of reality is that this divine power causes *both punishment and salvation*: WA 19.377.10ff. (*Der Prophet Habakuk ausgelegt*. 1526): "Denn es macht grossen mut, wenn einer weis und gewis gleubt, das nur eyn Gott sey und der selbige unser Gott, unser heyliger sey und mit uns halte. Was konnen den thun alle götter auff erden? Weyl du denn alleine Gott und unser heyliger bist, wir aber dein volck, das alles ynn deinen henden stehet, so sey uns gnedig und las uns nicht sterben noch gar verderben durch die Babylonier, sondern nur gestrafft und gezüchtiget werden, das doch samen uberbleybe deynem volck, wie du verheyssen hast"; *Ib* 219.28ff. (*Der Prophet Jona ausgelegt*. 1526): "Gott hat uns damit beweyset, wie gewaltiglich er den tod und alle ding ynn seiner hand hat und wie gar leicht es yhm sey, uns zu helffen auch ynn unaussprechlichen und verzweyffelten notten, das wyr doch so gar schwerlich konnen gleuben. Er ist allenthalben gegen wertig ym tod, ynn der hellen, mitten unter den feinden, ja auch ynn yhrem hertzen. Denn er hatts alles gemacht und regiert es auch alles, das es mus thun was er wil."
[5] WA 23.133.19ff. (*Dass diese Worte Christi "Das ist mein leib" noch fest stehen* 1527, Dr).

56

Consequently, Luther follows the tradition of William of Ockham and Biel in emphasizing the Biblical view of the Almighty Creator, in contrast not only to the papal theologians but also to the zealots of the Reformation's left wing. With this interpretation of the first article of the Creed Luther can add to his doctrine of ubiquity an element which is based not on the speculations of reason but on God's own revelation.

3. From the end of the 1530's we have a detailed *exposition of the first chapter of St John's Gospel,* in which the belief in the creation is discussed in connection with John 1:3. God does not appear as a craftsman, who leaves the job when it is finished, or as a captain of a ship who leaves the work to his crew. God continues to be always present in His works, to create as long as He wishes so that His works will endure. Consequently, Jesus says that the Father is working and the Son also (John 5:17). We are not our own cause. The Almighty Father maintains all things by Himself alone.[6] Thus God is not only the prime mover, who then lets the world go its own way. He is also the direct instigator of every event.

As in Ockhamism the Biblical concept of omnipotence becomes a fundamental feature of Luther's theology.[7] By His present omnipotence the Creator acts through the secular order: vocation, office, government.[8]

LW 37.57f. Cf. WA 40.I.174.3f. (Gal. 1531/35, Hs): "Ideo universa creatura eius (sc. Dei) est larva." See also WA 42.95.25ff. (*Vorlesung über 1. Mose.* 1535–45).

[6] WA 46.558.20ff. (*Auslegung des ersten und zweiten Kapitels Johannis.* 1537–38, Dr).

[7] Cf. E. Hirsch (1918)8: "Welche von den vielen Aussagen Luthers über Gott haben wir nun voranzustellen? Darüber kann im Sinne Luthers kein Zweifel sein. Es ist die Herrlichkeit, die Gott hat als allmächtiger Schöpfer und Wirker der Welt. In jedem Wort Luthers schwingt als letzte grosse Voraussetzung *der Gedanke der göttlichen Allmacht* mit. Er ist von ihm mit herzhafter Entschlossenheit bis in die äussersten Folgen hinein bejaht worden. Allmacht hiess für Luther Alleinwirksamkeit." *Ib* 21: "Alleinwirksamkeit ist *das Rückgrat der Lutherischen Gottesanschauung.*" H. Olsson (1971)7 says: "Da Gott der Schöpfer ist, gilt, dass alles, was zur Schöpfung gehört, in Gott besteht, vom ihm erhalten und bewegt wird. Kein Ding der Schöpfung kann daher Gottes alles bewegender und treibender Kraft entgehen."

[8] See further E. Billing, *Luthers lära om staten* (1900), F. Lau, "*Äusserliche Ordnung" und "Weltlich Ding" in Luthers Theologie* (1933), H. Olsson (1934), A. Deutelmoser, *Luther, Staat und Glaube* (1937), H. Diem, *Luthers Lehre von den zwei Reichen* (1938), G. Törnvall, *Andligt och värdsligt regemente hos Luther* (1940), G. Buchwald, *Luther über die Welt als "Mitwirkerin" Gottes,* L 23 (1941)49ff., G. Wingren, *Luthers lära om kallelsen* (1942), F. Lau, *Luthers Lehre von den beiden Reichen* (1953), G. Hillerdal, *Gehorsam gegen Gott und Menschen* (1954), P. Althaus, *Luthers Lehre von den beiden Reichen im Feuer der Kritik,* LuJ 24 (1957)40ff., A. Hakamies, *"Eigengesetzlichkeit" der natürlichen Ordnungen als Grundproblem der neueren Lutherdeutung* (1971).

3.3.

By His dynamic power the Creator also gives rise to every historical event.[9] All this is an essential part of Luther's rich thought on Creation.

3.4. Criticism of Deus Otiosus

Influenced by Ockham and Biel, confirmed by his own study of the Scriptures, Luther experiences through faith the close, active omnipotence of God. Indeed, he criticises the theology which conceives the Creator as distant and inactive. As a result, he wants to reform not only an unbiblical doctrine of justification but also the view of the divine omnipotence which overlooked the Word and the faith.

1. If we return to *the exposition of the Magnificat* we find statements which should reflect the way in which Luther comprehended the notion of God in contemporary sermons and teaching. He then contrasts this passive idea of God with the concept of dynamic omnipotence derived from the Scriptures. For the God of the Bible is not a *deus otiosus*, but a power constantly active throughout creation.[1]

The error of the traditional notion of God is more dramatically described in a later *sermon*. The monks and the university theologians have a frigid opinion of God, holding that He sits far away and the angels perform before Him.[2] This is the Christian concept of creation, that the Almighty God has the whole world in His hand. People ignorant of God say that the devil inflicted evil. For they do not believe that satan is

---

[9] The basic study is H. Lilje, *Luthers Geschichtsanschauung* (1932). See further also H. H. Pflanz, *Geschichte und Eschatologie bei Martin Luther* (1939), E. Kohlmeyer, *Die Geschichtsbetrachtung Luthers*, ARG 37 (1940)150ff., H. Lamparter, *Luthers Stellung zum Türkenkrieg* (1940), E. Th. Pedersen, *Schöpfung und Geschichte bei Luther*, StTh 3 (1950)5ff., H. W. Krumwiede, *Glaube und Geschichte in der Theologie Luthers* (1952), H. Zahrnt, *Luther deutet Geschichte* (1952), P. Althaus, *Luthers Haltung im Bauernkrieg* (1952), G. Hillerdal, *Luthers Geschichtsauffassung*, StTh 7 (1954)28ff., G. Rost, *Luthers Schöpfungsglaube und Geschichtstheologie*, LR 6 (1958)2ff.

[1] WA 7.574.27ff (*Das Magnificat verdeutschet und ausgeleget.* 1521): "Den das wortlin 'Mechtig' sol hie nit heyssen ein still rugende macht, wie man von einem zeytlichen kunige sagt, ehr sey mechtig, ob er schon still sitzt und nichts thut. Szondern ein wirckende macht und stettige tetticheit, die on unterlass geht ym schwanck und wirckt. Den got ruget nit, wirckt on unterlass, wie Christus sagt. Johan. V. 'Mein vatter wirckt biss hieher und ich wircke auch'. Auf die weysse sagt S. Paulus Ephe. III. 'Er ist mechtig zuthun mehr den wir bitten', das ist: Er thut altzeit mehr, den wir bitten, das ist sein art, sso thut seine macht." Cf. also *ib.* 574.3ff.

[2] WA 11.188.17 (*Pred.* 1523). Cf. *ib.* 188.18ff.

subordinate to God. In affliction we know that God is working on us. Or when something else happens we understand through the Word and through faith that it comes from God. Thus, the point is as above: Prevailing theology and preaching is open to criticism, for it does not do justice to the belief in creation which holds that the Almighty has a hand in every concrete event in His creation.

2. In *The Bondage of the Will* Luther carries out a detailed analysis of the reason why God is alienated from the world. Aristotle describes a *deus otiosus*. When God is said to be the rational mind, *nous*, which has no object but itself, and when this self contemplation is identical with His eternal, blessed life, the will and deeds of God have no direct connexion with earthly phenomena. This is also the weakness of Erasmus' concept of God: The Almighty is alienated from the world:

> "It is just such a God that Aristotle, too, depicts for us, that is to say, one who drowses and lets all and sundry use and abuse his kindness and severity. Nor can Reason judge otherwise of God than Diatribe does here. For just as she herself snores away and despises divine realities, so she judges also about God, as if he snored away and exercised no wisdom, will, or present power in electing, discerning, and inspiring, but had handed over to men the busy and burdensome task of accepting or rejecting his forbearance and wrath. That is what we come to when we seek to measure God by human reason and make excuses for him, not reverencing the secrets of his majesty but insisting on prying into them."[3]

Reason can only conclude that if God is good, the direct agent in present evil cannot be God. God is alienated from historical and worldly events, and especially from those which cause pain. Man is not regarded as absolutely dependent on his Creator. Beneath Erasmus' denial of the bound will Luther also finds a *deus otiosus*.

3. The same criticism of Aristotle and Erasmus recurs later on. We often observe how much wrong occurs and how many unjust tyrants achieve good fortune and worldly success. If God is both almighty and righteous, He should, in all reason, prevent everything which is unjust. But, as things are, many wrongs unquestionably occur. Reason finds that if God exists He is unjust. For provided that God has power, wisdom, goodness, then He wills, knows and can help. But why does He not, asks

---

[3] WA 18.706.22ff. (1525), LW 33.171f. Cf. also WA 18.709.32: "otiosa Deus esse non sinit". Cf. the criticism of Aristotle already in WA 4.459.28ff (*Dictata super Psalterium.* 1513–15).

Erasmus. This question is unanswerable.[4] If we do not interpret omnipotence as total causality, we can, of course, defend the divine goodness and righteousness. When the divine power is not directly involved in every concrete happening a gap opens between the Creation and the Creator.

Here there are only two alternatives for reason: Either there is not a God, or, if He exists, He is unjust, inactive, foolish, vacillating and weak. Aristotle does not indeed attribute direct stupidity to God. Nevertheless, he robs God of wisdom insofar as God is content with the blessedness *per se*. He neither sees nor cares about our earthly needs.[5] According to Luther, both Aristotle and Erasmus make the mistake of not doing justice to the dynamic power inherent in the God of revelation and of faith. Reason goes too far in setting the norm for God. As a result, God is envisaged as distant and inactive. The believer's experience of his total dependence on God is overlooked.

Accordingly, we see clearly how Luther delimits the validity of the rational arguments setting a norm for God. Luther can indeed assert that even reason is compelled to admit that God's will must be realised, since it would be a caricature of God if He could make mistakes, or be too weak to enforce His will (3.2.). Luther's criticism of the double *necessitas* concept of scholasticism may thus be based on rational arguments.[6] Reason can reach no further however. When Luther presents God as being nearby and incessantly active in all earthly things and phenomena, he takes a critical view of the capacity of reason to reflect upon such things. Instead, we see how the Word and the faith stand out. Thus, an interpretation of the monergism in Luther, which only describes it as a rational and non-Christian idea, does not suffice. It is also

[4] WA 40.III.321.3ff. (*In XV Psalmos graduum*. 1532/33, Hs): "Si est deus, est iniustus; hoc argumentum stosst rationem. Si deus, est potens, quia debet esse; si potest, debet scire; si scit et potest, debet velle bona. Si non vult, est iniquus. Ergo si habet potentiam, sapientiam, bonitatem, tum vult, scit, potest iuvare; quare non fit? argumentum Erasmi. Est argumentum insolubile apud rationem. Res ipsa dicit manifeste contrarium." Cf. WA 18.784.1ff. (*De servo arbitrio*. 1525).

[5] WA 40.III.321.14ff.: "Aut deus non est; aut si est, iniustus, non valet, stultus, infirmus, impotens; sol mir der Geier! Sic scribit Aristoteles, helt deum ignarum, qui nihil videt, intelligit rerum in terris vel apud homines; non dicit stultum. Est eis nobilissimum et primum, sed quod praeter se nihil intelligat, consideret, curet. Non tribuit ei stulticiam, sed adimit ei sapientiam; sit contentus sua beatitudine in semetipso; non curat res humanas; non nostras necessitates vides, vides rem." Cf. also WA 18.785.8ff. (*De servo arbitrio*. 1525).

[6] Cf. H. Olsson, *Det dubbla necessitas-begreppet i skolastiken och Luthers kritik därav* (In: *Till Gustaf Aulén* 1939, 288ff.), H. Vorster (1965)86ff.,*ib.* 337ff, H. McSorley (1969)256ff., J. Wicks (1970)107ff.

necessary to pay attention to the role played by the Biblical revelation and the personal experience in faith. Consequently, there is justification for the hypothesis that Luther's concept of God's omnipotence, and of the necessity of present phenomena, is shaped by personal experience, derived from a Biblical pattern of God's omnipotence comprehended by faith.[7]

3.5. Evil from God

1. In *the first commentary on the Psalms* Luther discusses the problem of evil, presenting two doctrines. Firstly, we should confess God as "author" of all evil and neither grumble at, nor revile Him who inflicts it upon us but patiently accept the tribulation from Him. Secondly, evil is regarded as the punishment for sin.[1] Consequently, it seems that Luther is here referring to the phenomenon described by Medieval theologians as *malum poenae.* No comment is made concerning God's use of instruments to inflict this evil.

When Luther is preaching on *the first commandment,* he begins with a provocative question. If a Christian believes in God, the Father, Almighty, why then does he attribute to the devil the responsibility for setbacks and trials? Why does he not accept these as coming from God? Either the Christians' belief in the divine omnipotence is false, or they must admit their folly and ignorance of God's total power.[2] For man's self-confidence is, in this way, crushed by evil, and his faith founded upon God alone. Thus, evil has a good purpose, which God cannot teach the believer in any other way. The positive end only becomes obvious in

[7] *Sic* B. Hoffman (1976)107: "The truth of the matter may rather be that Luther felt that he indeed based both his theological determinism and his notion of the powerlessness of free will without grace on the biblical message as he experienced it with increasing intensity in his own life"; *ib.* 125f.: "The mystical, numinous dependence was at the center of Luther's deterministic idea of the will in *The Bondage of the Will.*" Cf.1.4.3.

[1] WA 3.223.36ff. (*Dictata super Psalterium.* 1513–15): "In *omnibus malis* deum authorem confiteri debemus et dicere: Quoniam tu foecisti, ideo tacendum et obmutescendum, ne murmuremus aut blasphememus contra eum. Et ipse orandus, ut auferat. Quia qui nescit, quis malum inferat, frustra fit impatiens et amovere nititur, sicut si ex loco ignoto telum iaculetur, et frustra irascatur passus." *Ib.* 224.3ff.: "Omnis correptio est propter peccatum: patet hic, saltem propter primum." Cf. WA 4.459.26ff.: "Ideo ad creaturas nobis nocentes maxime addidit hoc, ut discamus et in malis Deum laudare, quia mala fiunt verbo eius." Cf. also S. Normann (1933)117.

a monistic mode of interpretation. This explains Luther's pathos in deriving setbacks and trials from God. Nor is there assumed an "intermediate cause" between the Creator and the evil in Creation.

We find that Luther often emphatically brands the attribution by man of the cause of suffering and pain to the devil or other evil people as a transgression of the first commandment.[3] Luther evidently discerns a vital catechetic purpose in this teaching.

Some controversial sentences in the popular *expositions on the penitential Psalms* follow this line of reasoning. It is said that the Christian must in all suffering and tribulation first turn to God, confess, and accept pain as coming from God. It may emanate from satan or arise from man. For the Lord thus seeks to teach patience and the fear of God.[4] The evil can, accordingly, be mediated by the devil or human beings. In any case the Christian should look deeper and assent to God's

---

[2] WA 1.75.19ff. (*Pred.* 1516): "At nunc Christiani qui orant 'credo in Deum omnipotentem', et quod Deus omnia possit, omnia fecerit, omnia faciat, si obtingat ut amittant rem, formam, membrum, honorem, dicunt 'diabolus hoc fecit' et deficiunt, ad auxilium hominum vel daemonum currentes. Quod si interroges, an credant Deum omnipotentem, respondent 'omnino credimus'. 'Quare ergo non haec ab illo suscipitis?' Quid allegabunt? nisi quod false dicunt se credere aut agnoscunt suam insipientiam." Cf. WA 11.188.8ff. (*Pred.* 1523).

[3] WA 1.252.2ff. (*Eine kurze Erklärung der zehn Gebote.* 1518), cf. *ib.* 254.16ff. The same point of view is found in WA 1.259.20ff. (*Instructio pro confessione peccatorum.* 1518), WA 2.61.4f. (*Eine kurze Unterweisung, wie man beichten sol.* 1519), WA 2.104.11ff. (*Auslegung deutsch des Vaterunsers für die einfältigen Laien..* 1519), WA 6.15.2ff. (*Eine kurze Form, das Paternoster zu verstehen und zu beten.* 1519), WA 7.208.1ff. (*Eine kurze Form der zehn Gebote.* 1520), *ib.* 224.20ff., WA 10.II.381.3ff. (*Betbüchlein.* 1522), *ib.* 400.20ff. Only God puts on the cross according to WA 10.III.336.12ff. (*Pred.* 1522).

[4] WA 1.159.16ff. (*Die sieben Busspsalmen.* 1517): "In allem leiden und anfechtung sal der mensch zu aller ersten zu got lauffen, und erkennen und auffnemen, *als von got zugeschickt werde*, es kom von teuffel ader von menschen. Also thut hie der propheet, der yn diessem psalme nennet sein feind, aber tzum ersten leufft er zu got, und nympt die feindschafft seiner feind *nit von yhn, sunder von got an*, dan mit der weisse lernet sich die gedult und forcht gottis. Wer aber den menschen ansehet und nit von got an nympt, wirt ungedultig und gottis vorachter u." We have a slightly different version of this text in WA 18.480.2ff. (1525). H. Obendiek, *Der Teufel bei Martin Luther* (1931)47 n.15, P. T. Bühler (1942)211 n. 5 and H. Beintker (1954)104f. discuss what conclusions can be drawn from Luther's words here. Cf. WA 1.418.5ff. (*Decem praecepta Wittenbergensi praedicata populo.* 1518): "Non sic B. Augustinus: Quando nos sumus sani, tunc maxime concupiscentiae morbus est insanus, Non quod quaerenda sit mala valetudo, sed quod illata *per deum* ut optimus nuncius dei sit excipienda, quia nullum bonum sine voluntate dei quaerendum est." H. J. Iwand (1974)97ff. has some illuminating passages from Luther on the good purpose of suffering. Cf. also WA 5.321.13ff. (*Operationes in psalmos.* 1519– 1521), WA 6.14.32ff. (*Eine kurze Form, das Vaterunser zu verstehen und zu beten.* 1519), WA 7.224.15ff. (*Eine kurze Form der zehn Gebote.* 1520), WA 10.II.478.34ff. (*Betbüchlein* 1522); *ib.* 400.15ff.

positive purpose: to subdue sin and to make the individual conform to the divine will.

This aspect emerges clearly in another *popular work*:

"The second form of discipline which we receive at the hands of others is when men or devils cause us suffering, as when our property is taken, our body is sick, and our honor is taken away; when everything moves us to anger, impatience, and unrest. For *the work of God* rules in us according to his wisdom and not according to our judgement; according to his purity and chastity, and not according to the will of our flesh. God's work is wisdom and purity, but our work is folly and impurity. It is these that we must cause to rest."

"Therefore, to destroy such works of ours as well as the old Adam in us, *God overwhelms us* with those things which move us to anger, with many sufferings which rouse us to impatience, and last of all, even with death and the abuse of the world. By means of these he seeks nothing else but to drive out of us anger, impatience, and unrest, and to perfect his own work in us, that is, his peace."[5]

In the first place evil emanates from "men or devils", then from God. We lack a detailed description of the internal relationship between these phenomena. Luther's interest would seem to be quite different. He seeks to emphasize that reason and flesh are automatically impelled to sinful impatience and grumbling, and that it is good "practice" for faith to trust that the Almighty God has love as motive even when through agents He sends that which at first glance appears to be evil.

It is hardly surprising that also in the form of a sermon Luther suggests a way to peace and quiet, consisting of radical acceptance that all things come to pass in accord with the perfect will of God. When the believer is confident that nothing happens by chance, he can abide in the divine will and partake in the total peace.[6]

Luther is aware that many people protest against this interpretation. Cannot evil be caused by myself or by satan? Only if I know for sure that God Himself sent the evil can I be glad and satisfied with it.

[5] WA 6.247.26ff. (*Von den guten Werken.* 1520), LW 44.77. Cf. *ib.* 210.24ff., *ib.* 218.10ff., *ib.* 223.13ff.
[6] WA 10.I.1.315.18ff. (*Kirchenpostille.* 1522). "Solch unruge, unfrid und ubirdruss tzu meyden, ist nutz und nott der glawb, der da gewisslich dafur hallte, gott regire gleych und beschicke eynen iglichen ynn dem wessen, das yhm auffs aller nutzlichst und fuglichst sey, alsso das es nit mocht besser geratten, wenn er selb sollt gleych die wal haben." Cf. WADB 6.44 (*Randanmerkung.* 1522).

According to Luther, this mode of reasoning is a foolish and an unchristian enterprise, which reveals the disloyalty of the heart. Faith believes, on the basis of Mat. 6:28 and 10:29, that the Almighty Creator always steers His Creation in the smallest detail.[7]

2. The famous statements in *The Bondage of the Will* concerning the almighty, hidden God fit into this context. The hidden God has all things "under his mighty hand" and "neither deplores nor takes away death, but works life, death, and all in all".[8] While the terminology differs slightly, the thought is the same as before. Nothing has autonomy *vis-à-vis* God's actions, neither evil nor death. This relates to Luther's belief in the Almighty Creator of the first article of the Creed.

When we say that God promotes evil, it is we who are classifying evil as evil. But it is not evil in God's eyes. For the purpose is good. Here we see the idea that only by revelation can we comprehend how evil is transformed into good. "Many things as seen by God are very good, which as seen by us are very bad. Thus afflictions, calamities, errors, hell, and indeed all the best works of God are in the world's eyes very bad and damnable." Christ and the Gospel are not regarded as good by reason. "Consequently, how things can be good in God's sight which are evil to us only God knows, and those who see with God's eyes, that is, who have the Spirit."[9] Consequently, omnipotence is designated as good. The Almighty Creator of the universe is also the loving father who to the eyes of faith is revealed in the Son.

Even during this period, there is clearcut evidence that Luther stressed it as an important element of the Church's teaching that "alle trübsal", both the spiritual and the carnal, are inflicted by God, to admonish and incite to repentance.[10] In an exposition of the Psalms for a wider audience, Luther emphasizes that we must not only accept all tribulation from God but also thank Him therefore. Behind all sorrow the Christian ought to perceive the guidance of God, who reveals His goodness and

---

[7] WA 10.I.316.15ff. Cf, also WA 16.138.9ff. (*Pred. über das 2. Buch Mose.* 1524–1527), WA 17.II.22.11ff. (*Fastenpostille.* 1525), WA 17.II.474.19ff. (*Festpostille.* 1527).

[8] WA 18.685.1ff. (*De servo arbitrio.* 1525), LW 33.139f.

[9] WA 18.708.34ff. (*De servo arbitrio.* 1525), LW 33.175. Cf. WA 18.727.22ff.: "non sit dubium, afflictiones *a Deo* venire invitis nobis, necessitatemque afferant ferendi eas, velimus, nolimus; nec est in manu nostra eas avertere, licet exhortemur ad ferendas voluntarie."

[10] WA 26.212.4ff. (*Unterricht der Visitatoren an die Pfarrherrn.* 1527), Cf. *ib.* 206.22ff. Cf. also WA 28.210.1ff. (*Wochenpredigten über Joh. 16–20.* 1528/9, R): "Econtra si deus malum zuschickt, ferendum non fugiendum. Si schickt dir zu, ut egrotum sit corpus sine tuo consilio, noli murmurare sed fer. Ut hic dominus non quaerit nec fugit."

mercy in countless other elements.[11] Thanksgiving and praise to God would be impossible if the devil was the cause of the evil which crushes and humiliates mankind.[12]

3. A believer who does not attribute evil to God's handiwork stands for a Manichean conception which both Luther and Biel reject.[13] *The Exegesis of Ps. 51:10* sheds light on this. Here as before we seem to have *malum poenae* and not *malum culpae*. The Psalmist writes that this evil emanates from God, although it is mediated by the devil, who seeks to cast down the believer into despair. But God wants the Christian to see Him behind events and to turn to Him.[14] The works of the Creator appear negative to man, since He performs them through evil instruments. But the negative aims at something which is good.

Material from the same period confirms that the devil is not an independent force on a par with the divine omnipotence.[15] Simply because God is basically the origin of this evil, a Christian can assent to it.[16] Since all God's gifts are good, evil must also be something good, which we are to regard as "a precious treasure".[17] Thus the effect of the divine omnipotence embraces evil but it is always designated as good.

4. Luther's *Letters on the Cure of Souls* show that he applies this opinion in concrete situations. Evil in the form of sorrow and pain is derived from the Almighty Creator. Occasionally satan is mentioned as the instrument of God. When an evangelical pastor in Halle was murdered in 1527, Luther's letter of condolence to the Christians in the town said that the devil was the real murderer.[18] He goes on to write that the

[11] WA 31.I.74.12ff. (*Auslegung des 118. Psalms.* 1529–30, Hs). This point is stressed by K. Holl (1923)47.

[12] WA 31.I.170.2ff: "Sihe, wer das leiden, dulden, feste halten und beharren drinn kan, dazu Gott hierinn loben und dancken, als ders hertzlich gut meine, Sihe der singet diesen vers Ich dancke dir das du mich demutigest, Er spricht nicht Der teuffel demutigt mich, Sondern, Du, Du, Es ist dein gnediger wille, mir zugut, On deinen willen wurdes der teuffel wol lassen." Cf. WA 38.507.22ff. (*Annotationes in aliquot capita Matthaei.* 1538), *ib.* 510.38ff., WA 41.306.6ff. (*Pred.* 1535, Dr).

[13] WA 31.I.447.15 (*Der 147. Psalm, Lauda Jerusalem, ausgelegt.* 1532), WA 40.II.417.7 (*Enarratio Psalmi LI.* Hs 1532. /1538/), Cf. WA 40.III.516.14 (*Enarratio Psalmi XC.* 1534–35 /1541/), WATR 5.4.13ff. (1540). Concerning Biel see 3.1 n. 20 above.

[14] WA 40.II.416.10ff. (*Enarratio Psalmi LI.* Hs 1532 /1538/).

[15] WA 40.III.328.6ff. (*In XV Psalmos graduum.* 1532/33, 1540).

[16] WA 49.506.8ff. (*Pred.* 1544, R): "Sed quando Deus so schickt, das pestis, mors sol uns plagen, dicimus: In nomine Domini, weil du es lieber Got, wilt haben. Ich unterwerffe und gebe mich in istam servitutem."

[17] WATR 3.456.20ff (1537).

[18] WA 23.402.6f. (*Tröstung an die Christen zu Halle.* 1527), cf. *ib.* 404.19, *ib.* 406.29f., *ib.* 408.13, *ib.* 422.23ff.

3.5.

murder was committed by reason of "God's gracious and fatherly order". God was able "to use" the evil power.[19]

Nevertheless, the devil is rarely mentioned in these letters. An entire series of letters from the 1530's and 1540's say that illness and death come from God. No intermediate cause is referred to. Again, it is the omnifacient God of *The Bondage of the Will* whom Luther interprets in the pastoral care.

The condition is invariably that the will and works of God involve the highest good. The Creator always does only that which is "very good" (Gen. 1:31). Therefore, the Christian may be at peace with God's will, praise His goodness, open himself to God's positive intentions. However great the tribulation, however deep the sorrow and pain, Luther maintains that God's omnipotence is the direct or indirect cause, and that He always does that which is good.[20]

[19] *Ib.* 402.19ff., *ib.* 424.7ff. We observe the same change in *ib.* 473.18ff.

[20] WAB 7.117.8ff. (1534): "Es ist mir leid, dass Ihr *von Gott mit mehr Krankheit uberladen werdet;*... Aber will Euch denn Gott ja also krank haben, so wird sein Wille gewisslich besser sein denn unser aller,..." *Ib.* 305.3ff. (1535): "Er Antonius hat mir angezeigt, dass du Dich fast bekümmert umb den Sohn, den Gott gegeben und so bald wieder genommen hat. Aber was wollen wir draus machen? Wir müssen also lernen *Gottes Willen* erkennen, *dass er allein gut und heilig sei*; ob's gleich unserm Willen viel anders deucht, welcher ein irriger, vorgänglicher Dunkel ist;" *Ib.* 399.2ff. (1536): "Ich hab vernommen, wie *der liebe Gott Vater Euch hat heimgesucht und Euer liebe Hausfrauen von Euch zu sich genommen,*... Gott hat dies Leben also geordnet und gemässiget, dass wir darinnen sollen lernen und üben *die Erkenntnis seines göttlichen, allerbesten Willens*, damit wir uns auch prüfen und erfahren müssen, ob wir seinen Willen auch höher achten und lieben denn uns selbs und alles, was er uns zu lieben und zu haben auf Erden gegeben hat." WAB 8.190.6ff. (1538): "Nu aber E. f. g. *von dem lieben Vater im Himmel*, der uns Leib und Seele gemacht und gegeben, dazu hernach durch seinen lieben Sohn Jesum Christi wieder vom Fall und Tod Adam erlöst und durch seinen heiligen Geist in unser Herz die Hoffnung des ewigen Lebens gegeben hat, *väterlich heimgesucht wird und mit Krankheit beladen*, sollen E. f. G. ja sich nicht bekommern, sondern solchs gnädiges Heimsuchen mit Dankbarkeit annehmen"; *Ib.* 352.4ff. (1539): "Es ist mir kund worden, wie *unser lieber Herr Gott abermal sein Ruten ober euch hat gehen lassen* und ewer liebe Hausfraw zu sich selbs genommen...

DArumb lasset euch das Rütlein des lieben Vaters also schmertzen, das jr euch seines gnedigen veterlichen willens gegen euch viel höher tröstet,...

Mein Kethe lest hertzlich grussen und weinet bitterlich vber ewerm vnsal vnd sagt, wenn euch gott nit so lieb hett oder weret ein papist, so wurde er euch solch unglug nit lassen geschehen;" WAB 10.63.1ff. (1542): "Ich habe leider erfaren, wie *Gott, der liebe Vater, euch, ja vns auch, mit einer Ruten gesteupet* vnd den lieben Man M. Johannem Cellarium, ewren Hausherren, von euch vnd uns genommen, Daran vns allen wehe geschehen, ob Er wol in guter, seliger Ruge ist."

To sum up, we may say that "God the Father, Almighty" in the Creed for Luther implies God as the cause—directly or indirectly—of evil. But this is not an end in itself. God has also revealed Himself as the good Father, who can do no evil, although He uses evil and the devil himself for His purposes of mercy, when by means of evil He subdues sin in man.

3.6. Hardening of Heart from God

1. In his scrutiny of the *Epistle to the Romans*, Rom. 9:16 prompts Luther to describe, how all mankind rests in the hands of God: "they are all the instrument of God 'who works all things in all' (1 Cor. 12:6). So the cutting of wood is not of the ax but of the cutter and beating the dog is not of the stick but of the man who uses the stick."[1] This is the essential experience in Luther's perception of reality: Only that which God wills and does—be it good or evil—can Creation accomplish. Even hardening of heart should be interpreted in these terms:

> "This was clear in the case of Pharaoh, who wanted to inflict injury on the children of Israel, but could not. And thus God showed His power in him, so that he could not will anything, because he was hardened; and he could run even less than he could will."[2]

a) Therefore, the basic defect is attributed to *the perverted will of man*. Pharaoh wished to inflict on the Israelites harm which is against the will of God, and which is thus a sin. However much Luther emphasizes that man is only an instrument of God's sovereign will and action, yet the guilt for the hardness of heart so far lies with Pharaoh in person: "if one does not will or run, it is not of a merciful God but of the God who hardens"[3]. As in the previous tradition, we could here speak of *meritum obdurationis* in man's rebellious will.

b) But the divine omnipotence is the reason why this wilful opposition is exacerbated to the extent demonstrated in the hardening of heart. If, in order to defend the divine justice, we interpret this hardness of heart not as an aggressive action on God's part but as a passive concession, God's

---

[1] WA 56.399.8ff. (1515–16), LW 25.388f.
[2] WA 56.399.21ff., LW 25.389.
[3] WA 56.404.14f., LW 25.394.

will is nevertheless the determining factor.[4] In Rom. 9:17 Luther provocatively emphasizes that the power of God aroused the rulers of Egypt in order to demonstrate to the children of Israel their impotence, and induce them to cry out to God for liberation. Yet, the object of God's actions may also be Pharaoh. The divine power brings about "the perdition of others".[5] This point, that God's close, active omnipotence does not overlook evil people but drives them deeper and locks them within their own selfishness, however, is at this stage only asserted in the form of the lecture and not addressed to the public at large.[6]

c) At the same time the perspective is never lost, that God's work is always—even in the apparently wholly negative hardness of heart—*something totally good*. The good purpose is partly that God's great power becomes manifest,[7] partly that God is given the greater honour through the elect. Seen not as merely an end in itself, but as a means of good purposes hardening of heart is an expression of God's paternal omnipotence. "He wills it (*sc.* the evil) so that the opposite good

---

[4] WA 56.92.30ff. (Gloss to Rom. 9:18): "Et licet hic multi laborent de Induratione Pharaonis Velut excusare Deum ab Iniustitia volentes dicentesque: Deus Non Indurat, Sed 'Indurat' i.e. indurare permittit—Sed hac ambage nihil efficiunt. Paulus enim recta via ingreditur dicens: 'Quem vult, indurat'. Quia etiamsi permittere tantum dicatur, Nihilominus hoc 'permittere' habent concedere volente Deo fieri, quia clare dicit: 'Quem vult, indurat' i.e. indurare permittit. Quia etiam sequitur: 'Nunquid potestatem habet?' " Cf. *ib* 384.20ff.

[5] *Ib*. 404.9f: "Potest et alius et forte melior esse, Quod potentia hic non in salvationem, Sed perditionem aliorum accipiatur", LW 25.393. Cf, the fact that the punishing God gives "spiritum mendacii" (WA 56.179.28f.), "spiritum compunctionis" (*ib*. 431.19ff.), or "den bossen geist" (WA 1.218.16ff. *Die sieben Busspsalmen*. 1517).

[6] See further WA 7.144.33ff. (*Assertio omnium articulorum M.Lutheri per bullam Leonis X u*. 1520): "Quomodo potest sese ad bonum praeparare, cum nec in potestate sit suas vias malas facere? Nam et mala opera in impiis deus operatur, Ut Prover. XVI. dicit 'Omnia propter semetipsum operatus est dominus, etiam impium ad diem malum', Et Ro. I. 'Tradidit illos deus in reprobum sensum, ut faciant quae non conveniunt', Et IX. 'Quem vult indurat, cuius vult miseretur.' Sicut et Exo. IX. de Pharaone dicit 'in hoc ipsum excitavi te, ut ostendam virtutem meam in te.' ideo enim est terribilis deus in iudiciis et operibus suis." Luther does not repeat these sentences in his popular exposition for the general public, cf. WA 7.445.30ff. (*Grund und Ursach aller Artikel D. Martin Luthers*. 1521). Becoming more courageous later he dares to touch on these thoughts in sermons, *e.g.* WA 15.644.4ff. (*Pred*. 1524): "'Nomen': ibi aufert omnem potentiam creaturarum et dat deo q.d. 'magna fecit', qui habet vim omnium creaturarum, ut nemo glorietur se quid facere, sed deus omnia in omnibus operatur, eciam in diabolo et malis." Cf. WA 16.140.1ff. (*Pred. über das 2. Buch Mose*. 1524–27) quoted in 4.2.6 n. 5, WA 25.265.16ff. (*Vorlesung über Jesaja*. 1527–29). See also W. von Loewenich, *Pharaos Verstockung*, (In: *Von Augustin zu Luther*, 1959)161ff.

[7] WA 56.404.18f: "Volens (sc. Deus), Quod in perditione eius magnificetur virtus eius."

may shine forth so much more brightly."[8] Luther has no intention of describing an Almighty God who stands totally beyond good and evil. Instead, he articulates a deeply rooted belief that God's action is always qualified as good. Consequently, we can already discern the conflict and unity of salvation and rejection which we shall discuss in more detail in the context of predestination (4.2.6. and 4.5.5.).

2. *The Bondage of the Will* may be regarded as a massive defence of the harsh view that "free choice is a mere empty name, that it is God who works both good and evil in us, and that all things which happen come about by sheer necessity".[9] Since the will and works of God are in fact inscrutable, it is with some hesitation that Luther consents to continue his line of thought on "how God can be said to work evils in us, such as hardening, giving men up to their lusts (Rom. 1:24), leading them astray, and so forth". Thus, his chosen starting-point is the view of God's omnipotence which is expressed, *inter alia*, in 1 Cor. 12:6. This is the very passage which was of great importance for the argument in the corresponding context in the lecture on Romans.[10]

a) Luther lucidly describes and defines how the guilt for hardness of heart lies in human evil and perversion. This he does by images which also appeared to some extent in the exegesis of Romans. The fact that it is difficult to ride a lame horse is primarily the fault of the horse and not the rider. The blunt edge of the axe, and not the carpenter who wields it, causes the poor result. So man's *self absorption* and lack of conformity with the will of God are the essential cause of the hardness of heart. "It is the fault, therefore, of the instruments, which God does not allow to be idle, that evil things are done, with God himself setting them in motion."[11] Consequently, Pharaoh is himself culpable for his hardness of heart insofar as his inmost being is characterized by wilful egoism.[12] Here Luther draws two boundaries. Firstly, he emphatically rejects all speculations that God somehow, in His omnipotence, is also the source

---

[8] *Ib*. 182.28f., LW 25.163. Cf. further 4.2.6 n. 1–4.

[9] WA 18.667.21ff. (1525), LW 33.112. Cf. G. Rost (1966)121f.

[10] WA 18.709.5ff., LW 33.175. Cf. above n. 1 and 3.2 n. 3.

[11] WA 18.709.21ff., LW 33.176. Cf. WA 18.711.2ff. See further H. Vorster (1965)415ff. about "Das Bild vom Reittier und Psalm 7:22f."

[12] WA 18.711.27ff. Cf. R. Seeberg (1917)143, G. Ljunggren (1928)435f., R. Bring (1929)290ff, *ib*. 331ff, G. Rost (1966)122ff.

of original sin.[13] Secondly, there is in this context indeed a doctrine concerning man's "free will": the sinner does not will or commit sin under compulsion but spontaneously consents thereto. Psychologically speaking, man experiences his possession of free will. At the same time we are, in theological terms, dealing with a will in bondage, *i.e.* the theory which Luther primarily emphasizes.[14]

b) The ungodly remain part of God's Creation. Therefore they also remain in the Creator's power. In this essential theonomy, which is implied by the theory of *the divine omnipotence*, lies the cause of the escalation of present evil to the point of hardness of heart: "Now, this evil will of his would not be set in motion or hardened if left to itself, but when the omnipotent Mover drives it along with inevitable motion like the rest of the creatures, it must of necessity will something. Then, as soon as he presents to it from without something that naturally provokes and offends it, it becomes as impossible for Pharaoh to avoid being hardened as it is for him to avoid either the action of divine omnipotence or the aversion or badness of his own will."[15] In this way the vision of the close, incessantly active God of the Bible, whom Luther personally experienced in faith, is the great source of inspiration and the driving force of his attempt at analysis.

c) At times we get a glimpse of the well nigh self-evident premise, that *the goodness of God* removes the conception of hardening of heart as an evil which is an end in itself: "God cannot act evilly although he does evil through evil men, because one who is himself good cannot act evilly."[16] Therefore, it is possible to see, in part, the good resulting from Pharaoh's hardness of heart. The power of God is revealed. The children of Israel are strengthened in the belief in God as their redeemer.[17] At first glance, the divine omnipotence may appear to be an ethically

[13] Luther is always very clear on this point, see *e.g.* WA 56.180.32ff. (*Rom.* 1515–16), WA 18.708.31ff. (*De servo arbitrio.* 1525), *ib.* 709.28ff., *ib.* 710.31ff., *ib.* 711.2ff., WA 39.I.518.5ff. = Drews 449 (*Die dritte Disputation gegen die Antinomer.* 1538), WA 39.II.361.3ff. = Drews 858 (*Die Promotionsdisputation von Petrus Hegemon.* 1545). There is also a consensus among the scholars on this issue, cf. R. Seeberg (1917)143, K. Holl (1923)48, G. Ljunggren (1928)436f., R. Bring (1929)286ff., E. Seeberg (1929)160f., *ib.* 166f., L. Pinomaa (1938)139ff, H. Beintker (1954)101, D. Löfgren (1960)45ff., P. Althaus (1963)106f.

[14] WA 18.634.21ff., cf. WA 56.385.32ff. (*Rom.* 1515–16). See further D. Löfgren (1960)115f, H. Vorster (1965)337ff., *ib* 349ff., G. Rost (1966)120f., K. E. Løgstrup, *Etiske begreber og problemer* (In: *Etik och kristen tro*, ed. G. Wingren, 1971)250.

[15] WA 18.709.16ff., *ib.* 711.27ff., LW 33.179. Cf. 4.2.6 n 13–17.

[16] WA 18.709.29ff., LW 33.176.

[17] WA 18.714.6ff., This is stressed by E. Hirsch (1918)22f., P. Althaus (1963)106, cf. W. Elert (1931)104.

indifferent power, with the result that the pious man approaches identity with the divine will and the ungodly is alienated still further. But on closer scrutiny, this divine omnipotence appears for Luther invariably qualified as good.[18] The notion of God is assumed to be characterized at its most profound by perfect goodness.

3. Luther seems to stick to this interpretation of the hardening of heart. For there are signs indicating that in "table talk" he returns to these ideas and briefly repeats them. Other reasons could also be adduced as evidence that the theses on the hardness of heart in *The Bondage of the Will* were approved by Luther much later.[19]

3.7. Both Monism and Dualism

We have seen how tribulations, suffering and death, according to Luther, come from God (3.5.), and how the exasperation of man's wilful rejection of God into hardening of heart is done through the divine omnipotence (3.6.). The Luther scholars starting from the concept of God, especially the idea of divine omnipotence, have consequently interpreted the power of evil in this *monistic* perspective: the devil is "Gottes Teufel".[1]

[18] A. Runestam in his introduction to the Swedish translation of *De servo arbitrio* (1925)68 and T. Bohlin (1927)276ff. develop a thesis on the ethically unqualified omnipotence. But this is rejected by most other scholars, *e.g.* G. Ljunggren (1928)436ff., R. Bring (1929)266ff., L. Pinomaa (1938)139ff., H. Olsson (1971)16, cf. also G. Rost (1966)121f., *ib.* 126. See further 4.5.5 n. 39–40.

[19] WATR 4.642.34ff. (1540): "Quem vult, indurat, explicatum. Quidam dixit: Domine Doctor, est indurare in scripturis proprie aut figurate accipiendum?—Doctor respondet: Proprie, et non active, quia Deus non agit mala, sua autem omnipotentia agit omnia; ergo ut reperit hominem, ita agit. Pharao natura malus est; Deus agit, ergo pergit esse malus Pharao. Induratur autem, quia Deus non impedit suo spiritu et gratia illos impios conatus. Quare vero non impedierit, nostrum non est quaerere." Concerning *De servo arbitrio* see WAB 8.99.5ff. (1537). Cf. WATR 2.298.33ff. (1531), WA 38.556.27ff. (*Annotationes in aliquot capita Matthaei.* 1538). *ib* . 557.27ff. Luther does not abandon his necessitarian conception in later years, cf. the discussion in H. McSorley (1969)356ff.

[1] H. Obendiek (1931) starts his extensive dissertation with an interpretation of the omnipotence of God (*ib.* 37ff.). "Damit ist für Glauben und Leben die allein berechtigte Dynamik einer *ausschliesslichen Monarchie Gottes* herausgestellt" (*ib.* 38). Obendiek depicts the devil's dependence on God (*ib.* 59). This theory is observed by other scholars, see further Th. Harnack I (1927)254ff., K. Holl (1923)48, *ib.* 90f., H. Bornkamm, *Christus und das 1. Gebot in der Anfechtung bei Luther*, ZSTh 5 (1927)453ff., R. Bring (1929)67, *ib.* 155ff., *ib.* 164f., *ib.* 221, *ib.* 229, *ib.* 254, *ib.* 276ff., *ib.* 283f., *ib.* 301, L. Pinomaa (1938)88, *ib.* 93, *ib.* 95, *id.* (1940)119, *ib.* 125, H. Beintker (1954)100ff., P. Althaus (1963)147f., G. Ebeling (1964)256f, H.-M Barth (1967)197ff.

We have also seen traces of *dualism*, when man was regarded as a personage on a par with God, with personal responsibility for his sins and shortcomings, in that his own will, and not the divine omnipotence, originally gave rise to *malum culpae* (3.5–6.). Scholars who were pre-occupied with the dualism between God in Christ and satan were also able to produce an abundant material showing that the devil might appear as God's adversary, endowed with a real power all his own.[2] Therefore, scholars have felt called upon to oppose an isolation of the monistic aspect.[3]

In his exegesis of 2. Thess. 2:4, Luther depicts both the monistic and dualistic outlook, in order to demonstrate that the two modes of interpretation are correct and worthy of equal emphasis.

1. The *second lecture on the Psalms* describes in one passage how man does not realise his own lack of righteousness, but interprets his status as goodness and piety. He thus becomes the instrument of the devil. God is bereft of His honour. Luther goes on to say that it is, therefore, impossible for the devil to set himself above the divine power, namely above God as He is "by nature". So far the monistic perspective holds good.

Nevertheless, satan can elevate himself above human worship of God, above the proclaimed, worshipped and adored God, *i.e.* God as He

---

[2] *Sic* G. Jacob, *Der Gewissensbegriff in der Theologie Luthers* (1929). In contrast to K. Holl he begins with the conflict between God and satan (*ib.* 6ff.). He is aware of the conception of *deus absconditus* (*ib.* 23 n. 1). However, he makes the devil the cause of all afflictions (*ib.* 38).

P. Th. Bühler (1942) shares Jacob's general opinion of the fundamental battle between God and the devil (*ib.* 1ff.) while maintaining that the afflictions come from satan. But after the victory is won through faith in Christ man can perceive the omnipotence of God as good and even consider *deus absconditus* (*ib.* 210ff.).

H. Beintker (1954) returns to the interpretation of K. Holl in emphasizing God's action in affliction (*ib.* 38ff.). Consequently, he objects to Bühler's view (*ib.* 102).

Finally, the Christology of Luther is the starting point for H.-M. Barth (1967)16ff. Thus he shows the autonomy of the devil (*ib.* 123ff.). Consequently, he has very little interest in *deus absconditus* (cf. *ib.* 185ff.).

Cf. also concerning this dualism Th. Harnack I (1927)256ff., *ib.* 263ff., R. Seeberg (1917)172f., G. Aulén (1927)170ff., *ib.* 187, *ib.* 207ff., *id.*, *Den kristna försoningstanken* (1930)176ff., *ib.* 185, R. Bring (1929)155ff., *ib.* 165ff., H. Obendiek (1931)53ff., *ib.* 59ff., L. Pinomaa (1938)41, *id.* (1940)119, *ib.* 127, P. Althaus (1963)145, G. Ebeling (1964)277.

[3] H.-M. Barth (1967)197: "Daher ist es einseitig, sogar falsch, zu meinen, der Teufel fungiere in Luthers Theologie grundsätzlich nur als 'Mittel', 'Werkzeug' oder 'Handlanger' Gottes, als 'Gottes Teufel'. Er hat vielmehr nach Luther tatsächlich eine von Gott unabhängige und wider Gott gerichtete Existenz." Cf. G. Aulén (1927)208ff.

appears in the thoughts and feelings of men through the Word and through faith. This is the dualistic aspect.[4]

2. 2. Thess. 2:4 is similarly developed in *The Bondage of the Will*. No power can set itself above God "in His essence and His majesty". His might controls all existing phenomena according to His perfect will. But the antichrist can set himself above the preached and adored God, *i.e.* above the word and the liturgy through which God is made known, and connected with us. Thus, monism and dualism are placed on a par, so that both are joined with two other, major concepts, namely the hidden and the revealed God.[5]

It seems then that Luther, firstly, makes a deliberate distinction between the divine will which is always sovereign, and the divine will which can be impeded by, *e.g.*, the devil. This fundamental difference recalls that recognised by Biel and other scholastic theologians[6] who talked about *voluntas beneplaciti consequens* and *voluntas signi*. Luther's distinction between two connotations in the concept of God's will leads to the antinomy that it is both possible and impossible to resist the divine will. Yet, Luther sees both aspects as so important and so true that he retains them in despite of his otherwise radical criticisms of the distinctions made by scholasticism.

---

[4] WA 5.330.40ff. (*Operationes in Psalmos*. 1519–21): "Sic Apostolus II. Tessa. II de impiorum principe Antichristo dicit, quod extolletur non simpliciter super deum, sed supra id, quod colitur aut quod dicitur deus, seu ut graece dicitur, super omnem dictum deum et cultum, ut indicet supra deum, ut in sua natura est, nihil posse extolli, sed ut est predicatus, cultus, adoratus, idest super culturam dei, hoc est in opinione et affectu hominum, apud quos solos praedicatur et colitur per verbum et fidem."

[5] WA 18.685.7ff. (*De servo arbitrio*. 1525): "Et ne meam hanc esse distinctionem quis arbitretur, Paulum sequor, qui ad Thessalonicenses de Antichristo scribit, quod sit exaltaturus sese super omnem Deum praedicatum et cultum, manifeste significans, aliquem posse extolli supra Deum, quatenus est praedicatus et cultus, id est, supra verbum et cultum quo Deus nobis cognitus est et nobiscum habet commercium, sed supra Deum non cultum nec praedicatum, ut est in sua natura et maiestate, nihil potest extolli, sed omnia sunt sub potenti manu eius." We can also establish that the same interpretation of 2 Thess. 2:4 is to be found in later material, *e.g.* WA 42.634.16ff. (*Vorlesung über 1. Mose*. 1535–45): "Haec dixi, ut intelligeretis, quid sit Deum esse: ac convenit sententia cum eo, quod Daniel de Antiocho: Paulus autem de Antichristo dixit, quod scilicet elevabitur super omne, quod Deus est, et omnem cultum. Antichristus, hoc est Papa et Turca, non extolluntur super Deum in substantia sua, qui est incognitus et 'absconditus Deus' ut Esaias appellat: Sed super Deum in praedicamento relationis, qui est Deus praedicatus verbo, et manifestatus cultu." Concerning the hidden God, see further 4.3.2 below.

[6] This is noticed by *e.g.* J. B. Hygen, *Guds allmakt og det ondes problem* (1974)35f. Cf. also 3.1.1 above.

Secondly, he emphasizes that the Christian should be concerned first and foremost with Christ the crucified, who is the source of wisdom, with the God who is revealed in the death and resurrection of Christ.[7] As a result of trust in the *deus revelatus* the *deus absconditus* is designated as good even when He promotes suffering, hardness of heart and death. Even if the concealed God destroyed all mankind, the believers who possess the Holy Spirit are convinced of God's goodness. For the Christian knows the manner in which evil benefits him.[8] Thus, the vital condition for the acceptance by the Christian of evil as a gracious gift of God, the Father, Almighty (3.5–6.) is this: On the cross Christ subdued, overcame and transformed all evil into good. As a result of faith in Him, this victory and re-assessment of all values become an existential reality for the Christian.

3.8. Conclusions

Luther follows William of Ockham in appropriating rational arguments in order to demonstrate that God is Almighty. Reason accepts the truth of this doctrine, and to some extent convinces itself thereof. Yet, there is no evident proof of the theological aspect of the divine omnipotence as the immediate cause of all that happens.

Both Biel and Luther place the emphasis on God's close and active omnipotence, which they are prompted to believe by the revelation. This divine omnipotence is according to Luther directly and unceasingly active in the believer's personal life, in society and in history. The theology which makes God a static and abstract entity far from the events of real life is therefore subjected to harsh criticism.

As for the relationship between the divine omnipotence and evil Luther proves to be near to the Medieval tradition, which derives evil (*malum poenae*) from God, and sin (*malum culpae*) from mankind. Both in his popular instruction and his counselling letters, Luther maintains that the Christian ought to accept evil as coming from the hand of the Almighty Creator, and learn the positive elements to be derived therefrom with regard to conversion and increase in faith.

Luther as well as Biel interprets hardness of heart in the terms mentioned above. Hardness is rooted in human sin, which here, may be

---

[7] WA 18.638.24ff. (*De servo arbitrio*. 1525), *ib*. 689.22ff. quoted in 4.5.1 n. 16 below.
[8] WA 18.708.8f. quoted in 4.5.5 n. 36 below, WA 18.709.1ff. quoted in 4.5.5 n. 37 below.

considered as *meritum obdurationis*. But God promotes the hardening of heart by His unceasingly active power which always wills and does good. The individuals who perceive with the eye of faith can to some extent discover God's positive purposes.

Like Ockhamistic theology Luther regards the Almighty will of God as the power which must win in the long run, and which nobody can resist. Nevertheless, there is both a dualistic and a monistic outlook: the devil can set himself above the *deus revelatus*. Yet, the devil is dethroned and defeated by the almighty God in Christ. And this triumph is given every Christian through faith in *Christus Victor*.

4. The Predestination

4.1. Background

1. Since the theology of Ockham and Biel strongly emphasizes *divine omnipotence* in order to bring out the Biblical conception of God, as we saw in the preceding chapter (3.1.1.), the divine election is also accentuated.[1] The eternal and immutable Creator is wholly free in respect of His creation. Predestination derives from the free counsels of God.

The nominalism of the Late Middle Ages also distinguishes between two different aspects of the divine power; *potentia absoluta* and *potentia ordinata*. The first term connotes the idea that God can in principle do anything which does not imply contradiction. He is His own cause, not dependent on anything. But all things depend on Him. In the doctrine of justification this prompts Biel to preach "grace alone". Concerning predestination this results in the vindication of *predestinatio ante merita*. The term *potentia ordinata* indicates that God usually acts with the help of the laws which He freely institutes. Thus, Biel can accentuate the importance of deeds for justification and election, the issue being *predestinatio post merita*. The expressions *potentia absoluta* and *potentia*

---

[1] L. Grane. (1956)53f., *ib.* 58, *ib.* 62f., *ib.* 66. The earlier attempts to define the doctrine of predestination in the theology of Peter Lombard, Thomas Aquinas, and Duns Scotus are discussed *e.g.* in W. Pannenberg (1954)29ff, *ib.* 45ff., *ib.* 69ff., *ib.* 88ff., *ib.* 90ff. Concerning Thomas see literature in H. McSorley (1969)138ff. Cf. 1.4 n. 22.

[2] A short history of the two concepts *potentia absoluta* and *potentia ordinata* is to be found in W. Pannenberg (1954)133ff. In another paper, *Der Einfluss der Anfechtungserfahrung auf den Prädestinationsbegriff Luthers*, KuD 3 (1957)112, Pannenberg sums up: "Der Grenzbegriff der potentia absoluta ist vielmehr nur ein Hilfsmittel des occamistischen Positivismus: Er deklariert die Unableitbarkeit der nun einmal geltenden Heilsordnung." But the detailed analysis in H. A. Oberman (1963)30ff. shows that the dialectics of God's two "powers" have a more profound theological and philosophical significance, and that both "orders" are highly relevant. So *potentia absoluta* proves to be of actual importance: "The realm of the *potentia absoluta* is not merely hypothetical and the sum of all noncontradictory possibilities. It is also founded on conclusions drawn from a few deeds which God in fact performed, according to biblical authority, where he deviated from the laws now in force, the *potentia ordinata*" (*ib.* 45). This interpretation is confirmed in H. Junghans (1968)236:"denn Gott konnte in der Schöpfung, in der er normalerweise durch seine potentia ordinata wirkte, auch durch seine potentia absoluta wirken." The lines of thought from the two "orders" to the doctrines of justification and predestination are drawn in H. A. Oberman (1963)175ff., *ib.* 186ff.

ordinata do not *per se* appear in Biel's *Coll Liber I Distinctio* 40 or 41, the fundamental passage for his teaching on predestination. Yet, it is important for the systematic comprehension to bear them in mind.[2]

On the one hand, man is absolutely dependent on God and His will. On the other hand, man's free will and personal responsibility are of vital importance. These two lines of thought may be described as the two conceptions around which Biel's doctrine of predestination revolves. Consequently, he is also compelled to contend with the tension between the idea that *God* really predetermines, and that *man* at the same time has a personal responsibility.

Nevertheless, I also wish to emphasize that Biel tried to set forth a unitary doctrine of predestination, in which the divine and the human action are organically fused. The disparate and contradictory traits in Biel's doctrine of election were accentuated by earlier scholars. But recent research has stressed his *intention* to *form a unitary* predestination doctrine.[3] In my opinion, it is essential to presume both the unity and the complexity in an interpretation of Biel's theory of predetermination.

2. Predetermination seems *prima facie* to be merely God's prescience of what will happen in time and in eternity.[4] The divine activity is not causative but cognitive in nature. At the same time, however, Biel can, in a parallel tenet, use the term *praeordinatio* as a synonym of *praedestinatio*.[5] This must mean that God not only passively foresees future events but also actively decrees them. Biel does not make any sharp distinction between prescience and predetermination. One is tempted to recall the important distinction between *potentia absoluta* and *potentia ordinata*. In His "absolute" might God has established that the "ordained" power is to apply with regard to man's acquisition of grace in the present and of glory in the future life.

One aspect of this is Biel's identification of *predestination* with God's own being. Predetermination is not only a hypothetical construction of

---

[3] *Sic* H. A. Oberman (1963)193: "The organic unity of the doctrine of justification reappears in the doctrine of predestination: there is no trace of the often-claimed ambiguity and the lack of clarity in this understanding of the movement from eternity to history as a movement from freedom to commitment." Cf. further *ib.* 187ff., *ib.* 192ff., *ib.* 206ff.

[4] Coll I, Dist. 40, q.1, A: "Circa primum notandum primo circa illum terminum 'praedestinatio', quod praedestinatio (ut dicit *Magister* dist. 35 et etiam 40) est praecognitio Dei de salvandis et bonis gratiae, quibus hic liberantur et in futuro coronabuntur. Ex quo patet quod praedestinatio est quasi species providentiae."

[5] *Ib.*: "Solet autem praedestinatio sic describi: Est praeordinatio alicuius creaturae rationalis ad gratiam in praesenti et gloriam in futuro." Cf. also E. Wolf (1927) 169.

minor significance. It is in fact an attribute of the Godhead.[6] Anything which may be said of God may also be said of the election. Since God is eternal the predestination is eternal.[7]

A "more strict" interpretation of God's prescience, according to Biel, demonstrates the way in which we are to interpret the *rejection*. Man himself is the cause of the sin and guilt which result in eternal damnation. Here Biel follows Peter Lombard's teaching. God foresees that by reason of man's own unworthiness the individual deserves rejection. God is not *auctor* but *praecognitor* with regard to the guilt.[8] Consequently, retribution is not arbitrary, but is an effect of the individual's personal guilt.[9] There is a fixed connection between God's passive precognition of human guilt and the punishment which must be imposed and exacted in accordance with the just order established by God in the creation. This I call *reprobation*$_1$: God has predetermined that the individual who remains in sin and incurs personal guilt must suffer eternal punishment.

Therefore, Biel finds no difficulty in using the concept "predetermination" of both the salvation of the elect and the damnation of the rejected. Man himself to some extent creates the essential conditions for his final salvation or rejection. Yet, God has established the decisive order of justification, whereby the individual is rewarded or punished. Biel goes so far as to follow up Augustine's anti-Pelagian writings, using "determinatio" of both predestination and reprobation.[10] Predestination and reprobation "presuppose" the same feature in the

---

[6] *Ib.*: "Ex quo sequitur quod praedestinatio non est aliquod imaginabile in Deo, distinctum quomodocumque a Deo, ita quod non est aliquis actus secundus adveniens deitati, sed importat Deum, qui est daturus alicui vitam aeternam."

[7] *Ib.*: "Secundo patet quod praedestinatio ex parte Dei est aeterna."

[8] *Ib.*, B: "Alio modo capitur magis stricte pro praecognitione sola, quam habet Deus de damnatione reproborum. Et hoc modo respectu eiusdem est praescientia et reprobatio, licet 'reprobatio' aliquid addit, scilicet praeparationem poenae aeternae. Est enim reprobatio praescientia culpae et praeparatio poenae, ut dicit *Magister*. Vel est ordinatio alicuius creaturae ad poenam aeternam. Et haec poena est effectus reprobationis. Non autem culpa, per quam reprobatur, meretur aeternaliter puniri, eo quod culpae Deus reprobans non est auctor, sed solum praecognitor, ut clare ostendit *Magister* in Textu dist. 40."

[9] Cf. *ib.*, Dist. 41, q.1, F; *ib.*, G, sum. 6 (quoted in n. 19 below).

[10] *Ib.*, Dist. 40, q.1, C: "Pro articulo secundo est conclusio prima: 'Quaelibet rationalis creatura a Deo fuit aeternaliter praedestinata vel reprobata.' Probatur: Deus ab aeterno disposuit dare cuilibet creaturae rationali vel gloriam aeternam vel non dare. 'Et haec conclusio est determinatio *Augustini* libro De praedestinatione contra Pelagianos.'"

Godhead, but different things in creation. And predetermination is primarily associated with the essence of God.[11]

Yet, another consequence of the identification of the divine being with predetermination is that the concept *immutabilis*, which is attributed to the Godhead, is also relevant to the predestination. Indeed, God never predetermines anyone by necessity, since predestination is contingent. But when someone is predestined this decision is unalterable.[12]

The fact that God predestines and reprobates is further modified by Biel with help of the concepts cause and effect. Thus, it becomes clear that the point at issue concerns predetermination *sensu stricto*, and not merely prescience. The reason why God gives eternal life or eternal punishment depends solely on the counsel of the divine will. Nothing in creation is a cause. Predestination and reprobation are as unconditional as God Himself.[13] Here the rejection might be interpreted with the theory which I call *reprobation₂*: God has not predetermined to bestow grace, faith or eternal life; in consequence man remains among "the unenlightened", and by reason of his guilt is punished with eternal damnation.

Now, however, it seems as if this Augustinian reasoning will fall short of the mark. In Biel's view there is a parallel between election to eternal life and election to eternal death. Therefore, it would seem that I can only express this doctrine by formulating what may be designated *reprobation₃*: God has predetermined by a special decree not to grant grace, faith and eternal life, which means that the unbeliever remains in sin, and is rejected because of his personal guilt. Thus, we arrive at Calvinistic ideas of a special *decretum reprobationis*.

---

[11] *Ib.*: "'Prima pars patet, quia praedestinatio est ipsa Dei essentia, quae est necessaria. Undi isti termini 'praedestinatio' et 'reprobatio' pro eodem supponunt et idem omnino important in Deo, licet non in creatura' quam connotant."

[12] Peter was elected by God. This fact cannot be changed later, *ib.*, D. Cf. E. Wolf (1927)170 n. 6–7.

[13] Coll I, Dist. 41, q. 1, B: "Secundo notandum quod per causam quandoque intelligitur res aliqua, ad cuius esse sequitur aliud tamquam effectus. Illo modo manifestum est quod, cum praedestinatio et reprobatio sit divina voluntas, quae illi vult dare vitam aeternam, isti poenam perpetuam, quae voluntas nihil aliud est quam Deus ipse, nulla est causa ex parte creaturae ipsius praedestinationis neque reprobationis, cum ipsa sit aeterna et incausata. Et hoc est, quod *alii* dicunt quod praedestinationis effective sive ut actus divinus nulla est causa." Cf. *ib.*, D and I (quoted in n. 18 below). Cf. also WA 18.694.9ff. (*De servo arbitrio*. 1525). Cf. Augustine's view of reprobation in *e.g.* A. Adam, *Lehrbuch der Dogmengeschichte* I² (1970)271ff.

4.1.

These tenets would also express Biel's Biblical concept of creation. This emerges from what follows. Since, God is the Creator and Lord of the universe He owes nothing to anyone but is righteous in redeeming and rejecting the beings which He created according to His own arbitrariness.[14] This would seem to be an expression of the *potentia absoluta dei*.

The fact of the predestination, accordingly, stands, both as regards the positive and the negative aspects. Some individuals will be redeemed because their merits are accepted.[15] Others will be lost, since they are abandoned to sin and condemned. This double outcome originates from the will of God. An unconditional, eternal will to love, and an unconditional eternal will to wrath are apposed in God. A rational synthesis is impossible. When we see the double outcome and trace its roots in the divine will, reason is faced with a *contradictory concept of God*. It will be interesting to analyse the similarities existing between Biel and Luther on this point (4.2.6.).

3. Since I have discussed Biel's theology of predestination on the general level I go on in order to give a closer illustration of the concrete predetermination. We encounter the concrete *how* of predestination in, *inter alia*, Biel's comments on the contingency of the divine election. The mode of God's predetermination is not dependent on any higher law or compelling necessity. Predestination is contingent in the sense that man could just as well be preordained to something other than his actual fate.[16] As Creator and Conservator of the universe God is righteous in acting according to His will. His actions are invariably right. No one can call Him to account, why His deeds are such as they appear to be.[17]

---

[14] Coll I, Dist. 41., q. 1, G: "Deus tamquam universitatis creator et Dominus de creatura potest facere quidquid vult, sine iniuria creaturae. Hinc potest salvare quem vult et damnare sicut habens plenum dominium in re sua. Et ideo non iniuste vult et operatur quidquid vult et operatur, cui nemo dicere potest: 'Cur ita facis?' Iob 11, et Rom. 9: 'O homo, tu quis es, qui respondeas Deo? Numquid dicit figmentum ei, qui se finxit: quid fecisti sic?' Nullius igitur est debitor. Propter quod nulli facit iniuriam nec accipit personam."

[15] Cf. further in W. Pannenberg (1954)148, L. Grane (1956)66, H. A. Oberman (1963)193.

[16] Coll I, Dist. 40, q. 1, C, con 2-3. *Ib*. Dist. 41, q. 1, G, sum 2.

[17] *Ib*. sum 1 (quoted in n. 14 above). This point is, accordingly, found already in the Ockhamistic tradition, which questions the assertion in K. Holl (1923)50 and L. Pinomaa (1938)137 about the difference between Luther and the earlier tradition: "Denn im Unterschied von Duns und Occam ist Luther ernsthaft davon überzeugt, dass das göttliche Tun immer wirklich 'recht' ist, d.h. dass es einen Sinn hat und zwar einen Sinn, den auch der Mensch einmal wird begreifen können"; Rom 9:20 is also very important for Luther when he defends the justice of God in predestination and reprobation (see further 4.2.6 below).

Indeed, man cannot calculate on any other special principle or cause than God's will. This will is quite simply "prima regula in contingentibus". Thus, it is wrong to seek another cause, since no such cause exists.[18]

Biel firmly believes *that* God predestines and reprobates solely through His eternal and immutable will. In addition, however, he emphasizes that man can never know, on earth, *how* God actually elects, since this is a free act. In the following Luther passages we shall observe that even Luther accepts man's awareness that God unconditionally predestines and reprobates. But, Luther also repudiates human knowledge derived from reason of how the Godhead predetermines in the individual, specific case (4.2.2–5. and 4.3.2–4.).

4. First and foremost, Biel assumes *a free will* on the part of the individual. Therefore man has a personal responsibility, personal guilt and personal merit respectively. *Merita* are a necessary, but not a sufficient condition for the attainment of eternal salvation.[19] In order to express this line of thought Biel introduces a different concept of cause with a wider significance than that explained above. By *causa* and *effectus* we may mean the relationship between two different circumstances which are not related to each other by an Aristotelian theory of cause. For example, if you do not stand near enough to a fire, this may be described as the reason why you do not feel its warmth.[20] In this sense, man's own attitude with consequent merits or lack thereof are the cause of the predestination or reprobation respectively. This stress on human activity compels Biel to modify his theory of an actual predetermination on the part of God. God *foresees* that man will in time follow a specific course of action. And He *predetermines*, on the basis of man's merits or lack thereof, to crown him with honour for eternity or to

---

[18] Coll I, Dist. 41, q. 1, I: "Quare Deus creat animas, quas scit perpetuo damnandas? Solutio: Quia voluit, et est status. Voluntas enim divina prima regula est in contingentibus. Et si illius causa quaeritur, non invenitur, ut dicit *Augustinus* De civitate Dei." And further: "Indisciplinati autem est quaerere causam, ubi non est causa." Cf. *ib.* II, Dist. 20, q. 1, D, con. 4.

[19] Coll I, Dist. 40, q. 1, C, con. 2: " 'nulli adulto confertur vita aeterna nisi propter aliquod' eius meritum." *Ib.* Dist. 41, q. 1, G, sum. 6: "Statuit Deus nullum damnare poena sensus nisi pro culpa personali nec adultum salvare regulariter sine merito personali."

[20] *Ib.* B: "Alio modo capitur causa ut dicit 'quandam prioritatem unius propositionis ad aliam secundum consequentiam. Sicut si quaeritur causa, quare ignis non calefacit, quia non est approximatus passo. Et sic frequenter dicitur quod antecedens est causa consequentis. Et tamen non est proprie causa, quia nec causa efficiens, materialis, formalis vel finalis. Quando enim ab una propositione ad aliam est consequentia naturalis, et non econverso, potest aliquo modo antecedens dici causa consequentis, et non econverso'."

reject him for ever (reprobation₁).[21] This may be described as a case of *potentia ordinata dei.*

Thus, Biel can express God's universal redeeming will in a natural way. God is close to all, offering His grace, to those who do not "shut Him out". He does not begrudge the meed of salvation to any adult who does his duty. Biel is referring to Paul's words in 1 Tim. 2:4. [22] Consequently, when an individual acquires merit of his own free will he need not fear that the offer of divine grace will be particularistic. In this context *merita* are not only a necessary but a well nigh sufficient condition for redemption. The reservation that in the last resort God's gift of salvation is free and unconditional is overshadowed.

This illustrates Biel's view of *the certainty of redemption.* Only the individual whose faith endures to the end can know that he will be saved. Only then is the *absolute* certainty of eternal salvation granted. But no one knows for sure *in via.* A believer can possess grace today and lose it tomorrow. Or he may lack it now and acquire it later. Only God knows who will remain steadfast in love unto the end.[23] If we still wish to speak of some form of certainty of salvation for man *in via*, this must be designated *relative.* Our hope may be rooted in the objective words and promises of God. Nevertheless, we do not know whether this hope will be fulfilled. We can perceive in ourselves, or in others, signs that the believer is in a state of grace: love of Christ, fear of the Judgement, and a will to obey God. These criteria are *subjective*, however, and can only give rise to a postulated idea of the individual's salvation. As we shall see in what follows, there is a very important distinction here between Biel and Luther[24] (4.5.3–4.).

---

[21] *Ib.* D, con. 1: "'Dare est aliquam causam reprobationis, accipiendo causam secondo modo'; quia sequitur: 'Iste peccabit finaliter; ergo damnabitur'. 'Non enim est Deus prius ultor quam sit aliquis peccator', *Augustinus* XI Super Genesim ad litteram, et videtur esse crudelitatis punire innocentem." *Ib.* con. 2: "'Alicuius praedestinationis est aliqua causa vel ratio', secundo modo capiendo causam. Patet, 'quia aliqui propter meritum salvantur, ita quod, si non voluntarie mererentur, non salvarentur'. Horum praedestinationis est aliqua ratio, sicut reprobationis. Nam sicut damnandi reprobantur, quia praevidentur finaliter peccaturi, ita tales praedestinantur, quia praevidentur finaliter perseveraturi in caritate."

[22] *Ib.* G, sum. 7. Cf. also *ib.* H, con. 6 (quoted in n. 23 below).

[23] *Ib.* D, con. 2 (quoted in n. 21 above). *Ib.* H, con. 6: "In quibus (sc. virtutum opera) quisquis in finem perseveraverit (quod in homine est, cui sine sui culpa gratia non subtrahitur), indubitanter salvabitur. Quamvis utrum perseveraverit an ne, inevitabiliter ab aeterno Deus novit." See further E. Wolf (1927)172, H. A. Oberman (1963)219f.

[24] H. A. Oberman (1963)227ff., cf. *ib.* 219 n. 118: "A more perceptive description of the difference between the theology of late medieval nominalism and that of the Reformation on this point would be hard to find." Cf. also K. Holl (1923)148.

5. If we overlook Biel's doctrine of predestination we can find both unconditional and conditional predetermination, both monergism and synergism as regards God and man. This can to a great extent explain why *predestination afflictions* can but need not, arise in the late Medieval nominalism of Biel's teaching. It depends on which point comes to the fore to reign supreme in human consciousness.

Insofar as the individual reflects upon God's free, unconditional, rejection, this may create disquiet, doubt, and obsession concerning predestination. Even if man exercises his free will for good, it may happen that God will nevertheless disapprove of his merits as a qualification for salvation. Even those who are not predestined can use their free will aright.[25] When a human being becomes aware that in the last instance all things depend on the will of God, he will also understand that eternal damnation finally derives solely from God's will. This brings forth the affliction concerning predestination.

In His absolute supremacy God has decided that *potentia ordinata* is to hold good. But, this allows of exceptions. Laws can be changed. This possibility exists not only in principle but also in practice.[26] Notwithstanding that man does all in his power, he cannot be entirely sure that this will *de facto* lead to eternal salvation. God's action is, and remains, free and contingent.[27] Therefore, I maintain that it is not adequate to interpret *potentia absoluta* as a "Grenzbegriff" and "Hilfsmittel", excluding the possibility of actual predestination afflictions, and only assuming the uncertainty of personal merits. In my

---

[25] Coll I, Dist. 41, q. 1, E: "Hic autem bonus motus seu usus liberi arbitrii non est effectus praedestinationis, licet sit a Deo; quia communis est etiam non-praedestinatis."

[26] *Ib.* D, con. 3: "Alicuius praedestinationis nulla est causa vel ratio talis. Patet, quia aliqui 'ex gratia speciali ordinati sunt ad vitam, ita quod sibiipsis non sunt derelicti', sed praeventi, ne ponere possent obicem et ne possent peccare vel in peccatis permanere; sicut beata virgo Maria et Paulus a Domino percussus et illuminatus. In illis enim nulla videtur ratio, quare Deus illos praedestinet sic gratia praeveniendo, nisi sola Dei voluntas. Non enim potest poni ratio bonus usus liberi arbitrii; quoniam gratia praevenit usum liberi arbitrii in beata Virgine, cui fuit gratia concreata, et in Paulo fuit malus usus liberi arbitrii, quia saeviens in discipulos Domini percussus est." Already in E. Seeberg (1929)22 we read this: "Die Unterscheidung zwischen dem 'absoluten' und dem 'ordentlichen' Gotteswillen ist also doch *mehr als ein logisches Spiel oder eine Verlegenheitsauskunft;* sie ist der Niederschlag zweier Frömmigkeitsweisen, die nicht bloss im Nominalismus mit einander verbunden sind." See further n. 2 above the dialectics between the two "orders".

[27] Notes 16 and 18 above. Cf. E. Wolf (1927)175f., L. Grane (1956)66f., *id.* (1962)71f., H. A. Oberman (1963)193.

opinion one may well be obsessed by the divine predetermination within the framework of Biel's theology.[28]

But this idea of predetermination can be brushed aside. It is most important for man to invest all personal resources in not "shutting out God" but in accepting the grace which God offers to all penitents. The believer who endures to the end will "undoubtedly" be saved.[29] This is the normal principle, and is related to Biel's doctrine of justification, which might be interpreted as mainly semi-Pelagian.[30] It also indicates that Biel does not carry out his ideas of unconditional predestination and reprobation. A scrutiny of his sermons shows that his practical preaching does not explicitly deal with this theme.[31] In this respect we shall see how Luther gradually arrives at an understanding of predetermination which also pervades the sermon material and the more popular teaching (4.5.1–4.).

Last, but not least, I wish to stress the fact that Biel teaches the *unity of the concept of God*. Even if both the acceptance of those who have done what lay in their power and the rejection of those who have not is in the last resort derived from the divine will, and *ratio* here posits a contradictory image of God, he asserts firmly that God Himself is one. All things are one in the Godhead. The divine attributes are human metaphors which are devised to distinguish God's *opera ad extra*. It is not possible to define the essence of God *sensu stricto*.[32] The various divine attributes are not separate realities in God. The divine knowledge

---

[28] *Contra* W. Pannenberg (1957)112 (quoted in n. 2 above), *ib.* 113: "So hängt bei Biel die Ungewissheit der Erwältheit nicht mit einer Ungebundenheit der göttlichen potentia absoluta zusammen, sondern lediglich mit der Unbeständigkeit des menschlichen freien Willens. Niemand ist sicher, ob er nicht vor seinem Tode doch noch in Todsünden fällt und keine Vergebung mehr dafür erlangt. An dieser Lehre kann nur Unsicherheit über die eigene rechte Disposition entstehen, aber *keine eigentliche Prädestinationsanfechtung*"; This thesis is found already in E. Vogelsang (1932)31. But I cannot wholly agree with this, since my conclusion is more in line with G. Rost (1966)99: "Einmal wird erkennbar, dass Luther in der Tat schon zu einem Zeitpunkt unter Prädestinationsanfechtungen gelitten hat, an dem er den synergistisch-gabrielistischen Typ der Prädestinationslehre noch nicht verlassen hatte."

[29] Coll I, Dist. 41, q. 1, H, con. 6 (quoted in n. 23).

[30] See further the analysis in H. A. Oberman (1963)177, *ib.* 196. Sic H. McSorley (1969)99ff. who has a critical discussion of the exposition in L. Grane (1962)218ff.

[31] H. A. Oberman (1963)196.

[32] Coll I, Dist. 8, q. 5, A, con. 1: "Deus non potest diffinitione proprie dicta et primo modo accepta diffiniri. Patet, quia res incompositae simplices non possunt diffiniri; qualis est Deus." See further L. Grane (1956)54f., *ib.* (1962)69ff. Cf. also WA 42.294.1ff. (*Vorlesung über 1. Mose.* 1535–45).

might, for example, be described as identical with *essentia dei*.[33] And God's will is no other than God Himself.[34] With reference to God's action in creation, and His dealings with His creatures, we could speak of eternal wrath which condemns, and refuses mercy, and eternal love which confers grace. But in the Godhead all predicates are one. In the essence of God there is no conflict between predestination and reprobation, although this realisation cannot be proved, nor is it available for reason. I intend to demonstrate that Luther also sees the unity as the most profound element in his conception of God (4.5.5.).

4.2. Unconditional Predestination as a Primary Feature

4.2.1. The Natural and the Revealed Conception of God's Predetermination

1. We have analysed a relatively comprehensive Luther material, which gives evidence of a knowledge of God innate in all human beings (2.2–3.). We have also studied a few texts which maintain that God's omnipotence is an idea which is conceded, and indeed even proved, by natural reason (3.2). We shall now proceed to the divine predestination, in order to see whether this is also somehow comprehended in human knowledge.

It is hardly surprising that the book which devotes most attention to God's omnipotence as envisaged by reason, namely *The Bondage of the Will* (3.2.2), also asserts that all men possess an innate awareness that the Almighty Creator and Preserver of life determines and foresees the future.

In his defence of the doctrine of human free will Erasmus alleged that the picture of the predetermining God which Wycliffe taught and Luther accepted should not be incorporated in ordinary Christian teaching. For this would have disastrous consequences and lead to godlessness, despair and pessimism.[1]

---

[33] Coll I, Dist. 35, q. 1, C, con. 3: "Scientia, quae Deus est realiter, est ex natura rei divina essentia ab ea penitus indistincta, nec realiter nec formaliter, sed omnibus modis eadem essentiae, quibus essentia est sibiipsi. Prima pars patet, quia scientia est divina essentia; et non per considerationem intellectus; ergo ex natura rei. Tenet consequentia a sufficienti divisione. Prima pars assumpti patet, quia quidquid realiter est in Deo, est divina essentia."
[34] *Ib.* Dist. 41, q. 1, B (quoted in n. 13 above).

[1] *De libero arbitrio* I.a. 9–11.

Luther retorts that this pastoral caution is wholly unjustified. For this truth about God need not be taught. It is an innate archetype in all men. They speak of it freely and openly, not least poets such as Vergil:

"Hence the very common saying on everyone's lips, 'God's will be done'; and 'God willing, we will do it', or 'Such was the will of God'. 'So it pleased those above'; 'Such was your will', says Vergil. From this we can see that the knowledge of *God's predestination and foreknowledge* remained with the common people no less than the awareness of his existence itself."[2]

This general understanding of God's nature, that His will imposes necessity on everything, so that all things are predetermined, belongs to "the things that the poets and common people, and even their (*sc.* the wise men's) own conscience, regard as entirely familiar, certain, and true",[3] although those who would be wise are deceived and have refused to admit it.

These statements indicate, first, the close connection between Luther's natural theology and the knowledge of God's predetermination. Nevertheless, Luther mainly by reason of his exegesis of *The Scriptures* regards the idea of predestination as an immediate and genuine feature of

---

[2] WA 18.618.11ff. (*De servo arbitrio.* 1525), LW 33.41.
Surprisingly enough, G. Rost (1966) does not seem to take this important passage into consideration, although it strongly supports his fundamental thesis, *ib.* 56ff. I may also refer to his summary: "Vielmehr wurzelt er (*sc.* der Prädestinationsgedanke) primär in dem theologischen Fundamentalsatz von der Allwirksamkeit und Alleinwirksamkeit Gottes... Der grundlegende Satz ist für Luther auch ein Satz natürlicher Theologie. Gerade darum kann er in der exegetischen Auseinandersetzung mit Erasmus als durchschlagender Beweis für die Richtigkeit der Schriftauslegung Luthers angeführt werden" (*ib.* 177). Cf. also the positive assessment of G. Rost in A. Peters (1968)365.
Interpreting these statements in *The Bondage of the Will* K. Schwarzwäller, *Theologia crucis* (1970)129f. does not give them their due importance. Firstly, he maintains that Luther's sentences do not add anything to the exposition: "Die Pointe liegt hier darin, dass man diese Passage durchaus entbehren könnte, ohne dass etwas vermisst würde." Secondly, he has to admit Luther's references as adequate and convincing. At least implicitly he suggests a conclusion *a minore*. This is also summarized in Th. 15 (*ib.* 19). In this light Schwarzwäller's complete rejection in *sibboleth* (1969)97 of Rost's analysis and conclusion that Luther actually is arguing *a minore* in the case of natural theology on this point, seems to be unjustified. Concerning the predestination, Luther can prove his doctrine both by reason and Scripture indeed. That his method is similar to the theological reasoning of scholasticism and that the principle *sola scriptura* from the doctrine of justification is pushed aside, that is really another question! I will elaborate this issue in 4.4.1 below.
[3] WA 18.618.17f., LW 33.41. Cf. also WA 18.718.16ff., *ib.* 719.30ff.

the notion of God. Elsewhere, man's innate conception of predestination is not as important for the exposition as it is in *The Bondage of the Will.*

Secondly, the fact that the theory of predestination is an integral part of Luther's natural theology justifies us in supposing that the same dialectic between the *notitia* and the *usus* level, which we observed in natural theology, is present in the statements on predestination, provided that the theological reasoning is consistent. I shall discuss a fairly extensive material, which confirms the truth of this hypothesis (4.3.).

2. Without the truth revealed in the Bible man could not assimilate aright the innate knowledge of God (2.2–5.). Without enlightenment by Word and faith the believer could not understand that the Almighty Creator is constantly present and active throughout His creation (3.3–4.), even in evil and hardness of heart (3.5–6.).

Therefore, it is not particularly surprising to see that, according to Luther, the idea of divine predetermination has deep roots in the *Biblical* testimony.[4] The decisive proof of the truth of the doctrine of predestination is not its self-evidence but its strong support in the Scriptures. When, in the *Lecture on Romans*, after the exposition of Rom. 8:28f. Luther develops the conception of the divine election, he presents something which could be called a compendium of the Bible's doctrine of predetermination.[5]

Special emphasis should be laid on the fact that the following material on predestination is to a great extent Biblical exegesis—in the form of a lecture, a sermon or a commentary. An important purpose of the book *The Bondage of the Will*, when presenting predestination as a basic Christian doctrine, is to mediate the correct interpretation of the Bible.[6]

3. The account in the Scriptures of the *double outcome* of the Last Judgement is a completely uncontroversial *locus* in the discussion between Roman and Evangelical theologians.[7] Luther material from all ages provides evidence of the belief in a division of mankind into saved and lost at Christ's Second Coming.[8] Luther, as an OT exegete,

---

[4] This is stressed in *e.g.* L. Pinomaa (1938)147, P. Althaus (1963)238f.

[5] WA 56.383.25ff. (*Rom.* 1515–16). A detailed analysis in G. Rost (1966)76ff.

[6] Cf. the extensive exposition of principles of interpretation which is also to be found in *The Bondage of the Will* in WA 18.652.23ff. See further the analysis in 4.2.2.2, 4.2.3.2 and 4.2.4.2 below.

[7] There is *consensus* about CA 17.

[8] See *e.g* WA 56.193.12ff. (*Rom.* 1515–16), WA 5.576.7ff. (*Operationes in Psalmos.* 1519–21), WA 7.218.13ff. (*Eine kurze Form des Glaubens.* 1520), WA 10.II.393.3ff. (*Betbüchlein.* 1522), WA 26.509.13ff. (*Vom Abendmahl Christi. Bekenntnis.* 1528), WA 50.198.5ff. (*Die Schmalkaldischen Artikel.* 1537).

emphasizes the development which is to be found in the Bible from the temporal punishment in the Old Testament to the eternal damnation in the New.[9] If we are going to preach the Word of God we must mention both heaven and hell.[10] In Luther's view Holy Writ differs from all other books, since it asserts that God rewards men after this life with punishment or with salvation.[11] At the same time he conveys an impression of being comparatively restrictive with regard to a detailed presentation of the infernal torments.[12]

4.2.2. God's Foreknowledge

1. Already in the notes on Peter Lombard's *Sententiae* (*Liber I*) we find a fairly detailed discussion of the divine prescience and power, and of man's dependence on God. As a commentary on the whole of Dist. 38 c.1, Luther says that the *potentia* of God is the cause of created things. Yet, God's *praescientia* is no less causative. Since the creation is an

---

[9] WA 16.449.1ff. (*Predigten über das 2. Buch Mose.* 1524–27). Cf. also WA 18.694.9ff. (*De servo arbitrio.* 1525).

[10] WA 18.386.37ff. (*Ein Sendbrief von dem harten Büchlein wider die Bauern.* 1525): "Sollen wyr Gotts wort predigen, so mussen wyr ia das auch predigen, das den zorn verkundigt so wol als das die barmhertzickeyt verkundigt. Man mus auch von der helle predigen so wol als vom hymel und auff beyden seytten uber die frumen und bösen Gotts wort, gericht und werck helffen foddern, das die bösen gestrafft und die frumen geschutzt werden."

[11] WA 40.III.570.8ff. (*Enarratio Psalmi XC.* 1534–35). Cf. WA 25.380.4ff. (*Vorlesung über Jesaja.* 1527–29), WA 27.449.2ff. (*Pred.* 1528, R).

[12] Luther's interest is focused on the *present* hell in the anguish of the conscience. See further Y. J. E. Alanen, *Das Gewissen bei Luther* (1934)32ff. Nevertheless he does not totally ignore the *future* hell when the horror of the second causes the first. WA 19.225.12ff. (*Der Prophet Jona ausgelegt.* 1526) is illuminating. Another passage, WA 5.590.7ff. (*Operationes in Psalmos.* 1519–21), was noticed already in Th. Harnack I (1927)239. K. Holl (1923)32: "Das Eingeständnis, zu dem der Mensch sich entschloss, indem er sich vorbehaltlos als Sünder bekannte, war nicht nur ein Selbstgericht; es war, wenn anders ihm dabei Gott lebendig vor der Seele stand, ein Gericht, das Gott selbst an ihm vollstreckte. Damit rückt das 'Gericht'—ähnlich wie in den johanneischen Schriften, deren Worte beizuziehen Luther nicht verabsäumt,—aus der Zukunft in die Gegenwart, ins persöhnlich Erfahrbare herein." And further: "Das 'jüngste' Gericht selbst will Luther damit nicht aufheben. Es steht immer hinter dem Erlebnis in der Gegenwart und wirkt als Mahnung, sich ja nicht mit der Torheit der Selbstbelügung zu behelfen." This point is developed in E. Vogelsang (1932)36ff. and in E. Hirsch, *Drei Kapitel zu Luthers Lehre vom Gewissen* (in: *Lutherstudien I*, 1954)135ff. L. Pinomaa (1938)129ff. presents the material about the future hell. See also the exposition in P. Althaus, *Luthers Gedanken über die letzten Dinge*, LuJ 23 (1941)9ff. Cf. what is said about Luther's traditional doctrine of hell in S. & L. Aalen, *Bakenfor Inferno* (1955)40, *ib.* 73ff.

object of divine prescience it can also be said that the creation is the cause of the *praescientia dei*.[1] There is a total correlation between that which God foresees in eternity and that which occurs in time. Mistakes arise if prescience is considered to be an immutable rule in the Godhead, irrespective of events in creation.[2] Nevertheless *praescientia dei* is not the cause of sin. For sin is not committed by necessity, even if God foresees it. If it was bound to happen God would be the cause.[3] Thus far, Luther vigorously stresses the agreement between God's prescience and that which is foreseen. He explicitly attributes sin to man and God's prescience is considered merely cognitive.

Yet, at first he could also designate both *praescientia* and *potentia dei* as *causa creaturarum*. This reasoning is strengthened when Luther gives eternity priority over time, making time dependent on eternity. Man comprehends the time which is present for him. Yet, he is not the cause of its existence. Before God, however, all things exist in an eternal present.[4] God's eternal prescience is the primary cause of that which happens in time:

"Sicut nihil incipit futurum esse ex tempore, sed ab aeterno fuit futurum, ita praescientia dei."[5]

[1] WA 9.57.4ff. (*Randbemerkungen Luthers* 1509–1511): "zum Ganzen: Notandum, quod relativa
sunt sibi mutua causa essendi aut sunt neutrum utri causa, quia mutuo se ponunt: igitur licet divina potentia sit causa creaturarum, tamen praescientia dei non minus est causa creaturarum nec magis quam creatura est causa praescientiae dei: quia sunt relativa et mutuo a se denominantur."

[2] *Ib.* 57.21ff: "Error autem venit inde, quod imaginantur praescientiam esse quandam regulam haerentem in deo immutabilem, cum hoc sit falsum. Sed sic debent imaginari: sicut deus videns et objecta ei praesentia, ut nobis videntibus accidit. Totum illud includitur in praescientia."

[3] *Ib.* 57.31ff: "Bona ratio: quia si scientia ejus est causa scitorum peccatorum, igitur non erunt peccantium, sed illius quod est causa eorum: ergo sequitur, quod si praescivit peccata esse eorum false praescivit, quia suae praescientiae erunt." And further: "Sed tamen praescientia non est causa eorum, quia non necessario facit, si praescit: licet necessario agat, si sit causa."

[4] *Ib.* 58.21ff.: "Nunc igitur, sicut quod ego non possum nescire, quod in puncto mihi praesens videtur, et tamen non sum causa, quare hoc sit, immo possit non esse, ita coram deo sunt omnia."

[5] *Ib.* 59.4ff. I agree with the conclusion in S. Normann (1933)68: "Hermed har Luther, om enn indirekte, uttalt at det som skjer i tiden har en evig bestemmelse som sin kausative bakgrunn. Og når denne tanke forbindes med den ovenfor fremholte om den nødvendige virkeliggørelse av hvad der er gjenstand for Guds praescientia, er predestinasjonstanken dermed faktisk gitt." Indeed I question whether G. Rost (1966)92 n. 16 and 94 n. 29 is right in his assertion that Luther here makes a sharp distinction between *praescientia* and *praedestinatio*.

We observe, accordingly, that Luther, at least implicitly, understood God's prescience as a cause in eternity of that which occurs in time, although this does not apply to sin.

If we proceed to *Dictata super Psalterium* we can find more examples indicating that God's prescience implies a necessity, so that *praescientia dei* and *praedestinatio dei* cannot be strictly distinguished but are inseparably fused. Luther paraphrases as follows the words in Ps. 138:3 (Vulgate), that God understood the psalmist's thoughts from afar: " 'Intellexisti' in tua predestinatione 'cogitationes meas...' "[6] Even if we cannot infer too much from this brief exposition, yet, we can surely maintain that the dividing line between divine prescience and predetermination has here been blotted out. The cognitive and the causative are interwoven. The fact that this is by no means a fortuitous expression is shown by what follows. When the psalmist says in v. 6 that the divine knowledge is wonderful Luther offers a comment which confirms our interpretation. " 'Mirabilis' superior et incomprehensibilis 'facta est scientia tua' divina predestinatio, que est essentia tua,..." [7] God's foreknowledge and God's predestination are combined, so that one could assert that an identification takes place.

In connection with the exposition of Rom. 8:29 in the *Commentary on Romans*, that God knows in advance and has decided for man to be the image of His Son, Luther clarifies this by saying that God creates and redeems not with closed but with open eyes.[8] Although, it is sometimes believed that the blessing is given blindfold, yet, the divine prescience is there. The individuals whom God has selected to resemble His Son He also predestines to become like His Son. He is prescient that they will become—not that they will make themselves—conform to Christ.[9] *Praescientia* and *predestinatio dei*, so far as forgiveness is concerned, converge, as in the theology of Biel (4.1.2.).

When in Rom. 8:28 Luther treats the conquest of affliction concerning predestination he advises that the person assailed should boldly plunge into the truth of the God of comfort, turning away from "praescientia

[6] WA 4.432.15f. (*Dictata super Psalterium*. 1513–15). Cf. also *ib.* 79.5ff.

[7] *Ib.* 433.5f. I reach the same conclusion as S. Normann (1933)117f. and G. Rost (1966)93f. But I do not agree with Rost in discerning a great difference in this issue between Luther's *Randbemerkungen* and *Dictata*. When Luther identifies *praedestinatio* with *essentia Dei*, he is using the same words as Biel in Coll I Dist. 40, q.1, C, cor. 2 (quoted in 4.1 n. 11 above).

[8] WA 56.83.25f. (*Rom.* 1515–16): "Non enim clausis oculis creat et salvat Deus, Sicut Ioseph suspicabatur in patre suo Iacob in figura huius predestinationis."

[9] *Ib.* 83.27ff.: "Sit Constructio: Quos prescivit conformes fieri, Hos et predestinavit conformes fieri. Non quod suis meritis fieri tales prescierit, alioquin dixisset: Nam quos prescivit se conformes facturos." Cf. also *ib.* 84.24ff.

terrentis Dei".[10] The fact that prescience on the part of the God who terrifies causes the serious obsession concerning predestination, must mean that God's *praescientia* is here well nigh identical with God's *predestinatio*. Otherwise, it is difficult to understand why the prescience of the awe-inspiring God can inflict this terror on the conscience. We could suggest already at this stage of investigation of Luther's theological reflection a form of doctrine of double election.[11]

At this point we can also add a passage in the *Second Commentary on the Psalms*, which seems to imply that God's prescience has such a certain knowledge of damnation that the actual precognition is said to reprobate man.[12]

Luther's version of the New Testament translates the Vulgate's *praescire* and *predestinare* in Rom. 8:29f. by the German verbs *versehen* and *verordnen* respectively.[13] The thought of God's foreknowledge is so close to the idea of predestination that the former in practice includes the latter.

This is obvious in the famous *Preface to Romans*. [14] Romans 9–11 deals, in Luther's words, with "der ewigen versehung Gottes". But that which is described is the divine predestination. There is a remarkable parallel between the positive and the negative effects resulting from God's "prescience". This is the original source of faith and the accompanying liberation from sin, but it is even the source of nonbelief and consequent denial of redemption. If we assume that Luther took it for granted that freedom from sin involves redemption and persistence in sin implies damnation, we here encounter a theory of predestination which is

---

[10] *Ib.* 387.24ff.: "Ergo in veritatem promittentis Dei audacter ruat se transferat de prescientia terrentis Dei, et salvus et electus erit." Cf. further *ib.* 404.9ff.

[11] I would emphasize the judgement in K. Holl (1923)148: "Luther hat sich in der Römervorlesung zur strengen paulinischen Auffassung der Prädestination als vollkommen freier Wahl Gottes durchgearbeitet". Cf. *ib.* 45 n. 2: "Ausgesprochenermassen vertreten hat Luther die Lehre von der Alleinwirksamkeit Gottes erst seit der Römervorlesung." Cf. also E. Seeberg (1929)169.

[12] WA 5.385.33ff. (*Operationes in Psalmos.* 1519–21): "Ita mitius patitur ab hominibus, mundo, carne quam a daemonibus, qui peccatis, morte et inferno intentatis premunt, Mitius in passionibus sensualibus quam conscientiae pavoribus et confusionibus, Mitius propter satisfactionem, pro peccatis et reconciliationem dei speratam quam propter *aeternam et immobilem praescientiam dei reprobantem.*" For the anguish of predestination in *Operationes* see further *ib.* 172.1ff., 397.35ff., *ib.* 428.9ff., *ib.* 622.24ff.

[13] WADB 7.54 (*Das Neue Testament.* 1522)

[14] *Ib.* 22.26ff.: "Am neunden, zehenden und eylfften Capitel leret er von der ewigen *versehung* Gottis, da her es *ursprunglich* fleust, wer gleuben odder nicht glewben soll, von sunden los odder nicht los werden kan, da mit es yhe gar aus unsern henden genomen, und *alleyn ynn Gottis hand* gestellet sey, das wyr frum werden." Cf. also the following

conditional not upon any human quality but on God alone. Considering the rejection, this could be described as *reprobation*$_2$ (4.1.2.): Non-election to a share in the faith and the justification. However, it is obviously possible to see here a stark conception of reprobation, which derives the exclusion from grace from a direct decree of will on the part of God, which we have described as *reprobation*$_3$ (4.1.2.). In such a case Luther would be reaching conclusions about the rejection which exceed the thought of Augustine and come close to the tenets of Calvin! Hitherto we have illustrated the theoretical significance of the doctrine of double election. Later, we shall discuss the advice which Luther gives concerning its practical usage (4.5.1.1.).

2. In his book *On Free Will* in 1524 Erasmus maintained that the Christian's prime task is to comprehend God's mercy and infinite grace. The believer must not, according to him, in irreligious curiosity penetrate the profound, not to say superfluous, question of how God's prescience is compatible with man's freedom of action.[15] Luther directly contradicts Erasmus, saying:

sentence: "Aber nu Gott gewis ist, das yhm *seyn versehen* nicht feylet, noch ymand yhm weren kan, haben wyr noch hoffnung widder die sunde." The same text is reprinted in the Luther Bible in 1546, *ib.* 23.26ff. A similar train of thought is to be found in WA 10.I.1.672.11ff. (*Kirchenpostille.* 1522): "Item, das Euangelium leret, wie *gottis vorsehung* ewiglich gewiss sey. Sso leren sie, das sie stehe auff dem freyen willen und sey ungewiss. Und kurtzlich, gott und seynen namen bekennen sie, aber alles, was gott ordenett, will, thutt, setzt und macht, das tzureyssen sie, vortilgen und vordamnen es als die hohist ketzerey,..." It is noteworthy that *gottis vorsehung* is described with several verbs stressing God's initiative and exclusive work. In the letter to Hans v. Rechenberg in 1522 we have the same terminology and thought. The phrase "die gottliche fursehung und erwelung von ewickeytt" (WA 10.II.325.25f.) can best be interpreted as a hendiadys. The same applies to the exegesis of 2. Pet 1:10 in WA 14.22.13ff. (1523–24): "*Die erwelung und ewige versehung* Gottes ist zwar fur sich selb fest gnug, das man nicht feste darff machen." Concerning reprobation in the thought of Augustine and Calvin, see A. Adam (1968)347, F. Wendel, *Calvin*[4] (1972)280f., and W. A. Hauck, *Die Erwählten* (1950) *passim*. Cf. further WA 14.636.13ff. (*Deuteronomion Mosi cum annotationibus.* 1525); WA 18.618.13ff. (*De servo arbitrio.* 1525) quoted in 4.2.1 n. 2; *ib.* 723.34ff.; WA 19.552.16ff. (*Vier tröstliche Psalmen an die Königin zu Ungarn.* 1526); WAB 6.86.1ff. (1531); WAB 11.166.14ff. (1545).

[15] *De libero arbitrio* I.a.8: "Haec, inquam, tenere meo iudicio satis erat ad Christianam pietatem nec erat irreligiosa curiositate irrumpendum ad illa retrusa, nec dicam supervacanea, an deus contingenter praesciat aliquid,..."

An instructive exposition of Erasmus' position is given in Swedish by R. Bring, *Erasmus av Rotterdam och hans förhållande till Luthers reformation* (In: *Kristendomstolkningar* 1950)170ff. E. W. Kohls, *Luther oder Erasmus* I (1972) presents an extensive survey of both the primary material and the secondary literature. The history of thought concerning the freedom of will among the Humanists and their influence on Erasmus and Luther is discussed in B. Lohse, *Marginalien zum Streit zwischen Erasmus und Luther*, L 46 (1975)5ff.

"Est itaque et hoc imprimis necessarium et salutare Christiano, nosse, quod Deus nihil praescit contingenter, sed quod omnia incommutabili et aeterna infallibilique voluntate et praevidet et proponit et facit."[16]

This divine foreknowledge makes God's word and promise of salvation firm and secure. He who doubts that God pre-ordains and comprehends all things will inevitably find it difficult to believe in His promises and put his trust in them. One must be sure that He—since He promises—knows, can and will stand by His word.[17]

Erasmus would interpret the example of Judas with the help of the scholastic concept of the unconditional necessity (*necessitas consequentis*): with reference to God's infallible prescience and immutable will Judas was bound to betray Christ. But Erasmus also speculates on the conditional necessity (*necessitas consequentiae*): Judas could have changed his mind, which God could also have foreseen. The necessity is prompted by what Judas freely desired.[18] Luther emphatically maintains that the difference between the absolute necessity and the conditional necessity is a mere play on words. If God pre-ordained that Judas would be a traitor then Judas had to be a traitor. Neither Judas nor any other created being was capable of taking a different course of action or of changing his intention. This intention was

---

[16] WA 18.615.12ff. (*De servo arbitrio.* 1525) Cf. *ib.* 614.27ff.: "Altera pars summae Christianiae est Nosse, an Deus contingenter aliquid praesciat et an omnia faciamus necessitate." Cf *ib.* 614.39ff.

[17] *Ib.* 619.1ff.: "Si enim dubitas aut contemnis nosse, quod Deus omnia non contingenter sed necessario et immutabiliter praesciat et velit, quomodo poteris promissionibus credere, certo fidere et niti? Cum enim promittit, certum oportet te esse, quod sciat, possit et velit praestare, quod promittit. Alioqui eum non veracem nec fidelem aestimabis, quae est incredulitas et summa impietas et negatio Dei altissimi. At quo modo certus et securus eris? nisi scieris illum, certo et infallibiliter et immutabiliter ac necessario scire et velle et facturum esse, quod promittit." Cf. *ib.* 716.5ff.

[18] *De libero arbitrio* III.a.9: "Sed dixerit aliquis: Interim duplici nomine necessitas est in rerum eventis, quod nec praescientia dei falli possit nec voluntas impediri . . . Praesciebat deus et, quod praesciebat, aliquo modo volebat fore, ut Iudas proderet dominum. Itaque si spectes dei praescientiam infallibilem et voluntatem immutabilem, necessario eventurum est, ut Iudas prodat dominum, et tamen Iudas poterat mutare voluntatem suam aut certe poterat non suscipere voluntatem impiam. Dices: Quid se mutasset? Non fuisset falsa dei praescientia nec impedita voluntas, cum hoc ipsum praesciturus fuerit ac voliturus, quod esset mutaturus voluntatem. In his qui rem scholastica subtilitate discutiunt, recipiunt necessitatem consequentiae, consequentis necessitatem reiciunt."
Cf. also Luther's interpretation of this distinction between *necessitas consequentis (absoluta)* and *necessitas consequentiae (conditionalis)* WA 18.616.13ff; *ib.* 715.1ff. See further H. McSorley (1969)310ff. for a critical discussion.

4.2.2.

God's handiwork, since He moved with His omnipotence as He moves all other things.[19] When Erasmus would ascribe the cause both to God and to man Luther makes God the sole cause.

Human foreknowledge can fall short and go astray. But this is not the case with God. "De praescientia Dei disputamus; huic nisi dederis *necessarium effectum* praesciti, fidem et timorem Dei abstulisti, promissiones et minas divinas omnes labefecisti atque adeo ipsam divinitatem negasti."[20] Luther's reasoning leads to the conclusion that God's prescience is explicitly regarded as a *causa* which initiates an inevitable *effectus*, considering that which is fore-ordained. Luther cancels the entire question of what God does and what man does since he allows the divine prescience to be the cause of all that happens.[21] In fact, it seems to be a much more lucid and consistent idea of reason, that God's inscrutable prescience inevitably comes to pass with unconditional necessity than to construct a foreknowledge which is sometimes absolute and sometimes conditional.[22] Indeed, it is impossible to reconcile the doctrines of God's *praescientia* and man's *libertas*. When Luther seeks to propagate the first, the second falls.[23]

In the conclusion of this book the apposition of *praescit/praeordinat* and *praescientia/praedestinatio* re-appears. Each of these word pairs could be interpreted as a hendiadys. God's foreknowledge and predetermination are so inseparably fused that any judgement of the one term also applies to the other. This is Luther's concept of "God the Father, Almighty". The consequence is that he must deny man's free will.[24]

3. In the *Large Genesis Lecture* (Gen. 26:9) we find the same apposition of *praescientia* and *praedestinatio*, since the interpreter seeks to illustrate the background of the Incarnation. When God becomes man this involves a manifestation of that which He foresaw and pre-ordained.

---

[19] *Ib.* 715.18ff.: "Si praescivit Deus, Iudam fore proditorem, necessario Iudas fiebat proditor nec erat in manu Iudae aut ullius creaturae, aliter facere aut voluntatem mutare, licet id fecerit volendo non coactus, sed velle illud erat opus Dei, quod omnipotentia sua movebat sicut et omnia alia."
[20] *Ib.* 716.13ff.
[21] Cf. *ib.* 716.22ff.: "Ita Dei voluntas, quoniam est caussa principalis omnium, quae fiunt, videtur necessitatem nostrae voluntati inducere."
[22] *Ib.* 717.22ff.: "Nec est quaestio difficilis, imo nihil facilius etiam communi sensu, quam hanc sequelam esse certam, solidam, veram: Si Deus praescit, necessario fit, ubi hoc *ex scripturis* praesuppositum fuerit, quod Deus neque errat neque fallitur."
[23] *Ib.*717.25ff.
[24] *Ib.*786.3ff. Cf. *ib.* 618.13ff., *ib.* 723.34ff. Cf. G. Rost (1966)67.

Prescience and predetermination are one.[25] The exposition of Gen. 43:1-5 stresses that man may not scrutinize the "providentia Dei et necessitate praescientiae Divinae" but must adhere to the commandments and promises of God, and use creation for the maintenance of life. Speculations on such matters are not fitting. Nor is it necessary to know, "quod apud Deum necessarium est".[26] God will inevitably arrange that which He knew beforehand to come to pass. This reasoning is highly reminiscent of that found in *De Servo Arbitrio*. When *praescientia Dei* confers an absolute necessity on events we can also speak of a fixed connection between God's foreknowledge and the events predicted, be it for salvation or for damnation.[27]

4.2.3. God's Counsel and Will

1. In order to arrive at a relation between the divine prescience and counsel we can begin in *Dictata* with the paraphrase of Ps. 91:6 (Vulgate). This says that God's works are great in themselves, and that they will be great, when they are so acknowledged, which comes to pass through the Holy Spirit. "Sic etiam profunde facte sunt eodem modo: 'nimis profundae factae sunt' inscrutabiles carnali homini et humano sensui 'cogitationes tuae' providentia tua cuncta gubernans, consilia super salute generis humani."[1] To the expression "your thoughts" is

---

[25] WA 43.459.21ff. (*Vorlesung über 1. Mose.* 1535-45): "Sic enim suam voluntatem et consilium proposuit: Ego tibi praescientiam et praedestinationem egregie manifestabo, sed non ista via rationis et sapientiae carnalis, sicut tu imaginaris." Cf. WA 42.296.9ff; WA 44.528.8ff.

[26] *Ib.* 38ff: "Haec opponenda sunt illis qui disputant de providentia Dei et necessitate praescientiae Divinae, cum tamen nihil ad eos pertineant, neque enim ipsis hoc est necessarium, quod apud Deum necessarium est, sed promissiones et praecepta Dei amplecti debebant et uti creaturis conditis ad huius vitae conservationem,..."

[27] When Th. Harnack I (1927)91 rejects the thought that God's precognition is "eine bestimmende, kausierende Tätigkeit" he is right concerning human sin and guilt. But in other cases I must agree with E. Seeberg (1929)169f.: "Dem Gedanken Luthers, dass Präszienz und Prädestination bei Gott identisch sind, wodurch die feige Entkräftigung der Prädestination durch die Präszienz abgeschnitten wird, entspricht eine Deutung der Allmacht, welche die Allmacht in die unmittelbare Nähe der absoluten Lebendigkeit Gottes rückt." FC (Ep 11, SD 11) distinguishes between *praescientia* and *praedestinatio* in the same terms as Th. Harnack above. Thus, FC can maintain God's precognition of the evil in man without making God's predetermination the cause of this evil (BSLK 817 and 1065f.)

[1] WA 4.79.8ff. (*Dictata super Psalterium.* 1513-15). Quoted in 4.3.3 n. 3. According to Luther the whole psalm concerns "Confessio exultabunda Christi super providentia et operibus dei". (*ib.* 78.18f.). Cf also *ib.* 82.6ff., *ib.*234.13ff.

4.2.3.

added *firstly* God's *providentia*. In the manner described in the previous section (4.2.2) the divine *providentia* is not only cognitive but also causative. This is clearly shown here by the fact that this *providentia* is characterized as governing (*gubernans*) all things (*cuncta*). *Secondly*, God's counsel is related, in terms of the *salvation* of the human race, to this divine providence. In His providence God foresees and governs all accidental events. This also applies to His decision to redeem mankind. God's *consilia* are the active cause of redemption.

Luther goes on to mention in brief "consiliis et iudiciis dei profundis, que predestinationis et reprobationis dicuntur".[2] In this context the actual term *predestinatio* is used to describe the significance of the *consilia dei*, which confirms our findings in the exposition of the same psalm. Nevertheless an analogous description of *damnation* is given. Just as the divine counsel implies predestination the divine judgement means reprobation for the sinner.

In the introduction to the detailed interpretation of Rom. 8:28 he says that this verse deals with "materia predestinationis et electionis".[3] According to Luther, Paul's words mean that the salvation of the elect is not contingent but by necessity.[4] This election is conditional solely upon the "electione mera et immutabili voluntate sua".[5] The connection between the divine will and predetermination is so obvious to Luther that without further ado he uses the expression "predestinationis voluntas".[6] God's predetermination and election are the sole cause of *salvation*. This will with regard to the predestination is ineluctable.

We find evidence for the theory that Luther interprets the *rejection* as a *negative* parallel to salvation in the exegesis of Rom. 11:4. There he first explains how the faithful remnant remained in Israel. The fact that these people were left behind depended not on them but on God who allowed them to stay. Then Luther reflects on those who defected: "Quin etiam eodem verbo subindicat *seipsum esse authorem reprobationis aliorum.*" Then he strongly stresses God's initiative and

---

[2] *Ib.* 81.20f. (quoted in 4.3.3 n. 3).

[3] WA 56.381.17 (*Rom.* 1515–16)

[4] *Ib.* 381.27ff.: "Nunc autem, cum dicit: 'Quis Accusabit? Quis condemnabit? Quis separabit?' ostendit, quam non contingenter, Sed necessario salventur electi." Cf. further *ib.* 382.21ff., *ib.* 383.4ff.

[5] *Ib.* 382.3f. Cf. *ib.* 309.17ff.: "Cum infirmi essemus secundum tempus, licet iam coram Deo essemus in predestinatione Iusti. Quia in predestinatione Dei omnia facta iam sunt, que in rebus adhuc futura sunt."

[6] *Ib.* 382.8f. Cf. *ib.* 384.1ff.: "'Propositum' enim hic Dei predestinatio seu libera electio et deliberatio seu consilium dicitur."

work in the rejection: "ego reliqui, qui et idem abstuli".[7] Luther uses the verb *subindicat* to emphasize that he is reaching conclusions from a mere suggestion. According to this interpretation, God in His grace and blessing did not destine these people to remain behind. If the consequent rejection involves eternal punishment the phenomenon designated *reprobatio₂* (4.1.2.) is here present. If the rejection here is not merely the absence of election for salvation but explicit election for damnation we have *reprobatio₃*.

In the second *Lecture on the Psalms* on Ps. 5:12 (Vulgate) we find deterministic arguments. The purpose is to exhort to refrain from brooding on the eternal predetermination with regard to the double outcome. "We take wives, build houses, plant vineyards, buy possessions, and no one here first asks (*disputat*) whether or not it is *predestined,* that the wife will be chaste or a whore, that the house will catch fire or stand firm, that possessions will be destroyed or will endure. In brief, we begin and persist in all our deeds, especially our sins, with confidence, and we do not worry about God's *predestination* with them. In these things it is sufficient that *His counsel* transcends our daring. No one here is such that he does not ponder in advance, bother, worry concerning his capacity to achieve his ends before he scrutinizes and asks about *predestination*... Is it not for the same reasons that a leaf does not fall from the tree to the ground without *His will,* and that your soul is not redeemed without *His counsel?* Not a hair on your head grows without *His counsel,* nor do you eat bread, nor do you drink (without His counsel)."[8] Luther seems to start from the presumption that human actions and sufferings are in essence determined by the *consilium dei.*[9] For only if this circumstance is self-evident can it be a convincing

[7] Ib. 429.7ff. Cf. the hardening of the heart of Pharaoh in *ib.* 404.9ff. (quoted in 3.6 n. 5). Early in the material we find the thought that God is hewing with a dull ax (*sc.* the sinful man). Consequently, the result is very poor, WA 1.357.36ff. (*Disputatio Heidelbergiae habita.* 1518)

[8] WA 5.174.4ff. (*Operationes in Psalmos.* 1519–21). G. Rost (1966)68f. has noticed this passage. Cf. A. Gyllenkrok (1952)36, W. Joest (1967)310.

[9] Cf. WA 6.249.19ff.: "Wan nu der bosse geist solchen glaubenn, gottis ehre unnd gottis dienst gewar wirt, so tobet er und hebt an die vorfolgung, greifft an leyb, gut, ehre und leben, treibet auff uns kranckheit, armut, schande und sterben, das *got alsso vorhengt und vorordnet*". Later Luther sees God as the cause of evil: "dann es ist ein gross dinck, eine gute zuvorsicht zu got erhalten, ob er schon den tod, schmach, ungesuntheit, armut, zufuget,..." (*ib.* 249.24ff.). We can observe this point of view in Luther's concrete counseling, of people facing calamities and sudden death. "Aber nu sich ynn des leider die sache *durch Gottes gewalt und versehung* also gekeret hat, das der Turcke diesen jamer und elend hat angericht und das edle junge blut König Ludwig, E. K. M. liebes gemalh, nyddergeschlagen, hat sich mein furnemen auch mussen umbkeren"; WA 19.552.16ff. (*Vier tröstliche Psalmen an die Königin zu Ungarn.* 1526). Cf also *ib.* 553.2ff.

argument in this context. Concerning our decisions or deeds in our daily life we do not in fact speculate on predestination. Would not human beings have the same attitude with regard to the eternal life, especially as we have a specific commandment from God to trust in Christ and not to usurp knowledge of the divine counsel?

This causative aspect of God's counsel and will—with regard to both blessing and damnation—is to be found in Luther's *Sermons on Genesis* from the 1520's. The accounts of Jacob and Esau show, according to Luther, that their circumstances were conditional upon a previous decision in heaven which must later be enacted on earth.[10] Since God is the determining power in existence, and His counsels are wonderful, the devil, according to the printed text of the *Exodus Sermons*, is compelled to promote God's intentions.[11] Consequently the monism which is implicit in the doctrine of the divine omnipotence (3.7.) recurs here.

2. At the beginning of *The Bondage of the Will* Erasmus is criticized for being unduly conciliatory in seeking to avoid unrest and disputes. In Luther's view it is more important to tolerate temporal evil than to be afflicted by the evil which is eternal. "For the operations of God are not childish or bourgeois or human, but divine and exceeding human grasp. But you do not seem to see that these tumults and divisions are marching through the world by the counsel and operation of God (divino consilio et opere), and you are afraid lest the heavens should fall."[12] The concept of *consilium* takes priority over the events occurring in the world. Thus God's will has also predetermined the evil which comes to pass.

Therefore, Luther cannot allow human judgement or the idea of peace to be decisive. The consequence would be that God's Word was dependent on human whims and human authority. "Whereas Scripture says on the contrary that all things stand or fall by the choice and authority of God (arbitrio Dei et auctoritate), and all the earth should

---

[10] WA 14.325.15ff. (*Predigten über das erste Buch Mose. 1523/24*): "Sed quod minor praesit maiori, hoc est dei opus. Ist aber eins die art operum dei. *Sic est conclusum in celo*, et non aliter ibit, quam iis duobus pueris: quidam supplantant, quidam supplantantur, quidam divites, quidam pauperes, non in bonis, sed in spiritualibus rebus." Cf. WA 10.III.108.12ff. (*Pred. 1522*), WA 12.262.8ff. (*Epistel S. Petri gepredigt und ausgeleget. Erste Bearbeitung. 1523*).

[11] WA 16.204.19ff. (*Predigten über das 2. Buch Mose. 1524–27, Dr*): "Der Teufel ist ein Gott und Fürst der Welt, darümb so ist er mechtig und gewaltig, er kan zu weilen helffen, und Gott verhengts also, denn *Gottes Ratschlege* sind wünderbarlich,...." Cf. the same thought in n. 9 above.

[12] WA 18.627.18ff. (*De servo arbitrio. 1525*), LW 33.54. Cf also WA 18.631.36f.: "quid non indignationis ostendis erga Deum, quod talis iudicii sui consilium et ratione, non licet videre?"

keep silence before the Lord.''[13] The believer may not yield, even if the ungodly take offence and reason raises objections. Instead, we must implore the divine majesty in its awe-inspiring miracles and incomprehensible judgements, saying: Thy will be done on earth as it is in heaven.[14] So the interpretation of Jacob and Esau is similar here.

Erasmus had laconically rejected these examples, asserting that they were not explicitly concerned with the salvation of man.[15] At first Luther agrees. He stresses, however, the point which Erasmus overlooked: God's will decided before Jacob and Esau were born which destiny was to be theirs.[16] The divine counsel alone, and not human merits by means of free will, brought blessing and damnation. Luther holds that these effects concerned not only secular dominion but also spiritual. Thus these examples are relevant for the eternal kingdom and the eternal rejection.[17]

In his discussion of Ez. 33:11 (and 18:23, 32) Luther faces the problem of why some people are touched by the Law of God and others ignore it. This raises the question "de occulta illa et metuenda voluntate Dei ordinantis *suo consilio*, quos et quales praedicatae et oblatae misericordiae capaces et participes esse velit"[18]. As regards the *positive* election, the participation in God's eternal mercy, which is essential for salvation, God makes the decision *sua sponte*. The *negative* side would be that God did not pre-ordain certain individuals to share in His grace, so that they remain in sin and are condemned. We called this Augustinian view *reprobatio₂*.

Nevertheless Luther is not content with this. He says explicitly that God seeks the death of the sinner through His inscrutable will.[19] This is concerned with predestination. According to Luther, Christ scandalizes those who by "secreta illa voluntate maiestatis vel relicti vel indurati".

---

[13] *Ib.* 631.16ff., LW 33.60. We find this inclusive *omnia* in other important passages: WA 18.716.22f., *ib.* 786.3ff.

[14] *Ib.* 718.1ff.: "Hic igitur locus, hic tempus est, non Coricios illos specus sed veram maiestatem in metuendis mirabilibus et iudiciis suis incomprehensibilibus adorandi et dicendi: Fiat voluntas tua sicut in coelo et in terra."

[15] *De libero arbitrio* III.a.11: "Sed haec vox non proprie pertinet ad hominis salutem; potest enim deus velle, ut homo velit nolit servus sit aut pauper, ut tamen non reiciatur ab aeterna salute."

[16] WA 18.723.33ff.: "Quid liberum arbitrium iuvit Iacob? Quid obfuit Esau? cum iam praescientia et destinatione Dei uterque nondum natus nihilque operatus definitus esset, qualia esset recepturus, scilicet ut ille serviret, hic dominaretur."

[17] *Ib.* 724.3ff. From this exposition R. Hermann (1967)166f. discusses the question of *predestinatio gemina* .

[18] WA 18. 684.32ff., cf. *ib.* 689.18ff., *ib.* 690.9ff., *ib.* 20ff.

[19] *Ib.* 685.28f., cf. *ib.* 21ff. See further 3.5 n. 8 above.

4.2.3.

This means that they do not accept redemption in time.[20] Thus God's counsel leads to the fixation of temporal wickedness into something eternally evil. The hardening of heart becomes the rejection. Therefore Luther, like Calvin, seems to assume a special decree of reprobation when he asserts: "voluntas maiestatis *ex proposito* aliquos relinquat et reprobet, ut pereant".[21] This harsh theory of damnation has been designated *reprobatio₃*.

Indeed there is such an explicit expression thereof only in *The Bondage of the Will*. But above we have seen that this accentuated concept of rejection may be indicated both in the *Lecture on Romans* and the *Preface to Romans* in the translation of the New Testament. There are no indications that Luther rejected his own arguments used in the attack on Erasmus. Luther does indeed emphatically contradict Erasmus' interpretation of Ex. 4:21, stressing God as the driving force behind the hardening of heart.[22] Furthermore, he finds that Erasmus' figurative interpretation leads to at least as great difficulties as his own literal

---

[20] WA 18.689.28ff.

[21] *Ib.* 33f. In WA 56.381.12ff. "propositum Dei" was the cause of salvation. Here "ex proposito" is connected with reprobation. So we can see a parallel between the positive and the negative side of God's predetermination. See also the passage in WA 18.712.19ff. (n. 28 below). Concerning Calvin's doctrin of a *decretum reprobationis* see *e.g.* F. Wendel (1972)280f. where he explicitly refers to *De servo arbitrio*, WA 18.712f. as an interesting parallel.

The general characterization in B. Lohse, *A Short History of Christian Doctrine* (1966)187 seems to be quite right: "It used to be common to regard Calvin's teaching of the double predestination as one of his special peculiarities. Yet there can be no doubt that Luther, too, hewed a strict line with regard to predestination. At just this point both have in common an important feature. For both, the doctrine of predestination does not represent the focal point with reference to which all else is developed; rather, this doctrine is coordinated with the doctrine of justification and can be properly evaluated only within the framework of such coordination."

If there is a significant difference between Luther and Calvin concerning the twofold predestination this difference might—to a certain extent—lie in the question whether the reprobation of the predestination is considered in *a context of Supralapsarism, or of Infralapsarism*. We can establish that Luther tends to accept the latter view (n. 29–31), although he does not totally avoid the former conception (n. 28). As regards Calvin, he also seems to adopt a similar dualism. He can state that man sins "even as *God ordained* that he should, but he stumbles on account of *his depravity*...", F. Wendel (1972)281. Judging by suggestions in current literature on Calvin scholars are more prone to characterize Calvin's position as more Supralapsaristic than that of Luther, cf. *e.g.* A. Adam (1968)347.

Interestingly enough, in discussions with the Lutherans *the school of Calvin* finds arguments for its own doctrine in Luther's *The Bondage of the Will* according to G. Adam, *Der Streit um die Prädestination im ausgehenden 16. Jahrhundert.* (1970)46: "In dieser Theologie, die im ganzen den Eindruck einer wohlausgewogenen Vernünftigkeit vermittelt,

exposition.[23] He denies that God "has not determined by *his certain election* who are to be *saved* and who *damned*, but after offering to all men generally the forebearance that tolerates and hardens, then the mercy that corrects and punishes, he has left it to them to decide whether they want to be saved or damned".[24]

But Luther like Augustine, Biel (4.1.2.), and even Calvin assumes man's own sin and guilt. "For although God does not make sin, yet he does not cease to fashion and multiply the nature that has been vitiated by sin through the withdrawal of the Spirit, as a woodcarver might make statues out of rotten wood."[25] This argument is also illustrated by the pictures of the horseman riding a lame mount, and the timberman who chops with a blunt axe.[26] By his goading omnipotence, God is the cause of the hardness of heart and the rejection. But by his wilful rejection of God man himself carries the responsibility.[27]

One could say that God, by His decision not to amend the selfishness of human kind, is an accomplice in sin. One could also ask why God does not eliminate sin. But we are given no answer, since this is one of "the secrets of his majesty, where his judgements are incomprehensible". The fall and original sin could be included too. Luther retorts:

"The same must be said to those who ask *why he permitted Adam to fall*, and *why he creates us all infected with the same sin*, when he

---

ist die Berufung auf Luther nahezu konstitutiv. Es ist ja eines der theologiegeschichtlich interessantesten. um nicht zu sagen überraschendsten Phänomene, dass man sich im ausgehenden 16. Jahrhundert (erstmals wird dies Phänomen im Strassburger Streit zwischen Zanchi und Marbach in aller Öffentlichkeit sichtbar und greifbar) in der Prädestinationslehre reformierterseits auf Luther berief und—nicht nur im übertragenen Sinne, sondern tatsächlich—*den Lutheranern De servo arbitrio unter die Nase hielt, um zu zeigen, dass die eigentlichen theologisch legitimen Nachfolger Luthers die reformierten Theologen seien.* In diesem Sinne veranstaltet Kimedoncius im Jahre 1591 in Neustadt eine Ausgabe von Luthers De servo arbitrio. In diesem Sinne schloss Beza seine erste Entgegnung auf Andreäs 'Acta Colloquij Mompelgartense... 1587' hinsichtlich der Prädestinationslehre ausschliesslich mit recht ausführlichen Zitaten aus Luthers De servo arbitrio." See also J. Moltmann, *Prädestination und Perseverenz* (1961)81ff.

[22] WA 18.702.1ff. *Voluntas dei* is very closely related to *potentia dei* according to *ib.* 615.33ff.: "Voluntas enim Dei efficax est, quae impediri non potest, cum sit naturalis ipsa potentia Dei, Deinde sapiens, ut falli non possit."

[23] *Ib.* 705.18ff.

[24] *Ib.* 706.16ff., LW 33.171.

[25] WA 18.708.31ff., LW 33.174f. Cf. WA 18.710.31ff. See 3.6.2 above. See also F. Wendel (1972)281f.

[26] WA 18.709.21ff. Cf. also 3.6.2 n. 11 above.

[27] WA 18.711.27ff. (quoted in 3.6.2 n. 15 above).

could either have preserved him or created us from another stock or from a seed which he had first purged. He is God, and for his will there is no cause or reason that can be laid down as a rule or measure for it, since there is nothing equal or superior to it, but it is itself the rule of all things."[28]

Luther can go so far in taking a Supralapsaristic position. But he never pursues the argument to its last conclusion, that God originally created or promoted sin.[29]

Luther occasionally refrains from mentioning this fundamental exception in God's omnipotence. In consequence, his statements seem to be more monistic than they really are. In general terms Luther can depict God's will as "caussa principalis omnium, quae fiunt".[30] Yet, the implicit prerequisite for these ideas is that originally God neither wanted nor enacted sin. With a few exceptions, as the quotation above (n. 28), Luther is reflecting from an Infralapsaristic point of view.

An adequate account of the course of events in reprobation consists therefore in the statement that "God *by his own sheer will* should abandon, harden, and damn men".[31] Grace has no point of contact with human merits. But damnation afflicts mankind by reason of sin and guilt (*reprobation₁*). As a result no complete parallel exists between predestination and reprobation. Only insofar as we start from the fact that man is a sinner there is an analogy between the positive and the negative outcome. Purely of His own will God elects certain people and gives them grace in Jesus Christ. He abandons and hardens the hearts of others, so that they succumb to damnation because of their own guilt (*reprobation₂*). This comes to pass by a special decree of His will (*reprobation₃*).

3. We have cause to return to detailed discussions of the theory of predestination, not least in the large *Genesis Lecture* (the exegesis of Gen. 26:9). Luther takes the opportunity to criticize the fatalism which

[28] WA 18.712.19ff., LW 33.180f. See further the passages in 4.2.6 n. 10 below. Cf. WA 18.549.35ff. (*Sendschreiben an die Christen zu Antwerpen.* 1525), WA 24.97.3ff. (*In Genesin Declamationes.* 1527), WA 39.II.361.3ff. = Drews 858 (*Die Promotionsdisputation von Petrus Hegemon.* 1545). For similar thoughts in Calvin, see F. Wendel (1972)281.
[29] See further P. Althaus (1963)106f., H-M. Barth (1967)196ff.
[30] WA 18.716.18ff.
[31] *Ib.* 719.4ff., LW 33.190. Thus far, I would confirm the words in W. Joest (1967) 309f.: "Er (*sc.* Luther) hat die doppelte Praedestination vertreten, aber er hat sie nicht supralapsarisch begründet. Gott kann aufgrund der *faktisch* gewordenen Sünde auch verwerfen, weil seine Gnadenwahl frei ist. Er bringt nicht die Sünde erst herein, um auch verwerfen zu können." But cf. also n. 28!

asserts that it makes no difference how you live, act, or believe. If I am predestined I shall be saved whether I live virtuously or not.[32]

There is a direct reference to *The Bondage of the Will*, followed by an exposition of the distinction between *deus absconditus* and *deus revelatus*.[33] Obviously there is here no word of criticism of the doctrine of double predestination.[34] Luther seems in his lecture to make the reference in order to remind those who yearn for a more detailed account. Indeed, we do not know in detail how the *deus absconditus* has predetermined. Nevertheless, we know that events are ordained by "sua decreta et mysteria in abscondito". The term *decretum* here refers to the decision which God issues in His authority concerning mankind. In what follows "arcana Dei consilia" is used as a synonym.[35]

It is beyond doubt that Luther's aim is to refute a false conclusion from determinism, namely: If something is predetermined, then it will happen automatically so to speak.[36] In contrast, he stresses the belief in Christ and the use of the Word and the Sacraments. Nonetheless, the main theme of *De servo arbitrio* is confirmed: "esse omnia absoluta et necessaria".[37] Indeed, this concept of predestination is only developed in terms of its *positive* consequences for salvation and the certainty of redemption. The fact that predestination to eternal damnation is not mentioned in this context in no wise justifies us in concluding that Luther would deny it.

Other passages in the same *Lecture on Genesis* associate God's determining counsel with the *negative* idea of punishment and damnation. The interpretation of Gen. 15:13–21 says that God is long-suffering and patient and does not immediately punish the wrongdoers. But they do not

---

[32] WA 43.457.35ff. (*Vorlesung über 1. Mose.* 1535–45), LW 5.38ff. Several scholars have discussed this passage, *e.g.* Th. Harnack I (1927)175ff., R. Seeberg (1917)153, J. v. Walter (1940)128f., H. Bandt (1958)181, G. Rost (1966)73ff., *ib.* 85f. After Luther's death this material was adduced by many Lutheran theologians, see further G. Adam (1970)93.

[33] WA 43.458.35ff. Cf. also WAB 9.627.36ff. (1542) quoted in 4.3.2 n. 14.

[34] We can prove Luther's affirmative attitude to *De servo arbitrio* with WAB 8.99.5ff. (1537).

[35] WA 43.460.26, *ib.* 462.26. Cf. WA 44.65.22ff.

[36] WA 43.457.33ff., *ib.* 460.3ff., *ib.* 605.40ff., WA 44.78.6f.

[37] WA 43.463.5f. (quoted in 4.3.2 n. 16) Cf. WA 43.461.31ff. (quoted in 4.2.4 n. 15). Th. Harnack I (1927)176 correctly maintains that Luther does not deny the Necessitarian concept. But Harnack is wrong (*ib.* 179) in claiming that in later years Luther abandoned the double doctrine of predestination from *The Bondage of the Will*. I agree with the interpretation in G. Rost (1966)73ff., *ib.* 85f. The passage in WAB 9.627.33ff. (1542) is also relevant (quoted in 4.3.2 n. 14). Cf. also WA 44.77.39ff.: "Verum quidem est, eventurum, quicquid est praefinitum: sed illud addendum est, tibi id esse ignotum."

therefore escape scotfree. The time is determined, when they will be captured and duly punished for their evil deeds. St Peter says that the ungodly are spared until the Day of Judgement (2 Pet. 3:7); St Paul teaches that the punishment is postponed according to this counsel (*hoc consilio*), so that God can give scope for penance (Rom. 2:4).[38] This could perhaps be interpreted as meaning that we here have a case of *reprobation₃*: God's will has pre-ordained that some will not be granted mercy but wrath, as they are abandoned to their sin until the Day of Judgement. Anyway, in my opinion, the aging Luther did not renege on his previous teaching of double predestination. Indeed, it is more true to say that the accent shifted because of the new polemical situation which arose.[39]

4. To sum up, I wish to say: My analysis leads me to assume that the theory of the twofold election is implied in Luther's notion of God. To Luther God Himself meant unconditional predetermination.[40] It is not possible to neglect the fact that we here have a theoretical tenet by referring to its practical function, so that we may be critical of the doctrine but positive toward its effect on man.[41] Furthermore, it is difficult to avoid the conclusion that there is a great difference between Luther and some Lutheran theologians who intended to follow him, with regard to the mode of characterizing reprobation. Like Calvin Luther does not hesitate to follow his reasoning to the end, with the result that we find in his works *reprobation₁₋₃* and thus a double predestination doctrine. The *Formula Concordiae* and Lutheran orthodoxy based on this document avoid the extreme consequences of thought of God's omnipotence as they express only *reprobation₁* and a single theory of election.[42]

---

[38] WA 42.577.12ff. Cf. WA 44.67.29ff.: "Tolerat igitur Deus etiam improbos et peccatores ad declarandam immensam suam bonitatem et tolerantiam, sed usque ad illud tempus, quod est destinatum poenae, quando iam impletae sunt iniquitates eorum, da zeucht er die hand ab..."

[39] This is especially stressed in G. Rost (1966)71ff. Scolars in the last century maintained the same theory: J. Müller, *Lutheri de praedestinatione et libero arbitrio doctrina* (1832), J. Lütkens, *Luthers Prädestinationslehre im Zusammenhang mit seiner Lehre vom freien Willen* (1858)84ff., C. E. Luthardt, *Die Lehre vom freien Willen und seinem Verhältnis zur Gnade* (1863)85, *ib.* 135. This is an important argument in H. McSorley (1969)357f.

[40] *Sic* G. Ljunggren (1928)471, E. Seeberg (1929)150. Cf. G. Rost (1966)55ff.

[41] From WA 18.632.27ff. both W. Elert (1931)108 and P. Althaus (1963)245f. conclude that the theoretical doctrine of predestination is not relevant to Luther.

[42] R. Hermann (1967)166: "Das (*sc.* Esau und Jakob in WA 18.724.27ff.) ist eine harte Blockstelle angesichts des lutherischen Bekenntnisses, das eine Prädestination nur zum Guten kennt, so in F.C.XI."

G. Adam (1970)46: "Nun ist zuzugeben, dass die Lutheraner im Verlaufe des 16.

4.2.4. God's Immutability

1. Already in the first *Lecture on the Psalms* we find that Luther is prone to understand the divine counsel as immutable. He writes in a gloss to Ps. 138:4 (Vulgate) that God dealt with His Son according to "eterno consilio", when He was degraded upon the Cross. This is then identified with the divine predestination *vis-à-vis* Christ.[1]

The *Lecture on Romans* (Rom. 8:28) reiterates the element of immutability in the divine election to redemption and salvation. The tenet that the elect are necessarily redeemed is developed in terms of the fixed nature of God's will. Luther uses not only "immutabilis" but also "inflexibilis" and "firma" as appropriate epithets. The famous expression "eterna et fixa Charitas Dei" also occurs here.[2] The creation is "mutabilis". Therefore "immutabilis" may be a synonym for God.[3] In other words, the concept of God implies immutability.

When Luther interprets Rom. 11:29 he has reason to return to these views. God does not change, although human beings do. Therefore the elect are converted and restored by the God, who is steadfast, to the truth of faith.[4] The absolute reliability of the divine promises is dependent on God's immutability.

Material which also indicates the irrevocable rejection can be found in the *Second Lecture on the Psalms*. In Ps. 13:1 we encounter the assertion that the most difficult feat is to suffer "propter aeternam et immobilem

Jahrhunderts sich ohne Zweifel sowohl verbotenus wie auch sachlich von manchen Spitzensätze in Luthers De servo arbitrio entfernt haben, indem eben nur eine Seite des Problems enfaltet wurde: die positive Erwählung." Thus FC in Ep 11 and SD 11 connects predestination only with the election of the children of God, and sees the cause of reprobation in man's sin and guilt, BSLK 817 and 1065f. The responsibility for the unbelief and hardening of hearts lies with man and not with God, BSLK 1076 and 1085ff.

[1] WA 4.433.22ff. (*Dictata super Psalterium.* 1513–15).

[2] WA 56.381.29ff. (*Rom.* 1515–16), cf. also *ib.* 429.2.

[3] *Ib.* 383.4ff. Since God is immutable He rules man and world with an immutable necessity, *ib.* 386.3ff.: "Sed quos Indurat Deus, ii sunt, quibus dat voluntarie velle in peccato esse et manere et diligere iniquitatem. tales enim necessario sunt in peccato necessitate Immutabilitatis, Sed non coactionis."

[4] *Ib.* 440.2ff.: "Quia Nullius meritis neque demeritis mutatur consilium Dei. Non enim penitet eum sui doni et vocationis promisse, Quia illi nunc sunt indigni et vos digni. Non mutatur vobis mutatis, ideo revertentur et adducentur tandem ad veritatem fidei." E. Seeberg (1929)169f. emphasized Luther's thoughts on the immutability of God. Cf. also WA 2.513.5ff. (*In epistolam Pauli ad Galatas commentarius.* 1519): "Nam vere non sunt filii Abrahae nisi promissionis filii. Cum autem divina promissio et praedestinatio fallax non possit esse, sine difficultate et consequentia infallibili erit, ut omnes sint fideles qui promissi sunt, ut sic fides promissorum stet non necessitate operum et fidei illorum, sed firmitate divinae electionis."

praescentiam dei reprobantem".[5] I stress the element of inflexibility, inherent in reprobation, when the properties eternal and immutable are ascribed to the divine prescience.

When Luther is exhorted to draft a comprehensive reply to the papal bull, he touches in *Assertio omnium articulorum* on the relation in principle between God's sovereign omnipotence and man's total dependence thereon. He states categorically that the things and events which concern mankind are neither constant nor permanent. When we look "down" everything seems to be arbitrary and variable. But if we look "up", everything is necessary. For we live, do, suffer all things, not by our own wish but according to the will of God. In this perspective, the idea of human free will is modified. Whereas in truth everything we perceive changes and varies, there is no change or vacillation in God (James 1:17).[6] Again we note that Luther's concept of God, including the divine immutability, is so self-evident that it can be used as a convincing reason in an important theological debate about the view of humanity.

2. In *The Bondage of the Will* the divine immutability is presented as a basic quality of the Godhead. It appears already in the definition of "contingency" as the opposite of the arbitrary and the fortuitous. An immutable, permanent will is one of the attributes of God.[7] One of the essential characteristics of "the three *Parcae*" who are said to control destiny is their immutability. The thought of the heathen poets was here lucid and consistent.[8] Consequently, Luther can reflect on this fundamental divine attribute, both in the Scriptures (James 1:17 above) and in the human reason which is manifested in Vergil *et al.*

The immutability renders *the promises* of the Bible permanent and stable. Therefore the believer can be absolutely safe and sure:

> "For this is the one supreme consolation of Christians in all adversities, to know that *God* does not lie, but *does all things immutably*, and that his will can neither be resisted nor changed nor hindered."[9]

[5] WA 5.385.33ff. (*Operationes in Psalmos.* 1519–21) quoted in 4.2.2 n. 12. Cf. WA 5.618.21ff., *ib.* 622.18f. Concerning the immutable wrath of God cf. also WA 2.137.12ff. (*Ein Sermon von der Betrachtung des heiligen Leidens Christi.* 1519).

[6] WA 7.146.32ff. (1520): "Cessat liberum arbitrium erga deum, quod apparet erga nos et temporalia: illic enim, ut Iacobus ait (1:17), non est transmutatio nec vicissitudinis obumbratio, Hic vero omnia mutantur et variantur."

[7] WA 18.616.7ff. (*De servo arbitrio.* 1525): "Contingenter autem fieri dicitur (ne vocabulis abutamur) latina lingua, non ipsum opus contingens fieri, sed contingente et mutabili voluntate fieri, qualis in Deo non est."

[8] *Ib.* 618.6f.: "Inde finxerunt parcas illas tres, immutabiles, implacabiles, irrevocabiles."

[9] *Ib.* 619.19ff., LW 33.43. Cf. the whole exposition in WA 18.619.1–620.3.

If we continue our reading of *The Bondage of the Will*, we find that this immutability on the part of the Creator can equally well be combined with the *negative* outcome. In the examination of the theory of the rewards, Luther introduces the concept "sequela" as denoting the effect of faith/lack of faith, irrespective of merit. Heaven and hell await mankind as "sequela necessaria", even though the individual does not imagine such a reward.[10] God fulfils His promises immutably. But God is equally immutable in His adherence to His laws and the threats resulting therefrom. This renders the consequences inevitable and terrible: The wrath is immutable.

Luther draws attention to this in the account of Jacob and Esau. Their reward is determined before they were born.[11] The discussion concerns the interpretation of a quotation from Mal. 1:2f. in Rom. 9:13. Erasmus asserts that this passage should not be taken literally, since God neither loves nor hates as we do. Such qualities are, according to him, alien to God's nature, and His wrath does not refer to eternal damnation but to temporal chastisement.[12] Luther retorts that Erasmus has missed the point, namely how God loves. Nonetheless, this is also relevant:

> "We know quite well that God does not love or hate as we do, since we are mutable in both our loving and hating, whereas *he loves and hates in accord with his eternal and immutable nature*, so that passing moods and feelings do not arise in him."[13]

Here we find again, that God's immutability involves a common-sense tenet, which Luther uses as an argument because for him it goes without saying.

This exposition above is the most detailed and pregnant I have found. Side by side in the notion of God are apposed a hatred of the sinners, which is as eternal and immutable as God Himself, and a love which also is absolute and immutable. This abiding wrath cannot be subordinated to the love but seems to be purely an end in itself. The concept of God is characterized by an inevitable antinomy. Furthermore, there is no

---

[10] *Ib.* 694.9ff.: "Manet enim impios infernus et iudicium Dei, *necessaria sequela*, etiam si ipsi talem mercedem pro suis peccatis neque cupiant neque cogitent, imo vehementer detestentur, et ut Petrus dicit, execrentur. Ita manet pios regnum, etiam si id ipsi neque quaerant nec cogitent, ut quod illis a patre suo paratum est, non solum antequam essent ipsi, sed etiam ante constitutionem mundi." H. Olsson (1971)21ff, *ib.* 173, *ib.* 427ff. drew special attention to the thought of the reward in Luther's theology.

[11] WA 18.723.36: "Praemia decernuntur, antequam operarii nascantur et operentur."

[12] *De libero arbitrio* III.a.11. P. Althaus (1963)241 reasons along the same lines.

[13] WA 18.724.32ff., LW 33.199. Cf. WA 18.633.14ff., *ib.* 725.3ff.

possibility of avoiding this tension by referring to human merits, or vices. The specific prophecy concerning Jacob and Esau is generalised to apply to God's love and hatred "antequam mundus fieret, non solum ante meritum et opus liberi arbitrii."[14] In other words, these two divine qualities are not conditional upon any human property but only on God's counsel and will.

3. The large *Genesis Commentary* brings out these arguments with direct reference to *The Bondage of the Will.* This is most clearly seen with regard to the belief in the evangelical promises, and the resulting certainty of salvation. Once again there is a combination of two concepts, Luther's conception of God, which implies the immutability as self-evident, and the promises of salvation and justification revealed in the New Testament.[15] Men lie and deceive. But God never changes or betrays.[16] Thus, the immutability gives power and weight to the promises, so that the believers can experience how the whole issue of redemption is rooted in God Himself for evermore.

4. Finally, I wish to point out that Luther can also present *God as changeable* in a fashion which seems diametrically opposed to the statements concerning the divine immutability. Yet, such a contradiction does not exist. The comment on *deus mutabilis* deals with *deus in nobis.*[17] God's mutability corresponds to the vacillations of conscience and of faith. The point at issue is Luther's so called "religious transcendentalism."[18]

[14] *Ib.* 724.35ff.: "Atque hoc ipsum est, quod liberum arbitrium cogit nihil esse, quod aeternus et immutabilis sit amor, aeternum odium Dei erga homines, antequam mundus fieret, non solum ante meritum et opus liberi arbitrii, omniaque necessario in nobis fieri, secundum quod ille vel amat vel non amat ab aeterno, . . ." Here I agree with E. Seeberg (1929)175f. The wrath and the love of God are the only cause for the cutting off and grafting into the olive tree, WA 18.726.35f.

[15] WA 43.461.29ff. (*Vorlesung über 1. Mose.* 1535–45): "Ideo autem manifestavit se in carne, ut rapiat nos ex morte, ex carne et ex Diaboli potestate. Ex hac cognitione non potest non existere ingens gaudium et delectatio, quod *Deus est immutabilis,* et quod necessitate immutabili operatur, *neque se ipsum negare potest,* sed servat promissiones."

[16] *Ib.* 458.32f.: "Cum e contra haec nostra consolatio sit, tametsi nos mutemur, ut ad immutabilem tamen confugiamus"; *ib.* 462.13ff.: "Quia homo est mendax et fallax. Sed cum Deo non potest agi dubitative. Is enim non vult, nec potest esse mutabilis aut mendax." Cf. further WA 42.293.25ff., *ib.* 313.24f. The same thought is stressed in SD 11, BSLK 1084.

[17] WA 14.448.4ff. (*Predigten über das erste Buch Mose.* 1523/24): "Quomodo vinces deum? non potestas eius vincitur, sed in me vincitur, quia mutatur, quando nos mutamur. In nobis est, sicut conscientia nostra est, ipse in uno wesen manet, semper manet bonus, sed mihi interdum inculcatur tanquam iratus. Ita damnatis inculcatur, quasi sit iudex. Ita pro quo tenent, talis est."

[18] R. Seeberg (1917)47f. There is a critical analysis in A. Gyllenkrok (1952)27f. Cf. also G. Ljunggren (1928)168f., P. Althaus (1963)152.

4.2.5. God's Will to Particular Redemption Through Predestination

The Bible proclaims God's will to universal redemption. The best known passage is 1 Tim. 2:4. How does Luther interpret this and similar passages with reference to the reprobation?

1. When 1 Tim. 2:4 is quoted in an early *Second Day of Christmas Sermon*, its purpose is to prove that God seeks the salvation of all men and the damnation of none. Individuals also wish to live well and be saved. But man can always "shut the door" and resist the grace, in reliance on his own will and wisdom. Thus, this self-will remains as the root which is the cause of the damnation.[1] Luther's heavy emphasis on the primacy of the will, and on sin as wilful resistance to God, impels him to interpret the sinful will as the reason for the rejection.

Further evidence from the same period, especially the *First Lecture on the Psalms*, indicates that man's relationship with God does not depend on a particularistic predetermination but on man's willing acceptance, or rejection of God and of God's will. If any man refuses grace God cannot compel him.[2]

The interpretation of 1 Tim. 2:4 in *Dictata* is so short that it can be compatible with both an universalistic and a particularistic theory. The paraphrase and gloss on Ps. 93:9 (Vulgate) say that man is given the capacity of hearing and seeing by God through Christ, and not of his own merit. No one is enlightened except through Him. It is His wish that all men shall be saved. This can be expressed by analogy: no one is saved except through His gracious will.[3] Yet, we find a categorical denial that Christ's mercy is valid for all men in the interpretation of the Passion narrative. The crucified Christ in truth drank the cup of suffering to the dregs "pro electis suis", but not "pro omnibus".[4] Thus, the introduction of predestination in this context provokes the conclusion that the reconciliation is not for all. Particularism seems to be an irrefutable fact.

The excursus on Rom. 1:24 in the *Exegesis of Romans* discusses the relationship between God and evil. God is not the cause of evil when this carries the imprint of sin and guilt. On the other hand, evil as the

---

[1] WA 1.31.29ff. (*Pred.* 1514), and *ib.* 32.16ff.: "Igitur adeo radicaliter ista portio voluntatis inest, ut etiam in damnatis sola sit causa totius pene inferni, quod nolunt eum et volunt contrariam salutem inaestimabili vehementia."

[2] This is shown *e.g.* in S. Normann (1933)120f. Cf. also G. Rost (1966)94f.

[3] WA 4.89.36f. (*Dictata super Psalterium.* 1513–15): "Item 'Qui vult omnes homines salvos fieri' (i.e. nullus salvatur nisi eius bona voluntate)."

[4] *Ib.* 227.32f. I agree with S. Normann (1933)119, G. Rost (1966)95.

punishment of sin is rooted in God's will and actions.[5] But when Luther reflects further on these problems, he concludes that God nevertheless intends the evil which is outside Himself, and which is committed by others, *e.g.* a human being or a demon. For if God did not so wish it could never happen. Indeed, God really intends all men to be bound by the commandments. Nevertheless, obviously it is not His will that all should keep them. For in Luther's view, the problem is not solved by adducing the guilt of free will in this context. Thus we here have two tenets which are difficult to reconcile in a feasible manner. Firstly: All men are enjoined to obedience under the divine will. Secondly: God grants grace only to those whom He chooses, He is not willing to grant it to all. He reserves to Himself an election among men.[6] As a result universalism only applies to the demands of the Law. Particularism enters in with regard to the fulfilment of the commandments. Furthermore, particularism is a fact concerning the gift of grace (*Nec vult omnibus*). Luther is here hinting at what I have called *reprobation$_2$*. *Electio Dei* is the cause of divine actions which lead to the limitation of grace to a number of people who are not identical with all humanity.

The examination of the divine predetermination in Rom. 8:28 deals with a series of arguments against predestination. Indeed 1 Tim. 2:4 is a strong objection to the belief that God does not *a priori* intend the justification and redemption of all men. Yet, this Pauline quotation is not, in Luther's eyes, a convincing argument. For this, and similar statements are covered by the hermeneutic rule: they always apply solely to the elect.[7] This interpretation is directly followed by several verses repeating the previously stressed assertion, that Christ did not "absolute

---

[5] WA 56.179.27ff. (*Rom.* 1515–16).

[6] *Ib.* 182.4ff.: "Alio modo vult malum, sc. quod extra ipsum est et alius facit, puta homo Vel demon. Hec vera est. Quia si nollet, non fieret. Sic Ediverso Non vult bonum, Quia vult nos omnes obligari ad precepta, et tamen non vult omnes illa implere. Ergo omnia hec sunt Vera: Deus Vult malum, Deus Vult bonum; Deus non vult malum, Deus non vult bonum. Sed obstrepunt hic, Quia Liberum arbitrium est in culpa. Sed hoc secundum profundiorem theologiam nihil est." *Ib.* 182.14ff: "Hec enim duo quomodo consonent et quo Iudicio Iusta sint, sc. Quod Deus vult me obligari et omnes, et tamen *non dat gratiam, nisi cui velit, Nec vult omnibus, Sed electionem in illis sibi reservat*: hec, inquam, in futuro videbimus."

[7] *Ib.* 385.23ff: "Secundum. 'Deus Vult omnes homines salvos fieri,' Et pro nobis hominibus tradidit filium suum Et creavit hominem propter vitam eternam. Item: Omnia propter hominem, Ipse autem propter Deum, ut fruatur etc. Hec et alia iis similia sicut et primum facilia sunt. Quia semper hec dicta intelliguntur de electis tantum, Vt ait Apostolus 2. Tim.: 'Omnia propter electos' ".

pro omnibus" suffer and die on the cross.[8] Luther makes it completely clear that the particularistic doctrine of predestination is balanced by an equally particularistic concept of reconciliation.[9]

In the *Lecture on Hebrews* one or two years later, Luther confirms this interpretation with the support of further NT material. He adduces John 17:9 and 20, Mk 14:24 and Heb. 9:15. The point is, that Christ's intercession, sacrifice, and merits do not apply to all but to a small number of believers. This train of thought is classified immediately thereafter as the material dealing with predestination. It is complex, difficult, and beyond the comprehension of the weak intellect.[10] The belief in predetermination confers a particularistic limitation on the application of both Christology and the doctrine of justification.

2. Luther's *Translation of the New Testament* is enlightening. At 1 Tim. 2:4 the Vulgate has Latin equivalents to the original Greek text: God wishes *omnes homines salvos fieri*. But Luther does not use the German verbs *erlösen* or *erretten*, which would provide the most literal translation. Instead he says: God wishes "das alle Menschen genesen".[11] This verb means, *inter alia*, to recover (from an illness). While we cannot draw too far-fetched conclusions from this fact, yet, we may well say that the idea of eternal salvation in a future life is overshadowed. The incompatibility of the Pauline passage in 1 Tim. 2:4 with the idea of a double doctrine of predestination does not clearly emerge from the translation. Luther's concentration on the interpretation of 1 Tim 2:4 is also illustrated by the fact that his entire Bible later uses the verb *helfen* in the passive voice.[12] Nor does this carry overtones immediately suggesting an universal, eternal salvation. Thus, it is feasible to maintain that Luther's translation of 1 Tim. 2:4 can be reconciled with the theory of a particularistic will to salvation on the part of God.

Since Luther, at about the same time, wrote a personal letter on these issues to an individual who was wrestling with the problem of universalism *versus* particularism in the divine will to salvation, we have an important detailed explanation. The letter begins by saying that

---

[8] *Ib.* 385.28ff: "Non enim absolute pro omnibus mortuus est Christus, quia dicit: 'Hic est sanguis, qui effundetur pro Vobis' et 'pro multis',—*Non ait: pro omnibus*—'in remissionem peccatorum'."
[9] Cf. *ib.* 84.23ff.
[10] WA 57.c.212.24ff. (*Heb.* 1517–18) S. Normann (1933) 205 proves the particularism with other passages. Cf. also Luther's particularism in WA 1.564.35ff. (*Resolutiones disputationum de indulgentiarum virtute.* 1518).
[11] WADB 7.262 (*Das Neue Testament.* 1522). Cf. n. 18.
[12] *Ib.* 263 (*Aus der Bibel.* 1546).

throughout the history of the Church scholars have cited passages from the Bible in order to prove that there is in God no eternal wrath, *e.g.* Ps. 77:8ff. Furthermore, this line of argument was based on 1 Tim. 2:4, which Luther here translates: "Gott will, das alle Menschen selig werden".[13] But these and similar passages do not disprove particularism. When the psalms speak of the wrath of God as limited in time, this is only relevant to the saints who suffer oppression on earth. 1 Tim. 2:4 is interpreted in the following terms: It is God's will that we pray for all estates, instruct all, and assist all men both physically and spiritually.[14] Consequently the point at issue is that we shall pray for, and preach to, all men, since this is God's will. But He alone grants the redemption and recovery of the sinner. We note that "genesen" is here used, as in the *Translation of the New Testament*. Thus, the door to particularism is held open. Furthermore, Luther explicitly guards himself against the conclusion from 1 Tim. 2:4 that God will redeem all mankind. It is stated that a decisive *Vorverständnis* to the Luther version of 1 Tim. 2:4 lies in the Pauline tenet of election.[15]

The most detailed discussion of 1 Tim. 2:4 is to be found in *a sermon from 1525*. Since this sermon was submitted for publication, and reached the general public, we may assume that its interpretation was intended for common study. Luther begins by emphasizing that this Pauline quotation may not be read out of context. Instead we must consider it in its setting. Thus, we might arrive at the true interpretation.[16] This leads him to identify "all men" in v. 4 with the "all men" mentioned in v 1. He concludes: Paul is not speaking of the elect but of all mankind. If all humanity is meant, then 1 Tim. 2:4 must be an expression of God's wish to help all mankind.[17] The printed text is highly specific on this point.

[13] WA 10.II.322.12ff. (*Sendbrief an Hans v. Rechenberg*. 1522).

[14] *Ib.* 325.20ff.: "Weyl er nu solichs uns befilhet und von uns gethan haben will, spricht S. Paulus recht, Es sey Gottis will, *das yederman genese*, denn auf seynen willen geschehe es nicht, *Aber daraus folget nicht, das er alle menschen selig mache.*" A similar discussion of 1 Tim 2:1ff. is found in WA 6.238.1ff. (*Von den guten Werken*. 1520).

[15] WA 10.II.325.25ff.: "sonst were die gottliche fursehung und erwelung von ewickeytt nichts, darauff doch S. Paulus hartte dringt." Cf. also WA 12.262.8ff. (*1 Pet.* 1523): "Sie sind erwellt (spricht er). Wie? nicht von yhn selber, sondern nach Gottis ordnung. Denn wyr werden uns selber nicht kunnen zum hymel bringen odder den glauben ynn uns machen, *Got wirt nicht alle menschen ynn hymel lassen*, die seynen wirtt er gar genaw zelen."

[16] WA 17.I.160.3f. (R): "Prior et sequens sollen den verstand geben, oportet videas, wie ein text den andern dringt." Cf. *ib.* 17ff. (Dr).

[17] *Ib.* 13ff. (R): "Illic loquitur non de electis, sed omnibus. Sic hic loquitur Paulus de omni, da mit eim geholffen wirt." Cf. *ib.* 161.14ff. (Dr).

The detailed account must in this case go back to Luther himself. We have an explanation why the Luther translation of the New Testament has the wording it has.[18] Redemption, here, should not be regarded exclusively, as referring only to eternal salvation, but inclusively, as denoting help and restoration in time and in eternity. 1 Tim. 2:4 is an expression of God's general readiness to assist the whole of humanity.

With reference to 1 Tim. 4:10, Luther makes it perfectly clear that he supposes a general will by God to help all mankind, including heretics and pagans, and a specific intention to redeem the believers. Neither eternal salvation nor timely help in need, sickness or hunger come to pass without God.[19] On the basis of 1 Tim. 2:1, Luther also specifies the meaning of God's will that all mankind shall be helped. It is only under a peaceful, stable rule of law that all men can have the opportunity to hear the Word of God, to confess Him, and to practice their faith.[20] 1 Tim. 2:5 is also adduced: All mankind shares in the *general* good. The *special* good, however, is reserved for the elect through the mediator, Jesus Christ.[21] This is a new example of the particularistic application of Christology. In Luther's view, only the faithful may experience eternal salvation.[22] 1 Tim. 2:4 is interpreted as meaning that this Pauline quotation is compatible with the particularism of election. This passage cannot prove the universalism of salvation.[23]

The *Lecture on Timothy* a few years later gives a similar interpretation of 1 Tim. 2:4. Luther holds it as self-evident that this passage brings out God as the only source of help and redemption for mankind. But the question remains, whether eternal or temporal redemption is meant.

---

[18] *Ib.* 17ff. (Dr): "Darumb habe ich die wort: 'Qui vult omnes homines salvos fieri' so gedeuscht: 'Der da wil, *das yederman genese.*' Dergleichen offt ym Euangelio stehet 'Salvum facere' das ist: *genesen odder geholffen, nicht selig werden,* Also, das es nicht allein von jhenem leben odder ewigem leben zu deuten ist, sondern sol umb sich greiffen und allerley hülffe, beide, zeitlich und ewig umbfangen, Das er der einige heyland ist, durch wilchen allen geholffen wird, fromen und bösen, menschen und thier. Er wil, das sie alle *genesen,* wo sie hülffe durffen." Cf. *ib.* 2ff. (R).

[19] *Ib.* 8ff. (R) and *ib.* 25ff. (Dr). Cf. also *ib.* 163.8ff. (R) and *ib.* 31ff. (Dr).

[20] *Ib.* 162.3ff. (R), *ib.* 13ff. (Dr). Cf. also *ib.* 163.23ff. (Dr), *ib.* 164.14ff. (Dr).

[21] *Ib.* 165.6f. (R): "gut dei, eine trifft all in der gemeyn, die ander electos. Ita omnia trahit in bonitatem dei et dicit, quid credentes erkrigen speciatim." Cf. *ib.* 27ff. (Dr).

[22] *Ib.* 164.3f. (R), *ib.* 19ff. (Dr).

[23] *Ib.* 163.1 (R): "Ex hoc non sequitur, quod omnes salvos velit im himel." Cf. also *ib.* 14ff. (Dr). In WA 18.686.5ff. (*De servo arbitrio.* 1525) Luther writes that the God of the Gospel wills all men to be saved according to 1 Tim 2:4a. Thus he comes with the word of salvation to all. The fault lies in the human will which does not permit of salvation. This concerns the universalism which will be discussed in 4.5.1–2 below.

Augustine's comment can be applied to both. Nevertheless, Luther, for his part, considers that the verse refers to "generali salvatione: salvat a periculis adulterii, fornicationis, paupertatis, erroris".[24] He likewise cites 1 Tim. 4:10 in support of his interpretation. The universal redemption refers to a salvation which is not eternal.[25] Luther then refers to the context, especially 1 Tim. 2:1. We should pray for all men and all in authority, even if they are wicked and ungodly.[26] A new feature in this context is the comment that the words of St Paul bear upon a question of "voluntate praecepti". The divine will revealed in the Scriptures indicates beyond doubt the attitude which the Christian must adopt to his fellow men and to those in authority.[27] According to Luther, 1 Tim. 2:4b expresses God's will not only for the devout but also for all mankind. God seeks to enlighten all men—both good and evil—by the sun which He allows to shine upon humanity. Likewise His commandment is to preach the Gospel to all nations.[28]

Since the Gospel is proclaimed to all men, it nevertheless happens that many reject it. This fact depends solely upon "God's profoundly *secret* will".[29] In this way the eternal salvation, which is only conferred on the faithful by the mediator Jesus Christ and His satisfaction of God's wrath at the sins of men, is brought into being.[30]

3. Finally, there is a note on the Bible written by the aging Luther, giving a direct exposition of 1 Tim. 2:4. It does not concern the realization of the eternal salvation either. The emphasis is instead laid on the human, temporal conditions which are essential: read the Scriptures, hearken to the Word, be content, bring up children, derive nourishment from heaven and earth. Therefore, the devil devotes his attention to

---

[24] WA 26.35.25ff. (*1 Tim.* 1528).
[25] *Ib.* 38ff.: "Iste locus (1 Tim 4:10) plane discrevit 'omnes homines' ab 'fidelibus', quos salvat aeternaliter, illos non." Cf. *ib.* 37.8ff.: "Quid est cognitio veritatis? est cognoscere unum deum, a quo veniunt istae salutes temporales."
[26] *Ib.* 36.8ff. Cf. *ib.* 37.5ff.
[27] *Ib.* 36.15ff.
[28] *Ib.* 23ff.
[29] *Ib.* 31f. (quoted in 4.3.2 n. 12). Cf. also *ib.* 25ff. See further WA 39.I.578.23ff. = Drews 481 (*Die dritte Disputation gegen die Antinomer.* 1538): "At *non omnibus contritis* datur Spiritus sanctus. Cur sic et non aliter? Respondeo: Hoc nobis non est revelatum, sed reliquendum iudicio Dei"; WA 40.III.576.6ff. (*Enarratio Ps XC.* 1534/35): "Electi dei lassen sich todten, quia metuunt mortem et eternam iram; habent igitur 1. gratiam, quae est cognitio irae et sensus divini iudicii: istis 'servis' dei sei gnedig", WATR 1.515.10f. (1530–35): "Ut autem certi essemus de voluntate Dei, quos velit *salvos aut non salvos*, hoc voluit nobis per verbum manifestari, ..."
[30] WA 26.37.9ff.

marring the good which is primarily temporal in nature.[31] As a result this Pauline passage is not in direct conflict with the fundamental Luther attitude, that God's redeeming will with regard to the effective eternal salvation does not apply to all but only a small number of chosen people.

4. If we survey the material which has been analysed we can establish that the doctrine of predestination, which is related to the hidden Lord, occasionally results in a particularistic use of both Christology and the doctrine of justification.[32] It lies outside the scope of this work to investigate all Luther's sayings on Christology and justification, and see to what extent universalism or particularism is accentuated. My limited material nevertheless demonstrates that it is not always feasible to assert that Christ's atonement and predestination are wholly incompatible facets of Luther's theology.[33] In the following section (4.3.2.) I shall consider the idea of the hidden God, which I have only noted in this context, and demonstrate too that man can have some understanding of the *deus absconditus*, although much remains hidden. I shall thereafter (4.5.1–2) examine how, in his doctrine of justification by *deus revelatus*, Luther still stresses the vital importance of believing that this God really does wish to save every human being through Christ.

---

[31] WA 48.212.5ff. (*Bibeleinzeichnung.* 1542).

[32] E. Hirsch, *Zu Luthers deutscher Bibel* (In: *Lutherstudien II*, 1954)240 comments as follows on Luther's dependence on Augustine in the translation of 1.Tim 2:4: "Hier hat Luther den Widerspruch, in dem die Pastoralbriefe zur paulinischen Gnadenwahl stehen, sich zugedeckt, indem er die Stelle mit Augustin, darum doch wohl nicht minder irrig, auf die Hilfe in äusseren Dingen deutete. Aber nur dem, der den genauen Vergleich hier anstellt, fällt das auf; Luther hat—indem er eine ursprünglich gewählte bestimmtere Fassung (*sc.* "Gott will, dass alle Menschen genesen") aufgab—den Ausdruck so allgemein gehalten, dass der Sinn gerade noch in der Schwebe bleibt. So haben denn die Lutheraner bis auf den heutigen Tag die tiefere Meinung Luthers bei dieser Übersetzung nicht gemerckt und führen diese Stelle ruhig auf deutsch gegen die strenge Prädestinationslehre an." See further the following note.

[33] W. Elert (1931)103ff. has the headline "Versöhnung und Prädestination bei Luther in Disjunktion" when he gives an exposition of Luther's doctrine of predetermination. His conclusion (*ib.* 108) is that this doctrine is only of "subsidiäre Bedeutung." S. Normann (1933)515f., *ib.* 528ff. agrees with Elert's conception in stressing the universalism of the Gospel. M. Doerne (1938)75ff. and P. Althaus (1963)241 use the universal doctrine of justification to criticize the particularism inherent in the thought of predestination. In FC Ep 11, 1. Tim 2:4 is not discussed in the context of particularism, but only adduced as evidence of the universalism of the Gospel, BSLK 818. See further the emphasis on God's universal will to save in W. Pannenberg (1957)127.

4.2.6. The Antinomy in the Concept of God

My examination of various basic concepts, which disclosed that unconditional predestination and unconditional reprobation derive from Luther's conception of God, points toward a fundamental contradiction in the divine being. Eternal grace and eternal disfavour, eternal love and eternal wrath are placed side by side in the concept of God. The question then arises: Was Luther himself aware of contradictions in his concept of God?

1. A first scrutiny of this problem is to be found in the aforesaid excursus on the *Commentary on Romans*. Luther begins by asserting that this is true: God wills evil, or sin, and God is cognizant of evil, or sin. Yet, this can be refuted by the fact that the Scriptures do not discern God's will in the evil. In fact He hates the wicked. The thesis and the antithesis are indeed logically "contradictory".[1] Certainly an argument follows which defines the way in which God intends the evil and the sin, so that the contradiction is modified to some extent. Yet, the whole interpretation stipulates that it is God who promotes the wicked hardness of heart which must result in damnation. Reason may then protest: "Ergo sine culpa damnantur, Quia obligantur et non possunt implere Vel 'obligantur ad impossibile'." The Luther reply is a reference to Paul's comment in Rom. 9:20.[2] Thus, he by no means gives an argument which repudiates the conclusion that God bears the guilt for the damnation as being accurate *per se*. Logically speaking, God here seems in a contradictory fashion to be the cause of both salvation and rejection. Thus, we here find that Luther personally was aware of the contradiction inherent in his concept of God.

In association with Rom. 8:28 Luther is more outspoken in his discussion of the objection to the theory of predestination which is based on the inherent inconsistency of the image of God.[3] We have unmistakeable evidence that he regarded this objection as very embarrassing as it is the last and the strongest argument which reason can produce. Why does God incite men, as He does, to contravene His will? The contradiction can be stated in even more shocking terms: Why does He harden the human heart to the point that man will transgress the Law of God still further, with damnation as a result? "Ergo Causa est in Deo, quare peccent et damnentur." Luther's preceding three rational

---

[1] WA 56.181.24ff. (*Rom.* 1515–16).

[2] *Ib.* 182.28ff.

[3] *Ib.* 386.6ff. Cf. *ib.* 383.27ff.: "Secundo Obiectiones et exceptiones eorum, qui in Deum culpam transferunt, et argumenta eorum et motiva solvemus." Cf. further 3.6.1 above.

objections to his concept of God can be fairly easily repudiated by him. But this is more difficult. Indeed, he openly concedes: "Hoc est fortissimum motivum et principale." Luther again adduces Rom. 9:19f. He has no real comment to make on the conclusion that this is a question of a stark contradiction between the eternal love of God, which gives grace to the elect, and the eternal wrath which increases the guilt resulting in the condemnation of the rejected. The contradiction cannot be eliminated or modified.[4]

2. The interpretation of Pharaoh's hardness of heart and the accompanying problems with regard to the conception of God recur in Luther's *Sermons on Exodus* from the 1520's. The God who otherwise disapproves of sin and hardness of heart seems to ordain concerning Pharaoh's fate that the sin will be committed, as He hardens his heart.[5] The concept of God can be determined by *ratio*. This definition follows "the law". The principle of logical contradiction is relevant here. For God is said to be good. But to harden someone's heart is to commit a wrong act.[6] When reason finds a contradiction and protests against this Luther again refers to Rom. 9:20.[7] Properly used, "the law" indicates that which is good and right for man. Thus, the rational analysis arrives at this conclusion: "Nobiscum contrarium".[8] Concerning the notion of God, the contradiction has as its content: God does good, and God does that which appears to reason to be evil, and which results in reprobation. The cleavage between two contradictory features in the Godhead is transposed to a fundamental division between ˜divine and human judgements. Consequently, the purpose of Luther's exposition is not, in any way, to weaken the stark conflict by some form of rational synthesis.

---

[4] This is emphasized in G. Rost (1966)112. The antinomy between eternal goodness and eternal damnation is indicated in a letter, WA 10.II.322.8ff. (1522): "Denn es auch bey uns alhie unnd zu zeytten bey den aller höchsten leutten als Origenes und seines gleychen altzu hart, gestreng und *gotlicher güte also ungemess* gedaucht, das er die menschen so dahyn werffen und zur ewigen peyn geschaffen haben sollt."

[5] WA 16.140.1 (*Pred. über das 2. Buch Mose.* 1524–27): "Num deum (sic!) iubet peccare, cum indurat homines? cur damnat?" See further the discussion in G. Rost (1966)113 n. 24–25.

[6] WA 16.140.1ff. (quoted in 4.3.1 n. 7). Cf. *ib.* 143.4ff.

[7] *Ib.* 142.4ff.

[8] *Ib.* 142.7ff.: "Homo ideo dicitur from, das er thut nach dem gsetz, cum deo econtra. Sed opus ideo bonum est, quia deus facit. Ego aufs meinem werck muss ich in ein andern wegk treten, nempe in legem, ut lex die gut nemb von dem theter, scilicet deo. Nobiscum contrarium, nos probi fimus per legem vel spiritum sanctum, qui implet legem."

All Christians should, according to Luther, be aware of the antinomy involved here. This emerges from a *letter to the Christians of Antwerp*, which has been somewhat neglected by the scholars.[9] The document was written as a polemic against the belief that God's will is simple and straightforward! A Dutch zealot had taught that God does not want that which is wicked. So far Luther agrees. This he states in no uncertain terms. According to His *revealed will*, God does not intend sin. But He permits it in accordance with His *hidden will*.[10] Luther explicitly states that the issue in the concept of God is "diese zween willen". He therefore categorically rejects the theory of the Dutch theologian that we should assume "nur den eynen willen ynn Gott".[11] Luther here shows in unusually outspoken terms how his concept of God is contradictory. On the one hand God does not want sin, but on the other hand in His hiddenness He seeks and ordains it, with the consequence that man is damned.[12] He also wishes to take the sting from the contradiction argument by citing Rom. 9:20.

It is and remains a paradox that God effects both the good and the evil in us, rewarding the good and punishing the evil. Although it is true that God stands behind both courses of action yet, in Erasmus' view, such contradictory assertions should not be publicised.[13] But in *The Bondage of the Will* Luther confirms the antinomy. This applies first to the basis. If the tension were a human invention, it could be simply ignored. Yet, if the paradox is a synthesis of *Biblical exegesis* then its concealment would be wrong, just as it is immoral to refrain from clearly and lucidly informing people about the revelation of God in Scripture. Here again allusion is made to the Pauline passage in Rom. 9:18ff. Consequently, Luther is aware that the God who acts so paradoxically appears to be

[9] WA 18.547.1ff. (*Sendschreiben an die Christen zu Antwerpen.* 1525). Concerning this material see G. Ljunggren (1928)463f., S. Normann (1933)469f.

[10] WA 18.549.31ff.: "Aber da wolt er nicht hynan, das Gott, wie wol er die sunde nicht will, *so verhenget er doch, das sie geschihet,* und solch verhengnis geschicht ia nicht on seynen willen." Luther also sees a divine *permission* behind the Fall: WA 11.274.11ff. (*Von weltlicher Obrigkeit.* 1523), WA 18.712.29ff. (*De servo arbitrio.* 1525), WA 24.82.8ff. (*In Genesin Declamationes.* 1527), WA 42.114.12ff. (*Vorlesung über 1. Mose* 1535–45).

[11] WA 18.549.35ff.

[12] *Ib.* 550.6ff.: "Ich sage, Gott hat verbotten die sunde und will der selben nicht, Dieser wille ist uns offenbart und not zu wissen. *Wie aber Gott die sunde verhenget odder will, das sollen wyr nicht wissen, denn er hats uns nicht offenbart.*" For other passages on the same subject, see *e.g.* WA 7.548.12ff. (*Das Magnificat verdeutschet.* 1521), WA 14.480.24ff. (*Pred. über das 1. Buch Mose.* 1523/24), WA 15.415.21ff. (*Pred.* 1524), WA 40.II.86.1ff. (*Gal.* 1531/35), *ib.* 381.9ff. (*Enarratio Psalmi LI.* 1532/8). But God did not originally cause the sin, see 3.6 n. 13 above.

[13] *De libero arbitrio* I.a.10.

"stultus ille vel imprudens Deus".[14] Thus, both Luther and Erasmus may be said to be agreed on the interpretation that Luther's concept of God implies a contradiction.

Erasmus would modify the cruel and ruthless conception of God in Luther's literal interpretation: It is the divine forbearance *vis-à-vis* the sinners which leads to their intransigence, when they do not pray for a change of heart in response to the offer of grace.[15] Luther, however, asserts that God is just as "cruel" in Erasmus' interpretation as in his own. For Erasmus too agrees with the view that human free will, in fact, cannot do any good in itself. The will, even in Erasmus' view, becomes less and less free when confronted with the divine forbearance. Therefore, the conclusion is: Although the hardness of heart, and the resultant damnation, is provoked by God's patience, yet, God is represented as "crudelissimus", and as delighting in human suffering.[16] In other words, the consequences for the concept of God are no less embarrassing. It is "ratio humana" which sees God's twin attributes of goodness and harshness as stumbling blocks. The antinomy is solved, according to *ratio*, when the concept of God as hardening hearts is designated "absurd". Nevertheless, for Luther the demand for freedom from contradiction is not decisive. The same argument could according to him be used to negate all the articles of faith: the Incarnation, the Virgin Birth, the Crucifixion, the Resurrection.[17] Thus, Luther by no means takes the sting out of the contradiction, but confirms that it does exist according to ordinary human judgement. Our reason, however, is not neutral but partial because of our selfish desires:

> "These things (*sc.* hardening of sinners), Reason will repeat, are not the marks of a good and merciful God. They are too far beyond her comprehension, and she cannot bring herself to believe that God is good if He acts in this way, but *setting aside faith, she wishes to feel and see and understand how he is good and not cruel.* She would, of course, understand if it were said of God that he hardens no one, damns no one, but has mercy on all, saves all, so that with *hell abolished and the fear of death removed,* there would be no future punishment to be dreaded. *That is why she blusters and argues so* in attempt to exonerate God and defend his justice and goodness."[18]

---

[14] WA 18.630.22ff. (*De servo arbitrio.* 1525).
[15] *De libero arbitrio* III.a.2.
[16] WA 18.705.24ff.
[17] *Ib.* 707.12ff. Cf. *ib.* 719.4ff., *ib.* 729.7ff.
[18] *Ib.* 708.1ff., LW 33.173f.

4.2.6.

Thus, Luther is so well aware that his own conception of God is logically contradictory, that he ironically suggests an alternative concept of God which does not contain this paradox. He also knows from own experience how a human being can be shocked to the depths of despair so that he wishes he had never been born, when he sees the good God as the cause of hardness of heart and damnation.

Nevertheless, he will under no circumstances neutralize the contradictions in the notion of God, but rather accentuates them. The first and decisive is, of course, *the argument from Scripture*. The simple, literal interpretation of Holy Writ is fundamental for Luther's reasoning.[19] Secondly, there is *an argument from experience*, which supports Luther's "intransigence". The experience of the God who by sheer will abandons, hardens and condemns human beings involves a "salutaris desperatio" which is close to grace.[20]

3. Luther's doctrine of predestination thus implies a paradoxical concept of God. Therefore, I wish to confirm the conclusion already reached by Erich Seeberg, Gustaf Ljunggren, Ragnar Bring and Gerhard Rost.[21] I also wish to assert that many Luther scholars have given an excessively partial interpretation of the material, since they did not bring out the stark antinomies in the conception of God but more or less neglected the consequences of the theory of predestination, and followed up the unity of Luther's concept of God. They have assumed that one concept (faith, the love of God, the revealed God, Christology, or the doctrine of justification) was the organizing principle and the basis of the Reformation.[22] When they then include the predestination tenets of which they are, in fact, fairly well aware, then the only point of relevance is election to faith and salvation. The negative predestination was therefore either regarded critically—it is not a genuine expression of the evangelical theology[23]—or interpreted in terms of function; it is needed in

[19] WA 18.703.14ff.

[20] *Ib.* 719.9ff.

[21] E. Seeberg (1929)175f., G. Ljunggren (1928)472ff., R. Bring (1929)337, *ib.* 339ff., G. Rost (1966)128f., *ib.* 171ff. Cf. further 1.2 above.

[22] *E.g.* R. Seeberg (1898)285, K. Holl (1923)30f., G. Aulén (1927)172, *ib.* 176ff., E. Vogelsang (1929)15f., *ib.* 23f., *id.* (1932)20f., L. Pinomaa (1938)11ff., H. Beintker (1954)31ff., H.-M. Barth (1967)15ff., K. Schwarzwäller, *Theologia crucis* (1970)46ff. Cf. further 1. 2.1 above.

[23] *Sic* A. Ritschl (1889)222f., M. Doerne (1938)73ff., P. Althaus (1963)241ff.

the practical life of faith in order to induce humility and purity of faith[24], unless election to eternal damnation was not neglected or overlooked.[25]

4.2.7. Conclusions

1. Assuredly, Luther can sometimes present a philosophical or rational defence of his deterministic attitude. Nevertheless, he emphasizes the rigid doctrine of predetermination as revealed in the Bible and elicited by exegesis.

2. In both Biel and Luther prescience imperceptibly becomes synonymous with God's predestination. Unmistakeable similarities to Biel's theory are to be found in Luther's view on the selection of those who by God's providence would receive grace and those who would be denied it; indeed His prescience enshrined His predetermination. Here Luther linked God's irrevocable prescience, on the one hand, with the promises, revealed in the Bible, of grace for Christ's sake and, on the other hand, the warnings of damnation and punishment for sin.

3. Luther's observations on God's counsel disclosed that his theory was similar to Biel's. In the last resort God's will destined faith and disbelief, and thereby man's eternal fate: heaven or hell. God was designated not only as the origin of predestination but also, directly or indirectly, as *auctor reprobationis*. The individual is rejected on the grounds of personal guilt. When the sinner, however, was denied forgiveness and mercy, the reason lay deep in the divine counsel. The great difference between Biel and Luther consisted in the latter's categorical denial of every thought of merit as a condition for pre-determination. This idea of predestination is present not only in the conflict with the semipelagianism of the papal theologians in the 1520's, but also in the statements of the aging Luther. The theory of double predestination appeared as originally and manifestly given in the Luther conception of God, and not as the result of hindsight and arguments.

4. Further evidence that the double predestination is a primary feature of Luther's concept of God is to be found in connection with his observations on divine immutability. Luther considers it self-evident that

[24] Cf. *e.g.* W. Elert (1931)108, S. Normann (1933)517ff., L. Pinomaa (1938)143, *ib.* 146, H. Bandt (1958)137ff., P. Althaus (1963)245ff.
[25] Surprisingly little can be found in P. Th. Bühler (1942)59ff. and H. Beintker (1954)82ff. H. Olsson (1971)369ff. gives an extensive analysis of the relation between God and creation without discussing the doctrine of predestination. Cf. further how FC in SD 11 rejects the thought of an antinomy in the image of God, BSLK 1073f.

God is immutable. He emphasized more strongly than Biel the importance of divine immutability for the warnings and promises of Scripture. Thus, the theory of immutability is most important, not only for the theoretical teaching about God, but also in the practical life of faith.

5. We were able to establish a major difference between Biel and Luther in the interpretation of 1 Tim. 2:4. If anyone is not redeemed this depends, according to Biel, on his wilful rejection of grace. The reason why the universalism of the Pauline *locus* is not realized rests first and foremost with the individual. In Luther's interpretation the universalism is referred to the situation. God desires all mankind to hearken to the Gospel. The external circumstances in the form of a stable ruling which should guarantee that the Word can be freely and clearly preached ought to exist for all men, so that they have the exogenous possibility of being helped. The basis of particularistic salvation lies in a will to particularistic redemption on the part of the hidden God. This tenet was so fundamental that the application of Christology became particularistic. Christ did not suffer and die for all men but only for the elect. The doctrine of justification is also particularistic: the redeeming faith was not granted to all but only to those who were predestined to possess it.

6. Finally, we could establish that both Biel and Luther articulated contradictory conceptions of God. The divine will was the ultimate reason why certain individuals suffered eternal wrath. This could not rationally be reconciled with the belief in the eternal mercy which was granted to others. In the Luther material we also found signs indicating that he himself was well aware that logical criticisms could be made of his concept of God.

4.3. Predestination on Two Different Levels

4.3.1. God is His Own Law and Rule

Luther alternates between positive and negative statements on predestination, which may appear bewildering at first glance. This arises from the fact that he sees everything as depending on God's will, which in turn is free of all dependence.[1] In order to systematically understand this alternative, therefore, I start from the material which presents God as a law unto Himself.

[1] This aspect is stressed by *e.g.* R. Seeberg (1917)144 and K. Holl (1923)50. Concerning the background see 4.1.3 and *e.g.* H. Junghans (1968)234f.

1. The basic principles appear in the *First Lecture on the Psalms*. God is supremely exalted and subject to nothing and nobody. Apart from His will He knows no law. Precisely this is the essence of deity. Therefore, the created beings do not do what they want but that which God allows.[2] *Eo ipso* God stands for two things. He is the only free will in the universe, He is the law on which all things depend. It is an expression of Luther's belief in creation, that the Creator reigns supreme over His creation. The implications for mankind are, firstly: Man knows *that* God's will is the basis of being, secondly: Man is not, by the intellect, cognizant of *how* this will is going to shape the future.

The Lecture on Romans gives Luther an opportunity to illustrate these ideas still further. The gloss on Rom. 9:15 says that God's will knows no law or ordinance. It goes on stating that no man may know on whom God will have mercy and forgive.[3] Indeed, all men are sinners. But all are not punished in the same way. For no one can lay down a rule for God, whereby He will punish or reward.[4] Romans 8:38 also sheds light on this context. Paul was made aware of his election by a special revelation. We also have a sure knowledge of all the chosen people in the Bible. Even though it is certain that the elect will be saved, nobody is assured of being numbered among the chosen through any general law.[5] Since the creation cannot make demands on the Creator, neither can man accuse God or convict Him of injustice.[6]

Thus, we know that God predestines and reprobates. All things are dependent on God's will. But since this will is wholly free, being a law unto itself, man can never know by speculation the purposes of God.

In the *Sermons on Exodus* Luther expounds how man has a goal and a

---

[2] WA 4.262.33ff. (*Dictata super Psalterium*. 1513–15): "Quia nulli debet, nulli subiectus, solus altissimus, non nisi voluntatem suam habet legem. Quod est esse vere deum. Omnes enim alii non quecunque volunt, sed que permittuntur, faciunt."

[3] WA 56.91.19f. (*Rom.* 1515–16): "Et voluntatis eius nulla est lex Nullumque debitum omnino." *Ib*. 397.20f.: "Nemo sciet, cui miserebor et ignoscam, Nec meritis nec operibus nec ullis aliis poterit id certum esse ulli. Et ita est verbum timoris et humiliationis."

[4] *Ib*. 186.10ff.: "Non enim similiter omnes tradit et punit Deus, etiamsi aliquod simile peccent. Cuius ratio est occultum Iudicium eius et quia unus bona aliqua simul facit, alius non vel minus, Ita ut obstruatur os temeritatis, ne quis statim definiat regulam Deo, secundum quam Deus quodlibet peccatum puniat aut bonum premiet." Cf. further E. Seeberg (1929)147f.

[5] WA 56.86.20ff.: "Apostolus loquitur in persona sua et omnium electorum, quia de se certus erat *per revelationem*, quod esset 'vas electionis', Act. 9. Et de electis et nos omnes certi sumus. Licet enim certum sit electos Dei salvari, Nullus tamen certus est se esse electum *lege communi*." E. Seeberg (1929)153 refers to this thought.

[6] WA 56.91.18ff., *ib*. 396.9ff. Cf. 4.1. n. 17. Cf. further K. Holl (1923)50f.

4.3.1.

yardstick for his life, since this is determined by God. Yet, God is outside every goal and gauge. He who seeks to measure God's actions has not begun to understand Him. The divine will is above all laws. Therefore, I cannot understand the manner of His justice, although He is just, nor comprehend the nature of goodness, although God is good. Nor can God be said to transgress the Law.[7] "Ratio hoc non intelligit. Qui non intelligit deum sine lege esse, taceat, mit got ist eytel wil wil wil."[8]

We again observe that Luther is hinting at a twofold view of human awareness of the deity. Firstly, man knows *that* God holds life in His hand, giving it conformity and goals. Secondly, however, man does not comprehend *what* God has determined, since He follows no principle or rule which can be anticipated by reason.

2. Since, in *The Bondage of the Will*, Luther has presented mankind as wholly dependent on its Master, he denies man's free will in this relationship. *Liberum arbitrium* is exclusively a divine attribute. Thereby God has power over, and does, all He desires in heaven and on earth. The attribution of free will to mankind would be an usurpation of divinity. For this reason, the term should be reserved for the divine majesty.[9] God is the supreme Creator, on whom creation is absolutely dependent. Luther proceeds to develop the divine freedom. In answer to the question of why God allowed Adam to fall, and all mankind to be tainted by the same sin, Luther writes simply:

> "He is God, and for his will there is no cause or reason that can be laid down as a rule or measure for it, since there is nothing equal or superior to it, but *it is itself the rule of all things*. For if there were any rule or standard for it, either as cause or reason, it could no longer be the will of God. For it is not because he is or was obliged so to will that what he wills is right, but on the contrary, because he himself so wills, therefore what happens must be right. *Cause and*

---

[7] WA 16.140.7ff. (*Predigten über das 2. Buch Mose.* 1524–27): "Mea vita habet finem, mas und ist gefast, dei wesen non ita. Si ergo velimus ein mass suchen in dei opere, so hab wir schon gefelt. Cum ergo ratio non potest hoher khomen, murmurat: tamen hunc obdurat? non ergo bene facit. Hic deo statim fecit ein mass. Deus dat tibi legem et steck dir das zil, et non econtra. Non ideo est iniustum, quia facit, sed quia vult, ists recht. Quando volo mensurare voluntatem, hab ich gefelt, sed eius voluntas est super omnes leges.

Sed ego non intelligo, quod est bonum. Pharao obduratur, est malum in oculis tuis, videtur malum, et si tu ipse faceres, malum esset, sed quia deus facit, bene facit. Non habet regulam, mass, gesetz, ergo non potest transgredi ea." Cf. *ib.* 148.1ff.
[8] *Ib.* 148.3f.
[9] WA 18.636.23ff. (*De servo arbitrio.* 1525).

reason can be assigned for a creature's will, but not for the will of the Creator, unless you set up over him another creator."[10]

Thus, the consequence of the Creator's total independence *vis-à-vis* His creation is that man cannot establish any general principle to be followed by the divine actions. With regard to the future, man must always remain in doubt as to how God will shape it. We see again the implications for the doctrine of predestination. We know, by intellect, *that* God predetermines but we cannot comprehend *how*.

3. From the *Large Genesis Commentary* we may derive examples of the same attitude: God is a law unto Himself. Prompted by Gen. 6:5f. Luther delivers a detailed exposition on the use of anthropomorphic turns of phrase in Scripture. He justifies his fear of relying too much on anthropomorphism by saying that the essence of God is beyond our comprehension. The divine nature can be neither defined nor articulated.[11] In his exegesis of Gen. 29:31 he explicitly states that God is "sine regula".[12] Therefore, there is no point in seeking to understand the will and works of God, or why God governs in one way and not another.[13]

For Luther, God implies something quite different. His essence, His will and His works cannot, by means of curiosity and speculation, be grasped by our limited human intelligence. In the case of predestination, this means that the Creator is always free to elect and reject as He wills, and that created beings can never make certain prognoses of God's intentions in the future, on the basis of an universal law or rule.

---

[10] *Ib.* 712.29ff., LW 33.181. There are many similarities to Biel, cf. 4.1.3.

[11] WA 42.294.1f. (*Vorlesung über 1. Mose.* 1535–45): "Nam Deus in sua substantia plane est incognoscibilis nec potest definiri aut dici, quid sit, etiamsi rumpamur." *Ib.* 18ff: "Nam quid Deus in natura sit, definire non possumus. Hoc bene possumus definire, quid non sit." Cf. *ib.* 39f.

[12] WA 43.646.14.

[13] WA 44.65.23f., *ib.* 67.37ff. Accordingly, Luther emphasizes the incomprehensibility of God. WA 5.86.41ff. (*Operationes in Psalmos.* 1519–21): "Sicut enim deus est ineffabilis, incomprehensibilis, inaccessibilis, ita eius voluntas et auxilium praesertim in tempore derelictionis." *Ib.* 494.36ff. WA 18.784.11ff. (*De servo arbitrio.* 1525): "At cum sit Deus verus et unus, deinde totus incomprehensibilis et inaccessibilis humana ratione, par est, imo neccessarium est, ut et iustitia sua sit incomprehensibilis." WATR 2.112.14ff. (1532): "Das thun wir nicht, ideo Deus est nobis incomprehensibilis, incogitabilis; er wirt nicht begriffen, er will ungefast sein extra Christum." Consequently, God's goodness is also an incomprehensible entity, see further 4.5.5. n. 14. n. 34–36.

4.3.2. Deus Absconditus

Scholars have long discussed the multitudinous and complex views and experiences which Luther associates with *deus absconditus*. They have discerned at least two different meanings:

a. The God who hides His love and grace beneath a present experience of wrath and damnation in the human conscience.
b. The God whose election to eternal salvation, and to rejection now and in the future lies concealed.[1]

Since we are discussing predestination we may confine ourselves to the latter thought. Regarding the result in the previous section we ask the following question: Can the fact that Luther assumes the existence of this *deus absconditus* be interpreted as both an affirmation and a critical assessment of the idea of predestination?

1. When, in connection with Ps. 16:14 (Vulgate) in the *First Lecture on the Psalms*, Luther explains the expression "abscondita dei", he asserts that this refers to three things: firstly, to God's "approval" of mankind, secondly, to His "punishment", and thirdly, to His mode of revealing something through its opposite.[2] This is obviously a question not only of man's temporal but also his eternal justification and vindication.

---

[1] This division comes in part from F. Blanke, *Der verborgene Gott bei Luther* (1928)5ff., *ib.* 17ff. His view is accepted by H. Olsson, *Kyrkans synlighet och fördoldhet enligt Luther* (in: *En bok om kyrkan.* 1942)306ff. H. Bandt (1958)19ff. stresses that the fundamental problem is the tension between these two conceptions of the hidden nature of God. J. Dillenberger, *God Hidden and Revealed* (1953) gives a good survey of the questions in discussion. D. Löfgren (1960)237ff. analyses the hiddenness of God in predestination and the implications for the faith. K.-O. Nilsson, *Simul* (1966)61f. has a short exposition of the issue. Finally, a kind of summary is to be found in H. Olsson (1971)12ff. Cf. further B. A. Gerrish, *To An Unknown God: Luther and Calvin on the Hiddenness of God*, JR 53 (1973)263ff.

[2] WA 3.112.12ff. (= WA 55.II.1.2.127.11ff: *Dictata super Psalterium.* 1513–15): "'Abscondita dei' sunt triplicia. Primo secundum approbationem. Quia sic ea novit, que approbat, et ea nescit, que reprobat. Sic capitur hic... Secundo secundum punitionem. Sic novit et videt, que punit aut punire vult... Tercio magis ad propositum vel idem cum primo, 'Abscondita' sunt, que foris secundum hominem geruntur et in conspectu hominum patent. Talia enim, que sunt coram mundo aliquid, sunt nihil coram deo, ut I Cor. I. 'Infirma mundi elegit'". I agree with S. Normann (1933)118 in this interpretation. It is impossible to grasp God through the natural "light". Man must be enlightened by a "higher light", WA 3.124.29ff. (= WA 55.II.1.2.138.5ff.) E. Seeberg (1929) 144 points out this fact. And A. Adam, *Der Begriff "Deus absconditus" bei Luther nach Herkunft und Bedeutung*, LuJ 30 (1963)100f. derives Luther's terminology from the Bible and from Dionysius Areopagitus. Cf. further WA 3.124.32ff., WA 56.387.27f. (*Rom.* 1515–16) and WA 5.176.28ff. (*Operationes in Psalmos.* 1519–21).

On the one hand, Luther emphasizes the divine prerogative, *that* God approbates and reprobates. This fact is concerned just with *God's* concealed will and acts of salvation and rejection. On the other hand, Luther maintains that man does not know *how* this actually occurs. We have here the problem of God's *hidden* judgement. The pagan judges by appearances. But there his knowledge goes astray. For that which carries weight in the world is nothing before God. In other words, it is not possible, through reason, to draw adequate, specific conclusions concerning either *approbatio* or *reprobatio* from ostensible reality. This would involve an assent to the knowledge of predestination, *sensu abstracto*, which I have named as the *notitia* level. It would also imply a denial of speculations on its actual mode of action in terms of *usus* level.

Since God's will is concealed as regards the definitive counsel on rejection, we cannot deduce any true, concrete judgements concerning the fate of *godless* individuals. This mode of reasoning is documented in the *Second Lecture on the Psalms*. Ps. 13:7 (Vulgate) can, according to Luther, be interpreted as referring to the Jewish people, but also to all mankind. Thus, it is an illustration to the godless of all ages:

> "His ergo omnibus, cum omnia frustra dicantur atque fiant, tandem tradita causa *divino secreto* non habetur nisi reliquus gemitus, qui optet nec tamen desperet futuram in fine dei misericordiam, sicut et nos hodie Ecclesiae captivitatem optamus et speramus converti."[3]

In a situation in which all that is said and done to the wicked seems to be wholly in vain, therefore, we may not draw the conclusion: these are elected to rejection. We would rather sigh, and hope that God will finally have pity on them. But we do not know whether they are elected to this fate. In brief: we have no certain knowledge from inquisitive reason, of the objects of predestination and reprobation on the *usus* level. We possess a general awareness on the *notitia* level that their eternal destiny is sealed in the hidden will of God. Our only course is to leave the concrete issue to this secret decision.

A *Sermon* from 1522 firmly maintains the divine election but emphasizes the impossibility of applying the general doctrine of predestination in any specific case. Not even the *devout* can, through

[3] *Ib.* 428.9ff. Cf. *ib.* 173.7ff., *ib.* 623.1ff. (discussed in 4.3.3 below).

rational speculation, attain certainty, whether they are worthy of God's wrath, or His love.[4]

Thus, everybody has an abstract knowledge that the counsel of God determines whether or not man is worthy of grace. This is the *notitia* aspect of the concept of predestination. Man also knows that this will of God is hidden. In other words, he cannot be cognizant, as a result of inquisitive calculations, of whether just he is the object which is predetermined by God's will to receive love. The doctrine of predetermination cannot be transferred to the *usus* level.

2. Luther asserts in *The Bondage of the Will* that the Law must take its course in each human life, if the individual is to be capable of discerning sin and seeking grace. This is a general statement concerning *that* but not *how*. The latter, regarding the way in which some people are touched by the Law while others are not, is "another question", namely of God's concealed, terrible will which "ordains by his own counsel which and what sort of persons he wills to be recipients and partakers of his preached and offered mercy".[5] Further Luther maintains: "This will is not to be inquired into, but reverently adored, as by far the most awe-inspiring secret of the Divine Majesty, reserved for himself alone and forbidden to us much more religiously than any number of Corycian caverns".[6]

Thus, the *positive* tenets apply to the general rule that God in His sovereign counsel predestines certain people, by using the message of the Law and the Gospel. This I have called the *notitia* category. Yet, man should not try to specify the doctrine in concrete terms by curiously inquiring which particular individuals God has predetermined to be

[4] WA 10.III.108.12ff. (*Pred.* 1522): "Darnach sollt ihr von den Auserwählten dieses wissen. *Niemand weiss*, ob er Hass oder Liebe werth ist. Aber du hast zweyerley vor dir, nemlich *seinen verborgenen Rathschluss* und seine Gebote. Nun hat er dir geboten, dass du liebest und gläubest. Dieses thue du und lass indessen die Gnadenwahl dahinten." Since Luther is preaching this sermon in *Zwickau* this passage might be an attempt to correct the misleading doctrine of election held by T. Müntzer and others among the Zwickau prophets! Their opinion is described in 4.5.4 n. 17 below. According to *ib.* 194.12ff. the rich man in Luke 16:19ff. suffers "wie das Gott gefellet, denn *keyn gewiss regel* hyrauff gestellet werden mag. Daher ich nicht sagen thar, das der reyche man noch itzt allso leyde wie er datzu mal gelieden hatt, auch nicht leucken, das er noch sso leyde, denn es stehet ynn Gottis willkor beyderley." Cf. also WA 10.I.1.279.22ff. (*Kirchenpostille.* 1522).

[5] WA 18.684.30ff. (*De servo arbitrio.* 1525), LW 33.139. Cf. WA 18.729.1ff.: "Nec similitudo verbis coniunctivis sed indicativis profertur: *ut electi et reprobi sunt*, ita vasa honoris et ignominiae sunt." Cf. also A. Gyllenkrok (1952)58.

[6] WA 18.684.37ff., LW 33.139. Cf. WA 18.606.12ff., *ib.* 784.11ff. G. Adam (1970)46f. overlooks the fact that there are different aspects in Luther's conception of the hidden God.

touched by the Law as a prerequisite for the word of forgiveness. Luther's assessment becomes *critical* in the case of rational attempts to understand God's election on the *usus* level. Some laconic comments later in his presentation of the *deus absconditus* clearly express this vacillation between positive and negative evaluations:

> "It is enough to know simply that (*quod*) there is a certain inscrutable will in God, and as to what, why, and how far (*vero, cur et quatenus*) it wills, that is something we have no right whatever to inquire into, hanker after, care about, or meddle with, but only to fear and adore."[7]

Luther regards it as so important to clarify this dialectic that he once again stresses the point.[8] We know that God predetermines salvation and rejection. This knowledge of a general divine predicate is sufficient and necessary with regard to *deus absconditus*. Man cannot, however, by speculations know the specific predestination. It is and remains hidden in the Godhead until the Last Day. Thus, this change of aspect is implied by the "quod" and "cur et quatenus" of the election.[9]

3. The same theme, with minor variations, is repeated in what follows. When Luther is coming back to the same matter he often uses words and modes of expression reminiscent of *De servo arbitrio*. It is not surprising that, in the *Exegesis of 1 Tim. 2:4,* he has reason to emphasize *deus absconditus*. Paul exhorts us to pray even for the heathen. But he makes no further mention of the "inscrutable will" of the Godhead. For this will is "hidden and reserved to Him".[10] "Si volunt dicere nobis: *quare facit aliquos caecos* etc.? Sed illa est voluntas abscondita et incomprehensibilis."[11] This is not a subject for human understanding. For that which is above us is no concern of ours.[12]

---

[7] WA 18.686.1ff., LW 33.140. Cf. WA 18.689.18ff. Cf. also L. Pinomaa (1957)345.

[8] WA 18.690.1ff.: "Nec nobis quaerendum, *cur* ita faciat, sed reverendus Deus, qui talia possit et velit." Cf. *ib.* 712.19ff. Cf. also WA 18.549.35ff. (*Sendschreiben an die Christen zu Antwerpen.* 1525).

[9] Some comments were made on these dialectics by H. Bandt (1958)145f., E. Th. Pedersen, *Luther som skriftfortolker I.* (1959)78, G. Rost (1966)57, *ib.* 59.

[10] WA 26.36.7ff. (*Vorlesung über den 1. Tim.* 1528).

[11] *Ib.* 36.25ff.

[12] *Ib.* 31ff.: "Multi non cognoscunt: hoc pertinet ad *abscondissimam voluntatem,* sed voluntas, quae nobis tradita ad docendum, et comprehensibilis. Altiora ne quaesieris, qui scrutatur: Adam brach den Hals driber, quae supra nos nihil ad nos." Cf. the famous words in WA 18.685.5ff. (*De servo arbitrio.* 1525). Cf. also WA 39.I.578.23ff. (*Die dritte Disputation gegen die Antinomer.* 1539) = Drews 481 (quoted in 4.2.5 n. 29 above); WA 45.93.7ff. (*Pred.* 1537, R); *ib.* 96.4ff.

Although, we know little of the concealed God, nevertheless Luther makes the allegation that the divine will, at least occasionally, impels the sinner to blindness and hardness of heart. This is a general awareness on the *notitia* level. But as soon as any attempt is made to define this will, when man inquisitively asks "why" and tries to transpose his knowledge to the *usus* level with the help of reason, Luther bars the way with the comment "Nihil ad nos!".

When the Turkish threat again loomed towards the end of the 1530's, Luther was impelled to teach on predestination in his *Exhortation to Prayer against the Turks*. Many Christians had succumbed to fatalism. If everything is predetermined, it will come to pass. This is really true according to Luther. But we are not commanded to know what will happen. On the contrary, God has forbidden it.[13] Those who seek to know the secrets of the divine counsel and predetermination usurp the knowledge which only God is to possess, and thus transgress His Holy Commandments.[14]

Once more we see the alternation between the general and the specific knowledge which only God is to possess, and thus gransgress His holy doctrine preached by the Turks: That which is predestined by God must come to pass. But he allows this to be only a general tenet, a knowledge on the *notitia* level. When human beings try, by rational speculation, to apply this to specific phenomena, and classify "what is predetermined" they are grasping at the knowledge which is reserved for God alone. His counsel is and must remain concealed in its particular details.

Finally, when referring in the *Large Genesis Lecture* to the teaching expressed in *The Bondage of the Will* and elsewhere Luther goes on to say:

[13] WA 51.615.3ff. (*Vermahnung zum Gebet wider den Türken*. 1541): "Ja war ists *Was versehen ist, das geschicht*, Aber mir ist nicht befolhen, sondern viel mehr verbotten zu wissen, *was* versehen ist. Weil ichs nü nicht weis was versehen ist so heissts Gott versucht wer auff solch sein unwissen, hinein feret und verdirbt,..."

[14] *Ib*. 616.12ff.: "Die wolten uber das, so yhn geboten war, *Gottes heymlichen rat und versehung* auch wissen, Versuchten da mit Gotte, und ubertratten sein heiliges gebot." Luther explicitly makes a distinction in WAB 9.627.33ff. (1542): "Es ist ja die warheit, *was Gott beschlossen, Das mus gewisslich geschehen*, sonst wehr er ein lügner Inn seinen vorheissungen, Darauff wir unssern glauben setzen müssen, oder schendtlich feylen, Das ist unmöglich. Aber hier ist gleichwol *der grosse unterscheidt* zu halten, Nemlich was Gott uns offenbaret, vorheissen oder geboten hat, Das sollen wir gleuben, undt uns darnach richten, Das er nicht liegen werde. Aber was uns nicht offenbaret noch vorheissen hatt, das sollen wir, Ja können auch nicht wissen, uns viel weniger darnach richten,..." Cf. the touching consolation in WA 53.205.14ff. (*Ein Trost den Weibern, welchen es ungerade gegangen*. 1542).

"*a distinction* must be made when one deals with the knowledge (*notitia*), or rather with the subject, of the divinity (*subiecto divinitatis*). For one must debate either about the hidden God or about the revealed God. With regard to God, insofar as He has not been revealed, there is no faith, no knowledge, and no understanding. And here one must hold to the statement that what is above us is none of our concern."[15]

These statements can give the impression of wholly denying the knowledge of the hidden God (*nulla scientia et cognitio nulla*). Nevertheless, Luther can give us teaching about the *deus absconditus*. This is manifest from the conclusion:

"Among other things, however, I have written that everything is absolute and unavoidable (*esse omnia absoluta et necessaria*); but at the same time I have added that one must look at the revealed God, as we sing in the hymn: Er heist Jesu Christ, der HERR Zebaoth, und ist kein ander Gott, 'Jesus Christ is the Lord of hosts, and there is no other God'—and also in very many other places. But they will pass over all these places and take only (*tantum*) those that deal with the hidden God."[16]

Accordingly, the idea that everything comes to pass absolutely and by necessity is linked with the concept of the *deus absconditus*. Obviously Luther stands by his assertion of determinism concerning the hidden God. But he criticizes and refutes those who do not observe the correct balance between the concealed and the revealed God, and who, speculating, attempt to penetrate even matters which are, and must remain, hidden.

4. Consequently, we may conclude that in fact we know something of the hidden God which cannot, or should not be ignored, which is the case

[15] WA 43.458.35ff. (*Vorlesung über 1. Mose.* 1535–45), LW 5.43f.
[16] WA 43.463.3ff., LW 5.50. Cf. WA 42.313.20ff., *ib.* 645.28ff., WA 44.78.5ff.: "Repraehendenda igitur est stultitia, sive impietas potius eorum, qui omnia referunt ad praedestinationem, quae complectitur arcana Dei consilia et gubernationem nobis ignotam. Si Deus esses, tum liceret secundum eam procedere." Cf. also WA 52.140.25ff. (*Hauspostille.*1544), WATR 5.293.30ff. (1542): "Haec est nobis valde necessaria doctrina, et primum *distinguendum est de notitia vel abiectione divinitatis*, vel disputandum est de Deo revelato vel de notitia divinae voluntatis non revelatae. Ibi prorsus nulla est scientia. Hic est dicendum: Quae supra nos, nihil ad nos. Valde tamen Sathan obicit mihi obiectum impenetrabile. Non debeo scire, an sim praedestinatus ad salutem necne, sine verbo Dei, et quia ratio vult ita inquirere Deum, non invenit eum." See further E. Jüngel, *Quae supra nos nihil ad nos*, EvTh 32 (1972)223ff.

when this general cognizance is overshadowed, or totally subordinated to the understanding received through Christ.[17] This also means that it is too simple to say that the *whole* of Luther's theology is revealed theology, so that the doctrine of predestination, with reference to the hidden God, can only *indirectly* be an object of theology.[18] For Luther explicitly states *that* the hidden God predetermines without reservations. My analysis confirms the theory that the hidden God implies a "theoretical doctrine of the double predestination". This truth is relevant not only as regards the cure of souls but also on a general theoretical level.[19] The common purely *Christological* starting point in the Luther interpretation makes it difficult to do justice to his idea of the hidden God. It is also necessary to reflect on the *theological* premises with regard to the general relationship between God and the world.[20]

4.3.3. Abstract and Concrete Predestination

1. One of the psalms of praise, Ps. 91 (Vulgate), prompts Luther, in *Dictata*, to discuss the question of predetermination with special reference to human knowledge thereof. Verse 7 emphasizes that the Church of Christ does not show herself in her true colours to the outward glance. The whole of her spiritual structure is invisible. Therefore, her nature cannot be perceived by the eyes of the body but only by those of the spirit. This is why the foolish do not understand her.[1] In judging by the poverty and weakness of the Church the ignorant cannot comprehend that she is the creation of the great and mighty God. Yet, the believer, wise in faith, truly discovers God behind His opposite.[2]

---

[17] This is done by R. Seeberg (1917)153ff., T. Bohlin (1927)330. J. v. Walter (1940)122ff., is critical of R. Seeberg.

[18] W. Elert (1931)109f. *Deus absconditus* can be interpreted as a "central" thought in Luther's theology, L. Pinomaa (1938)150f.

[19] Cf. 4.2.6 n. 24.

[20] Both H. Bandt (1958) and H.-M. Barth (1967) are unduly negative in their discussion of the hidden God as a result of their more or less purely Christological approach to Luther interpretation, see 1.2 n. 11. FC in SD 11 has a doctrine of the hidden God in whom there is precognition of man's future belief or unbelief. But we are to avoid speculations about this knowledge and focus on the God revealed in Christ (BSLK 1079f.). Concerning the doctrine of the revealed and the hidden God in the theology of Calvin with reference to the theory of predestination, see *e.g.* H. Olsson (1943)34ff., *ib.* 79ff., *ib.* 555.

[1] WA 4.81.11ff. (*Dictata super Psalterium.* 1513–15)

[2] Cf. *ib.* 25ff.

Then Luther inserts an explanatory note:

"Non est putandum, quod hic propheta loquatur de consiliis et iudiciis dei profundis, que predestinationis et reprobationis dicuntur. Quoniam talia *nec sapiens* nec insipiens cognoscit, Rom. XI. 'O altitudo & c'."[3]

In other words, not even the believer can infer the election, or rejection, from the specific situation open to his eyes. Nevertheless, he knows intellectually that God really does predestine and reprobate. We may also say: It is possible to know in general terms—this is a knowledge on the so-called *notitia* level—that God predetermines to salvation and damnation. But neither the foolish nor the believer enlightened by faith can, by speculation, apply this general awareness to concrete objects *i.e.* to the *usus* level.

Turning our attention to the *Exposition of Romans*, we encounter the same arguments. They are lucidly presented in association with Rom. 9:15. Luther states that St Paul does not explicitly mention predestination, but evidently speaks in somewhat "indefinite" terms of the divine mercy. The vocabulary of Ex. 3:14 is equally vague: "I am who I am", or: "I shall be who I shall be." In this obscure mode of expression Luther sees a sign that man can only achieve a very blurred knowledge of predetermination. St Paul opposes those who curiously and restlessly pry into their own, or other's predestination.

On the one hand, it is a totally self-evident divine predicate that God predestines. Man can possess an "indefinite" understanding of this. Using my terminology I may say that this is awareness of election on the *notitia* level. On the other hand, man tries to express this general understanding in concrete terms: which specific individuals are elected. In other words, man seeks to transfer his abstract knowledge to the *usus* level. Yet, this is, in fact, impossible for the inquisitive *ratio* according to Luther. No obvious feature—merits, deeds or anything else—can be used to attain this specific knowledge of predestination and election. Only

---

[3] *Ib.* 20ff. I discussed another aspect of this text in 4.2.3.1. It is not unusual for Luther to emphasize the inner understanding through the holy Spirit. Cf. *e.g. ib.* 79.5ff.: " 'Quam magnificata sunt opera tua, domine', in se quidem magna sunt semper, sed magnificantur, quando magna esse cognoscuntur, quod fit per spiritum revelantem." This is clearly noticed already in K. Holl (1923)547ff. G. Ebeling, *Die Anfänge von Luthers Hermeneutik*, ZThK 48 (1951)172ff. gives an extensive analysis. A slightly revised version can be found in G. Ebeling, *Lutherstudien I* (1971)1ff.

when the election is fulfilled ("trifft") can we possess a certain knowledge.[4]

It goes without saying that this dialectic between general and concrete statements on predetermination is not only a matter of interest for the theologians. And in one of Luther's early popular writings on *ars moriendi* it emerges in association with the discussion of predestination affliction.

When the individual sees the concrete reality with his own eyes, and endeavours to reach definite conclusions, he risks going hopelessly astray. If he reflected on the specific objects of election for one thousand years, he still could not arrive at an adequate conclusion. A human being is, by means of speculation, unable to apply predetermination on the *usus* level. It is God's prerogative to know more than we can, to be cognizant of the particular election and damnation.[5] Nevertheless, we can understand up to the point that we comprehend the predicate *that* God predestines. This knowledge belongs to the *notitia* level.

2. When damnation in the form of Pharaoh's hardness of heart is discussed in the *Exodus Sermons*, the situation is different, since the issue is not concerned with the future, and we are not devoid of divine revelation as in the earlier texts. Exodus 7:3 says that God will cause the hardness of Pharaoh's heart. Consequently, by means of *revelatio*, we

---

[4] WA 56.397.13ff. (*Rom.* 1515–16), quoted in part in 4.3.1 n. 3. Cf. further *ib.* 115.19ff. In his lectures Luther presupposes the predestination, and at the same time warns against the application of this general theory in specific situations; WA 2.513.9f. (*In epistolam Pauli ad Galatas commentarius.* 1519): "Hoc loco (Gal 3:9) satis erat, imitationem Abrahae commendare, non promissionis et praedestinationis sublimitatem inculcare"; WA 5.173.7ff. (*Operationes in Psalmos.* 1519–21): "Debes enim velle nescire eius secreta, quae voluit te nescire, atque gaudere in hac eius voluntate, quam praecepit tibi observare in omnibus"; *Ib.* 623.1ff.: "Sic oportet piam animam velle nescire dei secretum super se nec scrutari maiestatem, ne opprimatur a gloria, Prover. 25., nec permittere, ut inducatur ad hoc impossibile, quo pelagus inscrutabile divinae sapientiae exhauriat et deum tentet." On this argument see H. Bandt (1958)79, G. Rost (1966)72.

[5] WA 2.690.10ff. (*Ein Sermon von der Bereitung zum Sterben.* 1519): "Mustu die helle und ewigkeit der peyn mit der vorsehung nit yn dir, nit yn yhrselbs, nit yn denen, die vordampt seyn, ansehen, auch nichts bekummern mit ssovill menschen yn der gantzen welt, die nit vorsehen seynd, dan sichstu dich nit fur, sso wirt dich diss bild schwind sturtzen und zu boden stossen: drumb mustu hie gewalt uben, die augenn fest zuhaltenn fur solchem blick, *dan er gar nichts nutz ist, ob du tausent jar damit umbgiengst, und vorterbet dich zu mall, du must doch gott lassenn gott seyn, das er wisse mehr von dir wan du selbs.*" Cf. also WADB 7.22.35ff. (1522), WA 10.III.194.17ff. (*Pred.* 1522).

have application in concrete terms of the fact that God condemns, *e.g.* by hardening someone's heart. This transposition, however, from the *notitia* to the *usus* level could not take place by means of *ratio*. For reason cannot here see any logical reason why God should harden Pharaoh's heart.[6] In his thoughts man is not content with the general insight into the divine predicate that God elects and rejects. *Ratio* will start "supra" and try to intellectually comprehend the Godhead in order to attach His will and actions to specific ends.[7]

In consequence, these expositions of Exodus fit the pattern which we previously established. When no special revelation is given, the believer can only state that God's will is inscrutable by *ratio*.[8]

3. A *Trinity Sermon* can demonstrate that my interpretation of Luther's basic idea here holds good. When he expounds Rom. 11:33 he states, first, that predetermination is the issue, secondly, that it lies concealed. "Es ist, inquit, zu unbegreifflich, quia impossibile, quod homo ex ratione intelligat, quid cogitet und im syn habe."[9] Firstly we possess a purely abstract knowledge *that* all existing things and events, including the incarnation, are founded on the divine counsel: this is the *notitia* level. Secondly, we cannot by rational prognoses reach a concrete understanding of *how* God shaped that which will come to pass. "Hoc consilium apud se habuit, nemo intellexit, nemo dedit consilium." "The ways" of God, *i.e.* His will in the actual situations of daily life, are

---

[6] WA 16.113.9ff. (*Predigten über das 2. Buch Mose.* 1524–27): "'Ego obdurabo': mirum, quomodo hoc fit?" And further: "Hunc locum maxime miratur ratio et scire vult et quando hoc invenire non potest, quies non est." *Ib.* 116.7f.: "Si vult deus rem aliquam, non quaerendum: cur, non habet magistrum, secundum quem diriget omnia, sua voluntas est suprema." Cf. *ib.* 136.10f., *ib.* 140.1ff., *ib.* 144.9ff.

[7] *Ib.* 114.5, *ib.* 143.11f., 147.1ff. E. W. Gritsch & R. W. Jenson (1976)154: "Luther recognized the temptation of 'theo-logic': to solve the mystery of the relationship between the God hidden in creation and the God revealed in the gospel through syllogisms."

[8] Cf. WAB 4.589.23ff. (1528) quoted in 4.5.1 n. 17. G. Rost (1966)73 is quite right in his conclusion: "*Formal* steht also die Prädestinationslehre fest, muss feststehen, da sie einfach zwangsläufig aus dem Gottesbegriff ergibt. *Ihr konkreter Inhalt* aber ist unerforschlich und darf und soll vom Menschen nicht erforscht werden." Cf. also WA 36.61.4ff. (*Pred.* 1532, R).

[9] WA 45.92.35ff. (*Pred.* 1537, R). Cf. further *ib.* 93.7ff.: "Praedicatio *rationis*, non *von innwendig her aus*, wie es Gott in sein Gottlichen rad beschlossen, ubi solus bey im allein, antequam oravimus, fecit, 'faciamus hominem', utque filius fiat homo, ut omnes credentes in eum."

beyond the comprehension of human reason.[10] The *usus* level lies outside the limits of reason.

In the large *Lecture on Genesis* Luther uses the scholastic concept *voluntas beneplaciti dei* to designate "substantialis voluntas Dei seu nuda Maiestas, quae est Deus ipse", although it would be more appropriate to associate "the will to please" with the Gospel.[11] Man can only pass superficial judgements on this divine being: "In Deo enim nihil est nisi divinitas et substantia Dei est eius immensa sapientia ac omnipotens potentia."[12] So profound an awareness of the divine predestination is accordingly accepted without reservations. But when man seeks to specify it in concrete terms, Luther consistently rejects every rational application of the general doctrine of predetermination. Indeed, he firmly warns his hearers against speculations and reflection on the actual predestination.[13] Accordingly, the late Luther material also contains a dialectic between the predestination on two different levels.[14]

It is undoubtedly true that there is, in Luther, in the concept of God a feature of "antipredestination".[15] It is also true that he warns against speculation on election.[16] But this is only half the truth. Unless it is made clear that on the theoretical level Luther has a positive interest in election, and that the critical comments on predestination only relate to

---

[10] *Ib.* 93.10ff. Cf. further *ib.* 95.10ff.: "*Cor humanum non potest scrutari dei iudicium*, ut dicere possit: hoc placet deo, hoc displicet, nisi mundano more, sed quae iudicia et viae dei in re salutis... Die iudicant und verdamnen, wollen leute furen, was got gefalle vel non. Sed nemo ex suo capite dicet: hoc dei iudicium, hoc vult, hoc non, quia impossibile scire homini hoc, quanquam uns unterstanden, ut deo rat geben und furschrieben, was er loben und verdamnen sol... *Sed quando ipse revelat, tum fit comprehensibile, quod er richtet vel verdampt, sind etlicher mas begreifflich, sed non gantz.*"

[11] WA 42.294.36ff. (*Vorlesung über 1. Mose. 1535–45), ib.* 295.39ff.

[12] *Ib.* 294.39f.

[13] *Ib.* 38ff.; *ib.* 295.1ff.: "De hac voluntate substantiali et divina nihil scrutandum, sed simpliciter abstinendum est, sicut a maiestate divina: est enim inscrutabilis nec voluit eam Deus proponere in hac vita"; *ib.* 313.20ff.: "Hic Sophistae de Electione disputant, quae fit secundum propositum Dei. Sed sepe monui, abstinendum esse a speculationibus nudae Maiestatis. Hae enim sicut est impossibile, ut verae sint, ita etiam minime sunt salutares"; *ib.* 670.26ff.: Perniciosa igitur et pestilens cogitatio est de Quare, ac certum affert interitum, praesertim cum ascendimus altius, et de praedestinatione volumus Philosophari. Sed meminerimus exempli Abrahae, quo docemur, quod coram Deo sit repuerascendum, et non disputandum, quomodo aut quare Deus aliquid praecipiat."

[14] Cf. WA 44.65.23f.: "Atque haec sunt mirabilia consilia Dei, de quibus non est disputandum, cur hac aut alia ratione gubernet mundum." Cf. further also WA 40.III.656.28ff. (*Enarratio capitis noni Esaiae. 1543-44/1546*).

[15] Th. Harnack I (1927)177ff., cf. E. Vogelsang (1932)84.

[16] This is stressed by *e.g.* L. Pinomaa (1938)149f., *id.* (1957)345, *ib.* 348.

the transposition to the concrete level by the inquisitive *ratio*, we will necessarily miss the point.

We can also establish that the motif research of the Lund school does not do justice to the dialectic in the material, when it regards "the religious motive" as the only issue of value in the doctrine of predestination. The "rational motive"—Luther's explicit acceptance of the abstract concept of election—is underestimated, as it is not considered to be a genuine element of the Reformation.[17] Only if we distinguish between an abstract and a concrete knowledge of the divine predetermination, can we focus on both the material which gives evidence of this belief and the documents which exhibit opposition to reflection on predestination.[18]

4.3.4. The Concrete Use of Predestination by Natural Conscience Is Diabolical

For clarity's sake we have endeavoured in a previous section (2.2.) to use concepts derived from formal logic. Now when we penetrate further, we can employ these to understand the way in which the application of God's judgement and rejection involves "affliction" ("Anfechtung"), and the reason why affliction concerning predestination is consistently designated as "diabolical".

1. In the *Second Lecture on the Psalms*, Luther describes how a serious *affliction* arises. It begins with a general feeling of fear, and a perception of the grim judgements of Holy Writ, especially those related to horrible threats and terrible examples of God's wrath. Biblical quotations which may provoke such reactions are, according to Luther, *e.g.* Matt. 12:30, Ps. 140:12, Matt. 23:13. The train of thought is presented as a practical syllogism:

> "Posita autem *hac maiore*, facile et pronum est, cooperante uniuscuiusque propria et naturali conscientiae infirmitate et scrupulositate, *minorem* subsumere et dicere: *tu autem es talis*."[1]

---

[17] *E.g.* G. Aulén (1927)220ff. Cf. also R. Bring (1929)337, T. Bohlin (1927)271f.

[18] Thus I agree with G. Rost (1966)75f.: "Der fundamentaltheologische Charakter von Luthers Prädestinationsauffassung bleibt also auch in der Genesisvorlesung bestehen. Sie ist in dem formalen Gottesbegriff verankert, den Luther auch für die Vernunft erreichbar hielt und *an dem er nie etwas geändert hat. Dagegen ist ihm in zunehmendem Masse die Grösse der Gefahr bewusst geworden, die darin liegt, dass die Vernunft des Menschen daran geht, diesen formalen Gottesbegriff mit konkretem Inhalt zu füllen.*"

[1] WA 5.620.37ff. (*Operationes in Psalmos.* 1519–21).

The vivid awareness of God's unrelenting anger, judgement and punishment for sin begins the first phase of affliction. This is the presentation of the *propositio maior* of the syllogism. The second phase means that the individual perceives in himself the qualities for which retribution is due. The expression of the logical subject in concrete terms appears clearly and laconically in "You are like that!" The person's conscience is touched. The *propositio minor* becomes an existential reality. The *conclusion* is inevitable: "God is angry with you and will punish you!" Then, the third and most painful phase of the affliction is a fact. The afflicted man sees hell yawn before him. His conscience is beset by ineffable horror and anguish.

The establishment of the meaning of predestination in concrete terms, *i.e.* the affliction concerning predestination, can be done in an analogous fashion. Man realises that God has predetermined to reject certain sinners for ever more. This is the *propositio maior*, or the knowledge of predestination on the *notitia* level. The believer perceives, through his conscience, that he is such a sinner. This is the *propositio minor*, or the application of predetermination on the *usus* level. The logical "conclusion" follows directly: God has predetermined to reject you for all eternity. This is the most terrible and intolerable of all afflictions, the affliction concerning predestination, which creates the extreme despair.[2]

2. Now we have also established that in his natural theology Luther accepts the *propositio maior* but consistently repudiates the truth of the *propositio minor*, and therefore the truth of the "conclusion" (2.2.). This also applies here. It is not God who erects the latter premise and the conclusion following therefrom. This comes from the devil!

Luther emphasizes this, at an early stage, in his *academic* lectures. The devil, or the prudence of the flesh, is the cause of this dangerous affliction. For, in the first place, this belief cannot come from God since it leads to the transgression of God's commands and to self-aggrandizement. Secondly, it cannot be of divine origin for it means that man tempts God and in a wrong way searches for certainty of his own predestination, or for the sight of a sign from heaven.[3]

[2] In 4.5.1–2 I shall further analyse Luther's instruction to Christians to prevent and overcome the affliction concerning election.

[3] WA 5.172.3ff. (*Operationes in Psalmos.* 1519–21): "Interim hoc satis est, Hanc esse periculosissimam tentationem, quam qua causa moveat diabolus vel sapientia carnis, ubi scieris, simul scies, quo remedio occurras. *Primum* itaque firmus esto ac certissimus, *hanc cogitationem non esse ex deo*, ideo omni studio expellendam, tanquam eam, quae deo tuo displiceat multis modis... Nec diabolus ulla causa hac inutili cura et noxia te occupat, quam ut interim *obliviscaris praecepti dei tui*, quo iuberis sperare et credere, simulque subdole te trahat in affectum et amorem tuiipsius, ut *incipias quaerere, quae tua sunt*...

Luther is no less outspoken in his *popular* writings, which were intended for the general public. Hell looms large, and increases when man looks upon it and thinks of it in time of need. Indeed, the devil accepts the true premise that there are sinners who will not experience grace but eternal punishment, since they are predestined thereto. And he tries to present yet another premise which is nevertheless false, namely that the individual in question actually is such a sinner so that the mendacious conclusion is inevitable: It makes no difference what you do, or believe, you are lost anyhow.[4]

The decisive part is missing when the believer does not clearly see that these thoughts are from the devil. This really is a question of a *tentatio diabolica*. It differs from the human affliction which is sufficient.[5] It is one thing to know that God reigns supreme, another to follow the devil and try to comprehend how God rules.[6] As a result of the divine revelation, we possess an information of that which we need to understand. The devil tries to entice man to speculate about God's will and escape the revelation.[7] This is, indeed, the original sin into which the devil inveigled man in Paradise, *i.e.* to become like God, to be

Secundo, non esse ex deo, etiam hoc indicio facile intelliges, quod his machinis duo maxima mala tibi intentat: primum, ut *tentes deum,* quod Christo in pinnaculo templi quoque intentavit. Conatur enim hoc te negocio occupare, ut *optes certus esse de tua praedestinatione aut signum videre de coelo.*" Cf. *ib.* 623.1ff. (quoted in 4.3.3 n. 4). Cf. further K. Holl (1923)148, H. Beintker (1954)82ff.

[4] WA 2.688.2ff. (*Ein Sermon von der Bereitung zum Sterben.* 1519): "Da zu hilfft ubir die mass seer, *das man gottis urteyl nit weyss,* da hin *der bosse geyst* die seel treybet, das sie sich mit ubrigem unnutzen furwitz, Ja mit dem aller ferlichsten furnhemen beladet und forschen sol gotlichs radts heymlickeit, ob sie vorsehn sey odder nit. Hie ubet *der teuffell* seyn letzte, groste, listigiste kunst und vormugen." Cf. further *ib.* 11ff. See also discussion in G. Rost (1966)163.

[5] WAB 4.590.37ff. (1528): "Quid igitur fatigari se sinit *a Satana* iis, quae sunt impossibilia?" Further: "Maxima pars fallitur, quod non credunt has cogitationes esse *tentationes Satanae,* ideo nemo fere eas contemnit aut ut contemnat pugnat, cum illae ipsae sint tela ista ignita nequissimarum nequitiarum spiritualium in coelestibus." And further: "Summa, haec est princeps tentatio et proprie diabolica, ideo humana tentatione satis est tentari." Cf. WAB 6.86.10ff. (1531): "Erstlich musset yhr feste ynn ewr hertz fassen, das solche gedancken gewislich des leidigen *teufels* einblasen und feurige pfeil sind."

[6] WA 36.61.4ff. (*Pred.* 1532, R). Cf. WATR 1.515.6ff. (1530–35). WA 40.III.341.7ff. (*In XV Psalmos graduum.* 1532/33, Hs).

[7] WA 45.95.31ff. (*Pred.* 1537, R): "Prius dixi ex revelatione aliquo modo nos scire, quae iudiciae et viae. Ibi Satan iubet tales hoher steigen, quam deus wil haben, ut forschen, an sint versehen, obs selig sollen werden, und faren *ex revelatione,* quam deus revelavit, in alia somnia, quae non revelavit". Cf. further *ib.* 96.20ff. Cf. also WA 51.616.7ff. (*Vermahnung zum Gebet wider den Türken.* 1541), WAB 11.166.6ff. (1545).

dissatisfied with the revealed truths which can make man holy, and seek to penetrate the divine secrets in order to discover the identities of the elect.[8]

3. Against this background we can understand why the scholars who emphasized God as the cause of the affliction pay little attention to the diabolical affliction concerning predestination.[9] A dualistic "philosophy" allows of a more detailed exposition of *satan* as the cause of this kind of affliction.[10]

I maintain that it is right and important to accentuate not only the *existential* side,[11] but also the theoretical aspect of this Luther material. The application of the general doctrine of predestination, *i.e.* the affliction concerning predestination is *intellectually* impossible to achieve by human resources alone.[12] However, in what follows, we shall see that the Lutheran tradition also teaches a form of certainty of election through *belief* in Christ (4.5.4.).

4.3.5. The Concrete Use of the Commands by Faith Comes from God

Finally, I wish to emphasize that as a counterpart to the negative value set on the concrete application of the predestination theory by reason and the human conscience, Luther often presents God's command as the positive material which the individual ought to apply to himself.

[8] WA 43.458.3ff. (*Vorlesung über 1. Mose.* 1535–45), cf. *ib.* 460.36ff., *ib.* 461.42ff. Cf. also WA 42.295.23ff., WA 44.77.36ff., WATR 5.293.14ff. (1542).

[9] K. Holl (1923)67ff. has the merit of showing how affliction is a decisive factor in Luther's theology. This *Anfechtung* would be easy if the devil was the cause. But now man can discover God behind the affliction (*ib.* 68f.). Through the revelation of God's law and wrath we have knowledge of our sin, and of our need for the saviour. So the victory by faith in Christ is "Beschreibung des Rechtfertigungsvorgangs" (*ib.* 75). Consequently, Holl pays little attention to affliction concerning election. Following Holl, E. Vogelsang (1932)30ff. analyses the affliction of predestination paying little attention to the demonic origin of this assault by satan. It is remarkable that the latest extensive dissertation about the affliction in Luther's theology, H. Beintker (1954)82ff. only refers to Ps. 22:8f. in *Operationes in Psalmos* and then describes "Ihre Beziehung auf Gott". He does not emphasize that it is a temptation from the devil, for man to know as much as God.

[10] G. Jacob (1929)38, F. Gerke *Die satanische Anfechtung in der Ars moriendi und bei Luther,* ThBl 11 (1932)321ff., L. Pinomaa (1938)175, P. Th. Bühler (1942)61.

[11] Cf. the title of Pinomaa's dissertation on the affliction: "Der existenzielle Charakter der Theologie Luthers".

[12] The Lutheran confessions are congenial to Luther in this train of thought, BSLK 1083 (SD 11).

In the *Second Lecture on the Psalms* Luther maintains that the commands contain the revealed will of God, which we have to obey. When the believer does this, God's predestination is "spontaneously" realised without the need for us to concern ourselves.[1] A somewhat later *sermon* lucidly expresses that man has two general principles before him: God's hidden counsel and God's command. Only the latter is to be applied in a specific situation.[2] *Letters* also contrast the good application of God's commands, with the diabolical attempts to specify the election.[3] The *Exposition of 1 Tim.* 2:4, with reference to the doctrine of predestination, also oscillates between a *voluntas praecepti*, meaning that the Christian ought to pray for and preach to all mankind, and a *voluntas abscondita et reservata*, meaning that man is not allowed to reflect on the identities of those elected and rejected respectively.[4] God has not commanded us to know, by reason, whether we are among the chosen. Nevertheless, His command reveals enough for human understanding and action. This matter is made manifest by Holy Writ.[5] The intellectual specification of the doctrine of predetermination is not revealed. We neither can, nor should, possess rational knowledge of it.[6]

By discussing Luther's teaching on God's commands we have touched on an issue which has been intensively debated by scholars, and which played a major role for Luther, namely the first commandment as the fountain-head of all faith, wisdom, and humanity.[7] This not only means a death-bringing demand. It is really a life-giving Gospel: God wishes to be our God in all the vicissitudes of life, in suffering, and in death. In what follows I shall shed further light on how this Gospel through Christ means protection against, and victory over the affliction concerning predestination (4.5.1.–2.).

[1] WA 5.172.27ff. (*Operationes in Psalmos*. 1519–21): "Neque enim aliud deus requirit, quam voluntatem suam nobis esse assidua sollicitudine commendatam. Quod ubi fecerimus, praedestinatio sua *sponte implebitur sine nostra cura*. Ille vero perversor primo vult, te de te sollicitum esse et postremo de dei praeceptis, ut sic te praeferas deo tuo nec super omnia eum diligas, immo nec deum habeas." Cf. *ib*. 172.8ff., *ib*. 173.7ff., *ib*. 174.13ff.

[2] WA 10.III.108.12ff. (*Pred*. 1522) quoted in 4.3.2 n. 4. Concerning *De servo arbitrio* cf. L. Pinomaa (1957)345, *ib*. 348.

[3] WAB 4.590.3ff. (1528), cf. *ib*. 589.15ff., WAB 6.87.3ff. (1531), WAB 11.166.6ff. (1545).

[4] WA 26.36.11ff. (*Vorlesung über den 1. Timotheusbrief*. 1528).

[5] WA 51.615.3ff. (*Vermahnung zum Gebet wider den Türken*. 1541).

[6] WAB 9.627.36ff. (1542). Cf. WA 43.458.3ff. (*Vorlesung über 1 Mose*. 1535–45), *ib*. 461.8ff., WATR 5.293.22 (1542).

[7] Cf. WA 5.171.11ff. (*Operationes in Psalmos*. 1519–21). The debate was started in essence by K. Holl (1923)73ff. Major contributions were made by *e.g.* H. Beintker (1954)31ff., D. Löfgren (1960)392ff., A. Siirala, *Gottes Gebot bei Martin Luther* (1956)44ff., G. Heintze, *Luthers Predigt von Gesetz und Evangelium* (1958)121ff. Cf. H. Olsson (1971)25ff.

4.3.6. Conclusions

1. Similarities between Biel and Luther, with reference to both basic attitude and terminology, can be traced in the view of God as His own law and ordinance. Both state the impossibility of depicting any course of action with regard to election which applies *a priori* to the Godhead. Furthermore, both derive God's freedom from the Biblical concept of God as "the Creator of heaven and earth". Therefore in Biel as well as Luther we can find confirmation of the theory set forth of a dialectic between the abstract "that" and the concrete "how" of predestination.

2. Both men are clear that God unconditionally elects to salvation and reprobates. The fact which lies concealed, and which Luther indicates by using the term *deus absconditus*, is that we do not know by reasoning, how the hidden God elects and rejects. In the main, the scholars have done justice to Luther's critical view in this context. But the positive aspect of *deus absconditus* has been overlooked or deprecated. On the *notitia* level Luther prompts the intellectual understanding of predestination. On the other hand, a negative view appears when he notices attempts by speculation to transfer predetermination to the *usus* level. In this respect, we can speak of a tendency to "antipredestination" in Luther's theology. Here, scholars have rightly drawn attention to the statements warning against prying and speculation on predetermination.

3. We now understand why Luther designated affliction concerning predestination as diabolical. It is an attempt by the individual to use his own judgement in translating awareness of predetermination from the *notitia* to the *usus* level. This is also an illustration of the original sin of trying, in disbelief, to usurp knowledge which belongs to God alone.

4. Finally, we observe that Luther invariably entices the Christians away from brooding and disquiet concerning the specific rejection, advising them to bear in mind the commands revealed by God. The Christian can be confident of meeting the divine will in these.

Thus, we have got a natural transition to the discussion of the relationship between the idea of predestination and the doctrine of justification. Since this relationship takes two forms, depending on which type of association is intended, it is appropriate to divide the following analysis into two main sections. The doctrinal and theoretical relationship is treated in 4.4. and the practical and existential in 4.5. According to my own terminology, we may say that the former section is mainly concerned with the *notitia* and the latter with the *usus* level.

4.4. Concerning Cause, Predestination Takes Priority over Justification

4.4.1. Predestination is Autonomous Vis-à-vis Justification

Luther's great discovery, and the message of the Reformation, is justification by faith, irrespective of human merits or deeds. It is irrefutable that this theme is of fundamental importance in his theology. Moreover, it is easy to understand that scholars have at times tried to derive the theory of predestination from the doctrine of justification. This can be implied by such expressions as: The predetermination is "the necessary extension of the doctrine of justification".[1] Or: The predestination is an extrapolation "from the confession of Christ".[2]

I have already implicitly maintained the invalidity of the theory that predestination is a rationalisation *post eventum*, based on the important doctrine of justification, when I demonstrated, in a previous section (4.2.), that the theory of predetermination is a primary concept in the reformer's notion of God.

I will assert that it is not predestination which is a consequence of justification, but justification which is an effect of predetermination.[3] In order to connect the preceding passage (4.2.) with this one, I first select some representative texts dealing with justification and predetermination, which give evidence of predestination in such a way that predestination appears in principle autonomous *vis-à-vis* the doctrine of justification.

1. I start with the *Interpretation of Romans* (Rom. 8:28ff.). Luther begins by stating that the entire passage Rom. 8:28–39 is dependent on the first verse, and that it deals with predetermination.[4] Even if the elect encounter all kinds of suffering, they will not fall from grace: "non contingenter, sed n e c e s s a r i o s a l v e n t u r e l e c t i".[5] Consequently, salvation is not brought about by human will or action but by the divine counsel.

According to Luther all are agreed that everything which belongs to creation in the eyes of mankind appears as "contingens in esse suo i.e.

---

[1] C. Stange (1928)88. Cf. Th. Harnack I (1927)142.

[2] K. Schwarzwäller, *Theologia crucis* (1970)101, cf. *ib.* 164f., *ib.* 185f. See further *id., Das Gotteslob* (1970)11 and *ib.* 53.

[3] Cf. the same thesis in G. Rost (1966)80ff.

[4] WA 56.381.14ff. (*Rom.* 1515–16).

[5] *Ib.* 28f.

mutabilis, Et non Deus seu immutabilis."[6] He asks: does that which God has predetermined come to pass by necessity? Indeed, he holds that all confess this to be the case. The fact that we believe certain phenomena to be fortuitous does not prevent God's certain predestination.

> "Quod Nulla est contingentia apud Deum simpliciter, Sed tantum coram nobis. Quia etiam folium arboris non cadit in terram sine Voluntate patris."[7]

Therefore, Luther can conclude this critical exposition with a kind of summary: It is a poor mode of expression when the concept *necessitas* sometimes refers to the subject (God) and sometimes to the *copula* (creation, time). In fact, it here concerns only the contingency of time, never of the subject.[8] Thus, predetermination is based not on justification but on the contingent creation's absolute dependence on the Creator who alone exists by necessity. Election is regarded as a special case of the absolute necessity which binds and governs all created things. Simply because the theory of predestination has this independence *vis-à-vis* the doctrine of justification, it can become an effective knife which, *inter alia*, excises the idea of human merit from justification and creates certainty of salvation.

2. These arguments recur on a wide front in the book *The Bondage of the Will*. Where Erasmus would avoid the complex questions of chance and necessity, Luther says in a programmatic *propositio*:

> "Est itaque et hoc imprimis necessarium et salutare Christiano, nosse, quod Deus nihil praescit contingenter, sed quod omnia incommutabili et aeterna infallibilique voluntate et praevidet et proponit et facit."[9]

In consequence, everything we do and everything that happens, come to pass by necessity and immutability if we consider God's will. And this is true, even when we think that it occurs by chance and that the turn of events could as well be different.[10] *Coram hominibus* much appears contingent, since we encounter it as if it were by chance and without our expecting it. But *coram Deo* all things come to pass by a necessary and

---

[6] *Ib.* 383.3ff. Luther's criticism of the distinction between *necessitas consequentiae* and *necessitas consequentis* is presented above (4.2.2.2).

[7] *Ib.* 19ff.

[8] *Ib.* 22ff. Cf. H. McSorley (1969)233f. who criticizes Luther's analysis of the twofold concept of necessity.

[9] WA 18.615.12ff. (*De servo arbitrio*. 1525).

[10] *Ib.* 31ff.

immutable will.[11] This train of thought once more gives Luther opportunity to contradict the scholastic distinction between the necessity which is dependent on the result, and the unconditional necessity. As in the *Lecture on Romans*, he finds the distinction worthless, since it adds nothing to the general human knowledge, namely that all things come to pass by necessity with reference to God. When we classify them as things without a necessary existence, it is no different from saying that the thing done is not God Himself but part of the creation.[12]

The principle underlying the arguments in *The Bondage of the Will*, therefore, is this theory that denies the autonomy of earthly phenomena in relation to the heavenly reality. A specific side of this total dependence is expressed in the doctrine of predestination. Therefore, this has its roots in the Luther concept of God. For this reason, the belief in God's predetermination can stand on its own feet with respect to the doctrine of justification. When predestination appears as an argument used for strengthening the doctrine of justification, it can therefore be designated as an autonomous argument, the tenability of which is only intelligible when its self-evidence is manifest.

3. The immutability of God, the immutability of His actions, His inability to deny Himself and His loyalty to His Word—these arguments do not derive from Christology. Because they are autonomous *vis-à-vis* Christology, they can be adduced in the late *Genesis Lecture* as a further argument for joy and delight in salvation.[13] This love of God holds good in all ages with the same certainty as the fact that God Himself is immutable and enacts His counsel by necessity in the liberation of believers from the forces of chaos. Luther is working with a combination of *two* different lines of reasoning. On the one hand, he assumes the truth of his proposition in *The Bondage of the Will*: "esse omnia absoluta et necessaria". This thought belongs to the hidden God. On the other, we must at the same time apprehend Christ as the revealed God.[14] The first aspect has its own truth and validity. But both are simultaneously present in the synthesis which constitutes the ground for the evangelical salvation.

4. We can carry out our reflection a little further. There must be a certain difference between a theology which interprets the Biblical

---

[11] *Ib.* 616.7ff.

[12] *Ib.* 13ff. There is a similar train of thought *ib.* 724.32ff.

[13] WA 43.461.29ff. (*Vorlesung über 1. Mose.* 1535–45), quoted in 4.2.4 n. 15. Cf. *ib.* 462.13ff., WA 44.528.38ff., WAB 9.627.33ff. (1542), quoted in 4.3.2 n. 14 above.

[14] WA 43.463.3ff. (quoted in 4.3.2 n. 16). Cf. WA 43.458.35ff.

concept of God's omnipotence as an ineluctable reality, on which everything is ultimately dependent, *i.e.* as a theological determinism, and a theology which does not consider "God the Father, Almighty, the maker of heaven and earth" in this way. For Luther there is no fundamental freedom for mankind *coram Deo*.[15] *Formula Concordiae*, however, does not assume that all things occur by necessity. It, rather, tells of man as having the freedom to reject the proffered grace. This results in a "broken" doctrine of predestination with respect to reprobation.[16] Since Luther's ideas on the absolute necessity do not carry the same weight in FC it is more apt to say of this than of the reformer that its tenets of predestination are an extrapolation from the doctrine of justification!

4.4.2. Predestination as Cause of Justification

Having established that the theory of predetermination is independent of Christology and the doctrine of justification, I hinted at the systematical context into which the thoughts of predestination as cause and justification as effect can be integrated.

1. Already in the first *Lecture on the Psalms*, we are able to observe that at an early stage Luther, in an apparently self-evident fashion, understood the divine election as the causative background to the enlightenment and renewal of mankind. Psalm 109:3 (Vulgate), as paraphrased by Luther, does not refer to Christ alone, but also to those who belong to Him. From the womb, *i.e.* Holy Writ, they are born "in filios adoptionis". This election took place before the light, which is equivalent to "from eternity", since God chose them from eternity to be born. These elect were born to this sonship through the divine birth by

---

[15] Cf. further 3.3 about God's omnipotence.

[16] Therefore FC in SD 11 is forced to stress the distinction between *praescientia* and *praedestinatio* (BSLK 1064f.). Cf. the critical questions in E. Schlink (1948)392: "Bekommen in dieser Lehre von der Verstockung und Verdammnis nicht vielleicht konkrete aktuelle Sünden ein isoliertes Übergewicht, das die grauenhafte Wirklichkeit des Sünderseins zurücktreten lässt? Entsteht bei diesen Aussagen über die mutwillige Verschuldung der Verdammnis nicht der Anschein, als ob hier eine Möglichkeit des Menschen vorausgesetzt sei, sich gegenüber dem Evangelium zu öffnen und offen zu halten?". And further: "Ist diese Ablehnung der doppelten Praedestination in der Unterscheidung von Gnadenwahl und Vorsehung nicht vielleicht trotz aller Scheu vor dem Geheimnis doch *der Anfang einer rationalen Auflösung des Geheimnisses der göttlichen Wahl*, wie sie dann in der lutherischen Orthodoxie offensichtlich wurde?"

the Holy Spirit.[1] When God, therefore, makes the believer be born anew by the Word and the Spirit, this event in time has a prehistory in God's eternal being.

An exposition indicating how Luther, on the basis of the actual Bible text, attributes to eternity priority over time, is to be found in the *Commentary on Romans*, Rom. 9:15. First, God has mercy through the predetermination present within Him. Then, God shows pity in the earthly reality. Since the latter is called "in effectu" we can draw the conclusion that the first act of mercy is the cause of the second. God's inner mercy is described in the present tense, and the external demonstration of pity in the future.[2] Since, without further ado, Luther understands predetermination as the cause which provokes an effect in the creation, we are given an indication of the self-evidence of predestination as background *sui generis* to justification. It seems impossible to convert the eternal election to a secondary construction, based on the doctrine of justification.[1]

The *First Lecture on Galatians* also suggests the way in which the divine predestination causes the incarnation of the Son and the sonship of the faithful. In the gloss on Gal. 4:4, Luther notes that by sending His Son into the world, God at the same time realises predetermination in a hidden fashion. Therefore, it is not time which prompts the mission of the Son, but rather the incarnation of the Son which brings time to its consummation.[3] There is an analogy in the gloss on Gal. 4:6, to the effect

---

[1] WA 4.234.13ff. (*Dictata super Psalterium.* 1513–15). "Consonat translatio nostra sic: 'Ex utero', scilicet scripture, 'genui te' et tuos in filios adoptionis 'ante luciferum', id est ab eterno, quia elegit nos ab eterno generari & c. Sic 1 Pet. 2. 'Quasi modo geniti infantes lac concupiscite'. Sed in talem infantiam generantur generatione dei ex spiritu sancto: ideo dicuntur 'ros infantie', ex matrice scripture nati". Cf. a similar train of thought in the interpretation of Ps 143:2 (Vulgate), WA 4.446.5ff.: " 'Protector meus... qui subdit ps. 17 populum' i. e. fideles per mundum 'meum' mihi predestinatum, ut meus sit, 'sub me' ". Cf. also WA 3.161.30ff., WA 4.37.13ff.

[2] WA 56.397.7ff. (*Rom.* 1515–16): "Grecus Sic: 'Miserebor, cuiuscunque misereor, et Commiserabor, quemqunque commiseror', q. d. cuius in presenti predestinatione misereor apud me, huius etiam miserebor postmodum in effectu, Ut sic presens tempus 'misereor' predestinantis misericordiam intrinsecam, tempus autem futurum predestinato exhibitam misericordiam notet. Sic etiam de 'commiserabor' ". Cf. *ib.* 84.24ff., *ib.* 89.15ff. An extensive discussion of Luther's conception of time and eternity can be found in H. Heimler, *Aspekte der Zeit und Ewigkeit bei Luther*, LuJ 40 (1973)9ff.

[3] WA 57b.29.23ff. (*Gal.* 1516–17): "Hic etiam notandum, quod subocculte simul predestinationem coexsequitur. Alioquin debuit pocius dicere: at ubi Deus misit filium suum, venit plenitudo temporis. Non enim tempus fecit filium mitti, sed econtra missio filii fecit tempus plenitudinis."

that the Holy Spirit makes us the children of God. The children are not the cause of the latter: those who are sons of God in His eternal plan for eternal predestination, whereby we are already the children of God, then the children do occasion the mission of the Paraclete.[4] Therefore, two phases are again at issue: God's predetermining counsel concerning the incarnation and the sonship, and its enactment in history. The former is the cause of the latter: Those who are sons of God in His eternal plan for the world must become sons in the temporal reality through the Holy Spirit.

Luther implicitly puts the connection between predestination and justification in a causal scheme in the *Preface to Romans* in his translation of the New Testament.[5] Man does not act as a cause in any sense. Only in God's hands have we the cause of righteousness in Christians. In this preface Luther presents his readers with a synthesis of his interpretation of St Paul's words. And Luther claims to expound not a speculative postulation of the doctrine of justification but the causative background of *iustificatio* as defined by the Scriptures.

2. It is God's secret and terrible will which, according to its counsel, decides which, and what kind of, individuals He will allow to receive and share in the grace which is preached and offered.[6] This is presented in *The Bondage of the Will* in apparently self-evident terms, so that it seems to be something more or less natural which does not call for further discussion. The divine predetermination is the cause and the human reception of the grace the effect.

3. When the false view of the divine monergism, which implies pure fatalism and which leads to contempt for the means of grace appears *c.* 1540, Luther does not repudiate *per se* the theoretical tenet that the individual who is predestined will be saved. For, generally speaking, his particular concept of God stipulates: "that it is the truth what God has decided and that must surely happen".[7] Consequently, God's counsel is the cause which must surely ("gewisslich") result in an effect, that God

---

[4] *Ib.* 30.23ff.: "Et hic quoque inverse loquitur. Nam ideo pocius efficimur filii, quia spiritus mittitur, quam econtra. Spiritus enim facit filios, non filii spiritum mitti faciunt, nisi respiciatur ad aeternam predestinacionem, ubi sumus eciam filii, antequam spiritus mittatur." Cf. WA 2.469.39ff. (*In epistolam Pauli ad Galatas commentarius.* 1519), *ib.* 534.15ff.

[5] WADB 7.22.26ff. (*Das Neue Testament.* 1522), quoted in 4.2.2 n. 14. Cf. WA 12.262.8ff. (*Epistel S. Petri gepredigt und ausgelegt.* 1523), WA 14.627.11ff. (*Deuteronomion Mosi cum annotationibus.* 1525).

[6] WA 18.684.32ff. (*De servo arbitrio.* 1525), quoted in 4.2.3 n. 18.

[7] WAB 9.627.33ff. (1542), quoted in 4.3.2 n. 14.

abides by His promises of justification *sola fide*. Luther also suggests at this period that God is responsible in principle for the events in which the Christians are involved.[8]

4.4.3. Predestination as Argument Against Human Merit

The conception of God as the sole cause of justification leads to the heavy emphasis laid on *sola gratia* and *sola fides*. This theme stands out more clearly when we remember the background, namely the major role which free will's acquisition of merit and God's prescience thereof plays in the theology of Ockham and Biel.

1. The Luther material on this issue is abundant. In the oft repeated polemic, affirmed by the doctrine of predestination, against the Catholic theory of merit, we encounter the main issue of the Reformation. If we return to *Dictata*, for a start, we find statements relating election to God's gracious will alone. Thus, the conclusion naturally follows that mankind is redeemed "non ex merito".[1] Since the material from this period is complicated and ambiguous, we cannot, however, draw any far-reaching conclusions.

In the *Lecture on Romans*, Luther's thoughts which were previously vague and ambiguous are more sharply defined. God allows His elect to be afflicted by all kinds of suffering and evil. He even lets them experience a foretaste of the rejection. For He shows them, thereby, that salvation is not bestowed on grounds of merit, but only as a result of His election and immutable will. "Quia si non per tot monstra duceret, multum relinqueret opinionis de nostris meritis".[2] Salvation is in no way

---

[8] *Ib.* 628.71ff.: "Als solt er (*sc.* Christus) sagen: 'last mein vatther und mich Sorgenn, was geschehen soll, gehett ihr hin undt thut, was ich euch heisse'." Cf. the parallel exposition in WA 43.457.32ff. (*Vorlesung über 1. Mose.* 1535–45). FC in SD 11 sees God's benevolence in Christ as the cause of the salvation of the elect, BSLK 1066.

[1] WA 3.116.25f. (= WA 55.I.1.2.144.25f.) (*Dictata super Psalterium.* 1513–15): "Meos, quia pro bona voluntate sua Deus salvos facit homines et non ex merito." Cf. WA 4.37.14f.: "'electis meis' Hebr. 'electo meo', qui secundum predestinationem eliguntur, non qui secundum carnem de electis nascuntur: ...'"; *ib.* 446.5f.: "'Protector meus' conservando liberatum 'et' ideo 'in ipso speravi' non in armis meis, virtutibus, meritis: ...'" And the gloss says (*ib.* 446.32): "Non confugit autem ad eum, nisi misericordia eius preventus et motus gratis sine merito." WA 9.59.22f. (*Randbemerkungen Luthers.* 1509–11) has been discussed by many scholars, but we cannot build any extensive reasoning on this sentence. See further E. Wolf (1927)178, W. Pannenberg (1957)116, G. Rost (1966)92f. L. Grane compares the anthropology in Biel and Luther, *id.* (1962)265ff.

[2] WA 56.382.1ff. (*Rom.* 1515–16).

derived from man himself or his actions. There are no words more calculated to terrify, humiliate and crush the arrogant assumption of merit than these.[3]

In terms of merit, Jacob and Esau were equals, belonging to the same *massa perditionis*, because both were evil "vitio originalis peccati" (Rom. 9:11).[4] Yet, the divine counsel is steadfast, unchanged by merit, or the lack thereof. God does not regret His gifts and His call through the promise (Rom. 11:29), even if some are unworthy and others worthy.[5] Therefore, it follows from the monergism of the divine grace that every thought of *merita previsa* comes to nothing. *Predestinatio sola gratia* is the only ground of salvation.

Thesis 25 of the *Disputation Against Scholastic Theology*, by Luther, attacks the doctrine of merit: the Christian hope does not derive from human merits but from suffering, which tears down the merits.[6] The believer does not share in the divine grace on the ground of his doing *quod in se est*. He can offer nothing but a lack of disposition to grace, yes, even a rebellion against mercy. Thesis 29 relates instead to the divine predetermination:

> "Optima et infallibilis ad gratiam praeparatio et unica dispositio est aeterna dei electio et praedestinatio."[7]

In contrast to the scholastic theology, not least that of Biel, who works with an interplay between human merit and divine mercy, Luther adduces solely God's election. Not only the radical conception of sin which regards man as wholly incapable of anything but evil before God, when he is separated from God's effective mercy, but also the monergistic image of God[8] prompts Luther to reject every theory of merit. Predestination is the only prerequisite (*unica dispositio*) for grace. In

[3] *Ib.* 386.26ff. Cf. *ib.* 83.27ff., *ib.* 394.24ff.
[4] *Ib.* 396.3ff. Cf. the long quotation from Augustine, *ib.* 405.3ff.
[5] *Ib.* 440.1ff. (Quoted in 4.2.4 n. 4). By excluding merits Luther maintains that our will is not at all the cause of salvation, *ib.* 89.15ff., *ib.* 385.13ff. It is well known that he once saw the justification conditioned by free will, *ib.* 382.26f. Cf. L. Grane (1962)326, *ib.* 328; H. J. Iwand (1974)92f.
[6] WA 1.225.15f. (*Disputatio contra scholasticam theologiam.* 1517): "Spes non venit ex meritis, sed ex passionibus merita destruentibus. Contra usum multorum." Cf. *ib.* 17ff. Cf. also WA 5.175.11ff. (*Operationes in Psalmos.* 1519–21).
[7] WA 1.225.27f. Cf. L. Grane (1962)372.
[8] Cf. WA 1.227.1ff.: "Gratia dei nunquam sic coexistit ut ociosa, Sed est vivus, mobilis et operosus spiritus, Nec per Dei absolutam potenciam fieri potest, ut actus amiciciae sit et gratia Dei praesens non sit. Contra Gab."

association with Gal. 1:15f., this point occurs explicitly, since election is said by Luther to happen before birth and therefore before every thought that man by his acts is able to acquire merit which God rewards.[9]

2. In *The Bondage of the Will*, Luther rejects Erasmus' theory that, in the interpretation of Mal. 1:2f. in Rom. 9:13, the issue concerns how God hates and loves. The question is rather: By what merit on our part does God love or hate? The very manner in which God loves, or hates, nullifies free will and human merit. God's love for, and His wrath against, mankind is eternal and immutable; before this world existed, not only before the merits and the acts of free will, God's will was established.[10] In this debate Luther excises the merits not only of the elect but also of the rejected. He quotes Erasmus' traditional attempts to solve the problem: God is said to hate those who are not yet born because he foresees that they will perform evil acts.[11] This is, according to Luther, based on a symbolical interpretation of the Malachi *locus* which he rejects. Neither those who come to faith nor those who remain in disbelief can plead any credit. This does not, Luther states, following St Paul, depend on any act of ours but only on God's love and hatred.[12] As a result, man is regarded as so utterly dependent on God for salvation, and destruction, that neither his merit nor the lack thereof make the slightest difference. His eternal destiny is rooted solely in God.

3. It is hardly surprising that, in his polemics against Rome, Luther occasionally returns to predestination and denies human merit. This is the case in some notes entitled *De loco iustificationis* from the year when the discussions on the *Confession* were held in Augsburg. Luther asserts that the Christians must be justified by faith alone without the deeds.

---

[9] WA 2.469.39ff. (*In epistolam Pauli ad Galatas commentarius.* 1519): "Quod autem placuerit ei sine meritis meis, id convincit, quod me in hanc sortem, antequam natus essem, segregarit et in utero matris meae me talem praepararit, deinde et per gratiam vocarit, ut iis omnibus intelligatis, quod fides et cognitio Christi non ex lege mihi venerit, sed ex praedestinante et vocante gratia dei"; WA 40.I.136.7f. (*In epistolam S. Pauli ad Galatas Commentarius.* 1531/35, Hs); *ib.* 140.1ff.: "Das ist praecise praecidere merita: Nobis confusio, deo gloria: Das gut, das ich solt thun, hat er beschlossen, cum essem in utero; non potui quaerere, venit ex mera et praedestinata gratia dei;" Cf. also WA 14.627.9ff. (*Deuteronomion Mosi cum annotationibus.* 1525), *ib.* 687.7ff.

[10] WA 18.724.27ff. (*De servo arbitrio.* 1525), cf. *ib.* 725.24ff.

[11] *Ib.* 726.17ff.

[12] *Ib.* 726.33ff.: "Sed hoc disputamus, quo merito, quo opere perveniant ad fidem, qua inseruntur, aut ad infidelitatem, qua exciduntur; hoc ad doctorem pertinet. Hoc meritum nobis describe. Paulus docet, quod nullo nostro opere, sed solo amore et odio Dei contingat". Cf. *ib.* 772.38ff.: "Si enim gratia ex propositio seu praedestinatione venit, necessitate venit, non studio aut conatu nostro, ut supra docuimus."

4.4.3.

"Quam falsum igitur est iustos propter opera futura praedestinari, tam falsum est propter opera *fidei* futura iustificari. Sed sicut praedestinationis gratia postea efficit opera ipsa *sola sine operibus eligens et vocans iustificandum et operaturum*, ita fides efficit opera ipsa sine operibus iustificans et peccata delens ante opera."[13]

Consequently, there is a very important *parallel between the idea of predestination and the doctrine of justification.* Simply because the election takes place before, and independent of, all human efforts and merits, this can be an argument that faith justifies before, and independent of, the deeds. I will elaborate the implications of this doctrine further (4.5.4.).

Luther directs a fierce attack on every idea of merit in his *Exposition of John 14–15.* He has opportunity to emphasize *electio sine merito,* especially in association with John 15:16. He maintains that Christ designates as friends those who have had no dealings with Him, yes, those who have never known Him:

"This blasts and condemns all the presumption toward God of the pseudo saints, who want to do and merit enough to reconcile God and to make Him their friend.[14]

Thus, the election has to a great extent become a weapon against the anthropology and the doctrine of merit of the Roman theologians. But at the same time, it is essential to remember that this rejection of merits comes to pass in order to make certainty of justification possible.

4. There is a long tradition among *evangelical* Luther scholars of presenting predestination as a convincing argument against the idea of merit acquired by free will, and of emphasizing the significance of the polemical situation. Sympathy is not seldom expressed with Luther's struggle against the false concept of merit but rarely with the deterministic doctrine of predestination *per se.*[15]

A *Catholic* expert on Luther has arrived at similar conclusions. He admits that Luther actually defends the Catholic tradition when, on the

[13] WA 30.II.659.25ff. (*De loco Iustificationis.* 1530).
[14] WA 45.697.18ff. (*Das XIV. und XV. Kapitel S. Johannis.* 1537), LW 24.258. Cf. WA 45.697.31ff., *ib.* 698.4ff.
[15] Already in Th. Harnack I (1927)117, *ib.* 127, *ib.* 133, *ib.* 142, *ib.* 174f. Here, scholars have found "the religious motif": G. Aulén (1927)220, L. Pinomaa (1938)143. See also A. Th. Jørgensen, *Luthers kamp mod den romersk-katolske semipelagianisme under særligt henblik paa hans prædestinationslære* (1908)48ff.

basis of the idea of election, he rejects the semi-Pelagian theory of free will and its merits. But he objects to Luther's determinism.[16]

4.4.4. Predestination as the Ground for Steadfastness

Since Luther takes his stand on the Augustinian tradition, it is not surprising to see that *donum perseverantiae* is associated with *electio dei*.

1. In a *Christmas Sermon*, probably from 1514, Luther reflects upon the world as in certain respects resembling hell. For every doomed individual, every dying sinner, begins to blaspheme. He will continue to do so for ever more. The elect, on the contrary, are fortified by grace, so that even in death and hell—not to mention temporal mischief—they praise God. Without grace the rejected are weak so that they not only fear death and hell but every other affliction.[1] Accordingly, it is grace alone which fills some individuals with faith, joy, and praise. Others who are denied this grace also lack its effects in their lives.

In the *Lecture on Romans* (Rom. 8:28ff.) we may observe that pre-determination is said to exclude not only man's free will and merit, but indeed his capacity to remain steadfast in the faith when assailed by various kinds of affliction:

> "For how could a man possibly break through all of these things in which he would lose hope a thousand times, unless *the eternal and fixed love of God* led him through them and *the Spirit* were present to aid our infirmity and to intercede for us with groanings which cannot be uttered?"[2]

When the elect are beset with despair, tormented by the devil, the world and the flesh, and feel that their own efforts are fruitless, God

---

[16] H. McSorley (1969)312f.; *ib.* 353: "When we turn to *Luther's strictly biblical concept of man's enslavement by sin,* however, we recognize at once a doctrine of *servum arbitrium* that is *fully in conformity with the Catholic tradition* of Augustine, Anselm, Peter Lombard, Thomas Aquinas, *et al,* as well as with the teaching of the Second Council of Orange and of the Council of Trent;" *ib.* 354 n. 287: "The concept of merit which Luther rejects in his biblical argument (WA 18,769,24–771,33) is the Neo-Semipelagian concept of Gabriel Biel and other late Scholastics..."

[1] WA 1.38.35ff. (*Sermone aus den Jahren* 1514–17). Cf. WA 4.90.25ff. (*Dictata super Psalterium.* 1513–15): "Quia totum tempus, quo electorum populus in mundo est, dies afflictionis et mali sunt i.e. poenales. Et simul peccatorum dies boni (i.e. iucundi), sed hiis interim paratur eterna fovea: illis autem mitigatio eterna."

[2] WA 56.382.9ff. (*Rom.* 1515–16), LW 25.371.

guides them through these afflictions and delivers them, while they them-selves lament in desperation that they will and do so much evil and not the good which they desire.[3] This is maintained in the exegesis of Rom. 9:17. The idea of justification *sola gratia*, therefore, has this meaning for Luther: steadfastness is a gift of God which is bestowed by God alone.

2. When Erasmus pursues the theory that Luther's doctrine of God's omnipotence leads to incorrigible passivity, Luther retorts in *The Bondage of the Will* by referring to the bestowal and action of *the Holy Spirit* in the hearts of the elect. "Corrigenter autem electi et pii per spiritum sanctum, Caeteri incorrecti peribunt".[4] When we are confronted with suffering and affliction, and see all the evil which is perpetrated, and at the same time hear that all stands or falls with the divine will and authority, we cannot believe that we are beloved of God. Luther replies:

> "Nullus hominum credet neque poterit, electi vero credent, caeteri non credentes peribunt, indignantes et blasphemantes, sicut tu hic facis."[5]

This doctrine of *the divine monergism and predetermination* opens to the righteous a gateway to justification, an entrance to heaven, and a way to God.[6] Thus, in the sanctification and faith of the steadfast people, Luther does not rely on human qualities, or abilities, only the divine source. Despite severe objections and natural disbelief of the reprobate, the elect remain open to God's grace and Spirit. They cannot find the way themselves. But they are guided on the way of the Lord by His power.

3. For this reason, the elect can be described as sensitive not only to the Gospel but also to the Law. In the detailed *Exposition of Psalm 90* Luther says that God will frighten and destroy the whole human race in His anger.

Amid their fears and misgivings concerning the inconstancy of life and the darkness of death the chosen, however, are given the grace to recognize the judgement and wrath of God. When other people neither wish nor dare to be killed by this knowledge, the elect are steadfast in this respect as well, as they apply this negative insight to themselves.[7]

This is the hopeful tone with which Reformation theology resounds when preaching predestination. The elect will not only share in Christ

---

[3] WA 56.402.13ff., cf. *ib.* 404.1ff.
[4] WA 18.632.3ff. (*De servo arbitrio.* 1525)
[5] *Ib.* 8ff.
[6] *Ib.* 13f., cf. *ib.* 642.34ff.
[7] WA 40.III.576.5ff. (*Enarratio Psalmi XC.* 1534/35, Hs), quoted in 4.2.5 n. 29.

through faith but also know that God seeks to protect them in their great weakness against the devil, the world, and their own carnal desires, lead them, and guide them on the paths of righteousness, support them when they hesitate, comfort them, and sustain them in chaos and affliction.[8] Since justification as well as perseverance, however, is received *by faith alone* it will be necessary to complete this exposition by depicting the content of certainty of salvation (4.5.3.) and certainty of election (4.5.4.) on the *usus* level.

4.4.5. Predestination as the Basis of the True, Hidden Church

We have drawn the line from the divine election to justification and steadfastness. In conclusion, I would suggest that this line might naturally be extended to the view of the Church. When the chosen believer is justified and steadfast in faith, he also becomes a living part of the body of Christ, according to Luther's theology.

1. When Luther objects to the identification of the true Church with the external institution he refers back to the doctrine of Augustine, Wycliffe and Huss. In the *Leipzig Disputation* he quotes a number of the tenets for which Huss was condemned:

> "Inter articulos Huss est et ille 'Una est sancta universalis ecclesia, que est predestinatorum universitas', item alius 'Universalis sancta ecclesia tantum est una, sicut tantum unus est numerus omnium predestinatorum'."

He states that these derive from Augustine and were repeated by Peter Lombard. Indeed, he contends that Johannes Eck is also in agreement with them.[1] Consequently, the only conclusion which is wholly accurate places the true Church on a par with the host of the elect. This is obviously so self-evident that it calls for no further proof on Luther's part.

[8] Cf. FC in SD 11 in BSLK 1069. Cf. also Denz 806 and F. Wendel (1972)277 about the Catholic and the Calvinist opinion.

[1] WA 2.287.30ff. (*Disputatio I. Ecci et M. Lutheri Lipsiae habita.* 1519). Cf. WA 4.90.25ff. (*Dictata super Psalterium.* 1513–15), *ib.* 446.6f., WA 1.564.35ff. (*Resolutiones disputationum de indulgentiarum virtute.* 1518).

Concerning Luther's early view of the church, see further K. Holl (1923)288ff., H. Fagerberg, *Die Kirche in Luthers Psalmenvorlesungen 1513–1515,* Elert–Gedenkschrift (1955)109ff., S. H. Hendrix, *Ecclesia in Via* (1974) *passim.*

We find a continuation of this theme in the *Second Lecture on the Psalms*. Luther testifies in the form of a solemn, personal confession that the articles he defended as evangelical and Christian in *Leipzig*, namely the doctrine that "Ecclesia universalis est predestinatorum universitas" and the consequences following therefrom, were godlessly condemned in the 15th century. He also asserts that the Council at Constanza on this issue was a council from the devil. He then explicitly repudiates all who took part in it. If John Huss and Jerome de Prague were rejected for this teaching alone then they were wronged. "Ego sane *ignorabam* Lipsiae sensum articulorum eorum, quorum verba vidi esse christianissima".[2] Thus, if Luther at the *Leipzig* disputation defended Huss chiefly by adducing the authorities on which he based his theses, he later realised that Huss's tenets on the connection between predestination and the Church are in essence legitimately Christian.

When true Christianity is prompted by no more and no less than God's own election, this means, *inter alia*, that definite human promises can only be given in the case that the specific election is known. In his *On Monastic Vows* Luther draws the consequence: "Verum impossibile est hac conscientia voveri nisi ab iis, qui mirabiliter spiritu Christi intus ducuntur et serventur, hoc est, ab electis."[3] Accordingly, it is not feasible to give a promise of poverty, chastity, and obedience. The conscience does not know whether it will endure, since God alone decides whether the believer is among the elect.

2. Luther maintains, in *The Bondage of the Will*, that the Church is ruled by the Spirit of God, and that the holy are guided by the same Spirit. Christ will remain with His Church until the end of time. This Church is the foundation and the pillar of the truth. He then refers to the confession in our Creed:

> " 'I believe in the holy catholic Church'; so that it is impossible for the Church to err, even in the smallest article. And even if we grant that some of the elect are bound in error all their lives, yet they must necessarily return to the right way before they die, since Christ says in John 10(:28): 'No one shall snatch them out of my hand'."[4]

---

[2] WA 5.451.29ff. (*Operationes in Psalmos.* 1519–21). Cf. his evaluation of Huss in WA 6.454.22ff. (*An den christl. Adel deutscher Nation.* 1520) and WA 12.176.11ff. (*De instituendis ministris Ecclesiae.* 1523).

[3] WA 8.610.13ff. (*De votis monasticis.* 1521).

[4] WA 18.649.30ff. (*De servo arbitrio.* 1525), LW 33.85. Cf. further R. Hermann, *Gesammelte Studien* (1960)352f.

The premise for this argument is that the Church consists of the elect. These, who form the body of Christ, may be a minority, like the 7,000 men whom God allowed to remain faithful in the time of the prophet Elijah. The situation was similar during the Arian disputes in the Early Church. Only five bishops were left to the Catholic Church. Even during the period which followed, when Christians quarrelled about "adiaphora" the true Church was preserved, although "holy men" like John Huss were condemned and put to death.[5] The believer who is chosen and preserved in the truth belongs to the invisible, true Church. But since this election is hidden from men's eyes, it is neither possible, concerning specific individuals, to deny that they are holy and a part of God's Church, nor prove that such is the case, if another would refute it. "Fides vero nullum vocat sanctum nisi divino iudicio declaratum, Quia fidei est, non falli."[6] Accordingly, when faith has no divine revelation on which to build, it is only possible to say that both the individual elect and the totality of the elect, or the true Church, belong to the hidden mysteries. In other words, the positive and the negative aspect, which we established in the view of *deus absconditus* (4.3.2.) reappear in Luther's concept of the Church.

3. In his *Exegesis of John 14–15* the aging Luther stands by his correlation of election and the true, invisible Church. In John 15:5 he confirms that God once and for all stated that Christ is the vine and the Christians the branches, although there are people who would challenge this. Many will lay claim to being the vine and the branches, although they have no part in them.[7] Only the believers who share the quality of being true branches of the vine really are the Christian Church. In John 15:16 their status is confirmed by the election.[8]

---

[5] WA 18.650.13ff., *ib.* 31ff., *ib.* 35ff.

[6] *Ib.* 651.31ff. Cf. *ib.* 652.23: "abscondita est Ecclesia, latent sancti". Cf. also I. Öberg (1970)468ff.

[7] WA 45.665.35ff. (*Das XIV. und XV. Kapitel S. Johannis.* 1537): "Ich bin ja (spricht er) der Weinstock, und jr seid ja meine Reben, als wolt er sagen: Man wirds doch nicht anders machen, Es ist *ein mal beschlossen bey Gott*, das Ichs sein sol und kein ander, wie jr gehort habt, Weitter durfft jr euch nicht umbsehen, als solt jrgend ein ander Weinstock sein denn ich oder das jr oder andere solten warhafftige Weinreben sein fur Gott denn jnn dem einigen Weinstock, welcher Ich bin, Denn er hat wol gesehen (wie ich gesagt habe), wie es wurde zu gehen inn der Christenheit, wie sich wider diese lere finden wurden beide, wütige Tyrannen und falsche lerer, Und viel den namen wurden furen beide, des Weinstocks und der Reben, die doch jnen nicht zu gehoren."

[8] *Ib.* 697.9ff.: "*Durch mein erwelen und annemen heisst jr freunde,* die jr sonst von art nichts anders denn eitel Feinde weret, die weder von mir noch von Gott nichts wüsten, Nu aber Freunde seid allein daher, das ich euch so lieb gewonnen und so trewlich gemeinet,

It comes natural to Luther to develop these arguments along lines reminiscent of Augustine's *City of God*. A battle is fought in the world, from the beginning to the end. Cain also wished to choose God, so that He should look with favour on Cain's work and sacrifice, and not on Abel's. Until this hour, the world has persecuted those who follow in Abel's footsteps. For the world, like Cain, can do nothing else but say it does not wish to be chosen but to choose.[9] This brings us back to the Augustinian view of the Church, which Luther defended in the disputation against Eck.

4.4.6. Conclusions

1. Like Biel, Luther comprehends God as the sovereign cause of election and justification. The eternal decision within the deity involves the *causa sola* and the temporal realisation of justification is the *effectus*.

But when *Biel* in practice gives priority to "God's ordered power", and when this is interwoven with a semi-Pelagian theory of human will and merit, the great differences stand out. Man's own freedom of choice becomes a kind of ground for justification. Here Biel introduces another conception of cause and effect: the relationship between two different situations which are not joined as cause and effect, in the sense Aristotle used these terms, but are nevertheless associated.

On this point, *Luther* breaks with the "modern" tradition, on which he originally was educated. God alone decides whether we shall be devout and faithful. As a result of election, the sonship and the justification are a fact prior to, and independent of, human achievement. *Causa iustificationis* is unreservedly attributed to the divine predetermination.

2. This leads to a profound difference between Luther and Biel with regard to the view of free will and its merits.

With his theory of predestination *Luther* propounds an autonomous argument against the theology of merit presupposed by the *via moderna*.

---

das ich euch erlöset und jnns ewige leben gesetzet habe, Und sollet auch dadurch freunde bleiben und meiner freundschafft ewiglich geniessen, allein das jrs also beweiset, das ich euch nicht vergeblich also gemeinet habe." Cf. *ib.* 30ff., *ib.* 699.25ff.

[9] *Ib.* 699.1ff. A more extensive exposition is to be found in I. Öberg (1970)470ff. Calvin also drew inspiration from *De civitate Dei* according to F. Wendel (1972)282f. H. Olsson (1943)23 and F. Wendel (1972)296ff. stress that the doctrine of predestination leads to a distinction between invisible and visible church in Calvin's theology. Concerning the importance of the doctrine of *perseverance* in Calvinistic thought, see J. Moltmann (1961)51ff., *ib.* 81ff. For the *biblical order* in the parish, see A. Adam (1968)357.

If God alone is *sola causa iustificationis*, then it follows that human will and merit are denied any significance in this context. The only prerequisite for mercy is God's eternal election to grace. The divine love is eternal, so that it can never be anticipated by any temporal merits. According to the doctrine of justification, there can be no question of synergism between divine grace and human merit. The doctrine of sovereign monergism of grace in the concept of election is extended to the new theory of the justification by faith.

3. Perseverance is also derived, by Luther, from God's election in Christ. The very circumstance that the elect amid the suffering and trials have no reserves within themselves to support their faith shows that God's election is the real, active cause. Therefore, the divine predestination is also the ground for the Church. Insofar as election on the concrete level is hidden, the true Church is also hidden.

4.5. Concerning Faith, Justification Takes Priority Over Predestination

The two preceding sections contain several conclusions suggesting the significance of *faith* for the idea of predestination (4.3. and 4.4.). While I previously analysed the *theoretical* connection, asserting that predestination takes causative priority over justification, in this section I seek to demonstrate the *practical* priority of universal justification by faith over election. We might say that we go from the *notitia* to the *usus* level.

4.5.1. The Mode of Preventing Predestination Affliction

1. The interpretation of Rom. 9:16 is of great importance.[1] St Paul's comment that the election does not depend on man's will or exertion, inspires Luther to give a description of God's sovereignty. The will does not belong to the individual who exercises it, but to God who gives and creates it. Even at this stage, Luther adduces 1 Cor. 12:6, using the

---

[1] WA 56.398.9ff. (*Rom.* 1515–16). Cf. MPL 192, 633ff. (Lib. I, Dist. 41, q. 2) concerning P. Lombard. Cf. also WA 9.71.1f. (*Luthers Randbemerkungen zu den Sentenzen des Petrus Lombardus.* 1509–11), WA 3.117.31f. (*Dictata super Psalterium.* 1513–15), WA 4.61.17 (*Dictata super Psalterium.* 1513–15).

Already K. Holl (1923)45 clearly understood this point: "Aber die entscheidenden Antriebe dafür (sc. die Lehre von der Alleinwirksamkeit Gottes) finden sich bereits in der Psalmenvorlesung."

metaphors of the axe and the rod, together with the example of Pharaoh, which is of great importance in what follows.[2] He then explicitly repudiates the misunderstanding which can easily arise on this point: this sovereignty does not nullify human will and exertion. The sole consequence is that the benefits do not derive from man's own capacity. St Paul refers to the will and the exertion of those who are in harmony with God, *i.e.* to the Christian life in love and divine justification. The will and exertion of other human beings are irrelevant. Their will and exertion do not follow the will of God, notwithstanding that they seek and achieve great things.[3] With this exposition Luther has guarded himself against those who attribute power and merit to mankind *vis-à-vis* God. But he has also emphasized the importance of human submission to this divine power:

> "Yet here I am issuing the warning that no man whose mind has not yet been purged should rush into these speculations, lest he fall into the abyss of horror and hopelessness; but *first let him purge the eyes of his heart in his meditations on the wounds of Jesus Christ*. For I myself would not even read these things if the order of the lection and necessity did not compel me to do so. For this is very strong wine and the most complete meal, solid food for those who are perfect, that is, the most excellent theology, of which the apostle says: 'Among the mature we do impart wisdom' (1 Cor. 2:6). But I am a baby who needs milk, not solid food (cf. 1 Cor. 3:1–2). Let him who is a child like me do the same. *The wounds of Jesus Christ, 'the clefts of the rock' (foramina petre), are sufficiently safe for us.* The strong and the perfect may discuss the first book of the *Sentences*, which properly should not be the first but the last book. Many today rush into this book heedlessly and strangely also become blinded."[4]

---

[2] See further WA 5.187.35ff. (*Operationes in Psalmos.* 1519–21), *ib.* 192.11ff., WA 6.125.21ff. (*Tessaradeka consolatoria.* 1520), WA 7.145.26f. (*Assertio omnium articulorum M. Lutheri.* 1520), *ib.* 146.9ff., WA 13.427.7ff. (*Prolectiones in prophetas minores.* 1524ff.), WA 18.614.9ff. (*De servo arbitrio.* 1525), *ib.* 709.10ff., *ib.* 753.29ff. Cf. also 3.6 above n. 1 and 11.

[3] WA 56.399.25ff. (*Rom.* 1515–16): "Quare ex isto textu non hoc sequitur, Quod Velle et currere hominis Nihil sit, Sed Quod non sue virtutis sit. Quia opus Dei non est nihil. At velle et currere hominis est opus Dei. Loquitur enim de Velle et currere secundum Deum i.e. de vita Charitatis et Iustitie Dei. Aliorum autem Velle et currere nihil est, qui non in via Dei volunt et currunt, licet magna Velint et valde currant."

[4] *Ib.* 400.1ff., LW 25.389f. Cf. WA 3.640.40ff. (*Dictata super Psalterium.* 1513–15), *ib.* 645.29ff.

The two aspects which we observed in the preceding context seem to be repeated here. *Firstly*, the individual who meditates on the wounds of Christ stands beneath the divine omnipotence. It is not human power which thus purifies the "eyes of the heart". Man is made conform to Christ by the power of God. *Secondly*, the very condition for the releasing of God's power is that the individual has a certain attitude of faith, namely abiding in meditation on Christ's wounds. Man evades the plunge into the "abyss" and the blindness, which is the risk he would run if he adopted the train of thought described in Peter Lombard's first book, in which he expounds God's prescience and predetermination. Staupitz had given the advice, which is also found in St Bernhard of Clairvaux and contemporary literature, that the Christian who is afflicted ought to gaze on the suffering Christ. This advice might here come to the fore.[5] The context allows of the interpretation that the idea of conformity and the advice to meditate on Christ's suffering are two sides of the same thing.[6] *Thirdly* and lastly, it is important to emphasize that "vulnera Christi" not only "purify" the individual but also provide his protection and safety ("tuta satis"). Christ has, by His suffering and His death, vicariously plumbed "the depths of terror and despair".[7] Thus, justification through Christ takes priority over the doctrine of pre-destination.

When Luther later gives his advice concerning the doctrine of election, he does so in a passage reminiscent of the above exegesis of Rom. 9:16.

[5] Concerning St. Bernhard of Clairvaux, see A. Adam (1968)77ff. for introduction and literature. Luther's high opinion of Bernhard is manifest in *e.g.* WATR 3.294.34ff. (1533), WATR 5.154.15f., (1542), WA 43.581.11ff. (*Vorlesung über das 1. Buch Mose.* 1535–45). E. Wolf (1927)194ff. shows that it was only the counsel to meditate on the wounds of Christ which comforted Luther in his heavy afflictions as a young friar. Nevertheless he emphasizes Staupitz' interpretation of *Imitatio Christi* (*ib.* 162ff.), and reiterates the importance of the thought of conformity with Christ as a consolation to Luther in the affliction concerning election (*ib.* 217). But he is conscious of the lack of correspondence with the counsel to meditate on the wounds of Christ (*ib.* 194, *ib.* 215f.). Therefore he tries to demonstrate a connexion between the conceptions of Staupitz and Luther.

Cf. the discussion in W. Pannenberg (1957)120ff. But E. Vogelsang (1932)72f. argues that Wolf has concealed the antinomy and arrived at an incomplete harmony. G. Rost (1966)139 does not consider Wolf's exposition convincing either. But both Vogelsang and Rost agree with Wolf that Luther found victory in his affliction of predestination in meditation on the wounds of Christ.

[6] After analysing the context I, in fact, arrive at the same conclusion as G. Rost (1966)139. I claim that Wolf is at least right in his intention of showing a connexion between the thought of Christ's wounds and the thought of conformity with Christ.

[7] WA 56.400.2f. Cf. Luther's dicta on Christ's vicarious suffering, when he like a man faced eternal damnation, *ib.* 392.8ff.

He thereby warns against the risk of starting from the theory of predetermination without adopting Christ.[8] He forcefully exhorts his readers to gaze upon the suffering Christ, in order to be safe and certain through His wounds:

> "Therefore fix your eyes upon *the heavenly picture of Christ, the Christ who for your sake went to hell and was rejected by God as one damned to eternal perdition, as He cried on the cross, 'Eli, Eli, lama sabachthani.* My God, my God, why hast thou forsaken me?' Behold, in that picture your hell is overcome and your election (vorsehung) assured, so that if you but take care and believe that it happened for you, you will certainly be saved in that faith (sso wirstu yn dem selben glauben behalten gewisslich)."[9]

Christ's descent into "hell" accordingly involves a vicarious action whereby the faithful attains certainty of salvation. As regards the cure of souls, it is not primarily the idea of predestination, but the Christology which each believer ought to apply to himself ("fur dich geschehn"). The other than God. This implies the divine omnipotence and steadfastness remarkable and surprising. The agent in this context can hardly be another than God. This implies the divine omnipotence and steadfastness which recalls the description of God's almighty power in Rom. 9:16 which has been analysed above.[10]

We encounter pastoral advice along similar lines in the *Preface to Romans.* Luther indicates the danger which arises when individuals begin to reflect seriously on the divine predetermination, starting from the first article of the creed and not the second. The entire foundation of human safety can begin to shake and fall.[11] Luther gives general instructions on how to treat the idea of election. In essence, these fill the pattern which we previously observed: Follow the order in Romans. First, believe in Christ and the Gospel, so that you see your sin and His grace. Then you

---

[8] WA 2.690.10ff. (*Ein Sermon von der Bereitung zum Sterben.* 1519), quoted in 4.3.3 n. 5. Cf. WA 2.688.2ff., quoted in 4.3.4 n. 4.

[9] *Ib.* 690.17ff. Translation from L. Pinomaa (1963)99. See further H. Appel, *Anfechtung und Trost im Spätmittelalter und bei Luther* (1938)121ff. A similar text can be found in WA 5.622.37ff. (*Operationes in Psalmos.* 1519–21).

[10] Concerning the work of God within the believer see further *ib.* 176.1ff.

[11] WADB 7.22.35ff. (*Das Neue Testament.* 1522): "Aber hie ist den freveln und hochfarenden geystern eyn mal zu stecken, die yhrn verstand am ersten hie her furen und oben an heben, zuvor den abgrund gotlicher versehung zu forschen, und vergeblich da mit sich bekummern, ob sie versehen sind, die mussen sich denn selb sturtzen, das sie entweder vertzagen, oder sich ynn die frey schantz schlagen."

must fight against sin. In the cross and suffering you will come to understand the consolation of the doctrine of election. As in the earlier lecture on Romans, predestination is likened to the strong wine which cannot without further ado be given to spiritual children.[12] The condition that predetermination shall not lead to revulsion or despair is thus accomplished by the existential understanding of one's own sin, and the grace mediated by Christ.[13] First when the divine Law and the Gospel have had their effect, so that the believer knows that he is damned by his own acts but justified in Christ, despite his weakness and his failures in the struggle against sin, we have the "Sitz im Leben" presupposed for a true understanding of *electio dei* on the practical level.

2. According to *The Bondage of the Will*, the knowledge of *deus absconditus* has a certain validity on the *notitia* level (4.3.2.2.). But in actual living, every Christian ought to grasp the *deus revelatus*. In this sense God's will is preached in concrete terms, revealed, offered and worshipped.[14]

On the one hand, Luther rejects the disputes concerning the secrets of the divine majesty. Human presumption, which in constant perversion neglects essentials and invariably yearns and strives against God's will,

---

[12] *Ib.* 39f.: "Du aber folge diser Epistell ynn yhrer ordnung, bekummere dich zuvor mit Christo und dem Euangelio, ..." The same pastoral admonition can be found in WA 10.III.108.14ff. (*Pred.* 1522). Luther strongly underlines the importance of the humanity of Christ, cf. *e.g.* WA 10.II.325.27ff. (*Sendbrief an Hans v. Rechenberg.* 1522): "Solichs will ich, G. herr, euch zü liebe geschrieben haben und bitte, E. G. wolte die hoch und fliegende geyster ynn solichen sachen nichts handlen lassen, Sondernn, wie ich gesagt, *sie binden an Christus menscheyt, sich vorhyn stercken und leren, biss das sie gnügssam erwachssen.* Denn was solt uns *der mensch Christus* geben seyn zü eyner leyttern zum vatter, wenn wyr yhn lassen ligen unnd uber yhn hynfarn und mit eygener vernunfft gen hymel farn und Gottis gericht messen wollen? *Es wirt niergent bas denn ynn Christus menscheyt gelernet, was uns zü wissen nott ist,* Syntemal er unser mittler ist, und niemant zum vater on durch yhn komen kan." Cf. further *ib.* 323.20ff. Cf. also WA 14.23.10ff. (*Die ander Epistel S. Petri.* 1523/24).

[13] WA 16.114.2ff. (*Pred. über das 2. Buch Mose.* 1524–27), *ib.* 143.11ff., *ib.* 146.11ff. Cf. *ib.* 117.7ff., *ib.* 120.2f., *ib.* 148.3ff. Here Luther rejects those who start "supra" in God almighty. Instead he teaches that our beginning should be "infra" in the humanity of Christ.

Referring to the *Exodus* sermons G. Adam (1970)46 is right in asserting that on the *practical* level Luther coordinates predestination and Christology.

[14] WA 18.685.3ff (*De servo arbitrio.* 1525): "Aliter de Deo vel voluntate Dei nobis praedicata, revelata, oblata, culta, Et aliter de Deo non praedicato, non revelato, non oblato, non culto disputandum est." Cf. *ib.* 685.8ff.; *ib.* 25ff.

4.5.1.

must be revoked and restrained.[15] On the other hand, the positive, universal programme is clear:

"Let it occupy itself instead with *God incarnate*, or as Paul puts it, with *Jesus crucified*, in whom are all the treasures of wisdom and knowledge, though in a hidden manner (Col. 2:3); for through him it is furnished abundantly with what it ought to know and ought not to know."[16]

Notwithstanding that Luther, in *The Bondage of the Will*, chiefly discussed problems on the academic and intellectual level, and even went so far that theologians often criticized "Spitzensätze" of *De servo arbitrio*, the primary role of Christology emerges on the practical level. The doctrine of the ubiquitous, omnipotent God must necessarily be supplemented with a doctrine concerning the incarnate and crucified God. Through Him solely we learn what we need to know about sin, grace and justification.

3. This is the view of the mature Luther: In principle and in theory (the *notitia* level) God's omnipotence and election take precedence over justification, but in practical, concrete situations (the *usus* level) he instructs the Christians to start from the justification which is offered to all through Christ. We find it in letters of spiritual advice[17], sermons[18], exegetic lectures[19], and table talks[20].

---

[15] *Ib.* 689.18ff.: "Nos dicimus, ut iam antea diximus, de secreta illa voluntate maiestatis non esse disputandum et temeritatem humanam, quae perpetua perversitate, *relictis necessariis*, illam semper impetit et tentat, esse avocandam et retrahendam, ne occupet sese scrutandis illis secretis maiestatis, quae impossibile est attingere, ut quae habitet lucem inaccessibilem, teste Paulo." Cf. *ib.* 690.19ff.

[16] *Ib.* 689.22ff., LW 33.145f. WA 18.638.24ff.: "Nam et nos nihil nisi *Ihesum crucifixum* docemus. At Christus crucifixus haec omnia secum affert, ipsamque adeo sapientiam inter perfectos, cum nulla sit alia sapientia inter Christianos docenda, quam ea que abscondita est in mysterio et ad perfectos pertinet non ad pueros Iudaici et legalis populi *sine fide* in operibus gloriantis, ut 1. Corinth. 2. sentit Paulus, nisi tu Christum crucifixum docere aliud nihil vis intelligi, quam has literas sonare: Christus est crucifixus." K. Schwarzwäller, *Theologia crucis* (1970) *passim* interprets the Christology and the doctrine of justification as the main theme in *The Bondage of the Will*. For a critical evaluation of this thesis, see further 3.2 n. 4 and 4.2.1 n. 2.

[17] WAB 4.589.23ff. (1528): "Docendum est quidem de voluntate Dei imperscrutabili, ut sciamus talem esse, sed niti, ut comprehendas eam, hoc est praecipitium periculosissimum. Proinde ego soleo me coërcere isto Christi verbo, quod ad Petrum dixit: '*Tu me sequere!* Quid ad te, si illum volo manere?' siquidem et Petrus de alieno opere Dei disputabat, quid de Iohanne esset futurum"; *ib.* 590.40f.: "Primum vero exerceat *fidem promissionis* et opera praeceptorum, quibus perfectis videbit, an impossibilibus occupari debeat"; WAB 6.87.41ff. (1531): "Unter allen geboten Gottes ist das hohest, das man *seinen lieben Son*

164

4.5.2. The Mode of Overcoming Predestination Affliction

Luther was from his sojourn in the priory personally familiar with "the hell" of affliction concerning predestination.[1] And this problem of spiritual guidance he encounters among his parishioners and elsewhere. As we have seen, he can repudiate the inquisitive speculations of reason, and assert that any attempt at cognizance of the concrete election (4.3.4.) is a direct manifestation of the devil's seduction. Yet, it does not suffice if the Christian intellectually rejects the affliction of the predetermination. The feeling in his heart must also be eradicated. Here I follow up a line of reasoning which has already been suggested (4.3.5.).

1. Although predestination and the affliction caused thereby "exist as full reality" even in the early *Lecture on the Psalms*[2], the *Interpretation of Romans* is the first work to describe it in detail and range. This material allows of a more extensive analysis. The third and last section of the exposition of *Rom. 8:28* deals with the consolation inherent in the idea of predestination.[3] Deriving salvation wholly from the divine

unsern herrn Jhesum Christum sollen für uns bilden, *der sol unsers hertzen teglicher und fürnemster Spiegel sein*, darin wir sehen, wie lieb uns Gott hat und wie er so hoch als ein frumer Gott fur uns hat gesorget, das er auch seinen lieben Son für uns gegeben hat. Hie, hie, sage ich, lernt man die rechte kunst von *der versehung* und sonst nirgent"; WAB 11.166.14ff. (1545): "DAgegen hat uns Got sein sohn gegeben Iesum Christum, an den sollen wir teglich gedencken, und *uns in ihn spiegeln*, do wirt sich dann *die vorsehung* selb und gar lieblich finden."

[18] WA 45.96.4ff. (*Pred.* 1537, R): "Si vis in *seinen heimlichen rat* kriechen, so lasse deine cogitationes faren et *vade in praesepi et in cruce cum vulneribus*, quae tibi revelata. Si in ea revelatione te exerces, so wirstu mit lust und lieb ad alia komen. Si extra Christum per tuas cogitationes vis scire, quomodo deus tecum mit dir, so brichstu den hals. Qui scrutatur, den schlecht der donner. Sicut Satan suam sapientiam, quid deus sit, ideo in abgrund. Ideo halt dich der revelationis, quae gethan ist"; Cf. WA 36.61.4ff. (*Pred.* 1532, R).

[19] WA 43.458.28ff. (*Vorlesung über 1. Mose.* 1535–45): "Opponenda est autem cogitationibus istis *vera et firma cognitio Christi:* Sicut saepe moneo inprimis utile et necessarium esse, ut cognitio Dei certissima sit in nobis, et firma animi adsensione adpraehensa haereat. Alioqui inanis erit fides nostra"; Cf. *ib.* 459.7ff.; *ib.* 460.14ff.

[20] WATR 1.512.10ff. (1530–35); WATR 2.106.19ff. (1532), *ib.* 112.9ff. (1532), *ib.* 227.20ff. (1532), *ib.* 384.27ff. (1531), *ib.* 582.15ff. (1532); WATR 3.521.21ff. (1530–40); WATR 5.293.27ff. (1536). Cf. BSLK 818f., 1073.

[1] J. Köstlin & G. Kawerau I (1903)64f., O. Scheel II (1930)150. In WA 4.210.18ff. (*Dictata super Psalterium.* 1513–15) G. Rost (1966)96 discerns a probable hint at Luther's own afflictions.

[2] S. Normann (1933)120.

[3] WA 56.383.29f. (*Rom.* 1515–16): "Tercio Consolationes eorum, qui ex iis terrentur et huius materie dulcorationes ad spem inducendam moliemur."

sovereignty, Luther asserts that by His Words God works "per antiperistasim i.e. contrarii circumstantiam". For no words are more effective than these in terrifying, humiliating and crushing the arrogant assumption of one's own merits.[4] Consequently, it is in accord with the divine monergism which we tried to define above (4.5.1.1.).

The individual who experiences this fear and terror of the sovereign, predestining God has "optimum et felix signum" in this very emotion. For several Biblical statements praise the blessedness which is to be found in the contrition before God: Is. 11:2, 66:2, Luke 12:32, Is. 35:4, Ps. 112:1. Indeed, man has radical doubts about himself when the divine Word works awe before God.[5] In this very situation of affliction and contrition Luther exhorts to faith:

> "Therefore he who is overly fearful that he is not elect or is tested (tentatur) concerning his election, *let him give thanks for this kind of fear and rejoice that he is afraid,* for he knows with confidence that God, who cannot lie, has said: 'The sacrifice acceptable to God is a broken', that is, a despairing 'spirit; a broken and contrite heart (cor contritum et humiliatum), O God, Thou wilt not despise' (Ps. 51:17). Moreover, he himself knows what 'broken' means. Therefore *he should boldly lay hold on the truthfulness of the God who promises* and thus free himself (*transferat*) from the prescience of the terrifying God (*de prescientia terrentis Dei*) and be saved and elect."[6]

Thus, the feeling of damnation and terror can "work together for good", namely salvation. The Word says that every humble and contrite individual is near to grace and acceptable to God. The terror of the conscience, interpreted with the help of the divine promises, becomes a positive experience. The Christian can thereby be inspired to *bold faith* which overcomes the affliction concerning predestination. To the believer who loves God and accepts all things as His gifts, the suffering of the affliction of predestination is of benefit.

This background explains Luther's exposition of "tres autem gradus signorum electionis".[7] For the greater the damnation the Christian's *love for God* can accept without ceasing to love, the greater the sign of

---

[4] *Ib.* 386.24ff.

[5] *Ib.* 387.6ff.

[6] *Ib.* 387.20ff., LW 25.377f. I cannot see that this should be a consolation only for the "weak" as K. Holl (1923)149 maintains. Cf. G. Rost (1966)137, *ib.* 144.

[7] WA 56.388.3.

election. This truth is the more easily understood if a distinction is made between the qualities attributed by Luther to the *empirical* Christian and those discerned only in the *ideal* Christian.[8] The *first* grade of the signs of election is that you are content regarding this will of rejection of God and you do not murmur against God but rely on the fact that you are elect and you do not wish to be damned. The *second* level is an improvement on the first, being represented by those who are resigned and content in this feeling of condemnation, or in the desire for it, should God not want to save them but consider them among the reprobate.[9] Thus, we here encounter the concept of *resignatio*, which played so important a role in Luther research from K. Holl onwards. Finally, the *third* grade implies the best and highest sign of election. It is to be found among Christians who, in effect, resign themselves to hell if this is the will of God. This is probably the case with many at the hour of death. These are totally purified concerning their own will and "the prudence of the flesh". They know what this is: "For love is strong as death, jealousy is cruel as the grave"[10] (SS 8:6). We establish three truths:

a. *Resignatio ad infernum* is a *sovereign work of God.* Man is cleansed (*mundantur!*). The agent can hardly be other than God. His invincible love is a gift to the Christian.[11] It is God who tempers the believer in various ways.[12] *Resignatio ad infernum* thus cannot be a method which is accessible to man, and so leading to certainty of salvation. The insight into this truth is only possible in *God's good time* and to the extent allowed by Him. Man does not know how and when he will die. The Christian is at death probably free of self-love and ruled by the perfect love of God. In time God confers the love briefly and in moderation

---

[8] A. Gyllenkrok (1952)83ff. In W. Joest, *Gesetz und Freiheit*[4] (1968)124ff. there is a stronger emphasis on the ideal as a new "reality" and a new "world".

[9] WA 56.388.4ff.: "Primus eorum, qui contenti sunt de tali voluntate Dei neque murmurant contra Deum, Verum confidunt se esse electos et nollent se damnari. Secundus melior eorum, qui resignati sunt et contenti in affectu vel saltem desiderio huius affectus, si Deus nollet eos salvare, Sed inter reprobos habere."

[10] *Ib.* 10ff.: "Tertius optimus et extremus eorum, qui et in effectu seipsos resignant ad infernum pro Dei voluntate, Ut in hora mortis sit fortasse multis. Hii perfectissime mundantur a propria voluntate et 'prudentia carnis'. Hii sciunt, Quid sit illud: 'Fortis ut mors dilectio Et dura sicut infernus emulatio'". Cf. K. Holl (1923)149ff.

[11] WA 56.388.16ff.: "Hunc autem raptim et modice dat electis suis Deus in hoc mundo, immo periculosissima res est, hunc frequenter et diu habere; 'receperunt enim mercedem suam'".

[12] *Ib.* 19ff.: "Sed A m o r d e s i d e r i i Ille, inquam, est sicut infernus durus et robustus, et in hoc exercet suos electos Deus in hac vita miris modis."

(*raptim et modice!*). Yes, a frequently recurring and abiding *resignatio* is very dangerous.[13] This delimits still further resignation to hell as a way to certainty of justification. So, this is in line with the divine monergism previously analysed.

b. Luther is engaged in expounding St Paul's words that all things work together for good to those who love God. Therefore, it is natural for him to further reflect on *the essence of love*. He seeks to emphasize theories which do not refer to affliction and hell but to perfect love. It is the strength of ideal love which is underlined with the words that it is as strong as death and as cruel as hell. Therefore, he forcefully states that the purpose of the comparison is to indicate the perfect love.[14] As a secondary point only, he suggests a means of overcoming anxiety concerning the election.

c. When God actually does temper His elect in love He uses the uncanny means of permitting them to taste suffering and damnation.[15] In that way their love is increased and strengthened. Therefore, we must always understand the cross and suffering as underlying *amor* or *charitas*.[16] The reverse is also true: without such suffering the soul becomes apathetic and is indifferent, neglecting the yearning for God, and no longer thirsting for the living water.[17] The love of the empirical Christian for God, and all that this involves (trust in God, hope, and willingness to give up everything for God) is meant to be inculcated by contrition and damnation. In fact, no human love is so perfect that it cannot attain greater heights, because traces of sin impede the empirical individual.

Further, in *Rom. 9:2ff.* Luther's exegesis follows up a number of the lines he previously suggested. We shall survey them in the same order as before.

a. It is established that the love which endures rejection and damnation

---

[13] See n. 11 above.

[14] WA 56.388.14ff.: "Mira comparatio, Quod Amor comparatur rebus asperrimis, cum sit res mollis et dulcis, ut videtur. Sed verum Est: Amor complacentie Est dulcis, quia fruitur Amato." Cf. also *ib*. 24ff.

[15] See n. 12 above.

[16] WA 56.388.21f.: "Ideo Sub nomine Amoris Vel charitatis semper Crux et passiones intelligende sunt."

[17] *Ib*. 23ff.: "Sine quibus anima languescit, tepefit et Dei desiderium negligit neque sitit ad Deum, fontem vivum." This is an important point in "the theology of the cross." See further W. von Loewenich (1939)148ff.

is not natural for man but derives from the Holy Spirit.[18] Self-love is only eradicated by an overflowing infusion of the divine grace, or by an extremely rigid resignation.[19] This is, therefore, concerned with something which *only God* can achieve, and which man can but endure in subjection to the divine monopoly. It is nothing but God's action which can remove all obstacles to complete fellowship with Him. Man must open his heart to the alien work of God.[20] For, as we saw, the monergism does not nullify the importance of human activity and consent (4.5.1.1.).

b. Once more, in this text, reflections on *the essence of the perfect love* are the main theme. Luther emphasizes that St Paul writes these words after his conversion to Christ. His motive is love for his fellow Jews.[21] But without marking any distinct borderline Luther goes over to an exposition of the true love for God in the same way as before.[22] The common denominator of total love for one's neighbour and love for God is the willingness to surrender all one's rights for the sake of the beloved. The Christian consents to the will of God, even if this would condemn the believer to hell.[23] And further Luther asserts:

"But just as they thus conform themselves purely to the will of God, so also it is impossible that they should remain in hell. For it is impossible that the man should remain outside of God who has so completely (*penitus*) thrown himself upon the will of God. For he wills what God wills; therefore he pleases God. And if he pleases God, he is loved by him; and if loved, then saved."[24]

---

[18] WA 56.391.7ff.: "Iis autem, qui vere Deum diligunt amore filiali et amicitie, qui non est ex natura, Sed spiritu sancto solum, sunt pulcherrima ista verba et perfectissimi exempli testimonia."

[19] *Ib.* 22f.: "Sed Non extirpatur, Nisi per superabundantem gratie infusionem Vel per hanc durissimam resignationem." Cf. *ib.* 26ff.

[20] G. Rost's (1966)148 objections to K. Holl (1923)149f. on the grounds of the divine monergism are not wholly relevant. A. Gyllenkrok (1952)39 has an illuminating summary: "Was von dem einen Gesichtspunkt, dem empirischen, aus gesehen menschliche Aktivität ist, erscheint von dem anderen, nämlich von dem des Glaubens an die Autorität des Wortes aus, als menschliche Passivität und göttliche Aktivität. Luther arbeitet mit zwei verschiedenen Betrachtungsweisen, aber das hat nichts mit einem Widerspruch im eigentlichen Sinne des Wortes zu tun."

[21] WA 56.389.12ff., *ib.* 390.13ff.

[22] *Ib.* 23ff.

[23] *Ib.* 391.9ff.: "Tales enim Libere sese offerunt in omnem Voluntatem Dei, etiam ad infernum et mortem eternaliter, si Deus ita Vellet tantum, ut sua Voluntas plene fiat; adeo nihil querunt que sua sunt."

[24] *Ib.* 12ff., LW 25.381. Cf. also WA 56.392.1ff.

Such is the love of the ideal Christian. The most perfect example of the willingness of this love to descend into the darkness of hell is Christ. By reason of His love He was resurrected and liberated from the realm of the dead.[25] The believer who conforms wholly to the divine will is in perfect fellowship with God, even if he experiences suffering and anguish.

c. Now Luther, however, assumes that *in reality* there are very few who share in this perfect love of God. The great majority of Christians has a need of being cleansed of complacency, and trained in complete surrender through the pain of resignation.[26] This ordeal makes it possible for the Christian to know if he feels pure love for God. Only then can he realize that he no longer demands salvation and will accept damnation if God so wills.[27] This purification is regarded by Luther as an equivalent to the punishment in purgatory.[28] So the empirical Christian is always subject to God's will and acts tempering the believer in belief in, and love for, God. Consequently, we are wretched fools if we reject the trials in this life.[29]

Thus, by "the prudence of the flesh", man cannot discern the good, or understand the implications of perfect love. Perfect love consists in hating, condemning, and illwishing oneself. It is to see oneself as God sees us all, namely as sinners.[30] Luther goes on to declare:

> "For what is good for us is hidden, and that so deeply that it is hidden under its opposite (sub contrario). Thus our life is hidden under death, love for ourselves under hate for ourselves, glory under ignominy, salvation under damnation, our kingship under exile, *heaven under hell*, wisdom under foolishness, righteousness under sin, power under weakness. *And universally our every*

---

[25] *Ib.* 7ff.

[26] *Ib.* 391.17ff.: "Sed queritur, An Deus hoc unquam voluerit aut velit, Ut homo sese ad infernum resignet et ad damnationem sive ad anathema a Christo pro Voluntate eius tradat. Respondeo, Quod in plurimis et precipue in iis, qui sunt in Charitate seu amore Dei puro imperfecti. Nam illis Amor concupiscentie, tam profunde immersus, necessario extirpandus est."

[27] *Ib.* 24ff.: "Nunc autem nemo scit, an Deum pure diligat, Nisi experiatur in se, Quod etiam salvari non cupiat Nec damnari renvat, Si Deo placeret."

[28] *Ib.* 29ff. Further in E. Vogelsang (1932)40ff.

[29] WA 56.391.31.

[30] *Ib.* 392.17ff. G. Rost (1966)148 argues against Holl and others: "Die resignatio als Methode könnte von nichts anderem als dem Seligkeitsverlangen des Menschen bestimmt sein." This is not convincing. You can use a "method" just because it is the will of God without reference to your own advantage.

assertion of anything good is hidden under the denial of it, so that faith may have its place in God, who is a negative essence and goodness and wisdom and righteousness, who cannot be possessed or touched except by the negation of all our affirmatives."[31]

The principle underlying the resignation to hell, namely that God inflicts a great evil ("hell") to demonstrate something wonderful ("heaven"), can be said to be generalised! *Resignatio ad infernum* is an extraordinary term but is, in fact, a fundamental thought in Luther's theology. Only the individual who regards himself as a "lost" soul can understand and reach for the justifying grace. Just as both judgement and vindication are real, resignation to hell is made in all seriousness, and the fellowship with God remains intact.[32] At the same time, we can note that the hidden grace which can only be grasped by faith is represented as an *universal* offer. The particularistic predestination is brushed aside. K. Holl rightly interprets resignation to hell as encompassed by the frame of the emergent doctrine of justification.[33] However, I would emphasize that the idea of justification in the interpretation of Romans is expressed in terms which Luther inherited from traditional *humilitas* theology. A consistent use of the fundamental Law-Gospel-Dialectic does not appear until later.[34] It should also be observed that, for example, Johannes Tauler, who takes upon himself the task of interpreting the idea of

---

[31] WA 56.392.28ff., LW 25.382f. Cf. also WA 56.393.3ff.

[32] This is stressed by K. Holl (1923)151f., E. Vogelsang (1932)68f., R. Bring (1929)351, E. Seeberg (1929)150, and G. Rost (1966)145.

[33] K. Holl (1923)150: "Denn, so befremdlich es zunächst klingen mag, gerade in dieser Zuspitzung kamen gewisse Antriebe seiner Rechtfertigungslehre zu ihrer reinsten Ausprägung." G. Rost (1966)151 has the same point of view in spite of his critical attitude against Holl's exposition: "Aber auch das hinter der Resignatio ad infernum stehende Gedankengut verschwindet später nicht einfach aus Luthers Theologie. Jedoch es erfährt ebenfalls eine bedeutsame Umwandlung. Nur das Fundament bleibt, die accusatio sui und die Selbstverurteilung." Rost is following W. Pannenberg (1957)126 who supports his reasoning with WATR 1.174.28ff. (1532). But, like Pannenberg, Rost only quotes the first sentence in n. 81! If you read the following words you observe that Luther's motive is somewhat different: "Carlstadius aliquando dixit: Si scirem, das mich unser Herr Gott wolt verdammen, so wolt ich in die hell hinein traben. Sed est impie dictum. Deus dicit: Thue und glaub, was ich dir sage; das ander lass mich machen. So wollen sie es vor wissen sine et extra verbum." This is simply an admonition not to deal with the hidden, predestining God! See further 4.3.2–4 above.

[34] R. Josefson, *Ödmjukhet och tro* (1939)10, *ib.* 50ff. is probably right in showing how Luther uses the concept of humility in a new sense in his early lectures. See further the discussion in A. Gyllenkrok (1952)20ff. I. Öberg (1970)144ff. demonstrates that the penitence is consistently related to the Law and the Gospel from *c.* 1523.

resignatio ad infernum seems to be appreciated by Luther, simply because, like Luther, he was interested in the present and perfect justification.[35]

Finally, we may observe that *the belief in God in Jesus Christ* plays a key role. Only insofar as a man cannot see, his faith is real. The less he perceives the greater can his faith be. Now God is defined by the deed which Christ performed. Indeed, He was more condemned and abandoned than all the saints. "For He really and truly offered Himself to God the Father for the condemnation (damnationem) for us."[36] Thus Christ is not only an example but also a gift offered to all. A Christian faith can only be in truths hidden in God. Col. 3:3 applies here. Our life is hidden with Christ in God.[37] It means that the justification through Christ is invisible and internal. "Outside of you is everything which is seen and touched, but within you is everything which is believed only by faith."[38] If *fides rerum non apparentium* is a personal faith in Christ's vicarious act of reconciliation and justification, we have no right to say that *resignatio ad infernum* in this context would not be relevant to the concrete revelation in Christ.[39] Thus, I would also reject the opinion that Luther's commentary on Romans teaches merely the passive conformity to Christ as consolation for the afflicted, and not the active adoption of the divine revelation in Christ.[40]

[35] G. Wrede (1974)33. Cf. K. Holl (1923)150: "Deutlich steht Luther mit diesem Gedankengang unter dem Einfluss der Mystik. Seine Forderung berührt sich aufs nächste mit der *resignatio ad infernum* bei Tauler und dem Verfasser der Theologia Deutsch, in deren Gefolge später Molinos und Mme. de Guyon den *amour desinteressé* derselben Probe unterworfen haben."

[36] WA 56.392.7ff., LW 25.382.

[37] WA 56.393.5ff.

[38] *Ib.* 18ff., LW 25.383.

[39] *Contra* W. Pannenberg (1957)126. G. Rost (1966)150 n. 77 is unduly uncritical in his acceptance of Pannenberg here.

[40] A very distinct line is drawn between the lectures on Romans and the following material by W. Pannenberg (1957)125 and G. Rost (1966)150ff. But WA 56.387.20ff. (quoted in n. 6 above) clearly shows how far back the active aspect of the concept of faith can be traced. Other arguments can be presented. With reference to WA 56.393.29ff. Rost maintains (152): "Aber Luther würde es später nie mehr sagen, dass diese Anerkennung der göttlichen Gerechtigkeit genugtut." In WA 5.170.17ff. (*Operationes in Psalmos.* 1519–21), however, we read: "Hoc scilicet, primum agnoscas, id te meruisse et hoc peccatis tuis debitum, ubi prudens sis oportet, gratusque ac laudans hanc infirmitatem et tentationem feras, *tanquam saluberrimam satisfactionem pro peccatis tuis* iuxta illud Eccle. X." And further: "Atque hic in uno momento plus *satisfit pro peccato*, quam si multos annos poeniteas in aqua et pane."

When Luther has an opportunity to discuss the affliction concerning predestination in the *Second Commentary on the Psalms* (Ps. 5) his detailed exposition first emphasizes the intellectual aspect of understanding God's election.[41] In the context of further reflection on this point, the similarity to the *Commentary on Romans* becomes striking. For Luther again asserts that the will and the acts of God must be hidden from men, otherwise "there is no scope for either faith, hope, or love".[42] It is essential that we show absolute respect for the Word of the promise which is given by grace. Here, Luther refers explicitly to St Paul's letter to the Galatians, in which human *iustitia* does not consist in the Law but in the promise from God who gives blessing.[43] In other words, we have a situation in which, in the face of anxiety over the particularism of predestination, Luther sets the *universalism of the Pauline doctrine of justification.* As in the interpretation of Romans, we can get a glimpse of the divine sovereignty in the background: Faith, hope and love are only realized through suffering. Thus, the believer preceives in his heart the acts of God and the Words of God which are reaching for, purifying and touching his soul.[44] As in the interpretation of Romans, the believer descends into hell, surrenders all visible things, abandons all that is familiar, dies and goes down into the abyss. There the soul is blind, living only by faith, hope and love. Luther refers explicitly to "Theologi mystici". He admits, however, his ignorance of whether these mystics really understood that this purification does not take place through their own deeds but through the suffering of the cross, of death and of hell. "CRUX sola est nostra Theologia."[45] In order to describe the total destitution beneath the hand of God, Luther can, even later than the interpretation of Romans, express the *resignatio ad infernum* of the mystic! His thought is, however, modified by the

---

[41] *Ib*. 172.3ff. (quoted in 4.3.4 n. 3 above).

[42] *Ib*. 175.7ff.: "Adeo quicquid deus vult et facit, homo pulvis temerat, unum hoc aestuans, ut sit sine timore dei, hoc est sine deo, neque enim timeri posset, si non secreta de nobis cogitaret, nec tunc fides nec spes nec charitas locum haberet. Ve tibi furentissima impietas!"

[43] *Ib*. 11ff.

[44] *Ib*. 176.2ff. Cf. the importance of the Word of God, *ib*. 310.14ff. and *ib*. 546.4f.

[45] *Ib*. 176.21ff. Cf. further H. Beintker (1954)87ff., G. Wrede (1974)30ff. WA 5.397.35ff. is also illuminating: "Quin ego credo id radicatissimi mali et speciosissimi idoli in spiritu (ut ps. XXXI. vocat) non extingui, immo nec cognosci quidem unquam, nisi homo maioribus illis mortis, inferni, conscientiae seu fidei, spei, *praedestinationis* et id genus tentationibus vexetur." In this sense resignation to hell remains a basic principle of Luther's theology. See also WA 40.III.341.9ff. (*In XV Psalmos gradum*. 1532/33).

distinct emphasis on *God's* sovereignty. We cannot draw a sharp delimitation between the lecture on Romans and *Operationes in Psalmos*, nor assert that the consolation in the affliction concerning predestination is justified in a manner fundamentally new in the latter work.

In the exposition of Ps. 22 we find an interpretation which in its structure is reminiscent of the analysis of Ps. 5. Luther, as a word of consolation to every individual who endures the profound need and anguish, being plunged by the affliction concerning predestination into hell, *first* adduces the argument which applies primarily to the cognitive aspect.[46] *Then* he treats the characteristics of existential anguish of this affliction: "Deinde fide contra fidem pugnet." If the Christian feels that he is lost and rejected, he really believes this of himself. Only the bold confidence in the hidden justification can overcome this experience of wrath. For our redemption comes from another faith, not from perception. This new faith does not doubt that God does that which is the highest righteousness, whether He saves or rejects. It trusts in God's invisible justification, although an impressive human emotion and all the devils argue forcefully against it.[47] At the same time, it is important to remember that Luther, in the preceding expressive exposition of Ps. 22:2, strongly emphasized that Christ bore all sin, death and hell *pro nobis*.[48] Thus, the righteousness of God is defined by the reconciling acts of Christ. The belief in this *iustitia dei* is a belief in Christ.[49] So only the

---

[46] WA 5.622.24ff and *ib*. 37ff.

[47] *Ib*. 623.17ff.: "Deinde fide contra fidem pugnet. Cum enim *fides sit rerum non apparentium* et substantia sperandarum vehementer repugnat, immo fidem expugnat curiositas ista scrutandae maiestatis, posse et nosse salvare deum, non est fides in hac hora, id enim experimento evidentissime sentit. Item S. Petrum salvum fieri deo volente et omnes sanctos et electos aeque iam non credit, sed scit. Verum te et me velle salvum facere, hoc non apparet nec apparere debet. Haec voluntas incomprehensibilis est et esse debet. Ideo sola fide hic opus est, et ea fide, quae non dubitet, deum facere et facturum esse secum, quod iustissimum fuerit, sive servet sive perdat. Hic enim manet gloria et laus dei in ore nostro, cum deo non nisi iustitiam tribuimus in omni voluntate eius, etiam si hanc ipsam iustitiam non videamus, sed tantum credamus, tam potenter contrarium suadente humano affectu et daemonum persuasione."

[48] *Ib*. 603.7ff., *ib*. 604.10f., *ib*. 606.13ff.

[49] *Ib*. 621.29ff.: "Christus enim iustitia nostra est, 1. Cor.1., in qua per fidem constanter gloriamur, tanquam nostra propria, quando nostra satisfacere legi et stare in hac hora non potest." Cf. *ib*. 171.11ff. and *ib*. 606.15ff. I agree with G. Rost (1966)154: " Das erste Gebot, so wie es Luther hier versteht, steht in voller inhaltlicher Übereinstimmung mit der evangelischen Verheissung. Das Evangelium von dem in Christus gnädigen Gott ist Voraussetzung und Grundlage dieses Gebotes." H. Beintker (1954)152 shows how the work of Christ is decisive for the victory over the grave afflictions, according to *Operationes in Psalmos*.

justification by faith, offered to all for Christ's sake, can force the affliction of predestination's particularism to yield and vanish.

2. In *The Bondage of the Will* Luther expresses his former revulsion to the belief that God arbitrarily abandons, hardens, and condemns certain individuals. He admits that he himself was tormented by the thought of this unconditional predestination:

> "I myself was offended more than once, and brought to the very depth and abyss of despair, so that I wished I had never been created a man, before I realized how salutary that despair was, and how near to grace."[50]

Thus, on the one hand, the negative feeling is in fact a serious reality. It is indeed an experience of the dejection of hell to sink down into total desperation. We can catch a glimpse of the reason why the *resignatio ad infernum* of the mystic is highly relevant for the young Luther! On the other hand, according to the quotation from Luther, a door opens amid the negative despair. Not until the Christian feels the perfect damnation is he able to invoke the perfect grace.

When Luther generalises this personal understanding to apply to all mankind, he vigorously presents the necessity of faith if man is to attain the positive amid the negative:

> "Hence in order that there may be room for faith, it is necessary that everything which is believed should be hidden. It cannot, however, be more deeply hidden than under an object, perception, or experience which is contrary to it (*sub contrario obiectu, sensu, experientia*). Thus when God makes alive he does it by killing, *when he justifies he does it by making men guilty, when he exalts to heaven he does it by bringing down to hell*, as Scripture says: 'The Lord kills and brings to life; he brings down to Sheol and raises up' (1 Sam. 2:6). This is not the place to speak at length on this subject, but those who have read my books have had it quite plainly set forth for them.
>
> *Thus God hides his eternal goodness and mercy under eternal wrath, his righteousness under iniquity.* This is *the highest degree of faith*, to believe him merciful when he saves so few and damns so many, and to believe him righteous when by his own will he makes us necessarily damnable, so that he seems, according to Erasmus,

---

[50] WA 18.719.4ff. (*De servo arbitrio.* 1525), LW 33.190.

to delight in the torments of the wretched and to be worthy of hatred rather than of love.''[51]

This is not merely a theoretical reflection on the essence of faith but also a mode of giving comfort in the actual affliction. The life-giving forgiveness and justification come from the Gospel of Christ.[52] But the Word of grace is necessarily relevant only to those who are tormented by despair in the consciousness of their sin.[53] Thus by God's covenant alone there is hope for the tortured conscience.[54] The hidden good which faith must grasp is Christ. Therefore, *The Bondage of the Will* is not merely an abstract defence of God's monergism. It is as well a penetrating proclamation of the need for Christ.[55] So Luther preaches to every deeply tormented human being of the universal grace and justification in Christ. The particularism of the idea of predestination, and God's apparent injustice therein, is brushed aside on the pretext of the eschatological verification in "the light of glory".[56]

3. We can find expressive words concerning the boldness of faith if we consider Luther's *sermons* on what has become the classic text for this theme, namely Matt. 15:21–8. He says that at times God takes His hand from us, allowing all kinds of misery to beset us, so that we cry out. Yet, He turns a deaf ear, as if He does not know us, and lets us feel as we have no God. But amid these negative experiences He gives a form of compensation. We need have no doubts of His yes in heaven. His comforting Word is actually hidden with Christ in the heart. Therefore, Luther consoles every tormented Christian: The despair does not yield if the individual continues to dispute concerning election, but merely if he boldly insists that God does accept him in Christ, even though he can neither see nor perceive it.[57] Faith forces its way through striking

---

[51] WA 18.633.7ff., LW 33.62f. These sentences are fundamental to the interpretation in W. Elert (1931)108 and P. Althaus (1963)245. See further 1.2 n. 23–24 above.

[52] *E.g.* WA 18.766.25ff.

[53] *Ib.* 684.4ff.: "Sicut vox legis non fertur nisi super eos, qui peccatum non sentiunt nec agnoscunt, sicut Paulus dicit Romano. 3: Per legem cognitio peccati, Ita verbum gratiae non venit nisi ad eos, qui peccatum sentientes affliguntur et tentantur desperatione."

[54] *Ib.* 683.22ff.

[55] *Ib.* 744.14ff., *ib.* 779.21ff., *ib.* 786.17ff.

[56] Cf. WA 18.767.19ff., *ib.* 785.20ff. R. Bring (1929)344f. carefully examines how "the light of nature" and "the light of grace" correspond to reason and faith and also to the attitude of the egocentric and of the theocentric individual.

[57] WA 37.316.23ff. (*Pred.* 1534, R): "Ich hallts ja, quod velit gnedig sein et barmhertzig illis, qui clamant, *Das Jawort stecket jm hertzen*, ergo non disputo, an sim electus vel gentilis, Sed *hoc urgeo, das das Jawort da sey.*"

experiences of damnation and rejection, and attains the hidden blessings which Christ instils into the believer's heart. So these burdensome afflictions are at one and the same time a challenge and a reinforcement of faith, since faith is tempered and strengthened to overcome everything.[58] This insistence on God's acceptance presupposes that man overlooks the particularism of predestination, and instead concentrates his spiritual energy on the justification in Christ which is offered to all mankind.

If the Christian only would say fatalistically that all things are predetermined and nothing can be changed, the election is to either salvation or rejection, simply all that God has done, and does, through Christ and the sacraments would be wholly irrelevant. This is the starting point of the detailed reasoning in the *Large Genesis Lecture*.[59] But this is not only a theoretical reason for placing Christology in the centre. It is also the exhortation of the spiritual adviser to all Christians who are disquieted about the election. Such thoughts must be countered with a "vera et firma cognitio Christi".[60] Luther describes how this happens in practice. The union of the heart with Christ becomes a private, invisible relationship, which is the cure for the terrible disease which man experiences and sees. Health is realized by means of its opposite, namely the disease.[61]

In order to shed further light on the qualities of the Christian belief, Luther tells of a woman at *Torgau* who, sobbing, lamented her inability to believe. He recited to her the articles of faith and asked her at each point if she was convinced that all this was true, and that the events had occurred as described. She replied: I know that it is absolutely true but I

[58] *Ib.* 25ff.: "Hoc est exemplum fidei, das fides wil geubt sein, und darnach uberwunden alles, Non debemus verbum sic achten, Haec clamat, sie lesst ir das Jawort aus dem hertzen nicht nhemen, das er freundlich sey und helffe, sie lest irs unsern herr Gott selbs nicht nhemen, unser herr Gott helffe uns, das wir auch hinach komen, Amen." Cf. WA 44.68.9ff. (*Vorlesung über 1. Mose.* 1535–45).

[59] WA 43.457.35ff. Cf. *ib.* 459.25ff., *ib.* 460.3ff. Even Th. Harnack I (1927)148ff. emphasizes Luther's reasoning in this passage.

[60] WA 43.458.28f., quoted in 4.5.1 n. 19. Concerning the hidden God and the particularistic salvation "nulla est fides, nulla scientia et cognitio nulla" (*ib.* 39f.).

[61] *Ib.* 459.36ff.: "Id unum age, ut suscipias filium, ut placeat in corde tuo Christus in sua nativitate, miraculis et cruce. Ibi enim est liber vitae, in quo scriptus es. Idque unicum et praesentissimum remedium est istius horribilis morbi, quo homines in inquisitione Dei procedere volunt speculative et ruunt tandem in desperationem aut contemptum." It is noteworthy that the counsel to Luther once was a kind of parallel to this: "Staupitius his verbis me consolabatur: Cur istis speculationibus te crucias? Intuere vulnera Christi et sanguinem pro te fusum" (*ib.* 461.11f.). Cf. also *ib.* 393.9ff.

cannot believe it. This was, according to Luther, a diabolical illusion. He said to her: If you know that all this is true, there is no reason why you should lament your disbelief. Indeed, if you do not doubt that God's Son died for you, then you assuredly believe. For to believe is simply to accept these articles as certain and ineluctable truths.[62] Thus the faith which is referred to in this context contains an element of consent to and of trust in the doctrine of justification which is offered to all through Christ.

Moreover, God has given the Christian these invisible blessings by means of visible signs, which bestow the surest comfort. I see the water of baptism, I see the bread and wine of the Eucharist, I see the priest in his office. All these are universal means whereby God reveals Himself, and gives absolution, life, and beatitude.[63]

4.5.3. Certainty of Salvation

The idea of predetermination is not merely a dark background in the notion of God, which gives rise to affliction and despair. It also involves the conception of light which bestows further evangelical dimensions on justification by faith for Christ's sake. Therefore, Luther guides the thought of the Christian from the total forgiveness of sins, life and blessedness in Christ back to the doctrine of predestination. It is a very important purpose in this new approach to God. To the abiding and imploring faith in Christ God's sovereignty and immutability do not appear threatening and terrifying but consolatory and hopeful.[1]

---

[62] *Ib.* 460.14ff. See further S. von Engeström (1933)5ff., *ib.* 228ff., *ib.* 254ff. on Luther's concept of faith, which is not adequately interpreted in the school of A. Ritschl. Not being a Ritschlian, however, H. Bornkamm, *Luthers geistige Welt* (1947)87ff. stresses how faith victorious is "ein Wagnis, ein Sprung ins Dunkle". Evidently, it is also necessary to say that faith clings to something which is quite clear, namely the Christian *Credo*, or Christian doctrine.

[63] WA 43.462.16ff. Cf. *ib.* 606.2ff., WATR 1.506.16ff. (1530–35) *ib.* 2.562.7ff. (1532). The same pastoral counseling can easily be found in Luther's letters from different times, see quotations in 4.5.1 n. 17. In FC we have the same point of view, BSLK 1066ff.

[1] This aspect is clearly observed by *e.g.* R. Seeberg (1917)154f., C. Stange (1928)87ff. W. Link (1940)324f. discusses Tauler's certainty of faith based on the thought of predestination. Cf. H. J. Iwand (1974)90f.: "Die Wiederentdeckung der Prädestination gehört zu den Urelementen der reformatorischen Heilsgewissheit." The special value of the doctrine of predestination is stressed in W. Pannenberg (1957)134ff. See further on this issue K. Heim, *Das Gewissheitsproblem* (1911)220ff.

1. In the *Lecture on Romans* (Rom. 8:28) Luther lays particular emphasis on "the consolation" in the conception of predestination. This consists in the fact that the God, who elects, supremely and immutably effects salvation. The individual who is ruled only by "the prudence of the flesh" is repelled by the doctrine of the unconditional predetermination. He himself is reduced to nothing when reason understands "that salvation comes in no way from something working in itself but only from outside itself, namely from God, who elects". But those who are governed by "the prudence of the spirit" hold a different view. They "delight in this subject with an ineffable pleasure".[2] The fact that *God alone effects* all that is needed for salvation becomes a source of joy to the believer. As long as it is a question of human achievement of certain qualifications man can always worry about whether he has attained them. But when all of salvation is rooted in a God who elects, man too is free of his doubts, and free to experience joy at God's sovereign works. Nevertheless, we must not be too quick to read into this a fully developed doctrine of certainty of salvation.[3]

At the same time we need only to read a few more lines to see that *the divine immutability* too provokes a feeling of gratitude and content. God cannot be lying when He says: "The sacrifice acceptable to God is a broken spirit; a broken and contrite heart, O God, Thou wilt not despise"[4] (Ps. 51:17). In other words, the divine veracity of the promise means that the experience of contrition can be turned into a positive perception.

The Preface to Romans in the translation of the New Testament from 1522 also points to the liberating train of thought, inherent in the idea of the divine predestination.[5] Here the theoretical doctrine of the double election has a practical significance. The uncanny possibility contained in the reprobation is not expounded in detail. Instead, Luther emphasizes

---

[2] WA 56.386.24ff. (*Rom.* 1515–16), LW 25.377. Cf. WA 56.89.15ff., *ib.* 381.24ff., *ib.* 382.7ff. See also the analysis of the predestination as argument against human merits (4.4.3.).

[3] A. Gyllenkrok (1952)65ff. examines the material on the certainty of salvation. He finds in the lecture on Romans no real certainty arising from the Ockhamistic concept of faith. F. W. Schmidt, *Der Gottesgedanke in Luthers Römerbriefsvorlesung* (1921)222 does not carefully distinguish between justification and man's consciousness thereof. See also S. von Engeström, *Luthers tankar om frälsningsvissheten i Romarbrevskommentaren* (*Festskrift t. Nathan Söderblom.* 1926)141ff.

[4] WA 56.387.20ff. See further the context quoted in 4.5.2 n. 6. Cf. also how the divine immutability provokes both fear and hope, WA 5.385.33ff. (*Operationes in Psalmos.* 1519–21) and *ib.* 175.26f.

[5] WADB 7.22.26ff. (*Das Neue Testament.* 1522), quoted in 4.2.2 n. 14.

the tenet closest to his heart; the Christian's absolute, present security in God. The issue of salvation does not rest in human hands but wholly on *the almighty God.* That which in a different context could be the source of the most awesome *terrores conscientiae* here becomes the sweet feeling of certainty that God carries the responsibility for all things relating to man's salvation. The idea of predestination is presented as a further guarantee of the certainty of salvation.

At the same time, the concept of *God's immutability* resounds in these words. God not only takes upon Himself all responsibility for our justification. He also stands by His promises for evermore. The feature of immutability in the divine being ("nu Gott gewis ist") and in the divine election becomes an argument promoting further support for the certainty of salvation.

This is a teaching on God's predetermination which differs from that found in Biel and in Roman Catholic theologians. These allow God to effect a part and man, with his free will, another part of the realization of God's election. Thus salvation must be uncertain. According to Luther, this has two consequences. Firstly, "man tears apart" all that God Himself does. Secondly, man does not recognize Christ as the redeemer He truly is, but denies Him His' honour and allows Him to suffer once more.[6] Therefore, the Reformation is not only a Reformation of the doctrine of justification but also of the tenet of predestination.

2. In *The Bondage of the Will* we have already discussed various implications of *God's omnipotence.* The point of prime interest to us here is how Luther uses the conception as a basis for the certainty of salvation.

The statements on the usefulness and the necessity to teach that God works all in all are familiar. "Prima est humilatio nostrae superbiae et cognitio gratiae Dei."[7] For man cannot radically humble himself until he knows that his salvation lies wholly outside his own powers, counsel, efforts, and will, and that it depends totally on another's free decision, counsel, will, and works, namely on God alone. The believer who truly does not doubt that everything (*totum*) depends on God's will despairs of

[6] WA 10.I.1.672.11ff. (*Kirchenpostille.* 1522): "Item, das Euangelium leret, *wie gottis vorsehung ewiglich gewiss sey.* Sso leren sie, das sie stehe *auff dem freyen willen und sey ungewiss.* Und kurtzlich, gott und seynen namen bekennen sie, aber alles, was gott ordenett, will, thutt, setzt und macht, das tzureyssen sie, vortilgen und vordamnen es als die hohist ketzerey, das es offenbar ist, wie itzt Christus leyden geystlich erfullet wirt unter des Bapsts regiment." Cf. further H. J. Iwand (1974)95.
[7] WA 18.632.27f. (*De servo arbitrio.* 1525).

himself, makes no decisions, but waits upon God, who acts. He approaches grace and so is saved. Therefore, this is broadcast for the sake of the elect, so that they may be totally humiliated, crushed with regard to their own capacity, and saved by the power of God.[8] Grace effects all things. Salvation is rooted in God wholly and completely. This deprives the Christian of every idea that he can in any way contribute to the salvation of his soul. The unconditional election as a theoretical doctrine is, indeed, a stumbling block. But its practical value is very important. The Christian ought to clearly understand that every moment of salvation is dependent on pure grace.

The personal background of this accentuation is revealed by Luther's *Confiteor*.[9] It first presents the hypothesis that man could be given free will, and that he could be entrusted with something to help him strive after salvation. Yet, Luther would refuse. For he could not endure and keep hold of salvation amid so many sufferings and afflictions. He would constantly be compelled to work in uncertainty and to fight as one beating in the air, even if no demons, or dangers existed. If he lived and worked for all eternity his conscience could never find absolute certainty that he had done enough to satisfy God.[10]

Then, Luther points at the reality of the sovereign grace of God:

"But now, since *God has taken my salvation out of my hands into his*, making it depend on his choice and not mine, and has promised to save me, not by my own work or exertion but by his grace and mercy, *I am assured and certain* both that he is faithful and will not lie to me, and also that he is too great and powerful for any demons or any adversities to be able to break him or to snatch me from him. 'No one', he says, 'shall snatch them out of my hand, because my Father who has given them to me is greater than all' (John 10:28f.). So it comes about that, if not all, some and indeed many are saved, whereas by the power of free choice none at all would be saved, but all would perish together. Moreover, we are also certain and sure that we please God, not by the merit of our own working, but by the favour of his mercy promised to us, and that if we do less than we should or do it badly, he does not hold this against us (*nobis non imputet*), but in a fatherly way pardons and corrects us. Hence the glorying of all the saints in their God."[11]

[8] *Ib*. 30ff.
[9] *Ib*. 783.17.
[10] *Ib*. 17ff. Cf. *ib*. 604.33, *ib*. 605.6ff. See also R. Seeberg (1917)155.
[11] WA 18.783.28ff., LW 33.289. Cf. WA 18.646.2ff., *ib*. 656.9ff. John 10:28f. is also the Biblical support in WA 43.461.16 (*Vorlesung über 1. Mose.* 1535–45).

Here Luther is not merely the belligerent but also the spiritual adviser. He seeks to demonstrate to Erasmus that the human conscience is restless and insecure until God looms so large before him that He does all things. Therefore, Luther's purpose is to reform the humanized notion of God, according to which man has the option of co-operating with God in the justification.

We may also observe in this quotation how *God's immutability* involves a fundamental, divine quality with regard to the certainty of salvation. Instead of brushing aside "metaphysical" definitions of God Luther emphasizes them, because they play a vital role in the consolation of the Christian. The divine immutability is not only the issue in the admonitions of the Law, but also the guarantee of the abiding forgiveness of the Gospel. In this way, all that Luther has written in *De servo arbitrio* concerning the unchanging God[12] might be regarded as prolegomena to the new certainty of justification and redemption.

3. Since we have already adduced tenets from the *Large Lecture on Genesis* dealing with *God's omnipotence*, it should suffice here to refer to Luther's confirmation of the *deus absconditus* concept.[13] The validity of both the hidden and the revealed God emerges not least from the reflection on faithful trust in Christ: "Si hunc habes, tunc etiam Deum absconditum pariter cum revelato habes."[14] The faith is directed to the revealed God, whom we meet in the Incarnation, Christ's suffering, death and resurrection, and victory on our behalf. Thus, the absolute qualities of the hidden God are seen in their true colours. *A posteriori* we can face *Deus nudus*. Yes, the "metaphysical" attributes of this God are of fundamental importance in the orthodox faith in Christ. So the omnipotence of *deus absconditus* is vital for the Christian faith in *deus revelatus*.

Luther here also places special emphasis on *God's immutability*. The knowledge of Christ must confer a feeling of boundless joy and delight because God is immutable, and acts with unchanging necessity. He

---

[12] Cf. further 4.2.4 n. 7–14.

[13] WA 43.458.33ff. (*Vorlesung über 1. Mose.* 1535–45), *ib.* 463.5ff. (quoted in 4.3.2 n. 16).

[14] WA 43.461.26f. P. Meinhold (1936)406 says: "Der deus incarnatus und der deus absconditus sind identisch. Das spricht die Genesisvorlesung gerade so deutlich wie die frühen Schriften Luthers aus." He also refers to WA 43.461.23ff. Meinhold is right in speaking of Christ as the revelation of God's hidden righteousness and salvation. But if Luther thinks of *deus absconditus* as the God who imposes necessity on man and immutably works all in all, then we must say that *deus absconditus* contributes certain metaphysical attributes which do not come from the revelation of Christ and cannot be directly identified with *deus revelatus*.

cannot deny Himself but stands by His word.[15] Thus, the interpretation which seeks to do justice to perhaps the most important feature of Luther's teaching, namely the certainty of salvation, cannot repress the idea of the *deus absconditus*.[16] Instead it is necessary to single out God's sovereignty and immutability, precisely in order to show that the Gospel leads to the total liberation envisaged by Luther. In this sense the idea of predestination has a profound psychological meaning which even a Catholic scholar studying Luther can regard with sympathy.[17]

The *Lutheran confessional books* seem to follow the reformer, insofar as they base the certainty of salvation on God's sovereign, immutable will to grace in Christ.[18] It has also been suggested that the doctrine of justification, according to the *Council of Trent*, appears to be in some agreement with Luther, insofar as it emphasizes human weakness, sin, and deficiencies which create uncertainty and affliction with regard to salvation, at the same time as, gazing upon *God's* almighty and unchanging being, man with a firm hope expects redemption at the last.[19]

4.5.4. Certainty of Election

In a previous section (4.4.3.3.), I have indicated a parallel between the doctrine of justification and the idea of predestination. Now I am able to

---

[15] WA 43.461.30ff. (quoted in 4.2.4 n. 15). *Ib.* 458.28ff. speaks of "vera et firma cognitio Christi" which includes "cognitio Dei certissima". And this is a knowledge of the immutability of God. Cf. *ib.* 462.14ff. Cf. also WAB 9.627.33ff. (1542), WA 45.403.20ff. (*Viel fast nützlicher Punkt.* 1537).

[16] Cf. *e.g.* A. Ritschl I[3] (1889)220ff., R. Seeberg (1917)155.

[17] S. Shapiro, *Quelques réflexions sur la signification psychologique de la prédestination dans la Réform*, RHE 68:1 (1973)825f.

[18] BSLK 1084 (FC in SD 11).

[19] Cf. Denz 802 and 805. In the abundant literature on this issue, see further E. Schott, *Einig in der Rechtfertigungslehre?*, LuJ 26 (1959)1ff. containing a discussion of the well-known book by H. Küng: *Rechtfertigung—Die Lehre Karl Barths und eine Katholische Besinnung* (1957); A. Peters, *Reformatorische Rechtfertigungsbotschaft zwischen tridentinischer Rechtfertigungslehre und gegenwärtigem evangelischen Verständnis der Rechtfertigung*, LuJ 31 (1964)77ff.; The major investigation by H. G. Pöhlmann with the title *Rechtfertigung* (1971) reaches this conclusion: "Für beide Konfessionen ist respectu dei die Rechtfertigung *ganz*, nicht nur teilweise gewiss. Für beide Konfessionen ist aber respectu hominis das Heil ungewiss, weil der Mensch aus der Gnade herausfallen kann, weil der Mensch die Gnade sich geschenkt sein lassen oder nicht" (*ib.* 296); Cf. *ib.* 287ff. E. Iserloh (1974) has the intention of showing "weshalb in der Rechtfertigungslehre, dem 'articulus stantis et cadentis ecclesiae', heute keine kirchentrennenden Unterschiede mehr angenommen werden müssen" (*ib.* 5).

proceed and expound this similarity. The Christian who knows that he is justified by his actual faith is also aware of the fact that justification has its causative background in election (4.4.1.). The question arises, then, whether, by experiencing the effect (the justification), he could accept the cause (the predestination) and possess some form of certainty of election? Would it not be possible to cling to the living, bold trust in Christ and thus conclude that one is among the elect and that God will help in all difficulties in the future?

Luther assents to these questions in the material from both his youth and his old age, a fact of which scholars *per se* are well aware.[1] Nevertheless, no recent scholar has narrowly expounded the positive and negative aspects of this certainty of election.[2] Nor has sufficient attention been given to the question whether Luther maintains the importance of deeds for the certainty of election to the same extent as, apparently, Calvin.[3]

1. If we first consider the material from the *Lecture on Romans*, we can establish that Luther both accepts and denies the certainty of election. On the *one* hand, he reads Rom. 8:38f. and *denies* that anyone can be certain of election by means of an universal law. Only by a special revelation can a Christian know whether he is among the elect.[4] God allows many people at first to live an upright life, doing good. Nevertheless, they are not saved at last. Again God lets many commit evil deeds and yet changes them so that they are redeemed. Take, for example, Saul and Manasseh, and Judas, and the thief on the cross, and many open sinners. God rejected the learned with their spectacular good

---

[1] We find a survey of this material already in Th. Harnack I (1927)180ff.

[2] R. Seeberg (1917)153f. *et. al.* do not carefully analyse the exact meaning of the certainty of election in Luther's theology. To K. Holl (1923)112f., *ib.* 149 is due the credit of differentiating between a certainty *a priori*, which is denied by Luther, and a certainty *a posteriori* which is affirmed as a fruit of the justification by faith in Christ. The lack of *consensus* in the debate between S. von Engeström (1926)149f. and R. Bring (1929)351 is due to the fact that they are discussing two different topics. I see it as a lacuna in the paper of G. Rost (1966) that he does not deal extensively with this issue.

[3] Being a specialist on Calvin K. Holl (1923)149, however, only makes a short suggestion: "Wer es zu fassen vermag, dass er erwählt sei, der ist auch erwählt. Das ist der Weg, den Zwingli und Calvin später eingeschlagen haben." According to W. Niesel, *Die Theologie Calvins*[2] (1957)172ff. the good works are of minor importance as a sign of election in the thology of Calvin. See also F. Wendel (1972)275f. About experience and perseverance see J. Moltmann (1961)49ff.

[4] WA 56.86.19ff. (*Rom.* 1515–16), quoted in 4.3.1 n. 5. K. Holl (1923)112 rightly argues against F. Loofs that this passage deals with "Erwählungsgewissheit". Cf further E. Schlink, *Der theologische Syllogismus als Problem der Prädestinationslehre* (In: *Einsicht und Glaube. Festschrift f. G. Söhngen.* 1962)314f.

works. Thus, He even rejected one of the 40 martyrs[5], namely the one who finally lost his faith and fled. Neither merits nor anything else can demonstrate to us on whom God will have mercy and forgive. The election comes like a bolt from the blue.[6]

But, on the *other* hand, Luther does not hesitate to describe diverse *signa electionis*, as we saw above (4.5.2.1.). Here he affirms that the Christian may possess some form of certainty of election. The elect display specific characteristics. Assuredly it is not the reprobates who fear the hidden judgement of God, but the elect.[7] If a Christian conforms to God's will, and this conformity has different steps as we reported above, this may be designated an indication of the predetermination.[8] *The love for God*, amid the cross and the suffering, may be as enduring and as strong as hell. Such a circumstance reveals something about the individual's election. For so God tempers His elect.[9] By reason of his love the believer is given a sign of his election.

Since this invincible love, this overwhelming infusion of grace is a *divine gift*, the Christian can therefore, according to Rom. 8:30, apprehend the love and loyalty of the Giver. As he now owns it, he is now also chosen. Or, in other words, as a result of the actual effect he can accept the actual cause.

Furthermore, we can consider *faith*. The Christian who knows "with confidence" that God cannot lie when He promises mercy and forgiveness to the contrite heart, should boldly plunge into the truth of the God who makes the promises, and turn from the prescience of the God who comes with threats. So he will be saved and elect.[10] Thus, by the bold grasping of the promise of God in Christ, a person disquieted about predestination can not only overcome these terrors but also attain the firm ground of certainty of salvation and election. At least implicitly assurance of predestination, with faith as an essential premise, is suggested.

Firstly, it is important to observe that the present faith in Christ is the starting point. It is not a matter of a carnal or rational certainty of *fides qua* in the future. Election, therefore, does not mean that man is given proof of *donum perseverantiae*, resulting in false security. *Secondly*, faith

---

[5] WA 56.384.25ff.

[6] *Ib.* 397.19ff., partly quoted in 4.3.1 n. 3.

[7] WA 56.387.27f.: "Certe non est reproborum hominum, saltem in vita, pavere ad Iudicium illud Dei absconditum, Sed electorum."

[8] See further 4.5.2 n. 7–17.

[9] WA 56.388.19ff., quoted in 4.5.2 n. 12.

[10] WA 56.387.20ff., quoted in 4.5.2 n. 6.

in this context is at least a sign of predestination, so that the Christian, by reason of actual faith based on Rom. 8:30, can have a humble confidence in his election and an assurance of God's willingness to preserve him in the future. This thesis can be supported by the fact that in Rom. 9:10 Luther makes faith so clear an indication of election that the lack of it is directly explained as the lack of election.[11] So we may say that we here find the obvious traces of both uncertainty *vis-à-vis* the predestination because of *fides qua* in the future, and certainty on the grounds of *fides quae* (= God's sovereign and immutable mercy in Christ). The same opinion is to be found later in the works of the mature reformer.

Luther teaches not only an educated audience but also a wide public that there is no certainty of election, and that nevertheless this exists. He describes the *impossible* undertaking of a Christian abandoning faith and presuming to pry into the secrecy of God's counsel. Only the devil can drive an individual to the point of seeking extraordinary signs of God's will. The more a man follows satan on this issue, the more dangerous is his situation.[12] Luther asserts, however, that it is nonetheless *possible* to discover whether one is among the elect. In the picture of Christ, the Christian's hell is overcome, and his uncertain election confirmed ("gewiss"). The individual who accepts this, believing it happened *pro se*, will surely ("gewisslich") be preserved in the same faith.[13] This word of consolation is, in fact, given to Christians who will very soon die! When they are leaving this world, Luther wishes to give them comfort in their worry over the quality of their faith at the last moment of life.

Accordingly, Luther not only derives a certainty of justification but also a certainty of election from the faith in Christ. Insofar as this firm confidence exists, the trust in the truth of election is also present.[14] This

[11] WA 56.395.20ff.: "Quanto minus proderit Incredulis Iudeis, longe posterius natis, quod sint filii patriarcharum secundum carnem, si sine fide fuerint, i.e. si non fuerint electi a Deo!"

[12] WA 2.688.1ff. (*Ein Sermon von der Bereitung zum Sterben.* 1519), quoted in 4.3.4 n. 4.

[13] WA 2.690.20ff., quoted in 4.5.1 n. 9.

[14] WA 2.690.26ff.: "Alsso wan du Christum and all seyne heyligen ansihist, und dir woll gefellet die gnad gottis, der sie alsso erwelet hatt, und bleybst nur fest yn dem selben wolgefallen, *sso bistu schon auch erwelet*, wie er sagt Gen: 12. Alle, die dich gebenedeyen, sollen gebenedeyet seyn."

This point is also stressed in *Operationes in Psalmos* (1519–21). The speculations on the predestination come from the devil, according to WA 5.172.3ff. (quoted in 4.3.4 n. 3). But Luther can also in WA 5.173.7ff. maintain: "Debes enim velle nescire eius secreta, quae voluit te nescire, atque gaudere in hac eius voluntate, quam praecepit tibi observare in omnibus. *Amata autem hac occulti eius consilii voluntate iam praedestinatus es.*" There are other interesting passages in WA 4.712.40ff. (*Sermone* 1520) and WA 8.368.27ff. (*Evangelium von den zehn Aussätzigen.* 1521). In his sermons Luther teaches both that we cannot gain rational knowledge about election, and that we can start with Christ and realize that we are sons of God, *e.g.* WA 10.III.108.12ff. (1522).

is not to say that the Christian is *always* sure of possessing *fides qua*. We must bear the *exceptional* situation in mind in order to interpret that sentence ("sso wirstu yn dem selben glauben behalten gewisslich") adequately, namely as a special statement that "the gift of perseverance" will be given the dying Christian, merely, through faith in Christ. The main point is that "glauben" here refers to the belief that Christ has ensured the believer's election and perseverance. The summarizing Genesis quotation, where Abraham is regarded as a type for Christ, also has this meaning. All who look upon Christ, and accept His giving of the divine grace, bless Him. This has the result that they in turn are blessed by God, *i.e.* are given certainty of their election. In other words, we may claim that the term election here means, first and foremost, the underlying cause in the immutable God of actual certainty, which His chosen possess in Christ.

So far I have only maintained that Luther makes an *unspoken* distinction between a *certainty*, which the believer is given through Christ (*fides quae*) and an uncertainty which results from doubt of *fides qua* in the remote future and until the end of life. If we turn to a sermon of 1522, this distinction is defined in so many words. Here Luther is teaching the true, perfect faith. This consists of a firm belief that the individual has personally received grace and mercy from Christ. The believer is thereby set free from himself, becoming holy, devout, and righteous, a child of God, and certain of his salvation.[15] Then this is expounded as a state of *simul certus et incertus*.[16]

---

[15] WA 10.I.1.331.17ff. (*Kirchenpostille*. 1522). See further S. von Engeström (1933)170ff. on this immediate certainty.

[16] WA 10.I.1.332.4ff.: "Denn es soll hie nit furcht oder wancken seyn, das er frum und gottis kind sey auss gnaden, ssondern alleyn furchten unnd sorgen, wie er also bleybe biss anss ende bestendig, ynn wilchem alleyn alle fahr und sorg steht; denn *es ist alle selickeyt da gewisslich. Aber ungewiss unnd sorglich ists, ob er bestehe unnd sie behallt*, da muss man ynn furcht wandelln; denn solcher glawb pocht nicht auff werck odder sich selb, ssondernn alleyn auff gott unnd seyne gnade, dieselb mag unnd kan yhn auch nit lassen, dieweyl das pochen weret. Aber wie lang es weren wirtt, weyss er nit; ob yhn eyn anfechtung davon treyben mocht, das solchs pochen auffhöret, so höret die gnade auch auff. Das meynet Salomon Eccle. 9: Es sind rechtfertige und yhre werck ynn gottis hand, dennoch wirtt es alles ynn tzukunfftig ungewissheytt gestellet, das der mensch nit weyss, ob er gnaden oder ungnaden wirdig sey. *Er spricht nit, das es gegenwertig ungewiss sey, ssondernn tzukunfftig*, Darumb, das der mensch nitt weyss, ob er bleyben werd fur den anstossen der anfechtung." Cf. also WA 7.24.22ff. (*Von der Freiheit eines Christenmenschen*. 1520). Accordingly, *the perseverance* is certain concerning *God*, but uncertain concerning *man*. Luther stresses that the Christian is preserved by continually making a new beginning in faith, WA 5.474.2ff. (*Operationes in Psalmos*. 1519–21): "Non ergo liberum arbitrium hic

4.5.4.

Accordingly, the actual certainty which the believer possesses in Christ (*fides quae*) is total. It contains the certainty of really being justified, a child of God, and God's willingness to stand by in the future. If the believer were to die at that moment, he would unquestionably inherit eternal life! But the assurance is not total in the sense that man can, from his present situation, with carnal or rational security, know anything about the state of his faith (*fides qua*) in the distant future. The Christian must "importune" grace again and again in order to achieve certainty. There is always the risk that some affliction or doubt will impel him to cease from striving for grace in faith. No believer can, except by daily conversion and faith, be sure of God's willingness to give to faith the necessary *donum perseverantiae*. On this point, Luther is afraid of teaching a certainty of perseverance, leading to false security. This is the risk of the enthusiasts.[17] Thus, *in the certainty and uncertainty of the idea*

aliquid valet, nec satis est prima (ut dicunt) gratia, sed *perseverantia opus est, quae est non volentis hominis, sed sustentantis dei.* Et Emphasin observa, quod maius est perseverare quam inchoare, quia perseveraturis necessaria est sustentatio divinae manus... *Perseverantia autem quid est nisi continua inchoatio et indefessa resistentis tum diaboli tum peccatis gravatae naturae tolerantia?"*

[17] In a contemporary letter (1522) Luther objects to the conception of a special "scientia praedestinationis" claimed by Carlstadt, WAB 2.550.13ff.: "Mea sententia est haec, *nos debere fidere gratiae Dei, sed manere incertos de nostri et aliorum futura perseverantia seu praedestinatione,* ut ille (sc. Paulus) dicit: 'Qui stat, videat ne cadat' (1. Cor. 10:12), quamquam apostolos certos fuisse de sua salute non est dubium. Attamen David quoties, quaeso, metuit et plorat, ne proiiciatur a facie Dei!" K. Holl (1923)112, *ib.* 152 has the credit of noticing this point.

Luther obviously, in the practical teaching of Carlstadt and Müntzer on predestination, discerns a great danger of ignoring the fact that the Christian primarily has to listen to the words of Christ, WATR 5.49.1ff. (1540). Their approach to the question of certainty makes us our own God and forgets the importance of faith in unseen things, WATR 5.107.21ff. (1540).

In the early years of the Reformation, *Müntzer* is not aware of any disagreement with Luther in this issue. Writing to Luther in July 1520 from *Zwickau* Müntzer presents the erroneous doctrines of a Franciscan monk by name Tiburtius. Concerning the election the latter had taught: "Predestinatio est res imaginaria, non debet poni in fidem, ut per eam nos certos sciamus, sed in opera, a quibus non est avertendus populus, ut ardeat candelas et virtuosissima opera faciat populus mihi semper charus Zwickauiensis a 24 annis." Quoted from *T. Müntzers Briefwechsel* ed. by H. Böhmer and P. Kirn (1931)13.

Later however, the prophetical consciousness becomes stronger. He calls himself "servus electorum Dei". And he cannot accept Luther's ecclesiological teaching derived from Matt. 13:24ff. The clear division between the elected and the rejected is not to be postponed till the Last judgement. This is *e.g.* shown by E. Mühlhaupt, *Martin Luther oder Thomas Müntzer—wer ist der rechte Prophet?*, L 45 (1974)61. See also 4.3.2 n. 4 above.

When the conflict is sharpened Müntzer violently attacks Luther whom he ironically calls "the scribe". He criticizes Luther's interpretation of Matt. 13:24ff. An exposition of this

of election, we have a clear equivalent to the simul justus et peccator of the doctrine of justification.

2. Now, however, we also know that Luther not only teaches an internal justification by faith alone, but also an external by the *deeds* which result from faith. The internal is the primary. By this means the Christian is *iustus coram Deo.* Since, however, faith is never alone, but is accompanied by good works as the fruits of faith, man can acquire a *certainty* of his faith and justification from his external deeds.[18] Then the question arises: Is there any mention in Luther of a possibility which is otherwise discussed almost exclusively in Calvin, namely that by reason of his good works the Christian is granted confirmation of his election?

I hold that this question can be answered in the affirmative. Even in the Vulgate text 2 Pet. 1:10 reads: "quapropter fratres magis satagite ut *per bona opera* certam vestram vocationem et electionem faciatis"[19].

interpretation is to be found *e. g.* in I. Öberg (1970)472ff. The viewpoint of Luther in the doctrine of predestination seems to be too "neutral" to Müntzer: "Es dunckt die welt, ja auch *die unversuchten schrieftgelerten,* das allerunmuglichste dingk sei, das die nidrigen sollen erhoben und abgessundert werden von den bossen. Ja do, do ist der rechte, schwere, schire reiff, sie wollen den text Matth: 13 kein stat geben von der abssonderung der gotlossen von der auserwelten, sie haben doselbst imaginirt, aus einem alten balcken visirt, die engel mit langen spiessen die sollen absundern die guten von den bosen *zum jungsten tag.* Ich meine, sie konnen dem heiligen geist eine nase drehen. *Sie sagen unverschempt, das got seine urteil niemant offenbare,* drumb leuckenen sie solche engel, welche seint rechte boten gottes, zukunftig die guten von den bossen zu ssundern. das ist den guten fromen leuten (. wie Jr mercken kontt.) nit vor ubel zu halden, dan *sie seint neutrales,* das sein leute, die den zcoberbaum auf beiden schuldern tragen konnen. Sie sprechen aus dem bartthe die glaubwirdigen leute, *es kan niemant wissen, wer ausserwelt ader verdampt sei."* Quoted from C. E. Förstemann, *Neues Urkundenbuch zur Geschichte der evangelischen Kirchen-Reformation* (1842)242f. A short summary of the theme *Luther und Müntzer* is published by B. Lohse in L 45 (1974)12ff. The same author has given an extensive bibliography in the exposition *Thomas Müntzer in marxistischer Sicht,* L 43 (1972)60ff.

It is also noteworthy that the Pauline sentence in 1 Cor. 10:12 which Luther put forward in the letter above, later is interpreted in the same way as a pastoral admonition to the secure Christians to be vigilant, in *the Council of Trent* (Denz 806). *Calvin* uses this passage in a similar manner according to J. Moltmann (1961)46, *ib.* 48.

[18] Illuminating discussions are presented by G. Ljunggren (1928)360ff. and O. Modalsli, *Das Gericht nach den Werken* (1963)44ff. Cf. also A. Peters, *Glaube und Werk* (1962)106ff. In the Luther material, see *e. g.* WA 32.423.12ff. (Wochenpred. 1530/32).

[19] Luther translates: "Darumb lieben bruder, thut deste mehr vleyss, ewren beruff und erwelung fest zumachen" (WADB 7.316, *ib.* 317). But in his preface he emphasizes the importance of works for the certainty of faith: "DIsse Epistel ist widder die geschriben, die da meynen, der Christliche glawb muge on werck seyn, darumb ermanet er sie, das *sie durch gutte werck sich pruffen, und des glawbens gewiss werden,* gleych wie man an den fruchten die bewme erkennet" (WADB 7.314.2ff. *Das Neue Testament.* 1522).

4.5.4.

During the first half of the 1520's Luther preaches on this text. He starts from his own translation, which does not contain the equivalent "durch gute Wercke". But in his exposition Luther mentions the positive importance of the deeds.[20] He adduces the conception of the necessity of the fruit, whereby faith is strengthened and produces even more good works.[21]

Thus, the relationship between faith and deeds is reciprocal. It is the power of faith which provides the incentive for the deeds, in the same way as the tree produces the fruit. But the works have repercussions on faith. The deeds are a testimony which reinforces faith. Thus, the certainty of being called and chosen is increased. This assurance of election here means that the believer is assured that God has given and will give all that is necessary to the present faith, endurance, and salvation. So we have an extension of the grounds for certainty of election, as the works are regarded as the fruit of faith and election. At the same time it is still denied that any other form of certainty of election than this one by faith can be achieved. The individual who seeks to comprehend God's counsel, by the intellect alone, simply cannot achieve his ends.[22]

Later statements of Luther also establish the reality of this certainty of election. In the detailed *Exposition of Deuteronomy*, Luther distinguishes between prevenient and postvenient mercy. By the former type we are chosen, called, and justified before each action.[23] The postvenient mercy is when by deeds we confirm the prevenient grace in ourselves, and personally perceive it. Thus, the already justified are given peace, security and all good things, so that they can speak of another mercy and another peace and another gift or object, another certainty of the gift and

---

[20] WA 14.22.25ff. (*Die ander Epistel S. Petri.* 1523/24): "Also auch hye, wie wol der berüff und *die erwelung fur sich* starck genug ist, so ist sie doch nicht *bey dyr* starck und fest, weyl du noch nicht *gewis* bist, *das sie dich betreffe.* Darumb wil Petrus, das wyr uns solchen berüff und erwelung mit gutten wercken feste machen."

[21] *Ib.* 29ff.

[22] *Ib.* 23.10ff.

[23] WA 14.627.9ff. (*Deuteronomion Mosi cum annotationibus.* 1525). Luther is obviously referring to the order in Rom 8:30.

object received.[24] Luther, accordingly, is stressing the importance of the works for the Christian himself. In doing good deeds, the believer can not only experience (*sentimus*) the justification, but also the personal election. The deeds confer a manifest certainty that the faith works. Since this justification, which he experiences in time, is totally achieved by God's eternal counsel, according to Rom. 8:30, these works are also a confirmation of the election and of God's wish to preserve him. I wish to emphasize this summary strongly: *It is, throughout, the reference to the Godhead (fides quae), which conditions the certainty concerning the past, the present, and the future. If man turns his eyes upon himself (fides qua) he becomes uncertain.* He does not know whether he will, even in the remote future, possess this true faith, which is manifested in deeds.

All that which is to come, concerning his own ability, is unknown to him. Therefore, he must be active and seek to carry out the necessary works, *e.g.* to sow his seeds (Eccl. 11:6). For he does not know what will happen in the distant future, although he understands that it will come to pass by necessity.[25] The assurance of being chosen involves a present certainty of being chosen, preserved, and justified, since the confirmation comes through present faith and action.

---

[24] *Ib.* 12ff.: "*Subsequens est, ubi per opera certam facimus nobis ipsis et sentimus ipsam praevenientem misericordiam*, de qua dictum est: Convertimini ad me (quod fit misericordia praeveniente) et convertar ad vos (quae est subsequens misericordia, quae iam iustificatis pacem, securitatem et omne bonum confert, ut alteram possis dicere gratiam et alteram pacem seu alteram donum et rem, *alteram certitudinem* accepti doni et rei possessae). Ita hic vult dicere: si servaveris haec praecepta (quod tamen sine gratia non poterant), *senties ipsa rerum experientia dominum esse fidelem, ut terram et promissam donet et donatam conservet.*" Cf. WA 20.715.15ff. (*Vorlesung über den 1. Brief des Johannes.* 1527): "'Quoniam', quod sit nulla hypocrisis in nobis, fucus, sed syncera fides et charitas. 'Suadebimus': Si dilexerimus opere et veritate, est *testimonium externum de vocatione nostra,* ut Petrus, i.e. *stabilimur, quod sumus in veritate,* quia ex synceritate et veritate diligimus fratrem utcunque infirmum."
[25] WA 18.747.2ff. (*De servo arbitrio.* 1525)
In this divine necessity, which God imposes on creation, Luther also includes the perseverance of the faithful, *ib.* 754.10ff.: "recreatus nihil facit, nihil conatur, quo perseveret in eo regno, Sed utrunque facit solus spiritus in nobis, nos sine nobis recreans et conservans recreatos." Cf. also the well known words in *Grossen Katechismus* (1529), BSLK 657f.: "Quin etiam spiritus sanctus a sanctorum communione seu christianitate non discedit, sed *cum ea usque ad consummationem saeculi perseverat,* per quam nos adducit, ejusque in hoc utitur adminiculo, ut verbum praedicet atque exerceat, per quod sanctificationem efficit communionem amplificans, ut quotidianis incrementis crescat et in fide ejusque fructibus, quos producit, corroborata fortis evadat." I might also refer to an important passage in *den Schmalkaldischen Artikeln* (1537) III, 3, BSLK 448.

4.5.4.

3. I have thereby reported the essential features of Luther's theory of the certainty of election. He adds nothing essential in his old age, although he occasionally emphasizes different aspects. I can here content myself with a succinct survey of the principles stated.

a. The basic thought is and remains that the Christian receives certainty of election if, and only if, he *in actual faith* rests upon the divine promises in the Gospel through Christ. Faith alone justifies. The deeds are totally excluded from the doctrine of justification.[26] *Fides quae* bestows on the believer assurance, as the whole issue of salvation is transferred to God, who is certain. This present certainty may be regarded as a gift of grace, since it consists of *testimonium spiritus sancti* by the reception of God's Word.[27] This assurance of salvation also includes, in Luther's *pastoral letters,* a certainty of election and endurance, when man, on the basis of Rom. 8:30, reflects on the divine cause of his experience of justification and God's will to preserve him through Christ.[28] The believer who perceptively meditates on Christ's wounds, and His blood shed for us, will notice how election follows therefrom. For the Son of God became man in order to overcome the devil and to make the Christian certain of his election. This is the message of the *Large Lecture on Genesis.*[29] Furthermore, in *the table talks* we find the same argument: the belief in Christ *pro me* stops and removes not only the uncertainty of justification but also the doubt of election.[30] Thus, Luther also teaches an *ad hoc* certainty with regard

[26] O. Modalsli (1962)17ff., *ib.* 34ff. has a good exposition of Luther's teaching that faith alone receives the justification and that faith is never alone but followed by the works of love, which means that he stresses the judgement according to the deeds on the Last day.
[27] See *e. g.* K. Heim (1911)257ff., S. von Engeström (1933)170ff.
[28] WAB 6.87.47f. (1531): "Gleubet yhr, so seid yhr beruffen. Seid yhr beruffen, so seid yhr auch *versehen gewisslich."* Cf. WAB 11.166.14ff. (1545): "DAgegen hat uns Got sein sohn gegeben Jesum Christum, an den sollen wir teglich gedencken, und uns in jhn spiegeln, *do wirt sich dann die vorsehnung selb und gar lieblich finden."*
[29] WA 43.461.12ff. (*Vorlesung über 1. Mose.* 1535–45): "Intuere vulnera Christi et sanguinem pro te fusum. *Ex istis fulgebit praedestinatio.* Audiendus igitur est filius Dei, qui missus est in carnem, et ideo apparuit, ut hoc opus Diaboli dissolvat, et *certum te faciat de praedestinatione.* Ideoque tibi dicit: 'Tu es ovis mea, quia audis vocem meam. Nemo rapiet te ex manibus meis.'" Cf. WA 39.I.289.16ff. = Drews 191 (*Die Zirkulardisp. de veste nuptiali.* 1537): "Deus facit et vult facere in iustificatione et salvatione hominis omnia propter Christum, *propter hunc dilectum sumus vocati, electi et praedestinati et manemus dilecti Dei patris."*
[30] WATR 2.112.10ff. (1532): "In vulneribus Christi *intelligitur praedestinatio et invenitur,* non alibi, quia scriptum est: Hunc audite", WATR 5.294.13ff. (1542): "Ich will dir sonst *dein praedestination* offenbarn. Ich will ex non revelato Deo revelatus werden. Incarnabo Filium und will dir da einen zusetzen, das du sehest, an *sis praedestinatus."* *Ib.* 35f.: "Si illum vero cordis affectu, vera fiducia amplecteris, et *certo scis te esse praedestinatum ad salutem."* Cf. further WA 21.514.31ff. (*Crucigers Sommerpostille.* 1544).

to *fides quae* in the past, the present, and the future. The uncertainty relates to his own willingness to *fides qua* in the future. This seems to be a clear parallel to *simul iustus et peccator* in the doctrine of justification.

The *Lutheran confessional books* follow essentially the same lines in the teaching on the divine election. *Predestinatio Dei* is to be seen in Christ alone. The Holy Spirit bears witness to the Christian that he is a child of God, and, according to the Word, chosen already before the beginning of the world.[31]

b. At the same time the works have significance, since faith never stands alone but is accompanied by *deeds* as the fruit grows upon the tree. The elect have, indeed, by faith received all good things from God. But it does not therefore follow that they will not act, or live as their fancy takes them.[32] Outside the doctrine of justification, Luther forcefully accentuates the movement of faith towards deeds and the importance of the works, not merely as a help to the needy but also as an external proof to the Christian himself concerning his standing in the eyes of God. The very fact that a person realizes that salvation is effected by God alone, and therefore begins to pray for it to be given him, may be regarded as a sign of the election: "hoc facientes sumus praedestinati".[33] Citing 2 Pet. 1:10 Luther can even emphasize the importance of love for the faith of the Christian: Sign of love instils the comfort of finding oneself in the state of grace and confirms our calling.[34]

Even if we cannot draw too far-reaching conclusions from the brief comments by Luther we might say that this material at least raises the question of "a practical syllogism": If, in general, it is true that a chosen individual performs good works in faith, and if a person really could, by intellect, observe good deeds, done by him in faith, could he not conclude that he is among the elect?

---

[31] BSLK 1082, *ib.* 1072, *ib.* 1075 (FC in SD 11).

[32] WA 45.700.27ff. (*Das XIV und XV Kapitels S. Johannis.* 1538). In his preaching Luther also stresses the importance of works of faith, see the instructive survey in H. Ivarsson, *Predikans uppgift²* (1973)56ff.

[33] WATR 1.602.6ff. (1530—35).

[34] WA 39.II.248.11ff. = Drews 744 (*Promotionsdisp.* 1543): "Charitas est testimonium fidei et facit, nos fiduciam habere et *certo statuere de misericordia Dei*, et nos iubemur, nostram vocationem firmam facere bonis operibus. Et tunc apparet, nos habere fidem, cum opera sequuntur, wenn kein werck da sein, so ist fides gar verlhorenn, sicut et fructus sunt testimonia arboris." Cf. WA 39.I.300.9ff. = Drews 204 (*Die Zirkulardisp. de veste nuptiali.* 1537), WA 52.142.2ff. (*Hauspostille.* 1544).

4.5.4.

Here, concerning an assurance which is not derived by faith but by *reason*, my answer is negative. For this rational undertaking must be very problematical in Luther's theology, since the Christian only with reference to the faith in Christ is *totus iustus* but with reference to his own empirical state is *partim iustus/partim peccator*. In other words, it is difficult, not to say impossible, to establish empirically what is a good work, done in real faith, as long as the most devout Christian is still to some extent controlled by sin.[35]

The literature on Calvin shows that he interpreted 2 Pet. 1:10 in a manner reminiscent of Luther. Although, he stresses the deeds as the fruits of faith, they are of secondary importance for the certainty of election. As in the Lutheran theology, this assurance is based primarily on the faith in Christ, which holds fast to the Word and diligently seeks forgiveness and consolation by the sacraments.[36] When the *Formula Concordiae* later discusses 2 Pet. 1:10 the interpretation, so far, seems to agree with that of Luther.[37]

c. Considering the future *fides qua*, God alone can know for sure who will receive the *donum perseverantiae*. The Christian can only, by living faith, every day overcome the uncertainty and anguish concerning election again and again.[38] His task is, day by day, to grasp "praesentem promissionem et praedestinationem". Then, the *deus absconditus* will gradually be revealed. If the individual confidently clings to the revealed God, he is assuredly chosen and will understand the hidden God, yes, he already knows Him "de praesenti".[39] Thus, the believer gradually becomes aware that he is among the elect.

[35] For an introduction, see further A. Gyllenkrok (1952)79ff., W. Joest (1968)55ff., *ib.* 82ff. O. Modalsli (1963)73ff. gives an interesting application. Important is also the exposition by E. Schott, *Fleisch und Geist nach Luthers Lehre unter besonderer Berücksichtigung des Begriffs "totus homo"* (1928)50ff.
[36] H. Olsson (1943)579ff., W. Niesel (1957)174, *ib.* 179, F. Wendel (1972)274ff.
[37] BSLK 1084 (SD 11).
[38] WA 28.114.5ff. (*Pred. Joh 17.* 1528): "Estque consolationis plenus locus omnibus, qui tentantur per praedestinationem, wens den kunden mercken: 'Quos dedisti'. Si vis scire, wie du mit gott dran bist, iste textus dicit tibi. *Wie wol man kan nicht drauff reden, wers zukunfftig bleibt vel manebit, et tamen verum: qui audiunt manifestationem patris, suscipiunt nomen et credunt, illi sunt qui dati Christo de mundo a patre.*"
[39] WA 43.460.24ff. (*Vorlesung über 1. Mose.* 1535–45): "Sed nescio, inquies, an maneam in fide? Attamen praesentem promissionem et praedestinationem suscipe, et non inquiras curiosius de arcanis Dei consiliis. Si credis in Deum revelatum, et recipis verbum eius, paulatim etiam absconditum Deum revelabit. Quia, 'qui me videt, videt et patrem.' Ioannis 14. capite. Qui filium reiicit, amittit cum revelato DEO etiam non revelatum. *Si autem firma*

Here we may speak of a certain *consensus*. For *the Council of Trent* explicitly rejects the theory that a Christian could be certain of enduring to the end. This doctrine, however, is wrongly attributed to the evangelical schismatics.[40] The *Lutheran confessional books* again reaffirm that the Christian can only be comforted by God's mercy and loyalty, as long as he himself is actually living in the redeeming faith.[41] Obviously, Calvin holds a slightly different opinion.[42]

fide revelato Deo adhaeseris, ita ut cor tuum sic sentiat te non amissurum Christum, etiamsi omnibus spoliatus fueris: *tum certissime praedestinatus es,* et absconditum Deum intelliges: imo iam de presenti intelligis." Cf. R. Hermann (1967)167: " 'Erwählung' ist eben nicht vornehmlich die positiv ausfallende Möglichkeit im Unterschied zu der ebenso möglichen Verwerfung, sondern *eine Charakterisierung der Zukehr Gottes in Christo zu dem einzelnen Menschen."* Cf. further R. Hermann (1960)173f.

[40] Denz 805f. A discussion of the Catholic teaching on this point, with references to the Medieval opinion about the grace of perseverance, is to be found in J. Moltmann (1961)21ff. An interesting analysis is also given by H. G. Pöhlmann (1971)287: "Das Tridentinum hat die lutherische Glaubens- und Heilsgewissheit missverstanden;" And further *ib.* 289: "Die Kapitel 9, 12, und 13 und die Canones 13, 14, 15, 16 von Trid. VI treffen an Luther vorbei, was sogar die gegenwärtige römisch-katholische Theologie zugibt."

[41] BSLK 1073 (FC in SD 11). J. Moltmann (1961)66ff. and *ib.* 110ff. presents a survey of the discussion of the gift of perseverance in the Lutheran tradition from Melanchthon to the Lutheran orthodoxy.

[42] According to J. Moltmann (1961)59ff. there is a very significant difference between Luther and Calvin. It can be summarized as follows: "Beide Wege, der lutherische und über Luther hinausführende *Aktualismus* in der Glaubenslehre und der bucersche *Habitualismus* des frommes Bewusstseins, zeigen die Gefahren auf, zwischen denen hindurch *Calvin* seine Lehre von der *geschichtlich-eschatologischen perseverantia sanctorum* zu führen hatte, obgleich, wie die Analyse zeigte, schon bei Calvin selbst manche Neigungen für den Habitualismus der reformierten Orthodoxie vorliegen" (*ib.* 71).

As regards Luther, however, I question if this brief summary is sufficient. It is not too difficult to find out that Luther asserts many issues which Moltmann primarily ascribes to Calvin. Luther also has a strong "Ausrichtung auf das Eschaton" (*ib.* 41), as is shown by U. Asendorf (1967) *passim.* The conception of faith is in a high degree founded on the passage Heb. 11:1 (see further *e. g.* 4.5.2 n. 31, 47, 51), which is also done in the theology of Calvin according to J. Moltmann (1961)41f. God's faithfulness must be considered as a major divine feature in Luther's exposition too (cf. the section 4.2.4 above). Both Luther (see n. 47 below) and Calvin maintain that the perseverance of faith becomes a reality in time under the influence of the Word and the Spirit, J. Moltmann (1961)51ff. If there is a difference between the two theologians, it might be discovered in their doctrines of *the holy Spirit.* Calvin is more prone to teach a continuous inhabitation of the Spirit as the reason for the perseverance, *ib.* 52f., *ib.* 56ff. Especially after the traumatic separation from the enthusiasts such as Carlstadt and Müntzer who claimed the possession of the Spirit, Luther is more anxious to underline the outward hearing of the Word as the effective means by which the Christian receives the Spirit and the perseverance. For a short introduction in this topic see L. Pinomaa (1963)79ff.

Accordingly, here and now the Christian must live and grow in faith, and thus daily realize God's hidden plan for his life. Therefore *Luther is extremely zealous to teach and to exhort the Christians concerning the use of the means of grace.* As we saw above, he rejects passivity and emphasizes the importance of deeds. We have also noted that he repudiates the fatalism which he encountered in the doctrine of the epicureans and Turkish Islam.[43] The Christians shall instead execute God's commands "denn wird sich die versehung wol selbs und ungesucht finden".[44] If the predestination were wholly realized without the incarnation and the reconciliation, and all that God has done for the redemption of the world, these actions of God would be meaningless and superfluous.[45] The almighty God carries the responsibility for the realization of the promise in Rom. 8:30. Those whom He has chosen has He called, and those whom He has called He has also justified. "Ipse finem promissionum suarum non vult implere immediate, sed per media."[46]

In God's counsel the election is made once and for all. But it becomes reality in time for mankind by *co-operation* between the Creator and His creation. God could achieve His end without the co-operation of men. As it is, however, He has chosen to realize His purposes with the Christians "als mittarbeiter". By use of baptism, of Holy Writ, and of all created things in accordance with His revealed will, God's counsel is consummated.[47]

[43] See further above 4.3.2 n. 13.

[44] WA 51.616.6ff. (*Vermahnung zum Gebet wider den Türken.* 1541).

[45] WA 43.457.35ff. (*Vorlesung über 1. Mose.* 1535–45), cf. *ib.* 460.3ff.

[46] *Ib.* 606.2ff. Cf. also WA 44.78.5ff., *ib.* 528.3ff., WATR 5.293.7ff. (1542), WA 52.140.16ff. (*Hauspostille.* 1544).

[47] WAB 9.628.54ff. (1542). It is noteworthy that M. Seils, *Der Gedanke vom Zusammenwirken Gottes und des Menschen in Luthers Theologie* (1962)193f. in this letter finds "den 'cooperatio'-Gedanken Luthers, wie wir ihn kennengelernt haben, in seiner vollen Gestalt zum Ausdruck". On this theme, see further K.-O. Nilsson (1966)406, W. Joest (1967)317 n. 87, L. Grane (1968)80f. A survey is to be found in R. Prenter, *Luthers "Synergismus"* ? (*Festschrift F. Lau.* 1967)264ff. The importance of the public preaching as a means for God's giving of absolution is underlined by H Ivarsson (1973)17ff. A critical discussion of this thesis is presented in I. Öberg (1970)181f. As regards the view in FC (SD 11), see BSLK 1074 and 1085. Concerning Calvin cf. W Niesel (1957)171ff., *ib.* 180f.

4.5.5. The Unity in the Concept of God

A new element seems to appear in Luther's view of *Christ*. Assuredly, he takes his stand on the Christology of the Early Church. But nevertheless the doctrine of Christ as true God and true Man takes on a new tone.[1] Through Christ it is manifest that God's chief attribute is *love* which is as eternal as the Godhead itself. We can easily find evidence for that from all ages.[2]

It is also a new accentuation in Luther's concept of *living faith*. This implies not only a *fides historica* but also a committed faith that God's loving and saving acts apply *pro me*.[3]

It is also well known that Luther accentuates the significance of the true faith with the formula: as you believe, such is your relationship with God! For God, indeed, is wrath against him who believes that such is the case. And to those who believe in the divine goodness and mercy God really is manifest in these attributes.[4] More relevant material is further available.

---

[1] P. Althaus (1963)162: "Das ist der neue Sinn und Ernst des Gottseins Jesu Christi für Luther: Christus ist 'Spiegel des väterlichen Herzens Gottes', der, in dem wir Gott selbst haben. Man kann sagen: vor Luther fragten Kirche und Theologie überwiegend nach dem Göttlichen in Christus, suchten göttliche Natur, göttliche Lebendigkeit, göttliches Gewicht der Genugtuung. *Luther sucht und findet in Jesus Christus Gott selbst, den Vater in Person.*" For an extensive analysis, see further O. Bayer, *Promissio* (1971)298ff., M. Lienhard, *Luther témoin de Jésus-Christ* (1973) *passim*.

[2] WA 2.140.35ff. (*Ein Sermon von der Betrachtung des heiligen Leibes Christi.* 1519), WA 10.III.155.1ff. (*Pred.* 1522), WA 17.II.244.27ff. (*Fastenpostille.* 1525), WA 20.229.11ff. (*Pred.* 1526), WA 39.I.45.25f. = Drews 10 (*Promotionsdisputation.* 1535). Cf. WA 30.I.192.3ff. (*Der grosse Katechismus.* 1529), WA 33.399.20ff. (*Wochenpred. über Joh. 7:28f.* 1531), WA 43.462.34ff. (*Vorlesung über 1. Mose.* 1535–45), WATR 2.112.17ff. (1532).

[3] See *e.g.* WA 7.215.1ff. (*Eine kurze form des Vaterunsers.* 1520), WA 9.518.19ff. (*Pred.* 1519–21), WA 10.I.1.47.8ff. (*Kirchenpostille.* 1522), WA 10.I.2.24.2ff. (*Adventspostille.* 1522), WA 12.518.11ff. (*Pred.* 1523), WA 31.II.432.16ff. (*Vorlesung über Jesaias.* 1527–30), WA 39.I.45.16ff. = Drews 10 (*Promotionsdisputation.* 1535), WA 44.720.3ff. (*Vorlesung über 1. Mose.* 1535–45). Cf. W. von Loewenich, *Luther als Ausleger der Synoptiker* (1954)125: "In der ständigen Betonung des 'pro nobis' kommt das existenzielle Moment in Luthers Christusglauben zu besonders starkem Ausdruck. Ein Christusglaube, der nicht bis zu diesem 'pro nobis' hindurchdringt, ist für Luther ohne Wert." Cf. also W. Pannenberg (1954)149, O. Bayer (1971)274ff., H.-M. Barth, *Fides Creatrix Divinitatis*, NZ 14(1972)89ff.

[4] On this subject see A. Gyllenkrok (1952)26ff., P. Althaus (1963)152. Illuminating passages can be found in *e.g.* WA 8.8.18f. (*Deutsche Auslegung des 67. (68.) Psalmes.* 1521), WA 9.668.26ff. (*Pred.* 1519–21), WA 17.II.66.21ff. (*Fastenpostille.* 1525), WA 24.169.24ff. (*In Genesin Declamationes.* 1527), WA 33.132.11ff. (*Wochenpred. Joh. 6:46.* 1531), WA 37.589.8ff. (*Pred.* 1534, R), WA 40.II.342.16ff. (*Enarratio Psalmi LI.* 1532/38).

1. If we begin with the first *Lecture on the Psalms* we find fragmentary comments which are of interest. Luther emphasizes that fools cannot understand God since His will is hidden. It is not possible to comprehend the internal from outward signs. Therefore, only the faith which derives from the Holy Spirit can understand God aright. God is perceived as merciful only by the Christian who believes and hopes.[5] With regard to God Himself, it is established that He hates and eschews wrath and death since He did not create death. Nor does He delight in the destruction of the unbelievers.[6] This suggests a form of "gradation" of the Godhead. God's deepest desire is not wrath but love of life. The same emerges from what follows. The severe anger which retaliates not in order to educate and improve but to punish and destroy is merely an "effectus". Luther can say of it: "Non ipse in se."[7] The actual cause within the Godhead is thus not wrath. In other words, the point is that not even the wrath of damnation cancels out God's innermost nature, since it is only an external effect.

An early *sermon*, by Luther, may say that the elect are sustained by grace, so that even in death and hell they praise God when they accept their fate, recognizing it as an act of the God who is righteous, good, and true. The rejected, on the other hand, not only loathe death and hell but every affliction. So in all things they desire the converse of God's will and also oppose it with all their strength.[8] If we used the aforesaid mode of expression we could say: The reprobates perceive only the outward effects, while the chosen, through love and praise, embrace *deus ipse* and see Him as wholly good despite the external phenomena. Consequently, the notion of God apprehended by the elect is homogeneous in the sense that all that happens, including the decisive event which seems to be an end in itself, namely death/hell, is regarded as caused by "the most gracious will of God" (*voluntati optimae Dei*).

According to the *Lecture on Romans* man must be willing to face destruction, and even damnation, if Christ is to be his powerful, wise and

---

[5] WA 4.81.25ff. (*Dictata super Psalterium*. 1513–15), *ib*. 52.32ff., WA 3.199.30ff.

[6] *Ib*. 161.29ff. (= WA 55.I.1.2.266.12ff.)

[7] WA 3.591.34ff. See further A. Brandenburg, *Gericht und Evangelium* (1960)33ff.

[8] WA 1.39.4ff. (*Pred*. 1514): "Quia sicut per gratiam firmantur electi, ut etiam in morte et inferno benedicant Deum, nedum in quocunque alio incommodo temporali, tum haec omnia acceptant et approbant a Deo facta ut iusto, bono, vero &c. Ita sine gratia infirmi sunt reprobi, ut non tantum mortem et infernum horreant, sed etiam quodlibet aliud incommodum, ac sic in omnibus optant contrarium voluntati optimae Dei contra eamque toto nisu conantur, quia horrent talia sibi fieri."

good creator.[9] This is an universal fact: Everything spiritually good is hidden under its opposite, so that there is scope for faith in God. He is goodness and wisdom and righteousness, which cannot be possessed or touched lest we renege on all our affirmations of these things.[10] Thus, only an individual who, as a result of the experience of his eternal damnation, has lost his selfconfidence in the *ego* can attain to an existential knowledge of God's true goodness and righteousness. And indeed, the objection that the concept of God is characterised by an antinomy, since God both loves and hardens the heart, is refuted, solely by reference to the revealed fact that the will of the Creator cannot wrong the creation.[11] Nevertheless Luther's postulation of the unity of the notion of God shines through. For, on the one hand, it is impossible that evil emerges from God's own will in the same sense that a human being desires evil. On the other hand, God wills the evil, namely that which is outside Him and performed by another—a human being perhaps or an evil spirit.[12] Obviously we are here faced with a manifestation of the same reasoning as we observed in *Dictata*. God's *voluntas propria* does not seek damnation, God's *voluntas externa*, however, does, acting through external agents. The external is the shell; the kernel is God as He truly is.

The consequences are that God's external will, like the internal, is in fact good, and that the Christian should therefore understand all God's outward acts as good. This tenet emerges when Rom. 9:14 is interpreted.[13]

Consequently, God is always designated as the highest good. Therefore this may be a major reason for parenesis. The evil, including the reprobation, is really not evil. Only the perverted individual sees it as such. But faith affirms God's goodness in all things, and thus conforms

---

[9] WA 56.303.10ff. (*Rom.* 1515–16).

[10] *Ib.* 392.32ff., quoted in 4.5.2 n. 31.

[11] See further the exposition in 4.2.6 n. 3–4.

[12] WA 56.182.2ff.: "Quod Vult malum, dupliciter intelligitur (i.e. quod malum *ab eius voluntate* eliciatur *propria*, sicut homo vult malum, hoc est impossibile in Deo). Alio modo vult malum, sc. quod *extra ipsum* est et alius facit, puta homo Vel demon. Hec vera est. Quia si nollet, non fieret."

[13] *Ib.* 396.17ff.: "Deinde Cum Voluntas eius sit *summum bonum*, Cur non libenter velimus eam fieri summo studio, cum non possit esse mala ullo modo? At dicis: Mihi autem est mala? Absit. Nulli est mala. Sed Quia non attingitur eius voluntas nec fit ab illis, hoc est eis malum. Si enim vellent, quod vult Deus, etiamsi damnatos et reprobatos vellent, non haberent malum. Quia vellent, quod vult Deus, et haberent in se voluntatem Dei per patientiam." Cf. *ib.* 402.13ff.

with the divine will. The conception of God *per se*, which faith comprehends, is uniform, *summun bonum*.

In the exposition of Rom. 12:2, these arguments are further emphasized. God's will is "vere et naturaliter" good, gracious and perfect. But it is well hidden beneath the appearance of evil—that which is detested and creates despair—to our will and our so-called "good intention". The good will of God seems to be no other than the worst, most desperate will, belonging more to the devil than to God. So man has to surrender his own will and preconceived opinion and submit to a total repudiation of the righteousness, goodness, and truth which he previously embraced.[14] Thus from the fact that something is good because God wishes it follows a radical "theonomy" in the language of theology. Man cannot take his definitions of goodness and apply them to God. Instead, it is the Creator who defines for His creation what truly is good. The created beings can but accept this definition.

The attribute "good" is not here formally (*formaliter*) used of the divine will. But in an objective sense (*obiective*), i.e. with reference to man as the object of God's will. This will does not become good by our proving of it, but rather it is recognized as good by the person concerned.[15] Luther invariably accepts as axiomatic the naked assertion that the divine nature is in truth *summum bonum,* which faith confirms and experiences on the basis of the divine revelation in Christ, the importance of which I previously maintained in the *Lecture on Romans.*[16]

If we turn to the more popular expositions to be found in the *Exegesis of the Seven Penitential Psalms* we may also say that the pastoral concern is paramount. Psalm 130:5 describes how the person reborn in faith does not instruct God what to do but trusts in "gottis gutem willen".[17] It is the correlation between the living faith and the concept of God united in the idea of love which Luther proclaims, in order to instil hope and peace of conscience.

---

[14] *Ib.* 447.3ff.: "contrarius—Ita et voluntas Dei, cum sit vere et naturaliter 'bona, beneplacens, perfecta', Sed ita abscondita sub spetie mali, displicentis ac desperati, ut nostre voluntati et bone, ut dicitur, intentioni non nisi pessima, desperatissima et nullo modo Dei, Sed diaboli voluntas videatur, Nisi homo relicta sua voluntate et intentione bona submittat se in omnen abnegationem Iustitie, bonitatis, veritatis a se preconcepte."

[15] *Ib.* 450.7ff.: "Unde notandum, Quod ista Nomina 'Bona', 'Beneplacens', 'perfecta' non dicuntur formaliter de voluntate Dei, Sed obiective. Quia non per nostram probationem talis fit voluntas Dei, Sed cognoscitur esse talis; fit ergo 'bona' nobis, i.e. agnoscitur essa bona, 'Beneplacens', quia optime placet, 'perfecta', quia omnia perfecit, i.e. fit nobis 'bona, beneplacens, perfecta'."

[16] Cf. above 4.5.2 n. 36–40.

[17] WA 1.208.33ff. (*Die sieben Busspsalmen.* 1517).

The Heidelberg Disputation emphasizes, in a manner highly reminiscent of the interpretation of Romans, how God's works always give an illusion of being evil. Therefore, it falls to the Christian's lot to live by that which is hidden in God, *i.e.* "in nuda fiducia misericordiae eius".[18] The individual who lacks confidence in Christ sees only that which is obvious to experience and reason. But the believer sticks to God's *vere esse*, namely His mercy.

In Luther's *Exposition of the Lord's prayer*, this basic view is repeated. By teaching us to pray the Lord's prayer, God shows us the depth of His appreciation of "die lieb, die er selbs ist".[19] This is a play on the words in 1 John 4:16. It shows that this clearcut conception of God appeared self-evident to Luther: God is love. This is no less then a fundamental premise which does not require any special proof or scrutiny to be accepted as the truth.

In the *Second Lecture on the Psalms* we can make further observations. Luther gives a long exposition of Ps. 5:12. He emphasizes, *inter alia*, that the believer must abandon all his merits in order that his faith may be "spes purissima in purissimum deum".[20] Obviously, the epithet *purissimum* refers to the innermost being of God. Indeed we sometimes find a terminology indicating no specification of the God of wrath and the God of love. The struggle of the faith under attack is simply a battle with God *contra* God.[21] Nevertheless, the divine wrath is modified and expressed in relative terms. It is real only in the eyes of the person assailed. God is not "vere" angered and intransigent but attacks in order to prevail upon the Christian to hope for more from God's pure mercy than from his own merits.[22]

The conclusion can hardly be other than this: *purissimus deus* is identified with *deus misericors*. Therefore, according to Ps. 16:18, the divine truth itself will counter the diabolical lie when the Christian envisages this God: "dominum quam potest misericordissimum".[23] Thus, the Godhead is not merely merciful. It is the highest form of

[18] WA 1.356.32ff. (*Disputatio Heidelbergae habita.* 1518), *ib.* 357.1ff. Cf. WA 1.271.21ff. (*Zwei deutsche Fastenpredigten.* 1518).
[19] WA 9.128.1ff. (*Auslegung und Deutung des heiligen Vaterunsers.* 1518). These words are omitted in the following edition, in WA 2.86.7ff. (*Auslegung deutsch des Vaterunsers für die einfältigen Laien.* 1519).
[20] WA 5.166.18 (*Operationes in Psalmos.* 1519–21).
[21] *Ib.* 167.15, *ib.* 204.27. Cf. *ib.* 166.25ff., *ib.* 204.9ff., *ib.* 623.17ff.
[22] *Ib.* 166.25ff., *ib.* 36ff.
[23] *Ib.* 459.10ff. Cf. *ib.* 494.31ff.

mercy—perhaps we could say the totality of mercy. Judging by the interpretation of Ps. 6:6, hell is consistently defined by Luther as the inability to remember whom God truly is, or the incapacity to perceive the mercy of God, which comes to the same thing.[24] The believer who rests upon the divine promises of mercy leaves to God the anxiety of the double predestination.[25] This faith should be so strong and so certain as to negate "every contradiction" rather than disbelieve in the divine promises of forgiveness and love.[26]

This sheds an interesting light on diverse arguments in the *Confutation of Latomus*. Luther regards God's mercy not as an inherent quality but as *favor dei*, as is well known. But it is probably less well known, at least more seldom pointed out, that, according to Luther, this divine favour finally in truth creates peace of mind, so that the believer also *feels* that he worships a propitiated God. For this is the divine magnanimity, which makes the bones strong and the conscience joyful, secure, confident, since it dares all things, and even laughs at death trusting in this grace.[27] *Consequently, this is a question of a "charismatic" experience which confers certainty on the believer.* His heart embraces a God who is all magnanimity, notwithstanding that his intellect may find the divine goodness incomprehensible.

In other words, it is a question not only of a consideration of *totus homo* but also of a perception of *totus deus*. In the affliction of God's eternal wrath the individual feels utterly lost. God appears to him as total wrath. But by means of his faith in the propitiation in Christ, the believer perceives His total justification. Indeed, the Christian is "totus sub tota

---

[24] *Ib.* 209.36ff. Cf. *ib.* 590.30ff.

[25] *Ib.* 623.17ff. Cf. further *ib.* 69.21ff., *ib.* 109.27ff., *ib.* 117.31ff., WA 13.252.3ff. (*Praelectiones in prophetas minores.* 1524ff.).

[26] WA 6.88.31ff. (*Resolutio disputationis de fide infusa et acquisita.* 1520): "Primo, ubicunque est verbum Dei promittens aliquid homini, ibi necessaria est fides hominis, qui credat hanc promissionem esse veram et implendam adeo certe et firmiter, ut *potius omnem sensum, omnem rationem, omnem scientiam, omnem contradictionem, omnem creaturam deberet negare quam Dei verbo non credere.*" Cf. WA 6.126.24ff. (*Tessaradecas consolatoria.* 1520), WA 6.208.34ff. (*Von den guten Werken.* 1520), WA 7.786.1ff. (*Tröstung für eine Person in hohen Anfechtungen.* 1521).

[27] WA 8.106.10ff. (*Rationis Latomianae confutatio.* 1521): "Gratiam accipio hic *proprie pro favore dei, sicut debet, non pro qualitate animi,* ut nostri recentiores docuerunt, atque haec gratia tandem vere pacem cordis operatur, ut homo a corruptione sua sanatus, etiam *propitium deum habere se sentiat.* Hoc est, quod impinguat ossa et conscientiam reddit laetam, securam, imperterritam, nihil non audentem, nihil non potentem, ut quae mortem etiam rideat in fiducia ista gratiae dei." Cf. further S. Shapiro (1973)826.

gratia".[28] *This is inspired by a profound, personal experience of unity by reason of God's Word.* The explains why Luther, who with his intellect recognizes his own concept of God as contradictory, can nevertheless believe in his heart that God is wholly gracious and merciful. A kind of diversity between "doctrine and life" seems, accordingly, to exist.

2. This sheds light on two issues. *Firstly* it provides an explanation for the fact that faith both reaches for hidden things and recognizes them by experience, which appears contradictory. But there is a straightforward coherence. When the individual under attack is tormented by his conscience and his terror of death, the only hope of rescue is to trust in the divine promise of the invisible, not yet apprehended, blessings, which God will bestow in Christ. When the Christian clings to this, then finally the affliction will subside, and the conscience feel the total peace and mercy of God, which suggests a form of "mystical" experience of the Kingdom of God on the basis of the divine Word.[29]

Secondly, it is understandable that, in his descriptions of the divine love, Luther uses new and vivid images for this property. By his mode of expression, he demonstrates that God's whole being is love.[30] Look on such a phrase as: "God overflows with goodness!"[31] Naturally, in his

---

[28] WA 8.106.35ff.: "Habemus ergo duo bona euangelii adversus duo mala legis, donum pro peccato, gratiam pro ira. Iam sequitur, quod illa duo ira et gratia sic se habent (cum sint extra nos), ut *in totum effundantur,* ut qui sub ira est, totus sub ira est, qui sub gratia, totus sub tota gratia est, quia ira et gratia *personas* respiciunt."

[29] See the quotation in n. 27 above (*tandem!*). Cf. WA 7.546.24ff. (*Das Magnificat verdeutschet und ausgeleget.* 1521), *ib.* 548.4ff., WA 8.375.16ff. (*Evangelium von den zehn Aussätzigen.* 1521), WA 10.II.323.1ff. (*Sendbrief,* 1522), WA 14.448.4ff. (*Pred. über das erste Buch Mose.* 1523/24), WA 17.II.203.29ff. (*Fastenpostille.* 1525), WA 18.389.19ff. (*Ein Sendbrief von dem harten Büchlein wider die Bauern.* 1525), WA 54.186.8f. (*Vorrede zum 1. Bande der Gesamtausgaben seiner lat. Schriften. Wittenberg.* 1545): "Hic me prorsus renatum esse *sensi,* et apertis portis in ipsam paradisum intrasse." This is Luther's report of his discovery of the new meaning in the concept *iustitia dei!* Cf. also H. M. Müller (1929)121ff., S. von Engeström (1933)170ff. Comments on E. Vogelsang (1929)75 are to be found in A. Gyllenkrok (1952)18f. See also H. Gerdes (1958)50f., P. Althaus (1963)61ff., G. Müller, *Über den Begriff der "Mystik",* NZ 13 (1971)95f., B. Hoffman (1976)147ff. See further n. 37 below.

[30] WA 10.III.56.2f. (*Pred.* 1522): "got ist ein glüender backofen foller liebe, der da reichet von der erden biss an den hymmel." WA 10.I.1.100.19ff. (*Kirchenpostille.* 1522): "gottlich natur ist nit anderss denn eytell wolthettickeyt und, alss hie S. Paulus sagt, freuntlickeyt und leutselickeyt."

[31] WA 27.246.6 (*Pred.* 1528, R)

sermons on 1 John 4:16 Luther has reason to emphasize this.[32] This joy in presenting God as love can only, I presume, be inspired by Luther's personal experience of God as He is revealed in Christ.

3. Both for Erasmus and Luther it goes without saying that in His true nature God is righteous and compassionate.[33] The God who is wholly good and just cannot diverge from goodness and justice in His actions. Following the tradition of Duns Scotus Luther asserts: the definition of goodness cannot be based on what human reason stipulates, but true goodness is in accord with the will of God.[34] When reason is confronted with the theory that God, like a potter, can shape certain vessels for salvation and others for rejection, *i.e.* the doctrine of the double predestination, the "flesh" regards this as a negation of God's goodness and justice. It seems unfair, cruel and intolerable.[35]

> "Sed fides et spiritus aliter iudicant, qui *Deum bonum credunt*, etiam si *omnes homines* perderet."[36]

This statement may be said to represent one of the most provocative assertions in Luther's tenets on the uniform conception of God. Faith is so convinced of the innermost goodness of the divine being that not even an universal reprobation could undermine it! The issue which is here illustrated is partly that the concept of goodness is deprived of its conventional meaning, partly that faith in the Word confers a feeling of certainty which is so profound as to withstand almost all logical contradictions. Even if Luther emphasizes that faith believes in hidden truths, he suggests that it also contains an element of seeing and perceiving the divine goodness by those who possess the Holy Spirit. Accordingly, they see with God's eyes.[37] This certainty is so deep that it

---

[32] WA 36.424.2ff. (*Pred.* 1532, R): "Si deus pingendus, sol ichs malen, quod in abgrund seiner Gottlichen natur nihil aliud est quam ein feur und brunst, quae dicitur lieb zun leuten." *Ib.* 425.2f.: "eytel backoffen dilectionis ... eytel lieb." *Ib.* 426.4f.: "Si inspicis deum etiam leiplich, sind eytel flammen und feur charitatis in deo." *Ib.* 9: "eitel brunst und lieb". Cf. WA 41.618.7ff. (*Pred.* 1536, R), WA 45.99.33ff. (*Pred.* 1537, R), WA 49.785.4 (*Pred.* 1545, R).

[33] WA 18.615.18ff. (*De servo arbitrio.* 1525).

[34] *Ib.* 712.36ff. Cf. WA 16.141.4f. (*Pred. über das 2. Buch Mose.* 1524–27).

[35] WA 18.719.4ff., *ib.* 729.15ff. Cf. WA 16.398.8ff., *ib.* 418.6f.

[36] WA 18.708.8f. Cf. *ib.* 633.15ff. Cf. also E. Schlink (1948)393f.

[37] WA 18.709.1ff.: "Igitur quomodo sint bona coram Deo, quae nobis mala sunt, solus Deus novit et ii qui oculis Dei vident, id est qui spiritum habent." Cf. the clear statements in WA 19.224.16ff. (*Der Prophet Jona ausgeleget.* 1526): "Da mercke du, wilch eyn scharff gesichte

silences all rational objections since it allows the believer to experience God as wholly loving.

Faith will, finally, yield to vision for the children of God.[38] But at the same time, we must remember the thought that the rejected can never see God as wholly good, and this very lack is the root of their hell, as we said above. Even in this life, however, God's omnipotence is truly good. God's almighty power certainly to reason appears as an ethically unqualified force which lies beyond good and evil.[39] Faith, however, believes that God is really good in this power as well, *i.e.* that the omnipotence at heart may be designated as perfect goodness.[40]

4. This is *Luther's definitive theology*: the conception of God is fully consistent. In His heart God is gracious and willing to help and do good, and reluctant to show anger and punish. In Himself He is pure love, so that His nature and being are such that He cannot be moved to anger. He is love for all eternity. The damnation is only "His alien work", which goes against His merciful nature, since He is forced to such lengths by human evil.[41] "The internal" is God's own eternal, immutable being, which is goodness to an extreme degree. *This is God's own face which shines through Christ's incarnation, suffering, death and resurrection.*

Nevertheless, this is "the art above all arts, the supreme achievement of the Holy Spirit".[42] The Spirit's first gift of grace to His elect, however, is faith. Therefore, Luther can also say that faith alone sees and perceives God as "eitel uberschwengliche gnade und liebe". This is

das hertze müsse haben, das mit eytel zorn und straffe von Gott umbgeben ist und doch keyne straffe noch zorn, sondern *gnade und güte sihet und fulet...* Das heyst eyn ruffen des glaubens, wilchs sich *mus fülen ym hertzen, das er Gott treffe,* gleich wie Christus fulete, das eine krafft war von yhm ausgangen, da er der frawen den blutgang stillet. *Denn des geysts wort und werck fület man, das sie treffen und nicht feylen."* WA 28.189.7ff. (*Wochenpred. Joh. 17.* 1528): "Si coniicior in carcerem, puto totum mundum et deum adversari mihi. *Si non video, sentio datam mihi gloriam.* Tum credo et fides suo tempore experietur."

[38] WA 18.784.1ff., *ib.* 785.20ff.

[39] A. Runestam (1925)68, T. Bohlin (1927)276ff., G. Rost (1966)121.

[40] Luther research in Scandinavia has emphasized the context of *faith* as the decisive condition for perceiving the omnipotence of God as good, see G. Aulén (1927)220ff., G. Ljunggren (1928)436ff., R. Bring (1929)266ff., L. Pinomaa (1938)137ff., H. Olsson (1971)16. Cf. G. Rost (1966)121 n. 62. Cf. 3.6 n. 18.

[41] WA 31.I.69.7ff. (*Confitemini.* 1530), *ib.* 374.29ff. (*Die ersten 25. Psalmen.* 1530), WA 36.428.3ff. (*Pred.* 1532, R), WA 45.99.33f. (*Pred.* 1537, R), WA 42.356.21ff. (*Vorlesung über 1. Mose.* 1535–45). Th. Harnack I (1927)349ff. stressed that God according to Luther is absolute love and relative wrath. I think that G. Rost, *Der Zorn Gottes in Luthers Theologie*, LR 9 (1961)3 too easily rejects the thesis of Th. Harnack.

[42] WA 31.I.94.6f., cf. *ib.* 158.13ff. See K. Heim (1911)256ff.

the concept of God which is given through Christ.[43] It enables the Christian to surrender in faith and feel certainty because of the Word. Thus, the picture of God as "eitel liebe" becomes an existential knowledge which through the vicissitudes of life leads the Christian singing songs of praise.

The homogeneous image of God is of decisive importance. In all earthly sorrows, in suffering and in death the believers ought to preserve the idea of God's love—incomprehensible though it be—so that, through the Spirit and through faith, *they see and know the will of God as something which "is always better than our own will although the flesh sees it in completely different terms".*[44]

The uniform concept of God also means that the Christian lives in the hope of one day seeing God as He is in His nature and His majesty. *It is one and the same thing which man possesses in this life and in eternity. For God and all good things are identical.* The difference consists only in the form of the knowledge; here faith, there vision.[45]

---

[43] WA 32.328.31ff. (*Wochenpred. Mat. 5:8.* 1530/32): "Wenn du einen rechten glawben hast, das *Christus dein heiland sey* u. so sihestu slugs, das du *einen gnedigen Gott habst,* Denn der glaube leitet dich hinauff und thut dir Gottes hertz und willen auff, da du eitel uberschwengliche gnade und liebe sihest. Das heisst recht Gott schawen, nicht mit leiblichen augen (damit jn niemand kan sehen jnn diesem leben), sondern mit dem glawben, der sein veterlich freundlich hertz sihet, darin kein zorn noch ungnade ist. *Denn wer jn fur zornig ansihet, der sihet jn nicht recht, sondern nur ein furhang und decke, ja ein finster wolcke fur sein angesicht gezogen.* Sein angesicht aber sehen, wie die schrifft redet, heisst jn recht erkennen als einen gnedigen fromen vater, zu dem man sich alles guts versehen darff, welchs allein durch den glauben an Christum geschicht." Cf. WA 36.368.23ff. (*Pred.* 1532), WA 37.458.1ff. (*Pred.* 1534, R), *ib.* 538.13ff., WA 43.462.34ff. (*Vorlesung über 1. Mose.* 1535–45). *Ib.* 219.28ff. is illuminating: "Fides igitur conciliat contraria, nec est ociosa qualitas, ut Sophistae dicunt. Sed virtus eius est mortem occidere, infernum damnare, esse peccato peccatum, diabolo diabolum, adeo ut mors non sit mors, etiamsi omnium sensus testetur adesse mortem."
The Lutheran Confessions also maintain the unity of the concept of God which is grasped by faith in Christ, BSLK 1073f. (FC in SD 11).

[44] WA 53.205.14ff. (*Ein Trost den Weibern, welchen es ungerade gegangen.* 1542). See further the passages in 3.5. n. 20.

[45] WA 17.II.169.16ff. (*Fastenpostille.* 1525): "Es ist eyn ding, das wyr hie ynn diesem leben und ynn ihenem leben haben, Denn *es ist der selbige Gott und alles gut, das wir hie gleuben und dort sehen werden, daran ist keyn unterscheyd.* Aber die unterscheyd ist ym erkentnis, Das wyr den selbigen Gott auff eyne andere weyse hie ynn diesem leben und auff eyn andere weysse ynn ihenem leben haben. Die weyse ynn diesem leben ist, das wyr yhn nicht sehen, sondern gleuben. Nu ist der glaube eyn unvolkomen und tunckel sehen. Zu wilchem not ist das wort, wilchs durchs predigampt, durch zungen und weyssagen gefodert wird. Denn on das wort kan der glaube nicht bestehen. Aber die weyse ynn ihenem leben ist, das wyr yhn nicht gleuben, sondern sehen, wilchs ist eyn volkomen erkentnis, dazu nicht not ist

The homogeneous notion of God implies finally that the Luther interpretation can rightly set Christology, or justification, as an unifying
centre of Luther's theology.[46] This, however, means that care must be
taken to consider what kind of a centre is suggested. It is not a
theoretical doctrine, from which all the other *loci* could be grouped in a
logically coherent system. The abiding damnation in the reprobation falls
outside Christology and the idea of justification according to reason. But
*it is a deep existential conviction from which, on the basis of the Word
concerning justification by faith alone for Christ's sake, the Christian
regards God as total love, even in the eternal damnation of predetermination.*[47] Faith rejoices ineffably despite all the paradoxes of the concept of
God, because it has tasted the goodness of God. Using the words by
Pascal we might say: "the heart has its reasons which the mind knoweth
not".[48] *On the one hand, Luther emphasizes praedestinatio gemina in*

das wort, noch predigen, noch zungen, noch weyssagen. Drumb mus dasselbige denn alles
auffhören." Cf. WA 18.784.1ff. (*De servo arbitrio.* 1525), WATR 1.643.12 (1540).

[46] The doctrine of justification is in this sense "the master of all doctrines", WA
39.I.205.2ff. = Drews 119 (*Die Promotionsdisputation von Palladius und Tilemann.* 1537):
"Articulus iustificationis est magister et princeps, dominus, rector et iudex super omnia
genera doctrinarum, qui conservat et gubernat omnem doctrinam ecclesiasticam et erigit
conscientiam nostram coram Deo." See further W. Maurer, *Die Einheit der Theologie
Luthers,* ThLZ 75 (1950)245ff., H. Beintker (1954)49, R. Hermann (1960)384ff., K. G. Steck
(1963)144ff., E. Wolf, *Die Rechtfertigungslehre als Mitte und Grenze reformatorischer
Theologie* (In *Peregrinatio II.* 1965)11ff. F. Gogarten (1967)176ff.

[47] I agree with the short exposition in E. W. Gritsch & R. W. Jenson (1976)162: "The final
possible way is also within those bounds (sc. of the Lutheran confessions), and seems to
have been *Luther's own.* This is *to abstain on principle from all attempts to resolve the
division in our image of God.* On the one hand, we see God as the ambiguous will behind all
events good and evil—that there is a will behind all events, the gospel itself compels us to
affirm. On the other hand, we hear the gospel of God as pure and universal love. Given our
reason for believing in the world-Will in the first place, we must affirm that these two
images are one God." Referring to *predestinatio gemina* H. J. Iwand (1974)98 rightly stresses
both the antinomy and the unity of the concept of God: "Und so hat die Prädestination für
Luther *ein Doppelgesicht,* so dass sie dem, welcher sie nur *mit dem natürlichen Auge* ansieht,
das Bild eines grausamen, eines die Menschen blind dahingebenden Gottes bietet, der
gefühllos die einen stürzen, die anderen steigen lässt, während sie sich dem, der ihr *im
Glauben* begegnet, öffnet und ihn hineinlässt in ihr innerstes Geheimnis und dieses sich
dann enthüllt—*eben als das Geheimnis der Erwählung Gottes in Jesus Christus.*"

[48] I arrive at the same conclusion as B. Hoffman (1976)219: "Luther used the word 'feeling'
when he wrote of the necessary accompaniment to the historical faith called true or inner
faith. To him the feeling component of faith did not spell emotionalism, if this term be
taken to imply mandatory emotional states of excitement in an order of salvation. Feeling-
in-faith was rather an experience of God's comforting presence. This experience was
logically unregistrable just as love is unregistrable. Yet the inner 'knowing' made the

provocative terms. On the other, he lives by the experience of God's love in Christ, which is also revealed by the Biblical texts. In this sense there is here a certain dualism between doctrine and life.[49]

4.5.6. Conclusions

1. The exposition in Luther differs from the common theology of *potentia ordinata Dei* of Ockhamism both as regards affliction concerning election and its prevention or conquest. When the meritorious synergism within the theory of predestination is excluded, afflictions of predestination, in the true sense of the term, are a predominant spiritual problem, which is discussed not only in the academic lectures but also in material addressed to the general public. Where *via moderna* also refers to *merita hominis*, Luther exclusively preaches faith in Christ alone. As in Biel, the Gospel is certainly presented as an universal offer of grace. *Deus revelatus* is proclaimed to all mankind. The reflection on the Crucified One who died for the sins of the world, tasted eternal damnation, and gives eternal salvation, becomes the protection against, and victory over, every affliction concerning predestination. The particularism which is implied by the concept of *deus absconditus* is in fact overshadowed. Here, the truth seems to be that the doctrine of predetermination has no relevance whatever on the *usus* level.

2. When Luther contradicts the doctrine of penance taught by Biel and Ockham, he does so to a great extent because it left the Christian in doubt about the mercifulness of his God. Luther uses the theory of God's sovereignty to provide the foundation of a new, evangelical certainty of salvation. Furthermore, God's immutability becomes a central attribute, since it is linked with the promises of the Gospel. Thus, one element of the predestination theory—*electio dei*—plays a major role also on the practical level.

3. Biel emphasizes that the believer cannot now know whether he will remain in the state of grace until the end. The possibility of defection is always open. The only recourse is, day after day, *facere quod in se est*, then God will not refuse His grace.

difference between a true theologian and an unauthentic one. In this sense the *Schwärmer*, those who enjoyed the psychological emotions of their God-immersions, embraced a false spirituality. They *relied* on emotions and knew little about the feeling which accompanies the use of external spiritual symbols in the church."
[49] Cf. the term "Doppelgesicht" which H. J. Iwand (1974)98 uses (quoted in n. 47 above).

The present faith can, according to Luther, only confer a present assurance. His theology does not preach a certainty of possession of "the gift of perseverance" as a quality inherent in man. Daily conversion, daily repentance for sin, and faith in Christ, daily use of the means of grace are well to the fore in the catechetic teaching. The idea of predestination can never be a reason for fatalistic passivity.

The certainty of justification also involves a certainty of election. The believer whom God has justified is also called, and he who is called is also chosen, according to Paul's words in Rom. 8:30. Without contradicting the theory that the inquisitive speculation on the future outcome springs from the devil, and involves a usurpation of the knowledge which is reserved for God alone, Luther can clearly emphasize a present certainty of election when man turns the eyes of faith to God's eternal love revealed in Christ.

Against this background, it is easy to understand why, in his exegesis of 2 Pet. 1:10, Luther can, as candidly as Calvin, teach a certainty of election confirmed by the deeds of the believer. Faith in Christ never stands alone, but produces works as the good tree puts forth good fruits. These are the outward sign of the life of the inward faith.

4. However much *via moderna*, as represented by Biel, related election and rejection to *potentia absoluta dei*, and however contradictory the concept of God seemed to be, it was always assumed that these antinomies *ad extra* did not nullify the inward simplicity of God.

For Luther it is an existential necessity of the first grade to portray God as "eitel liebe", and to show the mode of perceiving Him in these terms. The doctrine of justification thus holds a key position. Moreover, the faith in Christ is the essential prerequisite if God in all His deeds, even in the eternal election to destruction, is to appear as the highest good.

But this is not a question of "mere faith". Luther is deeply convinced that faith comprehends God as He is in His purest and truest being. The "charismatic" experience of certainty is the psychological background to the ability of Luther to live with the most difficult contradictions in the concept of God. Luther hereby maintains that he actually feels and perceives the basic principle of the Christian revelation of God: God in all His acts is love.

Abbreviations

AASF	Annales Academiae Scientiarum Fennicae
AGTL	Arbeiten zur Geschichte und Theologie des Luthertums
AKG	Arbeiten zur Kirchengeschichte
ARG	Archiv für Reformationsgeschichte
BGLRK	Beiträge zur Geschichte und Lehre der reformierten Kirche
BSLK	Die Bekenntnisschriften der evangelisch-lutherischen Kirche
C	Catholica
CA	Confessio Augustana
Coll	G. Biel, Collectorium circa quattuor libros Sententiarum
Denz	H. Denzinger, Enchiridion symbolorum
Dr	Druck
Drews	P. Drews, Disputationen
Ep	Epitome
EvTh	Evangelische Theologie
FC	Formula Concordiae
FGLP	Forschungen zur Geschichte und Lehre des Protestantismus
FKDG	Forschungen zur Kirchen- und Dogmengeschichte
FKGG	Forschungen zur Kirchen- und Geistesgeschichte
Hs	Handschrift
JR	Journal of Religion
KuD	Kerygma und Dogma
L	Luther. Zeitschrift der Luther-Gesellschaft
LuD	Luther and the Dawn of the Modern Era
Luh	Lutherforschung heute
LuJ	Luther-Jahrbuch
LR	Lutherische Rundblick
LUÅ	Lunds Universitets Årsskrift
LW	Luther's Works (American edition)
MPL	J. P. Migne, Patrologiae cursus completus. Ser. I Patres latini
NT	The New Testament
NZ	Neue Zeitschrift für systematische Theologie und Religionsphilosophie
OT	The Old Testament
R	Georg Rörer's reports
RGG	Die Religion in Geschichte und Gegenwart
RHE	Revue D'Histoire Ecclésiastique
SD	Solida Declaratio
SDCU	Studia Doctrinae Christianae Upsaliensia
SLAG	Schriften der Luther-Agricola-Gesellschaft
StTh	Studia Theologica. Cura ordinum theologorum Scandinavicorum edita.
SVRG	Schriften des Vereins für Reformationsgeschichte
SvTK	Svensk Teologisk Kvartalskrift
ThA	Theologische Arbeiten
ThBl	Theologische Blätter
ThLZ	Theologische Litteraturzeitung

ThZ	Theologische Zeitschrift
UUÅ	Uppsala Universitets Årsskrift
WA	Weimarer Ausgabe. Werke
WAB	Weimarer Ausgabe. Briefwechsel
WADB	Weimarer Ausgabe. Die Deutsche Bibel
WATR	Weimarer Ausgabe. Tischreden
ZKG	Zeitschrift für Kirchengeschichte
ZLThK	Zeitschrift für lutherische Theologie und Kirche
ZSTh	Zeitschrift für systematische Theologie
ZThK	Zeitschrift für Theologie und Kirche
ZZ	Zwischen den Zeiten

Bibliography

Aalen, S. & L., Bakenfor Inferno. Oppgjør med tradisjonelle forestillinger om helvete, Oslo 1955.

Adam, A., Der Begriff "Deus absconditus" bei Luther nach Herkunft und Bedeutung, LuJ 30, 1963, 97ff.

—, Lehrbuch der Dogmengeschichte I², Gütersloh 1970.

—, Lehrbuch der Dogmengeschichte II, Gütersloh 1968.

Adam, G., Der Streit um die Prädestination im ausgehenden 16. Jahrhundert. Eine Untersuchung zu den Entwürfen von Samuel Huber und Aegidius Hunnius (BGLRK 30), Neukirchen — Vluyn 1970.

Alanen, Y. J. E., Das Gewissen bei Luther (AASF Ser. B. 29:2), Helsinki 1934.

Althaus, P., Die Bedeutung des Kreuzes im Denken Luthers, L 8, 1926, 97ff.

—, Luthers Gedanken über die letzten Dinge, LuJ 23, 1941, 9ff.

—, Luthers Haltung im Bauernkrieg (Sonderausg.), Tübingen 1952.

—, Luthers Lehre von den beiden Reichen im Feuer der Kritik, LuJ 24, 1957, 40ff.

—, Die Theologie Martin Luthers², Gütersloh 1963.

Appel, H., Anfechtung und Trost im Spätmittelalter und bei Luther (SVRG Jahrg. 56. H. 1. Nr. 165), Leipzig 1938.

Arnold, F. X., Zur Frage des Naturrechts bei Martin Luther, München 1937.

Asendorf, U., Eschatologie bei Luther, Göttingen 1967.

Aulén, G., Den kristna försoningstanken. Huvudtyper och brytningar, Stockholm–Lund 1930.

—, Den kristna gudsbilden genom seklerna och i nutiden, Stockholm 1927.

Bandt, H., Luthers Lehre vom verborgenen Gott. Eine Untersuchung zu dem offenbarungsgeschichtlichen Ansatz seiner Theologie (ThA 8), Berlin 1958.

Barth, H-M., Fides Creatrix Divinitatis. Bemerkungen zu Luthers Rede von Gott und dem Glauben, NZ 14, 1972, 89ff.

—, Der Teufel und Jesus Christus in der Theologie Martin Luthers (FKDG 19), Göttingen 1967.

Bayer, O., Promissio. Geschichte der reformatorischen Wende in Luthers Theologie (FKDG 24), Göttingen 1971.

Beintker, H., Die Überwindung der Anfechtung bei Luther. Eine Studie zu seiner Theologie nach dem Operationes in Psalmos 1519–21 (ThA 1), Berlin 1954.

Die Bekenntnisschriften der evangelisch-lutherischen Kirche. Hrsg. im Gedenkjahr der Augsburgischen Konfession 1930², Göttingen 1952.

Beyer, H. W., Gott und die Geschichte nach Luthers Auslegung des Magnificat, LuJ 21, 1939, 110ff.

Biel, G., Collectorium circa quattuor libros Sententiarum, Basel 1508.

—, Collectorium circa quattuor libros Sententiarum. Prologus et Liber primus. Hrsg. v. W. Werbeck & U. Hofmann, Tübingen 1973.

Billing, E., Luthers lära om staten, Uppsala 1900.

Blanke, F., Der verborgene Gott bei Luther, Berlin 1928.

Bodenstein, W., Die Theologie Karl Holls im Spiegel des antiken und reformatorischen Christentums (AKG 40), Berlin 1968.

Bohlin, T., Gudstro och Kristustro hos Luther, Stockholm–Uppsala 1927.

Bornkamm, H., Christus und das 1. Gebot in der Anfechtung bei Luther, ZSTh 5, 1927, 453ff.

—, Luther. Gestalt und Wirkung. Gesammelte Aufsätze (SVRG 188), Gütersloh 1975.

—, Luthers geistige Welt, Lüneburg 1947.

—, Luther und das Alte Testament, Tübingen 1948.

—, Probleme der Lutherbiografie, Luh 1958, 15ff.

Bouwsma, W. J., Renaissance and Reformation: An Essay in their Affinities and Connections, LuD 1974, 127ff.

Brandenburg, A., Gericht und Evangelium. Zur Worttheologie in Luthers erster Psalmenvorlesung (Konfessionskundliche und Kontroverstheologische Studien, hrsg. v. J.-A. Möhler Institut 4), Paderborn 1960.

—, Thomas und Luther im Gespräch, C 16, 1962, 77ff.

Bring, R., Dualismen hos Luther, Lund 1929.

—, Kristendomstolkningar i gammal och ny tid, Lund 1950.

Brunner, E., Der Zorn Gottes und die Versöhnung durch Christus, ZZ 5, 1927, 93ff.

Brunstäd, F., Theologie der lutherischen Bekenntnisschriften, Gütersloh 1951.

Buchwald, G., Luther über die Welt als "Mitwirkerin Gottes", L 23, 1941, 49ff.

Bühler, P. Th., Die Anfechtung bei Martin Luther, Zürich 1942.

Burkard, F. J., Philosophische Lehrgehalte in Gabriel Biels Sentenzenkommentar unter besonderer Berücksichtigung seiner Erkenntnislehre (Monographien zur Philosophischen Forschung 122), Meisenheim am Glan 1974.

Copleston, F., A History of Philosophy II, London 1959.

—, A History of Philosophy III, London 1960.

Denzinger, H., Enchiridion symbolorum, definitionum et declarationum de rebus fidei et morum, ed. I. B. Umberg, ed. 24–25, Freiburg in Breisgau 1942.

Deutelmoser, A., Luther, Staat und Glaube, Jena 1937.

Diem, H., Luthers Lehre von den zwei Reichen, untersucht von seinem Verständnis der Bergpredigt aus. Ein Beitrag zum Problem "Gesetz und Evangelium", München 1938.

Dillenberger, J., God Hidden and Revealed: The Interpretation of Luther's Deus absconditus and its Significance for Religious Thought, Philadelphia 1953.

Doerne, M., Gottes Ehre am gebundenen Willen. Evangelische Grundlagen und theologische Spitzensätze in De servo arbitrio, LuJ 20, 1938, 45ff.

Drews, P., Hrsg. Disputationen. Dr. Martin Luthers, Göttingen 1895.

Ebeling, G., Die Anfänge von Luthers Hermeneutik, ZThK 48, 1951, 172ff.

—, art. Luther II. Theologie, RGG³ IV, Tübingen 1960, 495ff.

—, Luther. Einführung in sein Denken, Tübingen 1964.

—, Lutherstudien I, Tübingen 1971.

Elert, W., Morphologie des Luthertums. Theologie und Weltanschauung des Luthertums, hauptsächlich im 16. und 17. Jahrhundert, I, München 1931.

Engeström, S. v., Luthers tankar om frälsningsvissheten i Romarbrevskommentaren (In: Till Ärkebiskop Söderbloms sextioårsdag, Stockholm–Uppsala 1926), 141ff.

—, Luthers trosbegrepp med särskild hänsyn till församhållandets betydelse (UUÅ 1933:1), Uppsala 1933.

Erasmus Roterodamus, D., De libero arbitrio diatribe sive collatio (Ausgewählte Schriften 4, hrsg. v. W. Welzig), Darmstadt 1969.

—, Vom freien Willen. Verdeutscht von O. Schumacher, Göttingen 1956.

Erikstein, E., Luthers Praedestinationslehre geschichtlich dargestellt bis einschliesslich 'De servo arbitrio' (Diss. Göttingen. Maschinenschr.), Oslo 1957.

Fagerberg, H., Die Kirche in Luthers Psalmenvorlesung 1513–1515 (Gedenkschrift f. D. W. Elert), Berlin 1955, 109ff.

—, A New Look at the Lutheran Confessions 1529–1537, St. Louis–London 1972.

Feckes, C., Die Rechtfertigungslehre des Gabriel Biel und ihre Stellung innerhalb der nominalistischen Schule (Münsterische Beiträge z. Theologie. H. 7), Münster 1925.

Förstemann, C. E., Hrsg. Neues Urkundenbuch zur Geschichte der evangelischen Kirchen-Reformation I, Hamburg 1842.

Gerders, H., Zu Luthers Lehre vom Wirken des Geistes, LuJ 25, 1958, 42ff.

—, Luthers Streit mit den Schwärmern um das rechte Verständnis des Gesetzes Mose, Göttingen 1955.

Gerke, F., Die satanische Anfechtung in der ars moriendi und bei Luther, ThBl 11, 1932, 321ff.

√ *Gerrish, B. A.*, To An Unknown God: Luther and Calvin on the Hiddenness of God, JR 53, 1973, 263ff.

Gogarten, F., Luthers Theologie, Tübingen 1967.

Grane, L., Contra Gabrielem. Luthers Auseinandersetzung mit Gabriel Biel in der Disputatio Contra Scholasticam Theologiam 1517 (Acta Theologica Danica 4), Kopenhagen 1962.

—, Gabriel Biels Lehre von der Allmacht Gottes, ZThK 53, 1956, 53ff.

—, Gregor von Rimini und Luthers Leipziger Disputation, StTh 22, 1968, 29ff.

—, Modus loquendi theologicus. Luthers Kampf um die Erneuerung der Theologie (1515–1518) (Acta Theologica Danica 12), Leiden 1975.

—, Protest og Konsekvens. Faser i Martin Luthers taenkning indtil 1525, København 1968.

Grislis, E., Luther's Understanding of the Wrath of God, JR 41, 1961, 277ff.

Gritsch, E. W. & Jenson, R. W., Lutheranism: The Theological Movement and Its Confessional Writings, Philadelphia 1976.

Gyllenkrok, A., Rechtfertigung und Heiligung in der frühen evangelischen Theologie Luthers (UUÅ 1952:2), Uppsala 1952.

Hägglund, B., De homine. Människouppfattningen i äldre luthersk tradition (Studia Theologica Lundensia 18), Lund 1959.

—, Theologie und Philosophie bei Luther und in der occamistischen Tradition. Luthers Stellung zur Theorie von der doppelten Wahrheit (LUÅ N.F. Abt. 1. 51:4), Lund 1955.

—, Renaissance and Reformation, LuD 1974, 150ff.

Hakamies, A., "Eigengesetzlichkeit" der natürlichen Ordnungen als Grundproblem der neueren Lutherdeutung. Studien zur Geschichte und Problematik der Zwei-Reiche-Lehre Luthers (Untersuchungen zur Kirchengeschichte 7), Helsinki 1971.

Hamel, A., Der junge Luther und Augustin. Ihre Beziehungen in der Rechtfertigungslehre nach Luthers ersten Vorlesungen 1509–1518 untersucht I–II, Gütersloh 1934–1935.

Harnack, Th., Luthers Theologie mit besonderer Beziehung auf seine Versöhnungs- und Erlösungslehre I–II (Neue Ausgabe), München 1927.

Hauck, W. A., Die Erwählten. Prädestination und Heilsgewissheit nach Calvin, Gütersloh 1950.

Heim, K., Das Gewissheitsproblem in der systematischen Theologie bis zu Schleiermacher, Leipzig 1911.

Heimler, H., Aspekte der Zeit und Ewigkeit bei Luther, LuJ 40, 1973, 9ff.

Heintze, G., Luthers Pfingstpredigten, LuJ 34, 1967, 117ff.

—, Luthers Predigt von Gesetz und Evangelium (FGLP 10:11), München 1958.

Hemberg, J., Religion och metafysik. Axel Hägerströms och Anders Nygrens religionsteorier och dessas inflytande på svensk religionsdebatt (SDCU 4), Stockholm 1966.

Hendrix, S. H., Ecclesia in Via. Ecclesiological Developments in the Medieval Psalms Exegisis and the Dictata super Psalterium (1513-1515) of Martin Luther (Studies in Medieval and Reformation Thought 8), Leiden 1974.

Hermann, R., Gesammelte Studien zur Theologie Luthers und der Reformation, Göttingen 1960.

—, Luthers Theologie, hrsg. v. H. Beintker (Gesammelte und nachgelassene Werke 1), Göttingen 1967.

Hick, J., Evil and the God of Love[3], Thetford, Norfolk 1974.

Hillerdal, G., Gehorsam gegen Gott und Menschen. Luthers Lehre von der Obrigkeit und die moderne evangelische Staatsethik, Stockholm–Lund 1954.

—, Luthers Geschichtsauffassung, StTh 7, 1954, 28ff.

Hirsch, E., Luthers Gottesanschauung, Göttingen 1918.

—, Lutherstudien I–II, Gütersloh 1954.

—, Review of the new edition of Th. Harnack, Luthers Theologie (1927), ThLZ 52, 1927, 39ff.

Hoffman, B., Luther and the Mystics. A Re-Examination of Luther's Spiritual Experience and his Relationship to the Mystics, Minneapolis 1976.

Holl, K., Gesammelte Aufsätze zur Kirchengeschichte I. Luther [2-3], Tübingen 1923.

Hygen, J. B., Guds allmakt og det ondes problem, Oslo 1974.

Iserloh, E., Luther und die Reformation. Beiträge zu einem ökumenischen Lutherverständnis, Aschaffenburg 1974.

Iwand, H. J., Luthers Theologie, hrsg. v. J. Haar (Nachgelassene Werke 5), München 1974.

Ivarsson, H., Predikans uppgift. En typologisk undersökning med särskild hänsyn till reformatorisk och pietistisk predikan[2], Lund 1973.

Jacob, G., Der Gewissensbegriff in der Theologie Luthers (Beiträge z. historischer Theologie 4), Tübingen 1929.

Jørgensen, A. Th., Luthers kamp mod den romersk-katolske semipelagianisme under særligt henblik paa hans prædestinationslære, København 1908.

Joest, W., Gesetz und Freiheit. Das Problem des tertius usus legis bei Luther und die neutestamentliche Parainese[4], Göttingen 1968.

—, Ontologie der Person bei Luther, Göttingen 1967.

Josefson, R., Den naturliga teologins problem hos Luther (UUÅ 1943:4), Uppsala 1943.

—, Ödmjukhet och tro. En studie i den unge Luthers teologi, Stockholm 1939.

Junghans, H., Ockham im Lichte der neueren Forschung (AGTL 21), Berlin–Hamburg 1968.

Jüngel, E., Quae supra nos nihil ad nos, EvTh 32 (1972) 223ff.

Kattenbusch, F., Luthers Lehre vom unfreien Willen und von der Prädestination nach ihren Entstehungsgründen untersucht, Göttingen 1875.

Köstlin, J. & Kawerau, G., Martin Luther. Sein Leben und seine Schriften I–II[5], Berlin 1903.

Kohlmeyer, E., Die Geschichtsbetrachtung Luthers, ARG 37, 1940, 150ff.

Kohls, E. W., Luther oder Erasmus. Luthers Theologie in der Auseinandersetzung mit Erasmus, I, Basel 1972.

Krumwiede, H. W., Glaube und Geschichte in der Theologie Luthers. Zur Entstehung des geschichtlichen Denkens in Deutschland (FKDG 2), Göttingen 1952.

Küng, H., Rechtfertigung. Die Lehre Karl Barths und eine katholische Besinnung. Mit einem Geleitbrief von Karl Barth, Einsiedeln 1957.

215

Lamparter, H., Luthers Stellung zum Türkenkrieg, München 1940.

Lau, F., "Äusserliche Ordnung" und "Weltlich Ding" in Luthers Theologie (Studien z. syst. Theologie 12), Göttingen 1933.

—, Luthers Lehre von den beiden Reichen, Berlin 1953.

Lienhard, M., Luther témoin de Jésus-Christ. Les étapes et les thèmes de la Christologie du Reformateur, Paris 1973.

Lilje, H., Luthers Geschichtsanschauung, Zürich 1932.

Link, W., Das Ringen Luthers um die Freiheit der Theologie von der Philosophie (FGLP 9 R. Bd. 3), München 1940.

Ljunggren, G., Synd och skuld i Luthers teologi, Uppsala–Stockholm 1928.

Löfgren, D., Die Theologie der Schöpfung bei Luther (FKDG 10), Göttingen 1960.

Løgstrup, K. E., Etiske begreber og problemer (In: Etik och kristen tro, ed. G. Wingren, Lund–København–Oslo 1971), 205ff.

Loewenich, W. v., Pharaos Verstockung. Zu Luthers Lehre von der Prädestination (In: Von Augustin zu Luther. Beiträge zur Kirchengeschichte, Witten 1959), 161ff.

—, Zur Gnadenlehre bei Augustin und bei Luther (In: Von Augustin zu Luther. Beiträge zur Kirchengeschichte, Witten 1959), 75ff.

—, Luther als Ausleger der Synoptiker (FGLP 10:5), München 1954.

—, Luthers Theologia crucis³, München 1939.

Lohse, B., Die Bedeutung Augustins für den jungen Luther, KuD 11, 1965, 116ff.

—, A Short History of Christian Doctrine, Philadelphia 1966.

—, Luther und Müntzer, L 45, 1974, 12ff.

—, Marginalien zum Streit zwischen Erasmus und Luther, L 46, 1975, 5ff.

—, Ratio und Fides. Eine Untersuchung über die ratio in der Theologie Luthers (FKDG 8), Göttingen 1958.

—, Thomas Müntzer in marxistischer Sicht, L 43, 1972, 60ff.

Lombardus, P., Sententiarum libri quattuor (In: MPL CXCII, Paris 1855), 520ff.

Lotz, D. W., Ritschl and Luther. A Fresh Perspective on Albrecht Ritschl's Theology in the Light of his Luther Study, Nashville, Tenn. 1974.

Luthardt, C. E., Die Lehre vom freien Willen und seinem Verhältnis zur Gnade in ihrer geschichtliche Entwicklung dargestellt, Leipzig 1863.

Luther and the Dawn of the Modern Era. Papers for the fourth International Congress for Luther research, ed. H. A. Oberman (Studies in the History of Christian Thought 8), Leiden 1974.

Lutherforschung heute. Referate und Berichte des 1. Internationalen Lutherforschungskongresses, Aarhus 18–23 August 1956, hrsg. v. V. Vajta, Berlin 1958.

Luther, M., Ausgewählte Werke II³. Vorlesung über den Römerbrief 1515/16 hrsg. v. H. H. Borcherdt & G. Merz, München 1957.

—, D. Martin Luthers Werke. Kritische Gesamtausgabe. Weimar 1883ff.

—, Luther's Works: American Edition, ed. J. Pelikan & H. Lehmann, St. Louis–Philadelphia 1955ff.

Lütkens, J., Luthers Prädestinationslehre im Zusammenhang mit seiner Lehre vom freien Willen, Dorpat 1858.

Maurer, W., Die Einheit der Theologie Luthers, ThLZ 75, 1950, 245ff.

McSorley, H. J., Luther: Right or Wrong? An Ecumenical-Theological Study of Luther's Major Work, The Bondage of the Will, New York–Minneapolis 1969.

—, Luther und Thomas von Aquin über die Prädestination (In: Oekumenica. Festschrift f. E. Schlink zum 60. Geburtstag, hrsg. v. R. Herrfahrdt & A. Gerwinat, Heidelberg 1963), 17ff.

Meinhold, P., Die Genesisvorlesung Luthers und ihre Herausgeber (FKGG 8), Stuttgart 1936.

Migne, J. P., ed., Patrologiae cursus completus. Ser. I. Patres latini, Paris 1844ff.

Modalsli, O., Das Gericht nach den Werken. Ein Beitrag zu Luthers Lehre vom Gesetz (FKDG 13), Göttingen 1963.

Moltmann, J., Prädestination und Perseverenz. Geschichte und Bedeutung der reformierten Lehre "de perseverantia sanctorum" (BGLRK 12), Neukirchen – Vluyn 1961.

Mühlhaupt, E., Martin Luther oder Thomas Müntzer, — wer ist der rechte Prophet?, L 45, 1974, 55ff.

Müller, G., Über den Begriff der "Mystik", NZ 13, 1971, 88ff.

Müller, H.-M., Erfahrung und Glaube bei Luther, Leipzig 1929.

Müller, J., Lutheri de praedestinatione et libero arbitrio doctrina, Göttingen 1832.

Müntzer, T., Briefwechsel. Aufgrund der Handschriften und ältesten Vorlagen hrsg. v. H. Böhmer & P. Kirn, Leipzig-Berlin 1931.

Naess, A., Empirisk semantik, Stockholm 1966.

Niesel, W., Die Theologie Calvins², München 1957.

Nilsson, K.-O., Simul. Das Miteinander von Göttlichem und Menschlichem in Luthers Theologie (FKDG 17), Göttingen 1966.

Normann, S., Viljefrihet og forutbestemmelse i den lutherske reformasjon inntil 1525, Oslo 1933.

Nygren, A., Agape and Eros. A Study of the Christian Idea of Love II. Authorized transl. by Ph. S. Watson, London 1939.

—, Augustin und Luther: Zwei Studien über den Sinn der augustinischen Theologie (Aufsätze und Vorträge zur Theologie und Religionswissenschaft. H. 3), Berlin 1958.

Nygren, G., Das Prädestinationsproblem in der Theologie Augustins (Studia Theologica Lundensia 12), Lund 1956.

Obendiek, H., Der Teufel bei Martin Luther, Berlin 1931.

Oberman, H. A., The Harvest of Medieval Theology. Gabriel Biel und Late Medieval Nominalism, Cambridge, Mass. 1963.

—, Headwaters of the Reformation: Initia Lutheri — Initia Reformationis, LuD 1974, 40ff.

—, Simul gemitus et raptus: Luther und die Mystik (In: Kirche, Mystik, Heiligung und das Natürliche bei Luther. Vorträge des Dritten Internationalen Kongresses für Lutherforschung, Järvenpää, Finnland, hrsg. v. I. Asheim, Göttingen 1967), 20ff.

Öberg, I., Himmelrikets nycklar och kyrklig bot i Luthers teologi 1517–1537 (SDCU 8), Uppsala 1970.

Olsson, H., Calvin och reformationens teologi I (LUÅ N.F. Avd. 1. Bd. 40. Nr. 1), Lund 1943.

—, Det dubbla necessitas-begreppet i skolastiken och Luthers kritik därav (In: Till Gustaf Aulén, Lund–Stockholm 1939), 279ff.

—, Grundproblemet i Luthers socialetik I, Lund 1934.

—, Kyrkans synlighet och fördoldhet enligt Luther (In: En bok om kyrkan av svenska teologer, Stockholm–Lund 1942), 306ff.

—, Den naturliga gudskunskapens problem enligt den senmedeltida nominalismen, SvTK 26, 1950, 372ff.

—, Schöpfung, Vernunft und Gesetz in Luthers Theologie (SDCU 10), Uppsala 1971.

Pannenberg, W., Der Einfluss der Anfechtungserfahrung auf den Prädestinationsbegriff Luthers, KuD 3, 1957, 109ff.

—, Die Prädestinationslehre des Duns Skotus im Zusammenhang der scholastischen Lehrentwicklung (FKDG 4), Göttingen 1954.

217

Pedersen, E. Th., Luther som skriftfortolker I. En studie i Luthers skriftsyn, hemeneutik og exeges, København 1959.

—, Schöpfung und Geschichte bei Luther, StTh 3, 1950, 5ff.

Pesch, O. H., Existential and Sapiential Theology— The Theological Confrontation Between Luther and Thomas Aquinas (In: Catholic Scholars' Dialogue with Luther, ed. J. Wicks, Chicago 1970), 61ff.

—, Die Frage nach Gott bei Thomas von Aquin und Martin Luther, L 41, 1970, 12ff.

—, Zur Frage nach Luthers reformatorischer Wende, C 20, 1966, 216ff., 264ff.

—, Freiheitsbegriff und Freiheitslehre bei Thomas von Aquin und Luther, C 17, 1963, 197ff.

—, Zum Gespräch zwischen Luther und Thomas, C 18, 1964, 27ff.

—, Die Theologie der Rechtfertigung bei Martin Luther und Thomas Aquin (Walbergerer Studien der Albertus-Magnus-Akademie 4), Mainz 1967.

Peters, A., Glaube und Werk. Luthers Rechtfertigungslehre im Lichte der heiligen Schrift (AGTL 8), Berlin–Hamburg 1962.

—, Reformatorische Rechtfertigungsbotschaft zwischen tridentinischer Rechtfertigungslehre und gegenwärtigem evangelischen Verständnis der Rechtfertigung, LuJ 31, 1964, 77ff.

—, Review of G. Rost, Der Prädestinationsgedanke (1966), ThLZ 93, 1968, 364f.

Pflanz, H. H., Geschichte und Eschatologie bei Martin Luther, Stuttgart 1939.

Pfürtner, S., Luther und Thomas im Gespräch: Unser Heil zwischen Gewissheit und Gefährdung, Heidelberg 1961.

Pinomaa, L., Der existentielle Charakter der Theologie Luthers. Das Hervorbrechen der Theologie der Anfechtung und ihre Bedeutung für das Lutherverständnis (AASF Ser. B. 47:3), Helsinki 1940.

—, Faith Victorious. An Introduction to Luther's Theology, Philadelphia 1963.

—, Methodische Gesichtspunkte zur Lutherforschung, LuJ 43, 1976, 109ff.

—, Unfreier Wille und Prädestination bei Luther, ThZ 13, 1957, 339ff.

—, Der Zorn Gottes in der Theologie Luthers. Ein Beitrag zur Frage nach der Einheit des Gottesbildes bei Luther (AASF Ser. B. 41:1), Helsinki 1938.

Pöhlmann, H. G., Rechtfertigung. Die gegenwärtige kontroverstheologische Problematik der Rechtfertigungslehre zwischen der evangelisch-lutherischen und der römisch-katholischen Kirche, Gütersloh 1971.

Prenter, R., Luthers "Synergismus"? (In: Vierhundertfünfzig Jahre lutherische Reformation 1517–1967, Festschrift f. F. Lau z. 60. Geburtstag, Göttingen 1967), 264ff.

—, Spiritus Creator. Studier i Luthers theologi², København 1946.

Die Religion in Geschichte und Gegenwart. Handwörterbuch für Theologie und Religionswissenschaft³, Tübingen 1957ff.

Ritschl, A., Die christliche Lehre von der Rechtfertigung und Versöhnung I³, Bonn 1889.

Rost, G., Luthers Schöpfungsglaube und Geschichtstheologie, LR 6, 1958, 2ff.

—, Der Prädestinationsgedanke in der Theologie Martin Luthers, Berlin 1966.

—, Der Zorn Gottes in Luthers Theologie, LR 9, 1961, 2ff.

Rückert, H., Die Weimarer Lutherausgabe, Luh 1958, 111ff.

Runestam, A., Swedish Introduction to M. Luther, The Bondage of the Will, transl. by G. Rudberg, Stockholm 1925.

Scheel, O., Hrsg., Dokumente zu Luthers Entwicklung² (Sammlung ausgewählter Kirchen- und Dogmengeschichtlicher Quellenschriften. N.F. 2), Tübingen 1929.

—, Martin Luther, I Auf der Schule und Universität³, Tübingen 1921.

—, Martin Luther, II Im Kloster³⁻⁴, Tübingen 1930.

Schlink, E., Theologie der lutherischen Bekenntnisschriften[3], (Einführung in die evangelische Theologie 8), München 1948.

—, Der theologische Syllogismus als Problem der Prädestinationslehre (In: Einsicht und Glaube. Festschrift f. G. Söhngen, Freiburg-Basel-Wien 1962), 299ff.

Schloemann, M., Natürliches und gepredigtes Gesetz bei Luther. Eine Studie zur Frage der Einheit der Gesetzesauffassung Luthers mit besonderer Berücksichtigung seiner Auseinandersetzung mit den Antinomern (Theologische Bibliothek Töpelmann 4), Berlin 1961.

Schmidt, F. W., Der Gottesgedanke in Luthers Römerbriefsvorlesung (Theologische Studien und Kritiken H. 3), Gotha 1921, 117ff.

—, Theozentrische Theologie im Nominalismus und bei Luther, ZThK 12, 1931, 359ff.

Schott, E., Einig in der Rechtfertigungslehre?, LuJ 26, 1959, 1ff.

—, Fleisch und Geist nach Luthers Lehre unter besonderer Berücksichtigung des Begriffs "totus homo", Leipzig 1928.

Schultz, R. C., Gesetz und Evangelium in der lutherischen Theologie des 19. Jahrhunderts (AGTL 4), Berlin 1958.

Schwarz, R., Fides, Spes und Charitas beim jungen Luther unter besonderer Berücksichtigung der mittelalterlichen Tradition (AKG 34), Berlin 1962.

Schwarzwäller, K., Das Gotteslob der angefochtenen Gemeinde. Dogmatische Grundlegung der Prädestinationslehre, Neukirchen-Vluyn 1970.

—, sibboleth. Die Interpretation von Luthers Schrift De servo arbitrio seit Theodosius Harnack. Ein systematisch-kritischer Überblick, München 1969.

—, Zur Struktur von Luthers Pneumatologie, LuJ 38, 1971, 26ff.

—, Theologia crucis. Luthers Lehre von Prädestination nach De servo arbitrio, München 1970.

Seeberg, E., Grundzüge der Theologie Luthers, Stuttgart 1940.

—, Luthers Theologie. Motive und Ideen I. Die Gottesanschauung, Göttingen 1929.

Seeberg, R., Lehrbuch der Dogmengeschichte II, Erlangen-Leipzig 1898.

—, Lehrbuch der Dogmengeschichte IV:1²⁻³, Leipzig 1917.

Seils, M., Der Gedanke vom Zusammenwirken Gottes und des Menschen in Luthers Theologie (Beiträge zur Förderung christlicher Theologie 50), Gütersloh 1962.

Shapiro, S., Quelques réflexions sur la signification psychologique de la prédestination dans la Réform, RHE 68:1, 1973, 823ff.

Siirala, A., Gottes Gebot bei Martin Luther. Eine Untersuchung der Theologie Luthers unter besonderer Berücksichtigung des ersten Hauptstückes im Grossen Katechismus (SLAG 11), Helsinki 1956.

Spitz, L. W., Headwaters of the Reformation: Studia Humanitatis, Luther Senior, et Initia Reformationis, LuD 1974, 89ff.

Stange, C., Studien zur Theologie Luthers I, Gütersloh 1928.

Steck, K. G., Lehre und Kirche bei Luther (FGLP 10:27), München 1963.

Steinmetz, D. C., Luther and late Medieval Augustinians: Another Look, Concordia Theol. Monthly 44, 1973, 245ff.

Stolt, B., Die Sprachmischung in Luthers Tischreden. Studien zum Problem der Zweisprachigkeit (Stockholmer germanistische Forschungen 4), Stockholm 1964.

Stupperich, R., Karl Holl als Lutherforscher, L 37, 1966, 112ff.

Törnvall, G., Andligt och världsligt regemente hos Luther, Lund-Stockholm 1940.

Vignaux, P., Justification et prédestination au XIVᵉ siecle: Duns Scot, Guillaume d'Ockham, Pierre Auriole, Grégoire de Rimini, Paris 1934.

Vogelsang, E., Die Anfänge von Luthers Christologie nach der ersten Psalmenvorlesung insbesondere in ihren exegetischen und systematischen Zusammenhängen mit Augustin und der Scholastik (AKG 15), Berlin-Leipzig 1929.

—, Der angefochtene Christus bei Luther (AKG 21), Berlin– Leipzig 1932.

—, Luther und die Mystik, LuJ 19, 1937, 32ff.

Volz, H., Luthers Randbemerkungen zu zwei Schriften Gabriel Biels: Kritische Anmerkung zu Hermann Degerings Publikation, ZKG 81, 1970, 207ff.

Vorster, H., Das Freiheitsverständnis bei Thomas von Aquin und Martin Luther (Kirche und Konfessionen 8), Göttingen 1965.

Vossberg, H., Luthers Kritik aller Religion, Eine theologiegeschichtliche Untersuchung zu einem systematischen Hauptproblem, Leipzig–Erlangen 1922.

Walter, J. v., Die Theologie Luthers, Gütersloh 1940.

V *Watson, Ph. S.*, Let God be God! An Interpretation of the Theology of Martin Luther, London 1947.

V *Wendel, F.*, Calvin: The Origins and Development of his Religious Thought⁴, London 1972.

Wingren, G., Luthers lära om kallelsen, Lund 1942.

Wolf, E., Staupitz und Luther. Ein Beitrag zur Theologie des Johannes von Staupitz und deren Bedeutung für Luthers theologischen Werdegang (Quellen und Forschungen zur Reformationsgeschichte 9), Leipzig 1927.

—, Die Rechtfertigungslehre als Mitte und Grenze reformatorischer Theologie (In: Peregrinatio II. Studien zur reformatorischen Theologie, zum Kirchenrecht und zur Sozialethik, München 1965), 11ff.

Wolff, O., Die Haupttypen der neueren Lutherdeutung (Tübinger Studien zur systematischen Theologie H. 7), Stuttgart–Berlin 1938.

Wrede, G., Unio mystica. Probleme der Erfahrung bei Johannes Tauler (SDCU 14), Uppsala 1974.

Zahrnt, H., Luther deutet Geschichte, München 1952.

Index of Names

Index of Biblical Passages

Index of Subjects

Doomed mass 16, 150
Dualism 10, 13, 15, 26, 50, 71–75, 140

Ecumenical dialogue 22
Ein Sendbrief von dem harten Büchlein wider die Bauern 88, 203
Ein Sermon von der Bereitung zum Sterben 134, 139, 162
Ein Sermon von der Betrachtung des Leidens Christi 106, 186, 197
Ein Trost den Weibern, welchen es ungerade gegangen ist 130, 206
Eine kurze Form, das Paternoster zu verstehen und beten 62
Eine kurze Form des Glaubens 87
Eine kurze Erklärung der zehn Gebote 62
Eine kurze Unterweisung, wie man beichten sol 62
Elect 68, 109, 112, 113, 117, 122, 123, 149, 153–154, 155–158, 184–196, 205
Election 26, 59, 76, 96, 101–102, 105, 110, 120, 127, 134, 136, 144, 146–147, 149–152, 157, 163, 173, 184–196
   doctrine of double election 91–92, 104, 112, 161, 179
   single election 104, 146
   signs 166–167, 185–186, 193
Enarratio capitis noni Esaiae 39, 136
Enarratio Psalmi II 44
   LI 65, 118, 197
   XC 88, 114, 154
Enthusiasts, see *Schwärmer*
Epicureans 34, 196
Epistel S. Petri gepredigt und ausgeleget 98, 112, 148
Eschatology 195
Eucharist 56, 178
Evangelium von den zehn Aussätzigen 186, 203
Evil
   eternal 16–17, 50–51, 98, 100
   from God 61–67, 74, 87, 98, 116–120
   temporal 15–16, 26, 50–51, 58, 62, 63, 65, 98, 149, 153, 176, 198
Exegesis of Ps 51, see *Enarratio Psalmi LI*

Exhortation to prayer against the turks, see *Vermahnung zum Gebet wider den Türken*
Experience 21, 60, 61, 70, 113, 120, 179, 184, 191, 202–203, 205, 208
   of free will 70
   of Wrath of God 126, 174, 176–177, 201

Facere quod in se est 150, 208
Faith 13–14, 21, 25, 26, 33, 35, 43, 49, 51, 58–60, 61, 87, 91–92, 120–121, 151, 201, 205
   in Christ 10, 72, 74, 119, 172, 174, 176, 182, 183, 187, 205, 208
   in the promises of God 166, 205–206
   objective 197
   of the *ego* 199
   of the highest degree 175–176
   sign of election 185–186
   true 132, 197, 207–208
Fastenpostille 64, 197, 203, 206
Fatalism 102, 130, 148, 177, 196, 209
Favor dei 202
Fides qua of predestination 185–188, 191, 193, 194
Fides quae of predestination 186–188, 191, 192–193
Fides rerum non apparentium 172–175, 195, 203
First Lecture on Galatians 147–148
   on the Psalms, see *Dictata super Psalterium*
Flesh 25, 63
Forgivness 129, 176, 178, 185, 194, 202
Formula Concordiae 104, 146, 149, 155, 178, 183, 193, 194, 206
Free choice 69, 158, 181
Fruits of faith 189–190, 194

General level, see *Notitia* level
Gentiles 34, 37, 38, 39, 40, 52, 127
Gewissen, see Conscience
God
   foreknowledge 77–78, 88–95, 121
   hidden, see *Deus absconditus*

Lef

GENERAL BOOKBINDING CO.

79   4   A

355NY2   340

QUALITY CONTROL MARK   6117